W9-BIO-739

 # *Sugar and Slaves*

The Rise of the Planter Class

in the English West Indies,

1624–1713

BY RICHARD S. DUNN

Foreword by Gary B. Nash

*Published for the Omohundro Institute
of Early American History and Culture,
Williamsburg, Virginia,
by the University of North Carolina Press,
Chapel Hill*

*The Omohundro Institute of Early American History and Culture
is sponsored jointly by the College of William and Mary and the
Colonial Williamsburg Foundation.*

© 1972 The University of North Carolina Press
Foreword © 2000 The University of North Carolina Press
All rights reserved
Manufactured in the United States of America

The paper in this book meets the guidelines for permanence and
durability of the Committee on Production Guidelines for Book
Longevity of the Council on Library Resources.

Library of Congress Cataloging-in-Publication Data
Dunn, Richard S.
Sugar and slaves: the rise of the planter class in the English
West Indies, 1624–1713 / by Richard S. Dunn; foreword by
Gary B. Nash.
p.   cm.
Includes bibliographical references and index.
ISBN 978-0-8078-4877-7 (pbk. : alk. paper)
1. West Indies, British—Social life and customs.   2. Plantation
life—West Indies, British.   3. Slavery—West Indies, British.
4. West Indies—History—17th century.   5. Sugar—Manufacture
and refining—West Indies, British.   I. Title.
F2131.D8   2000   972.9'03—dc21   99-089856

12 11 10 09 08   8 7 6 5 4

For Mary

Contents

❧ *Illustrations*

Sugar and Slaves

❧ Tables

✒ Foreword

Twenty-eight years after its original publication, *Sugar and Slaves: The Rise of the Planter Class in the English West Indies, 1624–1713* is still the best place to begin a study of slavery in the British West Indies. In addition, by providing a vivid account of early Caribbean slavery, it provides essential benchmarks for understanding what was different about slavery in England's North American colonies. The book has rewarded readers for many years because, like all lasting historical scholarship, it is an amalgam of deep archival research, methodological ingenuity, new perspectives, and literary grace. Happily, this reissue of the book will bring it before a new generation of readers.

Sugar and Slaves is a brilliant depiction of the outlaw English planters who came to the Caribbean in the early seventeenth century. Because they were the first English colonizers to build an economy on African slave labor, their history provides a comparative perspective on the origins of slavery in England's mainland colonies. Writing at the beginning of the social history tectonic plate shift of the late 1960s and early 1970s, Richard Dunn takes the reader inside the tropical island plantation world where displaced Africans and English colonists built a tobacco and sugar economy that mocked all that the English believed their culture stood for. The book begins in 1624, when the English gained their Caribbean foothold on the tiny island of St. Christopher. From that lonely outpost emerged a "cohesive and potent master class" of tobacco and sugar planters that spread to Barbados, Nevis, Montserrat, Antigua, and Jamaica. The book vividly portrays how the English planters created a living hell in a Caribbean Garden of Eden and how they accommodated themselves to the human wreckage involved in turning the islands into highly successful sugar-producing colonies.

The foreword has been adapted from an earlier essay, "The Work of Richard Dunn," *Pennsylvania History* 64 (Summer 1997): 11–25, with permission of *Pennsylvania History*.

Dunn did not intend to write this book when he went to London in 1962 to work at the Public Record Office on a book concerning the Glorious Revolution of 1688. Encountering a voluminous body of material on the early English colonies in the tropical West Indies, he shelved his Glorious Revolution project and threw in his lot with one of the most dynamic and important fields to emerge in the last half-century—the study of slavery in the Western Hemisphere. Sipping his pints at the Queen's Parlor near the Public Record Office, Dunn turned into a social historian. He announces this conversion in the preface to *Sugar and Slaves*, calling the book a "social history" and speaking of the social historian's search for elusive documentary evidence on the "shadowy and half-forgotten" English planters who came out to the islands and on the Africans by the hundreds of thousands who made their white owners the richest men in British America. This entry into slave studies has now occupied Dunn for more than thirty years.

Fully understanding *Sugar and Slaves* requires some appreciation of its methodology. When Dunn wrote the book three decades ago, he became part of the first cadre of American social historians taking cues from the illuminating power of family reconstitution, demographic analysis, and social structure studies, as pioneered by the French and English historians of the post–World War II period. New sources had to be ferreted out and analyzed with techniques not then taught in graduate school. Devouring path-breaking community studies on both sides of the Atlantic, Dunn searched out in London and the West Indies the unexamined sources from which a composite portrait of Caribbean colonial life could be created: passenger lists, estate inventories, tax lists, war compensation claims, early censuses, militia lists, parish records, land warrants, customs ledgers, and plantation records. Almost all colonial historians of Dunn's generation were schooled in analyzing literary sources, mostly penned by the uppermost members of society, and this made social history research frustrating, eye-straining, and often inconclusive—but also intriguing and exhilarating. Like moths drawn to the flame, the early social historians were seeking illumination but risking incineration.

In researching *Sugar and Slaves*, Dunn was faced with a far more formidable task than that confronting the New England social historians whose community studies were emerging in the early 1970s. Kenneth Lockridge's study of tiny Dedham, for example, is based almost entirely on four conveniently collected volumes of town and church records.[1] By contrast, Dunn's study of the rise of the sugar planters on six British West Indian islands is

---

1. Kenneth Lockridge, *A New England Town: The First Hundred Years* (New York: W. W. Norton, 1970).

painstakingly researched in far-flung and discouragingly incomplete records. The book, in sum, is a methodological tour de force.

In painting a convincing portrait when only some of the pieces of the canvas are available—always the case in studies of slave societies—literary finesse is the historian's best friend. Dunn's formidable descriptive power and carefully crafted language are part of what makes this book so compelling, as well as readable. For example, at the beginning of the book Dunn writes crisply that "the Englishmen who settled in the islands were not mythmakers in the heroic vein of Capt. John Smith, John Winthrop, or William Penn. They did not attempt calypso-style Holy Experiments, nor did they build palm-fringed Cities on a Hill. The most famous seventeenth-century Englishman in the Caribbean was Sir Henry Morgan, the buccaneer, which is rather like having Al Capone as the most famous American of the twentieth century" (xxiii).

Explaining how the English adapted painfully to the strange new tropical world they struggled to control, Dunn tells us:

> Seventeenth-century Englishmen attuned their lives to the weather, to seasonal change, and to the annual cycle of birth, growth, maturity, and death. But in the West Indies, they found a year-round growing season, year-round summer, and year-round heat. They were used to a moderate climate: moderately warm, moderately cold, moderately rainy, moderately sunny. But in the tropics they had to adjust their eyes to brilliant sunlight, and a palette of splashing colors: vegetation startlingly green, fruits and flowers in flaming reds and yellows, the mountains in shimmering blues and greens, shading to deep purple, the moon and stars radiant and sparkling at night, and the encircling sea a spectrum of jeweled colors form cobalt to silver. They found the Caribbean atmosphere to be volatile: blazing heat suddenly relieved by refreshing showers, and soft caressing breezes capriciously dissolving into wild and terrifying storms. In climate, as in European power politics, the Indies lay "beyond the line." (40)

At the end of *Sugar and Slaves,* Dunn's stylistic deftness and eye for the paradoxical make the reader think broadly about the English colonizers who did not go to Virginia or Massachusetts or Pennsylvania. He writes:

> Despite . . . close contacts, the islanders rapidly diverged from the mainlanders, most particularly from the Puritan colonists in New England. . . . The New Englanders, through their numerous elective offices and frequent town meetings, encouraged (indeed almost required) every inhabitant to participate in public life, but in the Indies the big sugar planters completely dominated politics. . . . In New England the young

were deferential to their elders, repressed their adolescent rebelliousness, and often waited into their thirties to marry and set up on their own, while in the islands there were no elders, the young were in control, and many a planter made his fortune and died by age thirty. In short, the Caribbean and New England planters were polar opposites; they represented the outer limits of English social expression in the seventeenth century. (337–38)

Dunn's eye for the paradoxical, the bittersweet, and the downright grim, ugly, and tragic is apparent in *Sugar and Slaves*. At the book's beginning, Dunn explains how the pioneering English planters "made their beautiful islands almost uninhabitable" (xxiii). Midway through his story, he expresses his dismay that "from New England to Virginia to Jamaica, the English planters in seventeenth-century America developed the habit of murdering the soil for a few quick crops and then moving along. On the sugar plantations, unhappily, they also murdered the slaves" (223). Most tragic is his exacting account of how English colonizers "turned their small islands into amazingly effective sugar-production machines, manned by armies of black slaves" (xxi) and how this altered English behavior, values, and ideas. In Dunn's hands, this is a depressing story of human degradation, of the brutalization of Africans, and of the self-brutalization of the English planters and overseers. The English sugar islands, Dunn tells us, were "disastrous social failures" by the early eighteenth century (340), and he barely withholds his scorn for the sugar planters.

It is revealing to compare *Sugar and Slaves* with Edmund Morgan's *American Slavery, American Freedom.*[2] Both Dunn and Morgan were known first as gifted historians of Puritan New England, and both turned from the literary sources on which Puritan scholarship was built to the records from which social history is now constructed. For both, asking questions about the character of life at the bottom of society altered their understanding of the motive forces shaping history. Turning from free- to slave-labor societies, both delineated themes, interpreted human behavior, and reached conclusions that made them seem like closet Marxists. Sugar and tobacco production, they explained, developed hand-in-hand with coerced and degraded labor: grasping for wealth, profit-maximizing English planters relentlessly sought overseas markets, ruthlessly exploited fellow humans, accumulated narrowly concentrated power, and resonated very little to liberal ideas and higher values. Both of their books, dealing with class formation and class tension, have a tone of moral outrage at the behavior of the storied freedom-loving English adventurers in the raw Darwinian colonies

2. Edmund Morgan, *American Slavery, American Freedom: The Ordeal of Colonial Virginia* (New York: W. W. Norton, 1975).

they constructed. Dunn gloomily ends *Sugar and Slaves* by concluding: "The stark dichotomy between the all-powerful sugar magnate and his abject army of black bondsmen was the ultimate expression in seventeenth-century English society of man's strenuous search for wealth in an era of primitive productive techniques" (341).

What of the power of ideas? In his chapter titled "Life in the Tropics," Dunn struggles to show how inherited ideas and values continued to matter in the British Caribbean—but only in limited ways. "In their basic living arrangements—food, clothing, and shelter—the early settlers," he explains, hung on to English customs (264). But in this persistence Dunn sees only cultural stubbornness or stupidity in clinging to English habits that ill suited the tropics. They foolishly wore cool-weather garb, ate the wrong food, and built houses absurdly. In all other matters, the English planters tragically abandoned what might have rescued them from the human wreckage they were creating: they turned their backs on the idea of representative assemblies in order to convert the assemblies into platforms for the master class, sabotaged the militia system because it interfered with sugar production, muzzled religion in order to prevent slave unrest, made common law a mockery by withholding due process from three-fourths of the population, and scoffed at education.

At the outset, Dunn imagined his book as mainly a study of the English planter class. Yet in the course of studying plantation records, data on sugar and tobacco exports, and literary sources revealing planter attempts to control the newly formed slave societies, he was led inexorably to the enslaved Africans themselves. Though thwarted by the limited evidence on "how the blacks themselves reacted to their treatment by the island planters" (xxiv), he found a wealth of material disclosing slave conditions and slave revolts on the English Caribbean islands. For example, his comparative analysis of slave revolts in Barbados and Jamaica is very instructive, focusing on the far greater chance of their succeeding on the north coast of Jamaica than in Barbados, Virginia, Maryland, or other English colonies where geographical conditions discouraged or thwarted African rebels. This judgment, contrary to that of Orlando Patterson, whose book on Jamaican slavery appeared as Dunn was finishing his study, has stood up to the present.[3]

Given the absence of the kind of sources that are available for later eras—slave narratives, detailed plantation records, and the like—Dunn was able only to begin the process of restoring to memory the lives of the enslaved Africans who made their English masters wealthy. Yet he briefly treats

3. Orlando Patterson, *The Sociology of Slavery: An Analysis of the Origins, Development and Structure of Negro Slave Society in Jamaica* (London: McGibbon & Kee, 1967).

African cultural retentions in the West Indies—language, religion, family structure, and names—and he lays the foundations for studying the inner lives of slaves. In his memorable chapter "Death in the Tropics," he exhibits his skills (later to be sharpened) as a demographic historian by isolating two key factors that dealt out death and impeded fertility so differently in the island and mainland slave populations: first, the especially lethal disease environment in the tropics; second the extraordinarily brutal slaveowners who directed a uniquely punishing crop regimen. Philip Curtin's *The Atlantic Slave Trade*, published three years before *Sugar and Slaves*, had noted the huge contrast between the natural increase of British slaves in North America and the demographic disaster of slaves nearly everywhere in the tropics, whether their masters were English, French, Spanish, Portuguese, or Dutch.[4] But Curtin had not explored the causes, mentioning only the possible factor of tropical disease. Dunn, along with James Walvin and Michael Craton in their studies of Worthy Park, a large Jamaican sugar plantation, nailed down the reasons for the disaster.[5] By the early 1970s, Dunn was on his way to a comparative study of African enslavement in mainland and island British America. In a series of essays published over the last two decades, he has used two extraordinary sets of plantation records, each covering more than a century, to compare slave lives in Virginia and Jamaica.[6]

Dunn's analysis of the heartless sugar system in the West Indies swam against the tide of emerging scholarship—what might be called the story of the "heroic enslaved African." *Sugar and Slaves* was published before Eugene

4. Philip D. Curtin, *The Atlantic Slave Trade: A Census* (Madison: University of Wisconsin Press, 1969).

5. Michael Craton and James Walvin, *A Jamaican Plantation: The History of Worthy Park, 1670–1970* (Toronto: University of Toronto Press, 1970); James Walvin, *Searching for the Invisible Man: Slaves and Plantation Life in Jamaica* (Cambridge, Mass.: Harvard University Press, 1978).

6. "A Tale of Two Plantations: Slave Life at Mesopotamia in Jamaica and Mount Airy in Virginia, 1799–1828," *William and Mary Quarterly* 3rd ser., 34 (1977): 32–65; "Masters, Servants, and Slaves in the Colonial Chesapeake and the Caribbean," in *Early America in a Wider World*, ed. David B. Quinn (Detroit: Wayne State University Press, 1982), 242–66; " 'Dreadful Idlers' in the Cane Fields: The Slave Labor Pattern on a Jamaican Sugar Estate, 1762–1831," *Journal of Interdisciplinary History* 17 (1987): 795–822; "Sugar Production and Slave Women in Jamaica," in *Cultivation and Culture: Labor and the Shaping of Slave Life in the Americas*, ed. Ira Berlin and Philip D. Morgan (Charlottesville: University Press of Virginia, 1993), 49–72; *Moravian Missionaries at Work in a Jamaican Slave Community, 1754–1835* (Minneapolis: Associates of the James Ford Bell Library, 1994); "The Story of Two Jamaican Slaves: Sarah Affir and Robert McAlpine of Mesopotamia Estate," in *Caribbean Accounts: Essays on the British West Indies and the Atlantic Economy*, ed. Roderick A. McDonald (Kingston: University of the West Indies Press, 1996), 188–210; "After Tobacco: The Slave Labour Pattern on a Large Chesapeake Grain-and-Livestock Plantation in the Early Nineteenth Century," in *The Early Modern Atlantic Economy*, ed. John McCusker and Kenneth Morgan (Cambridge: Cambridge University Press, 2000).

Genovese's *Roll, Jordan, Roll*, John Blassingame's *The Black Community*, and Herbert Gutman's *The Black Family in Slavery and Freedom*.[7] Hence Dunn was not in a position to address their arguments about the resilience of enslaved Africans, African inventiveness in creating new cultural forms, and the near-heroic maintenance of slave family structure. His analysis of African slavery, of course, is about the British Caribbean, but nonetheless it rubs uneasily against the new slavery paradigm constructed in the 1970s and 1980s that gives far more agency to the slaves than Dunn allows.

In *Sugar and Slaves* (and in subsequent essays), Dunn argues that, in the main, enslaved Africans lived unspeakably difficult lives, dying prematurely, struggling futilely to resist brutalization, and in the end awaiting deliverance at the hands of their oppressors. While never subscribing fully to Stanley Elkins's thesis that the crushing brutality of slavery in the English colonies numbed slaves into becoming "Sambos," Dunn traffics little with the idea of a "slave community" that became popular in the 1970s and 1980s.[8] Mostly he stresses how white brutality thwarted black ambition and achievement. In his essays since the first publication of *Sugar and Slaves*, he has not strayed from his conclusion that slave systems, whatever the religion and nationality of the masters, whatever the region or crop regimen, afforded little opportunity for coerced Africans to achieve very much or to rebel very effectively. An outpouring of scholarship on West Indian and mainland slavery has mostly confirmed this view.

The question of overt slave resistance is central to this argument about the semi-autonomous roles played by enslaved Africans. "The acid test of any slave system," writes Dunn, "is the frequency and ferocity of resistance by slaves" (256). However, even in Jamaica, Britain's most rebellious colony, African insurrectionists had little effect in bringing an end to slavery. Much more important in destabilizing the British death-dealing sugar economy were hurricanes, earthquakes, malaria epidemics, and French marauders. Ironically, Dunn notes, "the English planters, who treated their slaves with such contemptuous inhumanity, were rescued time and again from disaster by the compassionate generosity of the Negroes" (262).

Considering today's strenuous debates over "the objectivity question," a final note is warranted on Dunn's value judgments in *Sugar and Slaves*. Subtly threaded through Dunn's *Sugar and Slaves* is a quality that must be called moral. It appears in rueful comments, in wordplay signaling a raised eye-

---

7. Eugene Genovese, *Roll, Jordan, Roll: The World That Slaves Made* (New York: Pantheon Books, 1974); John W. Blassingame, *The Slave Community: Plantation Life in the Ante-bellum South* (New York: Oxford University Press, 1972); Herbert G. Gutman, *The Black Family in Slavery and Freedom, 1750–1925* (New York: Pantheon Books, 1976).

8. Stanley Elkins, *Slavery: A Problem in American Institutional and Intellectual Life* (Chicago: University of Chicago Press, 1959).

brow, in suggestive juxtapositions of material, and occasionally in passages expressing righteous outrage. Though a thoroughly professional historian with a decent respect for impartiality, Dunn is impatient with man's inhumanity to man, with unconscionable behavior, and quite pointedly with the massive contradictions of freedom-loving English planters creating hell on earth for Africans. The grandson and son of Presbyterian ministers, the nephew of Congregationalist and Episcopalian preachers, the descendent of Ulster immigrants to East New Jersey in the 1680s, Dunn has channeled his family's moral temperament into an academic career. There is hardly such a thing as a notable historian who is not a passionate historian. Dunn is both.

Gary B. Nash
University of California, Los Angeles

❧ Preface

This book is about those other English colonists who came to America in the seventeenth century, the ones who chose the Caribbean islands rather than the mainland, who settled in St. Christopher in 1624, Barbados in 1627, Nevis in 1628, Montserrat and Antigua in the 1630s, and Jamaica in 1655. Today these tropical adventurers are seldom mentioned in the same breath with the founding fathers of Virginia and Massachusetts. It is easy to forget that they were members of the same migration as the first Chesapeake and New England colonists, that they settled in the New World at the same time, in the same numbers, for many of the same reasons. They employed similar colonizing techniques and shared similar colonizing experiences. Tobacco was initially the staple crop in Barbados and the Leeward Islands as in Virginia and Maryland. Puritans and Quakers came to the Indies as to New England and Pennsylvania. Imperial strategists planned the seizure of Jamaica as of New York. The islanders established the same institutional arrangements as in North America: each colony was administered by a governor, council, and representative assembly, with parish churches, vestrymen, and justices of the peace at the local level, and a militia for protection. And yet—inexorably and very rapidly—the island and mainland plantations evolved into two separate communities.

Once the English colonists in the Caribbean learned how to grow and process sugarcane in the 1640s, they developed a life-style all their own. They turned their small islands into amazingly effective sugar-production machines, manned by armies of black slaves. They became far richer than their cousins in the North American wilderness. They lived fast, spent recklessly, played desperately, and died

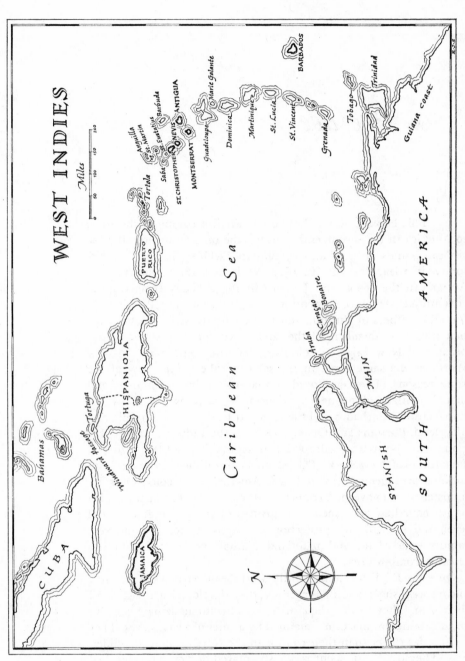

WEST INDIES

Miles

0   50   100   150   200

Bahamas

CUBA

JAMAICA

Tortuga

Windward Passage

HISPANIOLA

PUERTO RICO

Tortola

Anguilla
St. Martin
Saba
St. Eustatius
St. CHRISTOPHER
NEVIS
MONTSERRAT
Barbuda
ANTIGUA

Guadeloupe
Marie Galante

Dominica

Martinique

St. Lucia

St. Vincent

BARBADOS

Grenada

Tobago

Trinidad

Caribbean   Sea

Aruba
Curaçao
Bonaire

SPANISH   MAIN

SOUTH   AMERICA

Guiana coast

N

Map by Richard J. Stinely. (Adapted from an endsheet in Richard Pares, Yankees and Creoles: The Trade between North America and the West Indies before the American Revolution [Cambridge, Mass., 1956]; courtesy of Longman Group Limited of Great Britain.)

young. And although they persuaded the merchants and politicians at home that the sugar colonies were more valuable than the North American colonies, they could not persuade themselves to live in the Indies any longer than necessary. Indeed, they made their beautiful islands almost uninhabitable. By the close of the century, when Englishmen in the mainland colonies were turning into Americans, Englishmen in the islands had one consuming ambition—to escape home to England as fast as possible.

These sugar planters of the seventeenth century have become shadowy and half-forgotten men. They never wrote much about themselves—not caring to advertise their newfound wealth to the inquisitive authorities at home—and they have left few tangible remains in the islands. Hurricanes have obliterated nearly all of the old plantation houses with their furnishings, as well as the old churches, sugar works, and slave huts. The island towns have changed beyond recognition. Bridgetown in Barbados has been rebuilt repeatedly, thanks to a long series of disastrous fires and storms, and the old buccaneering capital of Port Royal in Jamaica lies thirty feet under water, thanks to the great earthquake of 1692. The books and papers belonging to the early planters have been rotted by tropical heat and devoured by vermin. Even their tombs are more likely to be found in London or Bath than in the island churchyards.

The Englishmen who settled in the islands were not mythmakers in the heroic vein of Capt. John Smith, John Winthrop, or William Penn. They did not attempt calypso-style Holy Experiments, nor did they build palm-fringed Cities on a Hill. The most famous seventeenth-century Englishman in the Caribbean was Sir Henry Morgan, the buccaneer, which is rather like having Al Capone as the most famous American of the twentieth century. Yet Morgan was perhaps the most authentic hero the English islands produced, for he and his daredevil companions spent their time attacking the proud Spanish foe, while the sugar planters of Barbados, Jamaica, and the Leeward Islands were busily exploiting their African slaves —a point not forgotten in these islands, which are 95 percent black today.

It is a shabby task in many ways, yet an illuminating one, to tell what these English sons of Adam did to the Garden of Eden islands they discovered and what the islands did to them. This book asks three principal questions: how did the early English planters in the West Indies respond to the novelty of life in the tropics? to the novelty of large-scale sugar production? and to the novelty of slave labor? The island planters, like their cousins in North America, were very conscious of the strange climate, strange food, and strange diseases they encountered, and it is worth asking how resourceful and resilient they were in adapting English habits to suit their tropical environment. They tried many ways of making money in the Caribbean, and it is worth examining why they concentrated so heavily on sugar and how they operated their plantations. They were the first Englishmen to employ massive numbers of African slaves, and their experience with Negroes is especially interesting because it tells something of the colonists' initial racial attitude and helps to explain the origin of the slave system in the Southern mainland colonies. To see how the blacks themselves reacted to their treatment by the island planters is scarcely possible, given the nature of the surviving evidence, yet there is a good deal of revealing information about slave conditions and slave revolts in the English Caribbean during the seventeenth century. Quite apart from the topic of slavery, there is special reason for the student of American colonial history to examine the social structure of the West Indian colonies. Economically interdependent, the two sections of English America were always in close touch down to 1775. During the seventeenth century, in particular, thousands of island colonists migrated to the mainland plantations. Study of the islanders' social milieu suggests who these migrants were, why they left, and what habits they brought with them to the mainland.

When I began to prepare this book, I wondered whether it would be possible to write the social history of the seventeenth-century West Indian pioneers, a people who left little literary evidence, who published no newspapers or almanacs or sermons, kept few diaries, left no attic trunks full of private papers—or much personal memorabilia of any sort. I was spoiled by having spent too much time in the company of the early New England Puritans, who wrote almost too much about themselves and preserved every laundry list for posterity. But it turned out that the inarticulate islanders had left more evidence than I had supposed.

There are several vivid contemporary travelers' accounts of life on the islands, including one—John Taylor's Baedeker-like description of Jamaica in 1688—that is still in manuscript. There are some excellent estate records of seventeenth-century sugar plantations, though many fewer than for the next century. Early maps of the English islands are exceedingly informative, not least because they often locate and identify the chief plantations. Numerous contemporary lists of passengers to the islands, indentured servants, convict laborers, militiamen, landholders, merchants, slave masters, taxpayers, officeholders, Jews, and Quakers—many thousand names in all—make it possible to reconstruct, at least partially, the rise of the planter class. Amongst the volumes of West Indian laws, sessional papers, and official correspondence housed in the Public Record Office in London there is material of great value to the social historian, such as the complete census returns for Barbados in 1680 and 1715 or the itemized compensation claims filed by the planters on St. Christopher after the French plundered their island in 1706. Last but not least, in such island depositories as the Jamaica Archives, the Jamaica Registry Office, the Institute of Jamaica, the Barbados Museum and Historical Society, and the Barbados Archives there is a mass of genealogical data that tells us a good deal about seventeenth-century family life and social structure—volumes of wills, inventories, deeds, land patents, vestry books, and parish registers. Social historians are currently quantifying this sort of documentation in order to discover the exact population pattern and familial structure of sample seventeenth-century English villages and New England towns. Unfortunately, the West Indian historian cannot do this, at least for the seventeenth century: his data are far too fragmentary, too unreliable, for precise demographic analysis. In many respects the early social pattern in Barbados, the Leeward Islands, and Jamaica remains illusive and mysterious. But something can be attempted, and in the following pages I will try to shape the miscellaneous evidence described above into a composite portrait of English life in the Caribbean three centuries ago.

I am deeply indebted to the John Simon Guggenheim Memorial Foundation, the American Council of Learned Societies, the American Philosophical Society, and the University of Pennsylvania for grants that enabled me to spend a year in England and to make three trips to the West Indies collecting materials for this book. Clinton V. Black of the Jamaica Archives, Philip Mayes of the Port Royal archeological project, C. Bernard Lewis of the Institute of Jamaica, and Neville Connell of the Barbados Museum and Historical Society assisted me very generously; they made my visits extraordinarily pleasant and profitable. Jeannette D. Black of the John Carter Brown Library has helped me with early maps of the islands, and Barnes F. Lathrop of the University of Texas, as literary executor to the late J. Harry Bennett, kindly loaned me microfilm from Bennett's collection. Professor Bennett was the pioneer in this field; had he lived longer, he would have written his own social history of the seventeenth-century English sugar islands, and I like to think of my work as in some sense a completion of his labors and a memorial to a fine historian. Other colleagues are becoming increasingly interested in the early history of the English islands; Carl Bridenbaugh and Richard B. Sheridan are each bringing out their own studies of the English Caribbean planters. I have profited greatly from exchanges of information and ideas with Professors Bridenbaugh and Sheridan, and I trust that the appearance of our three very different books will focus attention on a grossly neglected field. I also wish to thank Michael Craton, Stephen S. Webb, Mrs. Davis G. Durham, Otis P. Starkey, A. P. Thornton, Jack P. Greene, Peter Wood, Kenneth Lockridge, Jessica and Allen Ehrlich, Edwin Wolf 2nd, and Howard H. Peckham for helping me in various ways. My colleagues and students at Penn have patiently heard more than they cared to know about the sugar islands. James H. Hutson and Joy Dickinson Barnes have been wonderfully expeditious editors, and my other friends at the Institute of Early American History and Culture, Stephen G. Kurtz and Thad Tate, have encouraged me to get on with the job. Heidi Herrmann has done yeoman service preparing the manuscript. And my wife, Mary Maples Dunn, has helped me more than everyone else combined; this book is for her, with love.

❧ *Abbreviations*

Bar. Archives	Barbados Archives, Lazaretto, St. Michael
Bar. Mus. Hist. Soc.	Barbados Museum and Historical Society, St. Ann's Garrison
Blathwayt Papers	Blathwayt Papers, Colonial Williamsburg Research Library, Williamsburg, Va.
Br. Museum	British Museum
Cal.S.P.Col.	W. Noel Sainsbury *et al.*, eds., *Calendar of State Papers, Colonial Series, America and the West Indies*, 43 vols. (London, 1860–)
C.O. 1/1/1, etc.	Colonial Office Series, Class 1, Vol. 1, p. 1, Public Record Office
Coventry Papers	Coventry Papers of the marquis of Bath at Longleat (microfilm, American Council of Learned Societies, British Microfilm Project)
Deerr, *History of Sugar*	Noel Deerr, *The History of Sugar*, 2 vols. (London, 1949–1950)
[Duke], *Memoirs*	[William Duke], *Some Memoirs of the First Settlement of the Island of Barbados* (Barbados, 1741)
Harlow, *Barbados*	Vincent T. Harlow, *A History of Barbados, 1625–1685* (Oxford, 1926)
Harlow, *Colonising*	Vincent T. Harlow, ed., *Colonising Expeditions to the West Indies and Guiana, 1623–1667*, Publications of the Hakluyt Society, 2d Ser., LVI (London, 1925)
Hay Papers	Hay of Haystoun Papers relating to Barbados, Scottish Record Office, Edinburgh (microfilm, J. Harry Bennett Collection, University of Texas, Austin)

Helyar MSS	Helyar Manuscripts, Somerset Record Office, Taunton, England (microfilm, J. Harry Bennett Collection, University of Texas, Austin)
Hotten, ed., *Original Lists*	John Camden Hotten, ed., *The Original Lists of Persons of Quality . . . and Others Who Went from Great Britain to the American Plantations, 1600–1700* (London, 1874)
Jam. Archives	Jamaica Archives, Spanish Town
Jam. Hist. Rev.	*Jamaican Historical Review*
Jam. Inv.	Jamaica Inventories of Probated Estates, File 1 B/11, Jamaica Archives, Spanish Town. Vol. 1 (1674–1678), Vol. 2 (1679–1686), Vol. 3 (1686–1694), Vol. 5 (1699–1701)
Jam. Land Pat.	Index to Jamaica Land Patents, 1661–1826, File 1 B/11, Jamaica Archives, Spanish Town
Jeaffreson, ed., *Young Squire*	John Cordy Jeaffreson, ed., *A Young Squire of the Seventeenth Century. From the Papers (A.D. 1676–1686) of Christopher Jeaffreson*, 2 vols. (London, 1878)
Jour. Bar. Mus. Hist. Soc.	*Journal of the Barbados Museum and Historical Society*
Jours. of Jam. Assembly	*Journals of the House of Assembly of Jamaica, 1663–1826*, 14 vols. (Jamaica, 1811–1829)
Ligon, *True History of Barbados*	Richard Ligon, *A True & Exact History of the Island of Barbados . . .* (London, 1657)
Sloane, *Voyage*	Hans Sloane, *A Voyage to the Islands Madera, Barbados, Nieves, S. Christophers and Jamaica*, 2 vols. (London, 1707–1725)
Taylor MS	John Taylor, Multum in Parvo or Parvum in Multo. Taylor's second part of the Historie of his life and Travels in AMERICA. Containeing a full Geographical description of the Island of Jamaica . . . under the government of his Grace Christopher Duke of Albemarle. Manuscript, Institute of Jamaica, Kingston
Williamson, *Caribbee Islands*	James A. Williamson, *The Caribbee Islands under the Proprietary Patents* (Oxford, 1926)
Wm. and Mary Qtly.	*William and Mary Quarterly*

Sugar and Slaves

1 ≫ Beyond the Line

On May 22, 1631, a doughty gentleman from Essex named Sir Henry Colt boarded the ship *Alexander* at Weymouth in Dorset and began to keep a journal.[1] He was taking some servants to start a plantation in the island of St. Christopher,[2] which the English had begun to settle seven years before. Colt's pithy and detailed journal provides the best firsthand account we have of the infant English settlements in the West Indies. "Aboord we are," he writes. "Neyther doe we loose time, for we presently weigh Anchor, hoyse upp our sayles, puttinge ourselves to sea, takinge our Course South South West, alongst our English Chanell." On the second day out Sir Henry took his last sight of England, the Lizard in Cornwall, as his ship bore south toward the Bay of Biscay and the tropics.

Colt had equipped his party with enough food and drink to last the voyage and enough clothing and tools to last for a year or so once they reached America. He furnished his cabin in the *Alexander* with bedding, table linen, eating utensils, a stewing pan, wax lights, and a chamber pot. He tried sleeping in a hammock, but found that he got too cold and could not roll over, so he switched to a flock bed. He discarded his doublet, the quilted jacket worn by English gentlemen of the day, because it rotted in the humid heat, but the costume he says he wore still seems rather elaborate for a

1. The following paragraphs draw upon this journal, "The Voyage of Sir Henrye Colt Knight to the Ilands of the Antilleas . . . ," in Vincent T. Harlow, ed., *Colonising Expeditions to the West Indies and Guiana, 1623–1667*, Publications of the Hakluyt Society, 2d Ser., LVI (London, 1925), 54–102. Hereafter cited as Harlow, *Colonising*.
2. Since the 18th century this island has generally been known as St. Kitts, but in the 17th century both the English and French called it St. Christopher, the name that will be used in this book.

sojourn in the tropics: a long-sleeved shirt reaching to the knees, a suit of jerkin and hose (that is, a sleeveless jacket and puffed knee breeches), a handkerchief around the neck, a feathered hat, beads, boot hose, stockings, and shoes. Black shoes turned moldy in the Indies, so Sir Henry wore russet-colored shoes, and he brought a dozen pairs since shoes wore out fast. During the sea voyage he always wore a stomacher—the seventeenth-century equivalent of a sweater—to guard against the wind. On shipboard he and his men ate a monotonous diet of broth, porridge, pudding, bread, boiled biscuit, raisins, and cheese. They had a little fresh and salted meat, but ate sparingly of it. They drank brandy, wine, and herb-flavored "hott waters." Colt's liquor barrels were double-casked to prevent the sailors from tapping them.

The *Alexander* was armed with sixteen guns, but the danger of attack was so great that the captain formed sixty of the male passengers into squads of musketeers. She was a tightly run ship, with public prayers held three times daily, at ten in the morning, four in the afternoon, and eight at night. The godly, disciplined atmosphere on board sounds surprisingly similar to that described by John Winthrop in his journal one year before, when he sailed on the *Arbella* to Massachusetts. On Winthrop's puritanical ship, incidentally, there was considerable filching from the liquor barrels.

Like every transatlantic passenger in the seventeenth century, Sir Henry Colt found his voyage tediously long. "Suerly the Journye is great," he protested in midpassage, "and further by a 1000 miles then ever I supposed itt to be." The sea route from England to the Caribbean was in fact longer than to New England, but sailing ships generally covered the distance more quickly because they took advantage of the constant trade wind blowing toward the Indies. The *Alexander*, like practically all European sailing ships destined for the Caribbean, followed the route first charted by Christopher Columbus. She worked south past Portugal, Madeira, and the Canaries, picked up the trade wind, and headed west across the Atlantic. As his ship sailed south and west, Colt soon saw porpoises and grampuses, then flying fish and dolphins tinted with azure and gold, and beyond the Tropic of Cancer "we meet with the first Tropick birds, In colour, winges, flyinge not unlike our English swallowes but 4 times bigger and some are white." He complained of skimpy breezes, "like the languishinge motions of a dyinge man," but when the wind blew strong the *Alexander* ran ten leagues a watch, or 180 miles a day.

When they reached the latitude of Barbados, their first port of call, they had difficulty in reckoning their exact longitude, but knew that they could not be far from the island, the easternmost in the Caribbean. Barbados has a lower silhouette than most of the islands in the Indies and lies apart from its neighbors, ninety miles east of the main series of islands in the Lesser Antilles. Or as Sir Henry Colt puts it, Barbados is "like sixpence throwne downe uppon newmarkett heath." Throughout the century sailors had trouble finding it. In 1630, Colt tells us, many ships sailed past it by mistake, and once to the leeward of any Caribbean island a sailing ship had great difficulty in beating back against the wind. Thus the *Alexander* tacked warily for several days. In the small hours of the morning on July 1, a lookout in the forecastle cried "Land!" Colt could see nothing in the darkness and longed for daylight like "the woman with childe for her good howre." When day broke at last he was startled to find, less than a mile away, a white line of breakers, sand, and rocks, with wooded land rising steeply beyond. It was the craggy eastern coast of Barbados. Forty days had passed since they embarked from Weymouth, very good time by seventeenth-century standards, and not one passenger sick, which was almost miraculous.

Sir Henry stayed two weeks in Barbados while the *Alexander* took in some passengers and a cargo of fustic (a dyewood) and tobacco. The English had occupied this island for only four years in 1631, and their plantations were raw and straggling. Nevertheless Colt—like most subsequent visitors—was captivated by the place: "For to confesse truely all the Ilands that I have passed by and seen unto this day, not any pleaseth me soe well." He found no Indians and few species of wild animals on Barbados. The island was full of wild hogs, delicious to eat, which the planters were slaughtering at a terrific rate. They caught fish of many sizes and shapes in their nets, and some of Colt's fellow passengers went fishing at midnight. Colt liked stewed turtle: "The tast is between fish and flesh of veale." He disliked the sultry heat and daily summer showers and detested the stinging gnats and black ants. Squeaky lizards and other creatures cried strangely at night, pale yellow land crabs nipped his legs, great-throated pelicans nested in the trees, and turtle doves "singe us musick dayly into our shipp." What struck him most forcibly was the exotic tropical vegetation. Barbados was less densely forested than the other islands, but everything sprouted phenomenally fast and luxuriantly. Figs, oranges, lemons, pomegranates, pineapples, prickly pears, peppers, papayas, soursop, watermelons, muskmelons, guavas, plantains, cassava, cloves, and cinnamon were all growing on the island when Colt was there, and timber trees included cedar, locust, mastic, and fustic exported for dyestuff. "The palmito tree," he reported, "carryes his leaf like a ladyes skreen fann, or peacocks tayle, the fruit like a cabbidge but better."

Colt had many tart things to say about the English planters on Barbados. He found them a quarrelsome, drunken, and idle set of young men. The drinking was prodigious, if Sir Henry can be believed. Imitating the planters' bad example, he increased his liquor quota at meals from two to thirty drams! During his stay the *Alexander* was continually overrun by servants who came on board hoping to escape from the island or at least to avoid laboring in the fields. It took a full day to clear all visitors off the ship before she could set sail. Colt claims that in ten days he never saw any man at work in Barbados and he saw little evidence of defense against Spanish attack. The Barbadians had a fort and a watch house, but no organized militia or any open ground where militiamen could be drilled. They cleared their land as the Indians did, by slashing and burning, and it shocked Colt to see charred tree trunks, weeds, and brush, and desolate stumps six feet high standing or lying in the fields. They cultivated tobacco and cotton for export and wheat and corn for their own consumption. Although they kept cows and hens, they had no horses or oxen, which made transportation difficult and forced them to plant close to the seashore where the soil was thinner and the rainfall lighter than elsewhere on the island. Nevertheless, one planter served Sir Henry a feast of pigs, chickens, turkey, corn, cassava, and palm cabbage, boasting that he could entertain at the same rate every day of the year.

From Barbados, Colt sailed northwest to St. Christopher, a three-hundred-mile journey along one of the most romantically beautiful highways in the world. Passage lay through the principal islands of the Lesser Antilles: St. Lucia, Martinique, Dominica, Marie Galante, Montserrat, Antigua, and Nevis. This chain of islands, really half-submerged mountains, forms a parade of dark green peaks rising dramatically from the sparkling blue sea at twenty- or thirty-mile intervals. As he passed these islands Sir Henry noted how tall, rugged, and densely wooded they were. Martinique, Dominica, Guadeloupe, Montserrat, and Nevis all boast peaks ranging over 3,000 feet in height. Usually the voyage from Barbados to St. Christopher took three days, but it was tricky work for a sailing vessel. At night a ship veering too close to any of these isles on the Atlantic side might smash into outcroppings of rock and high surf. At any time of day sudden squalls could whip down the steep mountain sides, powerful enough to dismast a ship. It was safer to skirt the sheltered leeward coast of each island, but doing this a ship might lose the precious trade wind altogether and stand becalmed for hours. None of the islands Sir Henry passed in 1631 was as yet occupied by Europeans. Fierce Carib Indians inhabited Martinique, Dominica, and Guadeloupe. The Caribs of Dominica were reputed to weave excellent hammocks, and Sir Henry hoped to truck with them for one. As the *Alexander* coasted past Dominica, the captain fired a shot signaling his desire to trade. But to Colt's disappointment, no naked men appeared.

A few hours later they were off Guadeloupe. The ship's company was at morning prayers when suddenly they heard a gun and to their dismay sighted a fleet of twenty or more Spanish vessels bearing down upon them in full sail. England was at peace with Spain in 1631, but the Spaniards regarded the Indies as their private preserve, and if they could catch the *Alexander* they would certainly take her as a prize and likely kill her men. So Colt's ship ran for her life to open sea.

The two closest Spanish ships kept up the chase and, having the wind, overtook the *Alexander* in a few hours. The English prepared to fight, Sir Henry dispensing two great bottles of liquor among the men.[3] He watched the larger Spaniard approach within musket range before a voice cried out, "*Amayna pèrros, amayna pèrros, strike sayle doggs, strike sayle doggs*. After which a whistle is given, and off goeth ther ordinance which passed over our heads." The English returned fire briskly, and as the smoke cleared they saw the Spaniards backing off. But the danger was still great. The *Alexander* was far off course, leaking badly, and fearful that the main Spanish fleet would pounce on her once she regained the Leeward Islands. Furthermore, she could not warn the English colonists at Nevis and St. Christopher that the Spaniards were in the neighborhood. Only two years before a Spanish squadron of

3. Colt was personally most anxious to avoid fighting the Spanish, for he was a Catholic and had served in the Spanish army in Flanders.

similar size had chased the English off those islands temporarily, and it looked as though they were now trying again. The *Alexander* took four days, beating against the wind, to reach Montserrat, soon to be occupied by the English, but now uninhabited. Finding no sign of the Spaniards, she continued cautiously toward Nevis. On the horizon Sir Henry could see the conical mountain peak of Nevis rising over the lower slopes on the island "like the banquettinge house att Whitehall over the other buyldinges." To his great relief, all was safe at Nevis. The Spaniards had not attacked. The next day, July 21, Colt's ship crossed the narrow channel to St. Christopher and moored in the roadstead before the English fort, welcomed by volleys of shot from the militia and planters.

St. Christopher was an excitable, tension-filled place when Sir Henry Colt arrived in 1631. The English governor, Sir Thomas Warner, kept his men under tight military discipline, and for good reason. Three groups of people—English, French, and Indians—shared an island only sixty-eight square miles in size. The French settlers occupied both ends of St. Christopher, and the English were sandwiched in the middle. They agreed to pool forces in case of Indian or Spanish attack and shared highways, roadsteads, and salt ponds. But there was always friction. Shortly after Colt arrived some Indians shot arrows at an English fishing party at the salt ponds, and Sir Henry suspected they were really naked Frenchmen daubed with red annatto dye. He found breastworks erected at strategic points throughout the English sector. Field laborers were constantly being requisitioned for guard duty, and Colt stationed sentinels while he slept at night.

The Dutch were also on the scene. They held the neighboring island of St. Martin, traded freely with the French and English, and offered to join in warding off any Spanish attack. Colt entertained the governor of St. Martin at his house in St. Christopher and found him "the only temperate Hollander that ever I saw, or heard of, and a man of good appearance." It was at St. Martin that the *Alexander* had a dreadful accident. She was lading salt as ballast for the homeward journey to Europe when a thunderstorm suddenly brewed and a lightning bolt struck her mainmast. Six sailors, trying to furl the sails, were flung dead into the sea, the mainmast was shivered, and the sails burnt. Colt wondered why the lightning did not hit the Dutch ships riding close by, for he liked Dutchmen no better than the French—though he saw nothing wrong in shipping St. Christopher's tobacco crop to Holland to avoid paying the English customs duty.

Apart from the danger and excitement of living in an international cockpit, Sir Henry found the style of life in St. Christopher much like Barbados. Because the English had been in this island longer, their fields were larger and better cleared. Colt thought they produced better tobacco and fruit than Barbados. The terrain was more rugged and jungled, the water supply more abundant, the climate stormier and more humid. Colt says he found less drinking, quarreling, and idleness, but a man was killed in a fight soon after he came, and it was generally anticipated that the English servants at St. Christopher would desert to the Spaniards at the first opportunity rather than defend their masters.

Sir Henry soon found that starting a new plantation was harder work than he had supposed. First he pitched a tent and stored his goods by the seaside, then he set his servants to work clearing land and building a house on a hillside lot he had chosen half a mile above the sea. Formerly the Indians had planted sugarcane here, but now everything was overgrown. Colt had inadequate tools and no horses, so everything had to be carried by hand, and his men had a terrible time trying to chop down trees and root out vines. Tiring of his slow progress, Sir Henry decided to buy a house with cleared land at Palmetto Point and set his men to work planting peas, potatoes, and wheat. He wrote home for four horses, two cows, and forty more servants to man this "great plantation," but already he was looking for fresh adventures. He commissioned the captain of the *Alexander* to buy him in Holland a forty-ton pinnace mounted with six guns, which Colt intended to sail the next year from St. Christopher to the Spanish Main and trade with the Indians there. "For rest we will nott," said Colt, "untell we have doone some thinges worthy of ourselves, or dye in the attempt."

Buoyant as ever, Sir Henry Colt ended his journal on August 20, 1631, writing from his tent at St. Christopher. Nothing much more is known about him, except that by 1635 he was reported dead beyond the seas—one of many stout Englishmen who came out to the Caribbean in the seventeenth century and faded quickly from the scene.

§❧

Many such characters as Sir Henry Colt came to the Indies in the pioneer days, for everyone knew that the Caribbean was a stage for mettlesome gamblers. It was the Wild West of the sixteenth and seventeenth centuries, promising far more in the way of glamor, excitement, quick profit, and constant peril than the prosaic settlements along the North American coast. Colt and his fellows knew all too much about recent events in this exotic corner of the New World from the lurid pages of Hakluyt, Raleigh, and Purchas, not to mention such Spanish and Italian authorities as Peter Martyr, Oviedo, and Las Casas, whose coruscated accounts of the Spanish regime in the Indies had been translated into English. And if they were not readers, the English pioneers still heard ample tales about the gold and pearls that had been found in these isles and stories of Spanish cruelty, English robbery, and Indian and Negro slavery. They associated the Indies with incredible wealth and amazing savagery. Everything was larger than life. The English colonists expected—and rather hoped—that outrageous things would happen to them, and they armed themselves with a code of conduct that would never be tolerated at home.

By Sir Henry Colt's day the English had already been trading and raiding in the Caribbean for seventy years. Starting with John Hawkins's three slaving voyages in the 1560s, many hundred English ships and many thousand English sailors had cruised among the Antilles. Some had touched the islands only in passing, such as the half-dozen fleets that Sir Walter Raleigh dispatched to Virginia between 1584 and 1602, all of which paused en route in the West Indies.[4] Some had come looking for El Dorado, like Raleigh himself when he explored Trinidad and Guiana. But most had come to trade clandestinely with the Spanish colonists—or to seize their ships and loot their settlements. Here was the scene of Francis Drake's first outlandish exploit, where he stole £40,000 in silver, gold, and pearls in 1573. Here he returned in 1585 with thirty ships to sack Santo Domingo and Cartagena. Here was the favorite station for English privateers during the war years, 1585 to 1604, when they captured hundreds of enemy ships and carried home upwards of £100,000 per annum in sugar, hides, logwood, indigo, silver, gold, and pearls from the Spanish Main. Nor did English privateering and illicit trade stop with the Spanish peace treaty of 1604. It is probable that English investors—chiefly London merchants—put more money into commerce and piracy in the Caribbean from 1560

4. Similarly, in Mar. and Apr. 1607 the *Susan Constant, Godspeed,* and *Discovery* spent three weeks island hopping in the Caribbean; Capt. John Smith and his colleagues recuperated from a weary Atlantic crossing by bathing, hunting, and fishing in the eastern Antilles before they headed north for the James River.

to 1630 than into any other mode of long-distance, overseas business enterprise, even the East India Company.[5] Thus when Englishmen began to colonize in the Antilles in the 1620s, they were no babes in the woods. They were self-conscious heirs to Hawkins, Drake, and Raleigh, and as Sir Henry Colt put it, they could not rest until they too had "doone some thinges worthy of ourselves, or dye in the attempt."[6]

The Elizabethan war was still being fought in the Caribbean, for the Indies lay "beyond the line," that is, outside the territorial limits of European treaties. In America, might made right, and international law was suspended. It was the French and Spanish diplomats who first worked out this policy in 1559 when they could not settle their American counterclaims; the Spanish refused to surrender their "right" to exclude all foreigners from the Indies, and the French refused to abandon their "right" to go to the Indies, so the two parties agreed to disagree overseas while keeping the peace at home. Frenchmen and Spaniards who crossed the "line of amity," who sailed west of the prime meridian in the mid-Atlantic or south of the Tropic of Cancer, were expected to take care of themselves as best they could. Their fights in America were not to invalidate the peace settlement in Europe. On the same principle Spanish and English diplomats drew up peace treaties in 1604 and 1630 that deliberately sidestepped their rival pretensions in America.[7] The English remained free to settle unoccupied territory and trade with the Spaniards—if they could get away with it; the Spaniards remained free to exterminate the intruders and keep America a closed preserve—if they had the strength to do so. In practice Virginians and New Englanders had little to fear from Spain, living as they did so far removed from the closest enemy outposts. But in the Caribbean the English impudently perched athwart the

5. For a survey of Elizabethan activity in the Caribbean, see James A. Williamson, *The Age of Drake* (London, 1938), chaps. 4–5, 7–8, 12, 15, 18–19. For West Indian privateering, see Kenneth R. Andrews, *Elizabethan Privateering: English Privateering during the Spanish War, 1585–1603* (Cambridge, Eng., 1964), chaps. 7–8; Theodore K. Rabb, *Enterprise and Empire: Merchant and Gentry Investment in the Expansion of England, 1575–1630* (Cambridge, Mass., 1967), 61–66. For the continuation of anti-Spanish activity in the Caribbean, 1603–1641, see Arthur Percival Newton, *The Colonising Activities of the English Puritans: The Last Phase of the Elizabethan Struggle with Spain* (New Haven, Conn., 1914).

6. Harlow, *Colonising*, 91.

7. A. Pearce Higgins, "International Law and the Outer World, 1450–1648," in J. Holland Rose, A. P. Newton, and E. A. Benians, eds., *The Cambridge History of the British Empire*, I (Cambridge, Eng., 1929), chap. 6.

principal highway from Seville to Mexico and Peru. In 1629 a company of high-level English Puritans—numbering among them John Pym, the earl of Warwick, Lord Brooke, and Viscount Saye and Sele—sent colonists to occupy Providence Island off the Nicaraguan coast as a staging ground for raids against the Isthmus of Panama. In 1631 this company sponsored another privateering base at Tortuga, off the coast of Hispaniola, in deliberate continuation of the Elizabethan war with Spain. This was just at the time when Sir Henry Colt laid plans to buy an armed ship for trading in the territory of the Spaniards. "Next yeer I shall offend them," promised Colt.[8]

To live "beyond the line" meant more than a flouting of European treaty obligations. It meant a general flouting of European social conventions. The sixteenth- and early seventeenth-century record plainly showed that Spaniards, Englishmen, Frenchmen, and Dutchmen who sojourned in the tropics all tended to behave in a far more unbuttoned fashion than at home. White men who scrambled for riches in the torrid zone exploited their Indian and black slaves more shamelessly than was possible with the unprivileged laboring class in Western Europe. And they robbed and massacred each other more freely than the rules of civility permitted in European combat. Sir Henry thought the devil must have special power in America. "Who is he that cann live long in quiett in these parts?" Colt asked. "For all men are heer made subject to the power of this Infernall Spiritt. And fight they must, although it be with ther owne frends."[9]

For many years Englishmen had come to the Indies to fight, not colonize—this was the Elizabethan legacy. The travelers to the Caribbean whose reports were collected by Richard Hakluyt in *Principal Navigations of the English Nation* (1598–1600) and by Samuel Purchas in *Hakluytus Posthumus, or Purchas His Pilgrimes* (1625) had little or no desire to plant English colonies in the Caribbean. Their narratives are filled with naval battles, jungle marches, Indian ambushes, pestilential distempers, bloody sieges, and the sacking of Spanish towns. Hakluyt gives many pages of navigational instruction on how to sail from island to island, but neither he nor Purchas supplies much topographical description of

8. Newton, *Colonising Activities of the English Puritans*, chaps. 3–4; Harlow, *Colonising*, 101.
9. Harlow, *Colonising*, 73.

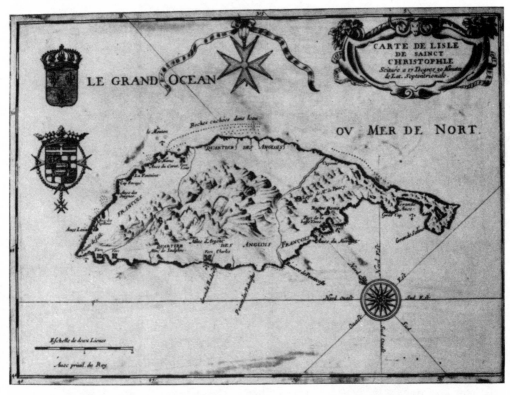

FIG. 1. The oldest map of St. Christopher, drawn by a French cartographer about 1654. (Courtesy of William L. Clements Library, University of Michigan, Ann Arbor.)

FIG. 2. *Two views from an unsigned map of Montserrat drawn in 1673, showing French ships attacking the island. Note the rugged topography, with plantations built high up the mountainsides. (Courtesy of John Carter Brown Library, Brown University, Providence.)*

the islands themselves, of the scenery, climate, flora and fauna, or economic geography. Travelers who touched at St. Christopher, Montserrat, Nevis, Guadeloupe, and Martinique [10] found little to say about these small islands, soon to be planted by the English and French. They observed Spanish sugar production in Hispaniola and Puerto Rico and pointed out the possibilities of English sugar production in Guiana—but cane growing was not the privateers' style.

One of the more telling points about these first English impressions of the Caribbean is their silence on the subject of African slavery. The Elizabethan sea dogs met plenty of slave ships and saw plenty of blacks in the Spanish settlements. Although their narratives sometimes mention "Negroes" or "slaves" in passing, these men showed no curiosity about the blacks, their African culture, their bondage, or their treatment by the Spaniards. It was harder to ignore the Carib Indians, who sometimes traded cordially with the English and sometimes shot at them with poisoned arrows. A number of reporters took pains to investigate and portray the Caribs' naked savage state. This rather curious differentiation between Africans and Indians was to be echoed again and again by later generations of English residents in the Caribbean—and by Englishmen in North America, of course, as well.[11]

It was easy to spin myths about the Indies, such as the legend of El Dorado—the golden man who lived in a golden city a few days' march inland beyond the jungles of the Orinoco basin. Englishmen tried desperately to find what Raleigh called "the Large, Rich and Beautiful Empire of Guiana." [12] But no one after Columbus could seriously entertain the grander myth that the Indies was perfect as well as rich—the seat of Elysium. Englishmen who came to the Indies rarely if ever adopted the romantic proposition of modern tourism that the Caribbean isles were bits and pieces of paradise.

10. Whether any Englishman touched at Barbados before 1624 is in doubt. Purchas reports a visit of 1605, but James Williamson challenges his accuracy in *The Caribbee Islands under the Proprietary Patents* (Oxford, 1926), 15–17.

11. Richard Hakluyt, *The Principal Navigations, Voyages, Traffiques and Discoveries of the English Nation . . .* , Everyman's Library (London, n.d. [orig. publ. London, 1598–1600]), VII, 87–88, 92–93, 96, 149, 154, 167, 171–172, 185–186, 219, 224–271; Samuel Purchas, *Hakluytus Posthumus, or Purchas his Pilgrimes, Contayning a History of the World in Sea Voyages and Lande Travells by Englishmen and Others* (Glasgow, 1905–1907 [orig. publ. London, 1625]), XVI, 52–56, 78, 90, 291, 321–322, 324–330, 347–348, 352–353, 362, 372–374, 381, 399–400.

12. See V. S. Naipaul's telling evocation of this myth in *The Loss of El Dorado* (New York, 1970).

Only one island in their experience had the attributes of Elysium, and that was Bermuda, which was *not* in the West Indies. This isolated miniature coral atoll, lying eight hundred miles north of the Caribbean and six hundred miles east of Carolina, seemed to the English to possess all of the merits of the tropics and none of the defects. Bermuda had a markedly cooler climate than the West Indies islands, too cool for optimum sugar production. The Spaniards had long thought it an accursed, enchanted place, the Isle of Devils, where violent storms blew up to catch passing ships and smash them against the coral reefs. But when a party of Virginia colonists was shipwrecked on Bermuda in 1609, they found it enchanting in an altogether different sense: beautifully green, bounteously fruitful, deliciously temperate. Even the Spaniards learned to admire the place. "It seemed," wrote a shipwrecked Spanish visitor in 1639, "we were entering some pleasant and delightful gardens where young trees grew among golden flowers. It all seemed to our eyes like Elysian fields." [13]

Bermuda was the ideal desert island, free from Indians, insects, gold mines, and international rivalry, a setting for escapism, solitude, and innocent beauty. Such poets as Shakespeare and Andrew Marvell were powerfully stirred by the image of this tiny refuge hidden in the bosom of the ocean. To Shakespeare, Bermuda was the dream habitation of Prospero, Ariel, and Caliban. To Marvell, the poet of green gardens, Bermuda was God's perfect garden:

> He gave us this eternal spring
> Which here enamels everything. . . .
> He hangs in shades the orange bright,
> Like golden lamps in a green night;
> And does in the pomegranates close
> Jewels more rich than Ormus shows.

No poets sang of Barbados, Jamaica, or the Leeward Islands in the seventeenth century. The Caribbee isles could boast delightful gardens, golden flowers, oranges, and pomegranates aplenty, but they were places of perpetual blazing summer, not sweet spring. And they were indelibly stained by tales of human greed and atrocity.

13. L. D. Gunin, trans., "Shipwrecked Spaniards in 1639," *Bermuda Historical Quarterly,* XVIII (1961), 15; see also William Strachey's "A True Reportory" and Silvester Jourdain's *Discovery of Bermuda,* pamphlets of 1610 recounting the English discovery of Bermuda, in Louis B. Wright, ed., *A Voyage to Virginia in 1609* (Charlottesville, Va., 1964).

ξ●

On his voyage to St. Christopher, Sir Henry Colt saw only one corner of the West Indies. There are three groups of islands in this vast archipelago: the Greater Antilles, the Lesser Antilles, and the Bahamas. The Greater Antilles are the four largest islands, in order of size Cuba, Hispaniola, Jamaica, and Puerto Rico. The Lesser Antilles stretch in an almost unbroken chain from Puerto Rico to the Venezuelan coast and include about forty habitable islands and a great many islets and rocks. The Bahamas, lying north of Cuba, include another thirty habitable islands and an even larger number of islets and rocks. Starting in the 1560s the English reconnoitered the entire archipelago, looking for likely places to trade, raid, and settle. During the seventeenth century they tried planting in all parts of the Indies and occupied sections of the South American and Central American coast as well as dozens of islands. But most of these settlements were temporary or casual. In the end the English concentrated their energies on half a dozen islands: Barbados, St. Christopher, Nevis, Antigua, and Montserrat, in the Lesser Antilles, and Jamaica in the Greater Antilles.[14]

Why these particular islands? They are not (except for Jamaica) among the larger Caribbean islands, nor are they compactly convenient to each other. On the contrary, the English settlers found themselves frighteningly cut off from their fellow countrymen in times of crisis and dangerously close to enemy territory. Yet the English did not select these six sites purely by accident. It was partly a matter of geography and partly a matter of European power politics.

From 1492 into the early seventeenth century, Spaniards were the only European peoples who occupied the West Indies. To the Spanish, the Caribbean islands were of minor importance compared with Mexico and Peru, so they only bothered to inhabit the Greater Antilles and Trinidad. They used these big islands to raise provisions—mainly cattle, plus a little cassava, corn, tobacco, and sugar—and they left the smaller islands to the Caribs. Strategically, however, the whole archipelago was vital to Spain. All traffic be-

14. The English also permanently planted Anguilla, Barbuda, and Tortola in the Lesser Antilles, and Eleuthera and New Providence in the Bahamas during the 17th century, but the settlements in these islands were tiny and insignificant.

tween Seville and Spanish America had to pass through the islands, and in order to protect the shipping route of their treasure fleets the Spanish tried hard to keep other peoples out of the Indies. They failed, of course, but during the sixteenth century the Spanish at least kept the Portuguese, French, English, and Dutch intruders in the Caribbean from planting colonies. Then the Anglo-Spanish war of 1585 to 1604 so exhausted the Spanish in the West Indies that after the peace treaty they could stop neither Dutch interlopers from taking over their trade routes in the Caribbean nor English and French colonists from occupying the fringe areas of the Indies. The Spanish squadron that chased Sir Henry Colt's ship in 1631 was less formidable than it looked.[15]

In the years between 1604 and 1640, English, Dutch, and French colonists—cooperating with each other against the Spaniards—selected their first colonizing sites in the Caribbean. This was the great age of Dutch commercial expansion, and the Hollanders turned the Caribbean almost into a Dutch lake. But it was the English who made the chief effort at colonization. Exact figures are unobtainable, but from what we know of shipping statistics and early island population figures it is reasonable to surmise that at least thirty thousand persons from the British Isles went to the Caribbean to colonize during the reigns of James I and Charles I. Commentators at the time placed the total much higher, and it is frequently asserted that more Britons migrated to the West Indies during these years than to North America. This, I think, is a distortion. Surviving evidence, which will be discussed later, indicates that the stream of migration to the mainland colonies was always larger, even before the English civil war. Yet it is certainly true that the English mounted a major colonizing effort in the West Indies during the early seventeenth century. They tried to plant in dozens of places and experimented with a wide range of colonizing techniques. They soon learned, however, that tropical settlement was tricky work. Their failure rate was strikingly high, for the great majority of the early English colonizing ventures in the Caribbean quickly folded.

Guiana on the South American coast was at first the favorite site.

15. For a fuller introduction to the history of the Caribbean in this period, see J. H. Parry and P. M. Sherlock, *A Short History of the West Indies* (London, 1956), chaps. 1–7; Sir Alan Burns, *History of the British West Indies* (London, 1954), chaps. 1–14; and especially Arthur Percival Newton, *The European Nations in the West Indies, 1492–1688* (London, 1933).

Inspired by Raleigh's search for the golden city of El Dorado in the Orinoco basin, the English tried repeatedly to plant in the no-man's-land between the Orinoco River (held by Spain) and the Amazon River (held by Portugal). Guiana settlements were started in 1604, 1609, 1617, 1620, 1629, and 1643, not to mention others that cannot now be precisely dated, but all of these ventures collapsed. The planters, poorly supported from home, were discouraged by their inability to find gold, decimated by fever, and chased away by Indian, Portuguese, and Spanish attacks. A different sort of failure was the Providence Company, chartered by the king in 1630 and operated by the chief Puritan politicians in England. This company managed the settlement of three islands in the western Caribbean: Providence (Santa Catalina) and Henrietta (San Andreas), near the Moskito coast of Nicaragua, and Tortuga at the entrance to the Windward Passage between Hispaniola and Cuba. The Providence planters grew plentiful crops of corn, tobacco, and cotton and tried to fashion a godly commonwealth analagous to the New England communities, but they soon diverted their energies to piratical expeditions against nearby Spanish settlements, and Tortuga was an outright pirate lair. The Spaniards captured Tortuga in 1635 and Providence in 1641 and closed down the Providence Company.[16] Meanwhile other English parties tried to settle at the southern end of the Lesser Antilles in Trinidad, Tobago, Grenada, and St. Lucia, but they too were quickly expelled by the Spaniards and Caribs.

The lesson from all these failures was obvious: settlement was only feasible in sites removed as far as possible from contact with the Spanish and Indian population centers. Englishmen who planted in the Indies in the early seventeenth century were forced to moderate, at least temporarily, their expectations of gold and glory. They had to pick secluded agricultural sites and start out as modest tobacco and cotton farmers. The only successful English settlements between 1604 and 1640 were in five of the more northerly islands in the Lesser Antillean chain—St. Christopher, Barbados, Nevis, Antigua, and Montserrat. Earlier travelers to the Indies had dismissed these places as mere watering stations. They were all small islands with apparently strictly limited potential. The land was obviously fertile, but mountainous, jungled, and hard to clear. There was no promise of nonagrarian development, for these is-

16. Early English efforts to plant in Guiana are traced in Harlow, *Colonising,* *lxvi–lxxxvii,* 132–174; the rise and fall of the Providence Company is fully discussed by Newton, *Colonising Activities of the English Puritans.*

lands lacked mineral deposits, pearl fisheries, or dyewood forests. Since they were situated on the eastern fringe of the Caribbean, the English colonists were in a poor position to trade or plunder on the Spanish Main, but on the other hand the Spanish rarely attacked them. Thanks to the trade wind, it was easier to reach the Lesser Antilles from London or Amsterdam than from Havana or Cartagena. The isolation and small size of these islands were probably psychological advantages, at least initially. The early settlers had a physical setting of manageable scale, a land they could hope to tame into a reasonable facsimile of the countryside they knew at home, unlike the planters on the vast North American seaboard who could only establish beachheads in a trackless wilderness.

It was no easy task to colonize even in the Lesser Antilles. The first permanent settlement (1624) in St. Christopher—the "mother colony" of the English West Indies—survived only because the English joined forces with the French on this island to collaborate against Spanish and Carib attacks. The two peoples pooled their talents to massacre the Indians in a sneak night attack, and in 1629 they withstood Spanish efforts to chase them off the island. But neither the English nor the French were satisfied to divide St. Christopher permanently, and for the next eighty years they jockeyed grimly for control of the place. The English in Barbados (1627) had a far easier time. They found this island marvelously suited to agriculture, and since it stands well east of the main Antillean chain, it became the first Caribbean port of call for provision ships from Europe or slave ships from Africa. The Caribs seldom visited here, and Barbados was the only English West Indian colony in the seventeenth century to escape invasion by the Spaniards or French. This island from the outset was the most populous and successful English plantation in the Indies, though at first the inhabitants were far from rich. Until the 1640s the Barbadians formed a simple community of peasant farmers.

The other early English settlements were all spin-offs from St. Christopher, in the Leeward group of islands, and were much less immediately successful. Nevis (1628), mainly one great mountain, offered less farmland than St. Christopher. Montserrat (1632) was a very small island with exceptionally rugged terrain, and Antigua (1632), although boasting considerable acreage and excellent harbors, was short of water. Nonetheless, these places proved to be far better sites than the other nearby islands occupied by the English—Anguilla, Barbuda, and Tortola—which were too barren and rainless for tropical agriculture. Scattered into many small and awkward sites, the Leeward colonists remained struggling peasant farmers for many years.

The French in these early times made much less of a colonizing effort than the English. They concentrated on three islands in the Lesser Antilles—St. Christopher, Guadeloupe (1635), and Martinique (1635) —and Cayenne on the Guiana coast. Since the French colonists were few in number and poorly supported, their English rivals could well have beaten them to Guadeloupe and Martinique. But the English held back because these places were so heavily populated by Caribs. It took the French many painful years to conquer and clear Guadeloupe and Martinique, but the struggle was worth it, for they acquired two of the larger islands in the Indies, with fertile soil and good harbors.[17] The Dutch, by contrast, picked up mere crumbs of land, despite their tremendous activity all over the Caribbean. Their chief base was Curaçao (1634), near the Venezuelan coast, well sited for trade with the Spanish Main and close to the salt deposits on Aruba and Bonaire, which they used to supply their home fishing industry. The Dutch also occupied St. Martin (which they shared with the French), St. Eustatius, and Saba—three of the most barren rockpiles in the Lesser Antilles. St. Martin had salt flats, and all three of these islands were conveniently close to English and French settlements, giving the Dutch traders handy bases for their commercial operations.

These infant outposts on the eastern edge of the Caribbean suddenly assumed a new significance in the 1640s when the English planters in Barbados—followed at a distance by the colonists in the other English and French islands—converted from tobacco to sugar production. This switch from a crop with minimum European market value to a crop with maximum European market value made the Barbados planters rich overnight. They consolidated their small farms into large plantations manned by squadrons of black slaves imported from Africa. The Barbadians were greatly helped by knowledgeable Dutch entrepreneurs who showed them how to process the cane, supplied them with Negroes, and bought their sugar to sell in Holland. At first the Caribbean sugar revolution

17. For French activity in the West Indies during the 17th century, see Stewart L. Mims, *Colbert's West India Policy* (New Haven, Conn., 1912); Nellis M. Crouse's two chronicles, *French Pioneers in the West Indies, 1624–1664* (New York, 1940) and *The French Struggle for the West Indies, 1665–1713* (New York, 1943).

was pretty well confined to Barbados; production in the Leewards, Martinique, and Guadeloupe did not become significant until the 1670s. Nonetheless, sugar did have a truly revolutionary impact upon the European pattern of colonization in the Indies. All of the English and French islands inexorably followed the Barbadian example, changing from European peasant societies into slave-based plantation societies. All of them came under the surveillance of the home authorities in London and Paris, who recognized the great value of their Caribbean possessions and took prompt steps to prevent Dutch middlemen from absorbing the profits of the sugar business. The English navigation acts of 1651 and following years were designed to tie the sugar planters to English ships, English merchants, and the home market. The Company of Royal Adventurers into Africa (1663) and its successor, the Royal African Company (1672), were given a monopoly on the slave trade to the English colonies. These mercantilist measures naturally precipitated conflict with the Dutch in the Caribbean, especially during the Anglo-Dutch wars of 1652–1654, 1665–1667, and 1672–1674. In 1667 the English suffered a major defeat in Surinam on the Guiana coast, where they lost to the Dutch a flourishing new sugar colony founded about 1650. But the loss of Surinam was more than offset by the acquisition of Jamaica.

The English seizure of Jamaica from Spain in 1655 was in part a demonstration of the aggressive self-confidence of the nouveau riche sugar planters who wanted additional Caribbean acreage to expand their production. But mainly it reaffirmed the old Elizabethan privateering tradition. As we have seen, the Englishmen who occupied Providence and Tortuga in the 1630s kept warm the memory of Hawkins and Drake by conducting a private war against Spain. And when these freebooters were chased away from Providence and Tortuga, many of them moved to the uninhabited forests of northern Hispaniola where they became buccaneers, rovers who hunted wild cattle and swine for their food and robbed Spanish ships and coastal settlements for their pleasure. Oliver Cromwell allied himself with these buccaneers in 1654 when he secretly sent a massive expeditionary force of eighty-two hundred men into the western Caribbean to conquer one of the principal Spanish islands. The two nations were at peace in 1654, but to Cromwell the Indies still lay "beyond the line." The Protector's troopers first tried to capture Hispaniola and failed miserably. Then they managed to occupy Jamaica, very lightly held by the Spanish.

The capture of Jamaica, strategically situated in the heart of the Caribbean, gave the English a matchless opportunity for plundering Spanish wealth. In the 1660s and 1670s Jamaica became the base for thousands of buccaneers, led by the redoubtable Henry Morgan, who preyed upon Spanish commerce or looted the coastal settlements of Cuba, Hispaniola, and Central America, then came roaring home to roister away their booty in the taverns of Port Royal, the wickedest city in the West.[18]

The annexation of Jamaica enormously increased England's sugar acreage, for this island was far larger than Barbados or St. Christopher. Potentially Jamaica could produce more sugar than all of the other English islands put together. In fact, however, sugar planting developed slowly in Jamaica. Until the 1680s the buccaneers vied with the sugar planters for control of the island, and the planters were chronically short of Negroes because the slave traders sold most of their black cargoes in the Lesser Antilles, closer to Africa. Jamaica did not surpass Barbados as the leading English sugar colony until about 1720. Nevertheless its annexation in 1655 provided the English sugar interests with as much Caribbean acreage as they wanted, for they feared that any further cane fields would glut production and drive down prices. Therefore, after taking Jamaica the English added no further significant territory to their Caribbean holdings for a century, until they took Dominica, St. Vincent, and Grenada during the Seven Years' War. This static policy—so different from English territorial aggrandizement in North America between 1655 and 1763—was not a sign of English apathy. Quite the contrary. It expressed the protectionist strength of the English sugar lobby.

In the French islands very much the same thing happened. Shortly after the English took Jamaica, the French occupied the western third of Hispaniola, and this new colony of St. Domingue (modern Haiti), much larger in area than Martinique and Guadeloupe, gave them as much sugar acreage as they could possibly use. The Dutch, for their part, had all the Caribbean trading posts they needed. Thus the English, French, and Dutch colonists stopped grabbing new islands in the closing decades of the seventeenth

18. One of these buccaneers, a Dutchman named Alexander Olivier Exquemelin, wrote a famous, firsthand account of the brotherhood, *De Americaeneche Zee Roovers* (Amsterdam, 1678), which was translated into English as John Esquemeling, *Bucaniers of America* (London, 1684), and ran through five English editions by 1699. For a modern account see C. H. Haring, *The Buccaneers in the West Indies in the XVII Century* (London, 1910).

century. Spain was by now much the weakest power in the Caribbean, though still in possession of the largest land area—Cuba,
eastern Hispaniola (the modern Dominican Republic), and Puerto
Rico—but the other European powers needed no further territory,
and they tacitly agreed to let Spain, the Sick Man of America, keep
the rest of its sprawling, undeveloped Caribbean empire. Indeed
both the English and the French authorities saw more profit in
trading with the Spanish colonists than in robbing them, and from
about 1680 onwards they tried their best to suppress the buccaneers.
Old habits died hard, however, and when the freebooters were expelled from Jamaica, St. Domingue, and the central Caribbean, they
simply transferred their activities north to the Bahama islands and
became outright pirates, preying indiscriminately upon the ships of
all nations. The Bahamas, with their numberless coral cays and
reefs, were ideal territory for pirate ships, which could pounce upon
merchant vessels passing through the Windward Passage or the
Florida Channel. Piracy flourished in the Bahamas from the 1670s
to the 1720s, until at last the English established a settled government over these islands.[19]

Buccaneers and pirates were no more destructive than the officially sanctioned fleets of English, French, Dutch, and Spanish war-
ships that cruised the Caribbean during the frequent wars between
1660 and 1713. The English and French were by now the most
bellicose powers in the West Indies, and their rivalry produced a
sort of balance of terror. The two nations, antithetical in religion
and politics, shared the same mercantilist economic postulates.
They competed against each other on the European market with
the same range of West Indian commodities, sugar being by far
the most important. Competition was keenest on St. Christopher,
inhabited by both English and French planters until 1689, but the
other English and French islands in the Lesser Antilles were within
sight of each other, and in the Greater Antilles, Jamaica and St.
Domingue were also near neighbors. The Anglo-French wars of
1666–1667, 1689–1697, and 1702–1713 proved very destructive in the
Caribbean—far more so than in North America. The aim was to
damage enemy property rather than to annex it. French and English

19. Englishmen first tried to plant on Eleuthera in 1648 and on New Providence in 1666, but neither of these Bahamian settlements took firm root until
after the Peace of Utrecht. See W. Hubert Miller, "The Colonization of the
Bahamas, 1647–1670," *William and Mary Quarterly*, 3d Ser., II (1945), 33–46;
Michael Craton, *A History of the Bahamas* (London, 1962), chaps. 1–9.

expeditions repeatedly raided each other's islands, carried off slaves, burned plantations, and seized shipping. St. Christopher was sacked seven times during these wars; Guadeloupe, Montserrat, and Antigua were pillaged twice each; Martinique, Jamaica, Nevis, and St. Domingue once each. But the peace treaties of Breda, Ryswick, and Utrecht always restored the status quo ante bellum, except that in 1667 the English ceded Surinam to the Dutch and in 1713 the French ceded their half of St. Christopher to the English. Otherwise, the Caribbean map remained essentially unchanged from the 1660s to the 1760s.

With the Peace of Utrecht the European nations in the West Indies at last settled down. The English, like their competitors, had what they wanted in the Caribbean. Their holdings were not large, but very valuable, and the sugar industry was booming. Old habits of greed and atrocity had been transmuted, though hardly abandoned. Englishmen in the Indies had learned how to exploit slaves more profitably than Spaniards. The sugar planters had discovered El Dorado after all.

This success story was not widely advertised to the world at large, for the island colonists publicized their doings very little. Back in the Elizabethan era, when English sailors knew the Antilles far better than the North American coast, reports from the New World centered on the Caribbean. But after 1607 the focus shifted decisively north.[20] Promoters of the Virginia Company, friends and foes of the Puritan communities in New England, and sponsors of the proprietary colonies in Carolina, New Jersey, and Pennsylvania circulated numerous accounts of their settlements, but the many thousand Englishmen who inhabited Barbados, Jamaica, and the Leewards during the seventeenth century rarely bothered to write descriptions of what they saw or did. Colt's journal of his Caribbean experience in 1631 is a rare document—and Sir Henry wrote for the private edification of his family back home; his journal remained in manuscript for three hundred years. None of the islands boasted a printing press, nor did the islanders use the London presses. During the entire course of the century eight or ten promotional tracts designed to lure immigrants to the Caribbean colonies were issued

20. See the year-by-year list of English geographical books and manuscripts, 1583–1650, compiled by E. G. R. Taylor in her *Late Tudor and Early Stuart Geography, 1583–1650* (London, 1934) , 177–298. According to my calculations, Prof. Taylor lists 68 works describing the Caribbean, Guiana, or the Spanish Main, 42 of them dated before 1607. She lists 139 works describing the Chesapeake and New England, only 15 of which predate 1607.

in England, whereas the Virginia Company sponsored some twenty propaganda pieces in the period from 1609 to 1612 alone.[21]

The seventeenth-century literature on the English sugar islands is deficient in quality as well as in quantity. The islanders were men of action, not reflection. They lacked the driving moral purpose and intellectual commitment of the New England Puritans, and they were less polished than the best of the early Virginia writers such as Robert Beverley. Nor could they match the keenest French Caribbean chroniclers of the day—Jean-Baptiste du Tertre and Jean-Baptiste Labat—who wrote minutely detailed multivolume accounts of their experiences in St. Christopher, Guadeloupe, and Martinique.[22] Nonetheless, the early island colonists have left us an invaluable medley of travel accounts, topographical descriptions, military journals, medical reports, commercial pamphlets, and propaganda tracts that go far beyond the privateering narratives collected by Hakluyt and Purchas before settlement began. In particular, Colt's journal of 1631, Richard Ligon's report on life in Barbados from 1647 to 1650, Christopher Jeaffreson's letters from St. Christopher, 1676 to 1682, and John Taylor's and Sir Hans Sloane's parallel descriptions of Jamaica in 1688 are marvelously sharp and evocative social documents. Characteristically, Ligon was the only one of these five gentlemen who published his observations during the seventeenth century.[23]

21. Jarvis M. Morse, who has surveyed the chief 17th-century writings on English America in *American Beginnings: Highlights and Sidelights of the Birth of the New World* (Washington, D.C., 1952), found 25 books and pamphlets worth mentioning on West Indian topics published between 1607 and 1713, as against 162 on North America (my count). A. W. Pollard and G. R. Redgrave, eds., *A Short-Title Catalogue of Books Printed in England, . . . 1475–1640* (London, 1926), and Donald Wing's companion *Short-Title Catalogue of Books Printed in England, . . . 1641–1700* (New York, 1945–1951) display an even more extreme contrast: six entries for Barbados, Jamaica, and the Leeward Islands as against 148 entries for the mainland colonies.
22. Jean-Baptiste Du Tertre, *Histoire générale des Antilles habitées par les François* (Paris, 1667–1671), Jean-Baptiste Labat, *Nouveau voyage aux isles de l'Amérique . . .* (Paris, 1722). For another ambitious and informative French report, see Louis de Poincy's *Histoire naturelle et morale des Îles Antilles de l'Amérique,* revised by Charles de Rochefort (Rotterdam, 1658, 1665) and translated by John Davies of Kidwelly as *The History of the Caribby-Islands . . .* (London, 1666). This English version is hereafter cited as Davies, *History of Caribby-Islands.*
23. "The Voyage of Sir Henrye Colt" was discovered among the manuscripts in the Cambridge University Library by Vincent T. Harlow and first printed in 1925 in Harlow, *Colonising;* Richard Ligon's *A True & Exact History of the Island of Barbados . . .* (London, 1657) was reissued in 1673, and is now

Much of the early literature on the island settlements was economic in character, for the sugar colonies were business ventures
primarily. From this perspective they were model plantations in a
mercantilist age. They promoted a favorable balance of trade by
supplying England with commodities that she must otherwise import from abroad. Whatever sugar was not consumed in England
could be sold in Europe. The islanders had no local manufactures
and depended on the home entrepôt for finished goods of all sorts.
Even in agriculture the sugar planters were far from self-sufficient,
and they bought large quantities of meat, fish, cheese, grain, and
lumber from North America and Ireland. Their bottomless appetite
for black labor supported the English slave trade to Africa. They
employed a significant portion of the English merchant marine and
supplied a growing sugar-manufacturing business at home. In a
few decades the English plantations in the Indies had developed
amazingly from the struggling little tobacco patches Sir Henry Colt
had seen in 1631.

Each of the Caribbean islands settled by the English in the seventeenth century has its own distinct personality, conditioned by local
geography and topography. It is important to remember that these
islands are widely separated from each other. The Jamaica planters
found themselves close to Spanish Cuba and French St. Domingue,
but a thousand miles west of the closest English settlements in the
Lesser Antilles. Barbadians had to pass two French islands in order
to reach their nearest English neighbors in the Leeward Islands. The
four English settlements in the Leewards were within sight of each

available in a facsimile edition of the 1673 printing (London, 1970) ; Christopher
Jeaffreson's letterbook was edited (very poorly) by John Cordy Jeaffreson in
1878 as *A Young Squire of the Seventeenth Century. From the Papers (A.D.
1676–1686) of Christopher Jeaffreson* (London, 1878) ; John Taylor's manuscript, Multum in Parvo or Parvum in Multo. Taylor's second part of the His-
torie of his life and Travels in AMERICA. Containeing a full Geographical description of the Island of Jamaica . . . under the government of his Grace
Christopher Duke of Albemarle, is still unpublished, a quarto volume of 256
closely written pages owned by the Institute of Jamaica, Kingston. It is hereafter
cited as Taylor MS. Sir Hans Sloane produced the two volumes of *A Voyage to
the Islands Madera, Barbados, Nieves, S. Christophers and Jamaica* (London,
1707–1725) many years after his return from Jamaica.

other, but also within sight of six French and Dutch islands. The set of the wind increased the distance between the English islands. Because of the trade wind, the Leeward Islanders could never get quick help from Jamaica and seldom from Barbados. A sailing ship could cross from the Lesser Antilles down wind to Jamaica in a few days, but had to beat up wind for weeks to make the return voyage. Even the short windward passage from the Leewards to Barbados could take a long time. In the hurricane season the wise sailor stayed out of the Caribbean altogether.

Among the six English Caribbean islands there is considerable topographical variation. The physical differences between Barbados and Jamaica, for example, help to explain why Jamaica, for all its size, took half a century to surpass little Barbados as a sugar producer. It is thus useful to discuss in brief detail the topography of each island.

The island of Barbados, the richest and most populous of the English colonies during the seventeenth century, is 166 square miles in area, 21 miles long, and 14 miles wide. It is shaped like a leg of mutton and consists of a series of coral terraces that rise gradually from the placid Caribbean coast and steeply from the dramatic Atlantic coast to a central plateau a thousand feet above sea level. There are no mountains or rivers in Barbados, and the dense tropical forest that originally covered the island was cleared during the first thirty or forty years of settlement to make way for cane fields. Today there remain only a few patches of thick woodland, such as Turner's Hall Wood, to suggest what the place looked like to the first English planters. By the late seventeenth century the island was as fully cultivated as it is today, a sea of cane accented here and there by a clump of trees, a sugar works, or a Negro village. The early planters tended to find Barbados more hospitable than the other Caribbean islands. Sir Henry Colt liked it even in its wild state, and once the place was cleared and planted it reminded homesick settlers of the gently rolling hills and green fields they had come from. Already in the seventeenth century Barbados was "little England."

The first planters settled along the Caribbean, or leeward, coast, sheltered from the wind and storms. There are no harbors on the Atlantic, or windward, coast, nor are there safe landing places amidst the surf, rocks, and limestone cliffs, so this side of the island was settled much more slowly. As the colony developed during the century the planters built four towns on the leeward coast: Bridgetown, the chief port, in Carlisle Bay, and the three subsidiary villages of Speightstown, Holetown, and Oistins. The land is fairly flat here, and the sea is crystal blue, warm, and tranquil, bordered by palm-fringed white beaches. In modern Barbados most of the tourist hotels are to be found along the leeward shore. The rainfall is lighter here than elsewhere on the island, and Bridgetown in particular tends to be hot, humid, and airless. But as soon as one heads inland the terrain changes completely. The land rises gently, and rolling hills dominate the scene. Climbing up from Bridgetown through terraced green hills and valleys, one reaches a steep escarpment four miles into the interior, and at the top of this coral retaining wall is the central plateau, or upland. Here, a thousand feet above sea level, the land stretches nearly flat, the temperature is noticeably cooler than along the leeward coast, and the breeze is constant and strong. At the eastern rim of this upland, Hackleton's Cliff drops abruptly down to the wild Atlantic coast, edged with coral rocks and pounding surf. This, the most wildly beautiful region in Barbados, was quickly christened the Scotland district by the early colonists. In Scotland the air is bracing, and there are sweeping vistas, rugged hills, and narrow canyons, and at the bleak northern tip of the island the sea dashes high against the rocks.

One early observer remarked of Barbados: "The Land lyeth high much resembling England more healthfull then any of hir Neighbors; and better agreeing with the temper of the English Nacion." [24] Others found the Leeward Islands or Jamaica healthier, but most agreed that Barbados of all the Caribbee islands most closely resembled England. Richard Ligon, who came in 1647, was enchanted by his first view of the terraced slopes. "For as we past along near the shoar," he wrote, "the Plantations appear'd to us one above another: like several stories in stately buildings, which afforded us a large proportion of delight." [25] Ligon found the island much better planted than in Sir Henry Colt's day, but the fields were only partially cleared, with provision crops planted between the boughs of felled trees, and he still could not travel around much because of the poor roads and impassable thickets and gullies. By the 1660s the colonists were complaining of a timber shortage, and it is evident that they had cleared the entire island and were cultivating all of

24. "A Briefe Discription of the Ilande of Barbados," Harlow, *Colonising*, 42–43.
25. Ligon, *True History of Barbados*, 20–21.

the arable land.[26] Gov. Jonathan Atkins reported in 1676 that the whole island looked like a beautifully planted green garden, and his successor, Sir Richard Dutton, echoed him in 1681: "It is one great Citty adorned with gardens, and a most delightful place." Gov. James Kendall was even more emphatic in 1690. "Itt is," he said, "the beautyfulls't spott of ground I ever saw." [27]

Unlike most of the Caribbean islands, Barbados has a very high percentage of arable land. Its coral limestone soil is thin but fertile. Its annual rainfall averages over sixty inches. When Dr. Hans Sloane visited the island in 1687, he remarked that Barbados had lost its original fruitfulness, and the Barbadians themselves were fond of complaining in the late years of the century that their soil was exhausted. But the complaint proved premature. By manuring their fields heavily and continually, the planters have kept them fertile. Today, more than three hundred years after the first sugar crop was raised on the island, sugar still accounts for 90 percent of Barbados's exports and supports the densest population in the Indies. Sugar grows much better, to be sure, in some parts of the island than in others. The leeward coast, where settlement first started, has thin, infertile soil as well as light rainfall. The Barbadians fairly quickly discovered that their best soil and most abundant rainfall are on the high central plateau and in the valleys to the south of this plateau. Here, shortly after mid-century, they laid out their largest plantations. Because the whole island is windswept, many of the early sugar planters used windmills to crush their cane. A pamphleteer of 1676 says he saw four hundred windmills perched on the slopes and ridges of Barbados, their flying sails a very pretty sight.[28] A number

26. David Watts ingeniously reconstructs the 17th-century pattern of Barbadian forest clearance in *Man's Influence on the Vegetation of Barbados, 1627 to 1800*, University of Hull Occasional Papers in Geography, No. 4 (Hull, Eng., 1966), chap. 3.

27. Sir Jonathan Atkins to Lords of Trade, Feb. 3, 1675/6, Colonial Office Series, Class 29, Vol. 2, 49, Public Record Office. Hereafter cited as C.O. 29/2/49; Sir Richard Dutton to William Blathwayt, Mar. 15, 1680/1, Blathwayt Papers, XXX, Colonial Williamsburg Research Library, Williamsburg, Va. Hereafter cited as Blathwayt Papers; James Kendall to earl of Shrewsbury, Aug. 22, 1690, C.O. 28/1/81.

28. *Great Newes from the Barbadoes* (London, 1676), 6. For a full discussion of Barbados's topography, soil, and climatic conditions, see Otis P. Starkey, *The Economic Geography of Barbados* (New York, 1939), chaps. 1–2; also Starkey's more recent *Commercial Geography of Barbados*, Indiana University Department of Geography Technical Report No. 9 (Bloomington, Ind., 1961), in his series of 12 reports on the commercial geography of British islands in the Lesser Antilles. The present population of Barbados is about 250,000.

of derelict stone windmills can still be seen on the island, but very few of them predate 1800.

It is interesting to compare the topographical information in two maps of Barbados, the first published by Richard Ligon in 1657 and the second by Richard Ford around 1674. Ligon's map is the earliest one we have of the island. He lived in Barbados from 1647 to 1650, and his map, which he probably drew himself, pictures the island as he knew it. Ligon was an acute observer but a crude cartographer. Nonetheless his map is fascinating, for it shows how undeveloped the island was in his day. Ligon charts the leeward shore where he lived with reasonable exactitude, but gives a misshapen outline of the windward coast, which he never visited. The interior hills and ridges are likewise very inaccurately placed. The map identifies 285 plantations by name of owner. The vast majority of these plantations hug the leeward shore; a few are to be found in the lush interior farmland of St. George's Valley, but none is located on the central plateau. According to this map the richest Barbados farmland was still virtually inaccessible, for the roads leading inland from the leeward coast all quickly petered out, except for one road that crossed the northern end of the island from Speightstown to Scotland. Ligon shows four churches along the leeward coast and fortifications at Carlisle Bay to protect Bridgetown. His map is decorated with vignettes of planters hunting wild hogs and chasing runaway black slaves in the unsettled parts of the island. He also inserts an exotic pair of camels; Ligon says that several planters imported these beasts and found them useful in Barbados, but did not know how to diet them.[29]

Richard Ford's map of Barbados, published only seventeen years later, shows how rapidly the island—and knowledge of the island—had developed. Ford was a surveyor who lived in Bridgetown, and his map charts the island and its principal inhabitants in minute, precise detail. He outlines the Atlantic coast as exactly as the Caribbean coast and indicates the interior ridges and hills far better than Ligon. Ford identifies 844 plantations by name of owner. Here again he is accurate, for the names on his map correlate very closely with the lists of landholders in the Barbados census of 1680—as will be explained more fully in chapter three. Ford's map even shows how

29. Ligon's map, "A topographicall Description and Admeasurement of the Yland of Barbados," was published in his book, *True History of Barbados;* see fig. 4, p. 63, in this volume. See Watt's analysis of this map in *Man's Influence on the Vegetation of Barbados,* 41–42.

many windmills, cattle mills, or water mills each plantation had. Six small patches of forest are all that remain of the pre-European vegetation. Every section of the island is fully planted, and the network of roads is almost as extensive as in modern Barbados. The four towns and the eleven parish churches are shown. Being a Quaker, Ford refused to put in the island fortifications, and he had no room for illustrative vignettes. His display of 844 plantations is really much more impressive.[30]

A few days' sail or an hour's flight northwest of Barbados are the Leeward Islands, which present a quite different scene. Barbados is physically isolated and self-contained, ninety miles east of the closest neighbor, St. Lucia, and one hundred miles east of St. Vincent. But the Leewards are a family of little islands, set close together and colonized in the seventeenth century by four rival European peoples—the English, Irish, French, and Dutch. Within a radius of seventy-five miles from Nevis lie ten habitable islands, of which three were settled by the English, two by the French, two by the Dutch, one by the English and Irish, one by the English and French, and one by the French and Dutch. The dominant feature of life in the Leewards during the seventeenth century was the close proximity of foreigners.

The principal English islands in the congeries—St. Christopher, Nevis, Antigua, and Montserrat—all proved to be more challenging sites for settlement than Barbados. They are miniature places; Antigua measures 108 square miles, St. Christopher, 68, Nevis, 50, and Montserrat, 33—and only about half of this total land area is arable. Antigua is low-lying, like Barbados, with a good deal of level farmland, but has no springs and suffers severely from drought. The other three islands have mountains ranging over 3,000 feet in height and hillside fields that are difficult to clear and subject to erosion. Collectively the four islands never supported as many colonists as Barbados during the seventeenth century or produced as much sugar. Today the situation remains the same. Their com-

30. *A New Map of the Island of Barbadoes* [London, *c.* 1674]. The map is unsigned and undated. Jeannette D. Black of the John Carter Brown Library has generously supplied me with information about Ford. This map was incorporated into the Blathwayt Atlas, a superb collection of manuscript and printed maps relating chiefly to English America, compiled by William Blathwayt in the early 1680s and now owned by the John Carter Brown Library, Brown University, Providence, R.I. A facsimile edition, Jeannette D. Black, ed., *The Blathwayt Atlas* (Providence, 1970), is also available. For a section of Ford's map, see fig. 5, p. 94.

bined population and agricultural production is far below that of Barbados. Only St. Kitts, which has the best land in this group of islands, now produces a large sugar crop. Despite the natural assets of rich soil, abundant rain, salubrious climate, and a year-round growing season, agricultural production in the Leewards has generally been somewhat marginal.

St. Christopher and Nevis, by far the most important of the Leeward Islands in the seventeenth century, are twins, separated by a three-mile channel. St. Christopher is shaped like an Indian club and Nevis is oval. Both have mountainous cores and similar topography. Both are spectacularly beautiful places, especially when approached by boat, with their darkly forested peaks rising elegantly from the sea. But seventeenth-century Englishmen associated mountains with savagery. English travelers at home reported that the Lake District was "rough with mountains" and "surrounded by crooked hills." Travelers to the interior of New England described the Berkshires as "long, tedious hills" and the White Mountains as "shattered rocks, without trees or grass, very steep all the way." [31] Such persons were not likely to see natural beauty in St. Christopher and Nevis. And so we find a French writer of 1658 describing the mountains of St. Christopher as "great and steepy," with "dreadful precipices," but he waxed enthusiastic at the man-made beauty of the planters' terraced farms. The neatly planted rows of bright green tobacco, pale yellow sugarcane, and dark green ginger, bordered by groves of trees, fruit orchards, and the red glazed slate of the plantation house roofs, "make so delightful a Landskip, as must cause an extraordinary recreation to the unwearied eye." [32]

The rugged character of St. Christopher is well illustrated in the oldest map we have of the island, drawn by a French cartographer around 1654. [33] This map charts the coast rather inaccurately and

31. Taylor, *Late Tudor and Early Stuart Geography*, 10; Charles S. Grant, *Democracy in the Connecticut Frontier Town of Kent* (New York, 1961), 3; John Winthrop, *Journal, 1630–1649*, ed. James Kendall Hosmer (New York, 1908), II, 86.

32. Davies, *History of Caribby-Islands*, 21–23. By the 18th century visitors to St. Christopher like William Smith and Janet Schaw were much more romantically attracted by the mountain scenery. See Gordon C. Merrill, *The Historical Geography of St. Kitts and Nevis, The West Indies*, Instituto Panamericano de Geografia e Historia, No. 232 (Mexico, 1958), 18; and [Janet Schaw], *Journal of a Lady of Quality, 1774–1776*, ed. Evangeline Walker Andrews and Charles McLean Andrews (New Haven, Conn., 1923), 120–127.

33. "Carte de Lisle de Sainct Christophle," in Jean-Baptiste du Tertre, *Histoire générale des Isles de St. Christophe, de la Guadeloupe, de la Martinique, et*

omits most interior details, but it shows the jagged range of volcanic mountains that spans the length of the island. Mount Misery, toward the northwestern end, is the tallest peak, 3,800 feet high and generally shrouded in clouds. The leeward, or Caribbean, coast of St. Christopher boasts some rich, though steeply pitched farmland. The scene today must be much as it was in the late seventeenth century. Verdant, jungled mountain slopes plunge down into neatly contoured fields, which in turn fall away step by step to sheer sea cliffs and occasional sheltered coves, where the black beaches are composed of volcanic sand. The soil in the terraced fields is volcanic ash, fertile and easy to work. Trees and crops are even greener here than in Barbados, because the rainfall is heavier. The temperature is generally a shade cooler also, especially a few hundred feet up the mountain slopes, and the island prides itself on excellent water. Dr. Hans Sloane in 1687 thought the English inhabitants of St. Christopher looked healthier and less sallow than elsewhere in the Indies.

The settlement of St. Christopher during the seventeenth century was severely impeded by its division between English and French colonists. The map of 1654 shows the curious way in which the two nations partitioned the island and also the forts they built to defend their respective quarters. The French occupied both ends of the island, and the English took the middle. This arrangement gave the French the best roadstead, at Basseterre, but the English had more good farm land. Both shared the salt ponds at the narrow southeastern end closest to Nevis. In the heights above Basseterre, the map shows the splendid château built by the French governor de Poincy to keep his subjects dutiful and to overawe the English. This château was an imposing three-storied structure with a double flight of stairs, surrounded by formal gardens and a high wall. Within the English quarter, the mapmaker's "Mine d' Argent" is wishful thinking, but the "Mine de Soulphre" on the water's edge is Brimstone Hill, the chief English citadel during French attacks. From the 700-foot summit of Brimstone Hill, now covered by eighteenth-century battlements, the early colonists had a panoramic view of the French quarter, as well as the Dutch islands of St. Eustatius and Saba a few miles offshore. English ships moored at Fort Charles on the leeward coast. There was no good landing place

---

autres dans l'Amérique (Paris, 1654). The same map, slightly revised, appears in du Tertre's enlarged *Histoire générale des Antilles.* See fig. 1, facing p. 12.

along the Atlantic, or windward, coast because of shoals, high seas, and cliffs. Since the mountains are impassable, the English had to travel through French territory to get from the leeward to the windward quarter. Likewise the French had to use English roads. St. Kitts still has only one highway, looping around the island through the cane fields that girdle the coast.

The Anglo-French competition over St. Christopher hastened the early development of neighboring Nevis. For most of the seventeenth century, Nevis was the most flourishing of the English Leeward Islands. This beautiful island ascends gracefully from the sea, its classically proportioned central volcanic cone 3,232 feet high and usually cloud capped. Lower hills stand to either side, leaving very little level land, and the slopes and lowlands are obstructed by great blocks and boulders. As in Barbados, there is an amazing contrast between the leeward and windward sides of the island. On the leeward coast the hillsides curve gently down to wide beaches and the placid Caribbean, while only six miles across there are bold cliffs and crashing Atlantic rollers. The early settlers placed their chief town, Charlestown, on the leeward coast, but its roadstead is even less protected from storms or attack than at Basseterre, St. Christopher. Sir Henry Colt, who saw Nevis only three years after settlement had started there, was anxious to visit its hot mineral baths, which could cure all maladies, or so he was told. In the eighteenth century a hotel was built for visitors who came to take the thermal waters. But Nevis also had a reputation for sickliness. Dr. Sloane considered the people here "more Swarthy, or of a yellowish sickly look, than any of the Inhabitants of these Islands."

In the early days the Nevis planters cultivated much land that is now scrub pasture or rain forest, especially on the windward coast. When Dr. Sloane climbed Nevis peak in 1687, searching for botanical specimens, he passed through cleared fields almost all the way up until he came to a patch of woods at the top. The upper slopes of the mountain are now heavily forested. Rainfall is rather lighter on Nevis than on St. Christopher, and the soil is generally thinner and much less carefully fertilized. The present yield per acre is very low. Nevis is a sleepy place today, though there are ruins of great plantation houses to show that it was once a bountiful sugar island.[34]

Antigua is an island with great natural assets, but settlement

34. Sloane, *Voyage*, 42, 46; Merrill, *Historical Geography of St. Kitts and Nevis*, esp. chap. 2; Otis P. Starkey, *Commercial Geography of St. Kitts-Nevis*, Ind. Univ. Dept. of Geog. Technical Report No. 7 (Bloomington, Ind., 1961).

developed more slowly here than in St. Christopher and Nevis because of the critical water shortage. Shaped like an ink blot, Antigua
is full of sheltered bays. The coastline is so irregular that in 1676
the governor, William Stapleton, despaired of finding anyone
who could draw a map of the island. Compared with its mountainous neighbors, Antigua is nearly flat, with a broad central plain
rimmed by low limestone hills on the windward side and higher
volcanic hills on the leeward side. The landscape is gentle and un-
dramatic, save for the magnificent heights at the southern edge of
the island, massively fortified in the eighteenth century, from which
the colony guardsmen could scan their own indented coast as well
as the mountainous silhouettes of Montserrat and Guadeloupe on
the horizon. Antigua's climate is exceptionally pleasant: dry, cool,
and breezy. But there are no rivers or springs, and the early colonists
had to catch and store rain water. Unfortunately they could not
catch much, for only forty inches fall annually in the central plain,
where the best farm land lies. Nevertheless, the early planters
cleared the acacia and logwood forests that covered the interior of
the island and converted it to cane fields. Since the entire island
is swept steadily by breezes, they erected windmills on every sun-
baked hillside. More than two hundred abandoned stone mills still
dot the island. As in Nevis, much of the seventeenth-century farm
land has reverted to scrub pasture. The Antiguans now depend
more on cotton than sugar and, most of all, on the tourist business.[35]

Montserrat was the smallest and the least important of the English
sugar islands. Nevertheless, it too gradually became a flourishing
place in the late seventeenth century—much more flourishing then
than now. This "saw-toothed mountain" island is a cluster of rugged
peaks, and its vertiginous fields (as in Nevis) are strewn with volcanic boulders. Christopher Jeaffreson described it as "a pleasant
and fruitful land, very rockie but a sandy soyle; the wayes uneven
and in some parts dangerous." The Montserrat planters never
produced large sugar crops, and today almost no sugar is grown
here.

The Blathwayt Atlas in the John Carter Brown Library contains
a fascinating manuscript map of Montserrat in 1673—in some ways
the most informative map we have for any English island in this
period—which demonstrates how difficult it was to plant this alpine
site. The anonymous mapmaker, unable to chart the interior of the

35. Arlin D. Fentem, *Commercial Geography of Antigua*, Ind. Univ. Dept. of
Geog. Technical Report No. 11 (Bloomington, Ind., 1961).

island, has drawn a series of seven coastal perspectives, as seen from a boat circling the island, and fitted them together so as to approximate the pear-shaped coastal outline of Montserrat. Three little towns are shown along the leeward coast: Plymouth (now the capital), Kinsale, and Stapletown (near the present village of Salem), the last named in honor of Governor Stapleton, whose large plantation is perched on the hill above. Eighteen other sugar plantations are identified by name of owner, some with windmills and some with water mills. Two forts, a church, customshouse, courthouse, and prison can be found on the leeward shore. Nowhere is level land to be seen. Many small farms precariously grip the sides of the tall Soufriere Hills, with land cleared almost to the top as at Nevis. Fewer settlements can be seen on the windward coast, for here the slopes with names like Bottomless Gutt (ravine) are too vertical for habitation. The map also depicts the international struggle for possession of this formidable little island. Off the leeward coast there is a naval battle in progress between French and English ships, and the French are headed toward the place where they landed in 1666 when they captured and sacked Montserrat. Off the windward coast three tritons carry the banners of France, Ireland, and England. Most of the early colonists on Montserrat were Irish, incessantly quarreling with the English, and the dark Irish triton looks glum at discovering that even in the remotest corner of the Caribbees he cannot escape English mastery.[36]

To move west a thousand miles from the Lesser Antilles to the island of Jamaica is to enter a new world. The climate and the colors and the sea are the same, but everything is on a grander scale. Jamaica is 4,450 square miles in area, close to the size of Connecticut, or ten times the combined area of Barbados, St. Christopher, Nevis, Antigua, and Montserrat. Today Jamaica has a population five times the size of the smaller English islands and boasts a considerably more diversified economy. True, it is still a relatively confined space, 145 miles long and 50 miles wide. Yet it has a continental feel. Jamaica has always been a wild place, not to be planted and tamed in a few years like the compact little Caribbees. The Arawaks had lived here for centuries without leaving

36. Montserrat Island, 1673, unsigned map in ink on vellum in Blathwayt Atlas. Sections of this map are reproduced in fig. facing p. 13. See also Jeaffreson, ed., *Young Squire*, I, 180; Otis P. Starkey, *Commercial Geography of Montserrat*, Ind. Univ. Dept. of Geog. Technical Report No. 6 (Bloomington, Ind., 1960).

much trace. The Spaniards had been here for 150 years, and their abandoned towns and plantations soon disappeared into the forest. The English in the seventeenth century only began to occupy Jamaica. They started to plant in many parts of the island, but mostly they congregated fairly close together along the southeastern coast. The two chief towns were here: Port Royal, the commercial and buccaneering headquarters, on its long sand spit at the entrance to Port Royal Harbor (now Kingston Harbor), and Spanish Town, or Santiago de la Vega, the former Spanish capital, a few miles inland. The seventeenth-century Englishman who disembarked at Port Royal found himself in one of the world's great harbors, with the majestic Blue Mountains piling up against the horizon—a bigger harbor and taller mountains than any at home. And if he traveled a few miles inland in any direction, he encountered precipitous mountains furrowed by deep gullies and rivers cascading through steamy jungles.

Among the various early maps of Jamaica, Edward Slaney's map of 1678 best depicts the topography of the island.[37] Slaney shows the many rivers, particularly numerous along the north coast where rainfall is heaviest. Dr. Sloane counted eighty rivers in Jamaica. Slaney also shows the mountain ranges crisscrossing the island. The tallest range is the Blue Mountains in the east, reaching a height of 7,400 feet. The central and western ranges seldom exceed 3,000 feet, but they are rugged enough. There is also a great deal of flat land in Jamaica, marked as savannas on Slaney's map. Most of the flat land is along the southern coast and particularly toward the western end of the island, where (as Dr. Sloane recounted) one can ride for miles without feeling the least ascent or seeing many trees.

By the time Slaney drew his map, plantations were scattered the full length of the south coast, from Morant Point in the east to Negril Point in the west. At the eastern end, the planters raised sugar around Morant Bay and indigo around Yallahs Bay. In the hot, dry plains adjacent to Port Royal and Spanish Town, they grew sugar, corn, and plantains. Up the Rio Cobre (or, as Slaney calls it, the Copper River) beyond Spanish Town is a rich interior valley where the early colonists cultivated cacao and sugar. Here it is foggy every morning, and the rainfall is heavy; Sixteen Mile Walk was

37. Edward Slaney's *Tabula Iamaicae Insulae* (London, 1678), Blathwayt Atlas. See fig. 3, opposite.

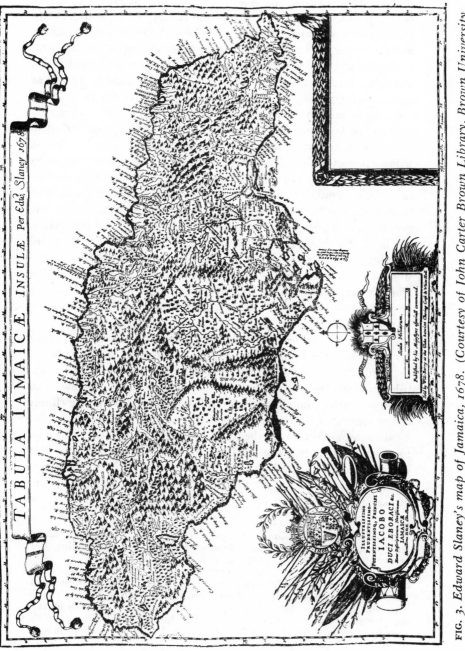

FIG. 3. *Edward Slaney's map of Jamaica, 1678.* (Courtesy of John Carter Brown Library, Brown University, Providence.)

called "the piss pot of the island." [38] West of Old Harbour, in the coastal plains watered by the Rio Minho, or Dry River, and the Milk River, indigo and sugar were planted. West of the Milk River, settlement was sparser. Small farmers lived here; they grew cotton, corn, and plantains and ranched cattle. The "Surranam Quarters" on Slaney's map near Bluefields Bay marks the settlement of a band of Guiana refugees, expelled from Surinam by the Dutch in 1670. In the interior western mountains are "Privateer Quarters," where the buccaneers hung out between raids, and "Banditi," or "Spanish Quarters," where the Maroons (escaped Spanish slaves) hid in the wildest sector of the island. Their descendants continue to live in this region, now called the Cockpit Country, still isolated from the rest of the island. The north coast of Jamaica, where most modern tourists stay, was not much settled in the seventeenth century. Sugar grows less well here because the rainfall is too heavy and the terrain too hilly. The early colonists tried ginger and cacao. Bananas and coconuts—the modern agricultural staples for north-coast farmers— were not yet recognized as export commodities. "Mantica Bay" on Slaney's map in the northwestern sector of the island is Montego Bay, the most remote and undeveloped corner of Jamaica in the seventeenth century.[39]

Dr. Hans Sloane, the physician and naturalist, lived in Jamaica for a year and a half, from 1687 to 1689. During his stay he gathered materials for a natural history of the island, which he later published in two folio volumes, profusely illustrated. Dr. Sloane tried to see as much of Jamaica as he could. In fact he stuck pretty closely to the region adjoining Port Royal and Spanish Town, but he did cross the mountains to see the north coast. It took his party two days to cover the twenty-five miles from Sixteen Mile Walk to the Rio Nuevo, and Sloane tells how he camped overnight near Mount Diablo in a hunter's hut on a bed of plantain and palm leaves, kept awake by the tree frogs and grasshoppers. During his stay on the

38. John Helyar to William Helyar, June 30, 1678, Helyar Manuscripts, Somerset Record Office, Taunton, Eng. (microfilm, J. Harry Bennett Collection, University of Texas, Austin). Hereafter cited as Helyar MSS.

39. Slaney's map locates many planters' houses, but seldom identifies them. Two other early maps of Jamaica, discussed in chap. 5, provide additional information about these planters. John Ogilby (1671) identifies 115 planters by name and crop; Charles Bochart and Humphrey Knollis (1684) similarly identify 467 planters. See also R. M. Bent and Enid L. Bent-Golding, *A Complete Geography of Jamaica* (London, 1966); Kit S. Kapp. *The Printed Maps of Jamaica up to 1825* (Kingston, 1968).

island Sloane collected eight hundred specimens of plants and made many observations about birds and beasts as well. A nineteen-foot alligator was caught near Port Royal while he was there, and he observed the carrion crow, or John Crow, the bald-headed black vulture that still skims endlessly everywhere over the Jamaica landscape looking for carrion. Dr. Sloane measured a carrion crow and found it had a four-foot wingspan.[40]

Everything about the Jamaica climate fascinated Dr. Sloane. "The Dews here are so great," he wrote, "as in the morning to drop down from the leaves of trees, as if it had rain'd. . . . One riding in the night perceives the greatness of the Dews, for he will find his Cloths, Hair, etc. very wet in a small time." Sloane learned what the tropical rainy season is like; the streets in Spanish Town became so flooded that he had to travel on horseback from house to house in order to visit his patients. He learned about tropical insects; one morning he found a patient disheveled because some ants had gnawed through his bedstead in the night and thrown the poor man to the ground. He learned what an earthquake is like; one day the room he was standing in suddenly began to reel, and he thought the house would collapse, but before he could get outdoors the shocks had passed. He learned something also of the untamed strength of the tropical forest; when he visited a ruined Spanish town on the north coast he found it all overgrown with tall trees, and when he saw an abandoned Spanish cacao walk he found that the trees had run wild and were shooting up seventy feet high. " 'Tis a very strange thing," Sloane remarked, "to see in how short a time a Plantation formerly clear'd of Trees and Shrubs, will grow foul" in Jamaica.[41]

To the early English colonists Jamaica was the most fascinating of the Caribbean islands. It was the largest and grandest place they knew in the Indies, the most fruitful, the most lushly tropical, in every way the most promising land for settlement. But it was also a thoroughly disturbing place: hot, wet, stormy, steamy, craggy, jungled, infested with insects and vermin. The colonists found the environment enervating, even corrupting. No one could say that life in Jamaica was like life at home.

---

40. E. St. John Brooks, *Sir Hans Sloane* (London, 1954), chap. 5. In the volume of plates illustrating his *Voyage to the Islands*, Sloane has a vivid picture of John Crow (plate 254).

41. Sloane, *Voyage*, I, *vii–xiv, xxxii, xlii–xliv, lx–lxxiii*, II, 294.

ॐ

Seventeenth-century Englishmen attuned their lives to the weather, to seasonal change, and to the annual cycle of birth, growth, maturity, and death. But in the West Indies they found a year-round growing season, year-round summer, and year-round heat. They were used to a moderate climate: moderately warm, moderately cold, moderately rainy, moderately sunny. But in the tropics they had to adjust their eyes to brilliant sunlight and a palette of splashy colors: vegetation startlingly green, fruits and flowers in flaming reds and yellows, the mountains in shimmering blues and greens shading to deep purple, the moon and stars radiant and sparkling at night, and the encircling sea a spectrum of jeweled colors from cobalt to silver. They found the Caribbean atmosphere to be volatile: blazing heat suddenly relieved by refreshing showers, and soft, caressing breezes capriciously dissolving into wild and terrifying storms. In climate as in European power politics, the Indies lay "beyond the line."

The early settlers constantly complained about the tormenting insect life on the islands. Jonathan Everard, newly arrived in Jamaica, especially disliked the gnats, or merrywings, "which doe so sting that one would be apt to dance without a fiddle." Richard Ligon, in Barbados, described how merrywings operate: "They are of so small a size, and so thin and aereall, as you can hardly discern them, but by the noise of their wings, which is like a small bugle horn, at a great distance: Where they sting, there will rise a little knob, as big as a pease, and last so a whole day." Ligon found mosquitoes more bothersome than merrywings, but of course neither Ligon nor any other seventeenth-century settler realized that mosquitoes transmit malaria and yellow fever and that they were the chief killers in the islands. To combat these stinging insects the colonists soon learned to clear the foliage around their houses, to set smoky fires, and to daub vinegar on the bites. To combat the ants and woodlice that devoured cloth, paper, and wooden articles inside their houses, they swept their floors frequently, stood their table legs inside cups of water, and hung shelves from the ceiling by tarred ropes for food storage. Cockroaches were likely to attack the colonists at night, unless they slept in hammocks. The skin of Barbados Negroes, Ligon said, looked currycombed from cockroach bites. Most hateful of all were the chiggers, which burrow under the toenails and ulcerate the feet. The embattled English wore shoes and stockings as protection against chiggers and kept checking their feet for bites.[42]

The other continual lament was about the humid heat. The Reverend Francis Crow protested that preaching one sermon in Jamaica exhausted him more than three sermons in England. "The constant heat," he wrote, "is so consuming night and day that here is a continual summer, without the least footsteps of a winter, either for frost or snow, cold or rain, or any sensible shortness of days." [43] In actual fact, a midsummer heat wave in any of the English mainland settlements considerably exceeded the hottest temperature in Jamaica, but of course the mainland heat was never continuous. In the islands, summer or winter, the thermometer is most commonly in the mid-eighties in the daytime and in the mid-seventies at night. Except in the mountains, it never sinks below sixty-five degrees, and only a few hot spots rise into the low nineties. All of the islands, except for interior pockets within Jamaica, are swept by the trade wind with alternating land and sea breezes. To feel comfortable in the West Indies one must take advantage of these breezes. But the early colonists, worried about hurricanes and enemy attacks, chose the most sheltered spots they could find for their chief towns. In Bridgetown on Barbados, Charlestown on Nevis, or Port Royal on Jamaica the weather was and is likely to be particularly muggy and oppressive.

Rainfall is far heavier in the Indies than in England, and it was undoubtedly heavier still in the seventeenth century, when the islands were more heavily forested than they are today. Most of the English islands now average at least sixty inches of rain per annum, with tremendous local variation. Jamaica has the widest range, from less than thirty inches annually at Port Royal to more than two hundred inches in the Blue Mountains. The smaller islands range from under forty to over eighty inches. The rainy season varies from island to island and from year to year, but generally extends from May to November. During the dry winter months there are frequent light showers. Seventeenth-century Englishmen were habituated to a wet climate, yet they found the Caribbean humidity

42. Jonathan Everard to William Helyar, Mar. 27, 1686, Helyar MSS; Ligon, *True History of Barbados*, 62–65; Davies, *History of Caribby-Islands*, 78–85, 146–151.
43. Francis Crow to Giles Firmin, Mar. 7, 1686/7, in Henry J. Cadbury, "Conditions in Jamaica in 1687," *Jamaican Historical Review*, III, no. 2 (1959), 55.

very trying. Knives, keys, needles, and swords were continually rusting, and clocks and watches seldom worked well.[44]

Then there were the hurricanes. The English on St. Christopher got their first taste of this West Indian speciality within nine months of their arrival, when a hurricane wiped out their first tobacco crop in 1624. And this was just the beginning of a long parade of ferocious wind-and-rain storms, which generally struck in August. It was easy to believe that these terrifying storms were the devil's work. An early disaster in St. Christopher was reported home in a London pamphlet of 1638: *News and strange Newes from St. Christophers of a tempestuous Spirit, which is called by the Indians a Hurrin-cano or whirlewind.* The excited author told how some of the colonists hid in caves, some lashed themselves to tree trunks, some climbed into hammocks suspended between two trees where they swung to and fro "like a Bell when it is rung." The force of the wind tossed men into the air "as if they were no more but ragges, clouts, or feathers." The pamphlet was illustrated by a crude woodcut showing a coal-black Carib Indian pointing to strange circles around the moon (the sign that a hurricane was coming), while broken branches fly through the air and houses topple from their foundations. This particular storm sank five ships and killed seventy-five men; damage would have been worse except that the Caribs warned the English to batten their hatches. Even so, the Caribs were to blame. If barbarous and sinful Indians had not lived on St. Christopher, God would not have punished the island.

Thirty years later the English were still deeply suspicious of the Caribs' ability to forecast hurricanes. St. Christopher and Nevis were hit in 1657, 1658, 1660, 1665, and 1667, and every time the Caribs on Dominica and St. Vincent sent a warning ten or twelve days in advance—obvious evidence that they practiced witchcraft and consorted with the devil. But one Nevis colonist bragged that he had learned how to read the sky for telltale signs, how to ride out a hurricane at sea, and also how to pack the goods in his storehouse so that they stayed dry and safe when the roof blew off.[45] This wisdom would have been useful to the Barbadians in 1675 when the worst hurricane of the century struck their island. Governor Atkins reported home that he had never seen a more amazing spectacle.

44. Ligon, *True History of Barbados*, 27.
45. Concerning Hurricanes and their Prognosticks, and observations of my owne Experience thereupon, Egerton Manuscripts, 2395/619–624, British Museum, London.

Two hundred persons were killed, and a thousand houses, three churches, and most of the sugar mills on the leeward side of the island were leveled—all in less than three hours. The force of the wind stripped trees bare of leaves and fruit and drove twelve merchant ships ashore, where they broke to pieces. Torrents of rain completed the havoc by unroofing the planters' storehouses and soaking their sugar.[46]

Six years later still another hurricane struck St. Christopher. "It was a little after midnight," a planter named Christopher Jeaffreson wrote, "when a great part of the roof of my dwelling-house began to fly away; several of my out-houses being allready down." Jeaffreson decided that it was time to leave. His slaves and servants had congregated in his house for safety, but he turned them out, locked the door, and pocketed the key—a vain gesture, as events soon proved. Bowled along by the wind, Jeaffreson and all but one of his people managed to reach a little hut, which rocked like a cradle in the storm, while rain pelted through the roof. "But to be wet was then no news to us." As soon as the storm abated, Jeaffreson went out to survey his property and found only one wall of his house standing and his two sugar works and outbuildings all knocked flat. What hurt the most was to see his sugarcanes smashed and his provision crops washed away. He quickly built a temporary two-room house, repaired his sugar works, and planted corn to feed his work force, but within six weeks a second hurricane unroofed his new house and swept away his new crop. Once again Jeaffreson reordered his battered plantation, but he sailed for England before the next hurricane season.[47]

Earthquakes and volcanos were also West Indies hazards, much rarer than hurricanes but even more terrifying. Three of the English islands—St. Christopher, Nevis, and Montserrat—are volcanic. The crater of Mount Misery on St. Christopher and the sulphur springs in the Soufriere Hills of Montserrat still show signs of activity. No eruptions have occurred recently in these islands, and none apparently occurred during the seventeenth century. Earthquakes are a different story. Tremors were felt repeatedly in Barbados, Antigua, Nevis, and Jamaica during the early years of settlement. In 1680 a major quake on Nevis toppled the town of Jamestown into the sea. But the most horrifying and damaging earthquake rocked Jamaica just before noon on June 7, 1692.

46. Sir Jonathan Atkins to Sir Joseph Williamson, Oct. 3, 1675, C.O. 1/35/231.
47. Jeaffreson, ed., *Young Squire*, I, 274–280.

In ten minutes, according to the reports sent home, this Jamaica earthquake of 1692 shook down most of the brick and stone buildings on the island. The Quakers, holding their monthly meeting at Spanish Town when the tremors began, rushed out into the meetinghouse yard "where the ground waving like to a sea, we could not stand but beheld the walls and houses shaken, as a man should shake a twigg, till they were laid flat around us." But the greatest damage was at Port Royal, the chief port, which stands at the tip of a long sand spit encompassed by the sea. At the first shock the sixty-foot, crenelated tower of St. Paul's church came crashing down. Next the wharves that lined the length of the harbor tumbled into the water. Whole streets of the chief merchants' houses, together with the town fortifications, sank after them. The sea gushed in, and hundreds of people were drowned or buried alive in mud, bricks, and crashing timbers. One lucky merchant, trapped in his shop when it was sucked into five fathoms of water, was swept "under earth and water a very considerable way until at last I got upon a floor of boards where multitudes lay about me most of them mortally wounded and I amongst them very little hurt."[48] The Jamaicans were so shaken by this disaster that they built a new port at Kingston, across the bay from Port Royal—seemingly a safer site, though Kingston was itself leveled by an earthquake in 1907.

Shocks and storms, heat and humidity, isolation and claustrophobia: these are among the common attributes of island life in the tropics. The cheerful face of the Caribbean—its fertility, beauty, and serenity—we hear much less about from the early colonists. This need not necessarily mean much. All reporters talk less about their joys than their tragedies. It is worth noting that Englishmen who came to the mainland colonies during the seventeenth century also talked constantly and habitually about the excessive heat and cold, terrific storms, and howling wilderness conditions they endured. They thereby spun the myth we have all been nurtured on, that pioneering life in North America was harder and more painful

48. Vivid firsthand accounts of the 1692 earthquake include the Jamaica Council's letter to the Lords of Trade, June 20, 1692, in J. W. Fortescue, ed., *Calendar of State Papers, Colonial Series, America and West Indies, 1689–1692* (London, 1901), #2278. Hereafter cited as *Cal.S.P.Col.;* Edmund Edlyne to William Blathwayt, June 20, 1692, Blathwayt Papers, XXII; Joseph Norris to Richard Hawkins, June 20, 1692, Norris Copy Letter Book, I, 27–30, Historical Society of Pennsylvania, Philadelphia; and Mordecai Lloyd to Thomas Lloyd, July 25, 1692, G. W. Norris Box, *ibid.* Six pamphlets describing this earthquake, published in 1692–1694, are cited on p. 187, n.55.

than life in old Europe. It is now apparent from seventeenth-century demographic studies that the opposite was more nearly true. The early mainland colonists, despite their lamentations, had a very brief starving time and soon lived better and kept healthier than their countrymen at home. Should we likewise discount the rhetoric about English sufferings in the tropics?

The answer, essentially, is no. The physical environment of the Caribbean islands *was* distressing to the early planters, especially when considered in conjunction with the social habits that they brought with them. Had the English pioneers been trying to escape from their acquisitive European culture, had they been craving for peace, simplicity, ease, and innocence, they might indeed have found paradise in the Indies. But the English were looking for El Dorado, not Eden. They had geared themselves for wealth, excitement, and violent combat, so they fought and played feverishly in the enervating heat, exploited the labor of white servants and black slaves, risked sudden death from mysterious diseases or the annihilation of their profits in smashing storms and buccaneering raids. The expectations the English brought with them and the physical conditions they encountered in the islands produced a hectic mode of life that had no counterpart at home or elsewhere in English experience. This is what it meant to live beyond the line.

2 🔊 Barbados
The Rise of the Planter Class

The English men and women who ventured to plant in the Caribbean isles created a society so radically different from the one they left at home—or from the mainland American settlements— that it requires an effort of imagination to recall their common origins. Of course the island and mainland colonists drew upon the same English cultural matrix. The Caribbee planters began as peasant farmers not unlike the peasant farmers of Wigston Magna, Leicestershire,[1] or Sudbury, Massachusetts.[2] They cultivated the same staple crop—tobacco—as their cousins in Virginia and Maryland. They brought to the tropics the English common law, English political institutions, the English parish, and the English church. Yet from the very beginning the island colonists developed their own life-style, and once they converted from tobacco to sugar, everything was bent by their eager embrace of African slavery.

The chief distinguishing feature of island society in the seventeenth century was the rapid rise of a cohesive and potent master class. By 1650 in Barbados and by 1680 in Jamaica and the Leeward Islands, the big sugar planters had taken charge. These people were genuinely *big* planters, particularly in Barbados, where in 1680 nineteen colonists owned two hundred slaves apiece and eighty-nine owned one hundred slaves. In all of the islands before

1. W. G. Hoskins, *The Midland Peasant: The Economic and Social History of a Leicestershire Village* (London, 1957) .

2. Sumner Chilton Powell, *Puritan Village: The Formation of a New England Town* (Middletown, Conn., 1963) .

the close of the century a few big landholders monopolized all the best sugar acreage, reaped most of the profits, managed island politics, and dominated their society in every way. These nouveau riche slave-owning gentry far outshone the leading Chesapeake planters of the day. They operated on the scale of county families at home, while rejecting most of the social values associated with the gentry in seventeenth-century England.[3]

The rise of the planter class in the English sugar islands is a story that has never been told. We have detailed political and institutional histories of the several Caribbean colonies in the seventeenth century [4] and excellent studies of Stuart colonial policy in the West Indies and of early English and North American commerce with the sugar islands.[5] But none of these works focus on the seventeenth-century sugar planters as a social group. By contrast, a number of historians have delineated the West Indian planter class in the eighteenth century, at the peak of its power.[6] Doubtless the

3. As depicted in such studies as Peter Laslett, "The Gentry of Kent in 1640," *Cambridge Historical Journal*, IX (1948), 148–164; Alan Everitt, *The Community of Kent and the Great Rebellion* (Leicester, 1966); C. W. Chalkin, *Seventeenth-Century Kent* (London, 1965); Alan Simpson, *The Wealth of the Gentry, 1540–1660: East Anglian Studies* (Chicago, 1961); Thomas Garden Barnes, *Somerset, 1625–1640* (London, 1961); William Bradford Willcox, *Gloucestershire: A Study in Local Government, 1590–1640* (New Haven, Conn., 1940); Mary Finch, *The Wealth of Five Northamptonshire Families, 1540–1640*, Northamptonshire Record Society, XIX (Oxford, 1956); and J. T. Cliffe, *The Yorkshire Gentry: From the Reformation to the Civil War* (New York, 1969).

4. Williamson, *Caribbee Islands;* Vincent T. Harlow, *A History of Barbados, 1625–1685* (Oxford, 1926); C. S. S. Higham, *The Development of the Leeward Islands under the Restoration, 1660–1688* (Cambridge, Eng., 1921); Agnes M. Whitson, *The Constitutional Development of Jamaica, 1660–1729* (Manchester, Eng., 1929); Frank Cundall, *The Governors of Jamaica in the Seventeenth Century* (London, 1936); Frederick G. Spurdle, *Early West Indian Government, Showing the Progress of Government in Barbados, Jamaica and the Leeward Islands, 1660–1783* (Palmerston North, N.Z. [1963]).

5. A. P. Thornton, *West-India Policy under the Restoration* (Oxford, 1956); George Louis Beer, *The Origins of the Old Colonial System, 1578–1660* (New York, 1908); Beer, *The Old Colonial System, 1660–1688* (New York, 1912); K. G. Davies, *The Royal African Company* (London, 1957); Davies, "The Origins of the Commission System in the West India Trade," Royal Historical Society, *Transactions*, 5th Ser., II (London, 1952), 89–107; Richard Pares, *Yankees and Creoles: The Trade between North America and the West Indies before the American Revolution* (Cambridge, Mass., 1956).

6. F. W. Pitman, *The Development of the British West Indies, 1700–1763* (New Haven, Conn., 1917); Richard Pares, *A West-India Fortune* (London, 1950); Richard B. Sheridan, "The Rise of a Colonial Gentry: A Case Study of Antigua, 1730–1775," *Economic History Review*, 2d Ser., XIII (1960–1961), 342–357; J. Harry Bennett, *Bondsmen and Bishops: Slavery and Apprenticeship on*

eighteenth-century planters deserve this attention. They owned more slaves and produced more sugar than their seventeenth-century predecessors. The grandest of them, such as the Beckfords and the Prices in Jamaica, were more spectacular figures by far than any of the pioneer sugar planters.[7] Still, the story of the early planters has its own interest and significance. These were the people who created the sugar and slave system in the English islands and made it work. They generated an aggressive dynamism that was not sustained by the gilded nabobs of the next century. Their land was fresh and their yield per acre was higher than it would be later. Their taxes and running expenses were lower. Fewer of them were absentees, so they managed their business interests more purposefully. And since world sugar production was still distinctly limited in the seventeenth century, they commanded much of the European market. Their only serious rivals were the Portuguese in Brazil, and it appears that the English Caribbean sugar producers caught and surpassed the Brazilians before the close of the century. They did not have to worry yet about competition from the French sugar islands or the Dutch in Surinam. In 1700 the English planters in Barbados, Jamaica, and the Leewards supplied close to half the sugar consumed in Western Europe.[8]

The planter class took shape initially and most decisively in Barbados. This island was not the first to be occupied by the English, but the Barbadians were the first Englishmen to take up sugar making in a big way. Two or three hundred Barbados planters took charge of the sugar business—and of the island—in the 1640s and 1650s, a full generation earlier than their counterparts in the Leewards and Jamaica. Throughout the century they retained control. Who were these tropical founding fathers, and how did they manage to develop, practically overnight, the most perfectly articulated colonial aristocracy in English America?

the Codrington Plantations of Barbados, 1710–1838 (Berkeley, Calif., 1958); Elsa V. Goveia, Slave Society in the British Leeward Islands at the End of the Eighteenth Century (New Haven, Conn., 1965); Lowell J. Ragatz, The Fall of the Planter Class in the British Caribbean, 1763–1833 (London, 1928).

7. For the Beckfords, see Richard Pares, Merchants and Planters (New York, 1960), 25; Richard B. Sheridan, "Planter and Historian: The Career of William Beckford of Jamaica and England, 1744–1799," Jam. Hist. Rev., IV (1964), 38–40. For the Prices, see Michael Craton and James Walvin, A Jamaican Plantation: The History of Worthy Park, 1670–1970 (Toronto, 1970), chaps. 3–6.

8. See the English, Portuguese, French, Dutch, and Spanish production figures compiled by Noel Deerr, The History of Sugar (London, 1949–1950), I, 101–112, 123–132, 193–203, 212–218, 233–240.

Initially the Barbadians showed little sign of developing a planter elite. The years from 1627 to 1640 constituted the tobacco age in Barbados. Caribbee tobacco was of poor quality, and no one made much money from it. Essentially the Barbados pioneers operated a subsistence economy. Their mode of life was every bit as homespun and crude as in the early days of Jamestown and Plymouth.

The colony suffered considerably from initial mismanagement. Sir William Courteen, a wealthy Anglo-Dutch merchant experienced in the Caribbean trade, organized a syndicate that sponsored the first settlement in 1627, sending out two shiploads of colonists under the command of John and Henry Powell. The Courteen syndicate sank about £10,000 into this venture, hoping for the same sort of returns as the London merchants who had invested in privateering expeditions to the West Indies in the 1590s.[9] Unhappily for Courteen, the earl of Carlisle, an influential courtier, soon challenged his control of the island. Both men obtained royal patents for Barbados. Both dispatched governors, settlers, and supplies. Courteen's and Carlisle's agents in turn were seized and banished; one governor was executed. By 1629 Carlisle obtained the upper hand. He was recognized as lord proprietor of all the English Caribbees, the Leeward Islands as well as Barbados. But Carlisle was an indolent absentee proprietor, interested only in collecting quitrents, and in 1636 he died, leaving his estate entangled in debts and his proprietary rights over Barbados in dispute. Effective management of the island in the 1630s was wholly relegated to Carlisle's governor, Henry Hawley, who made what profit he could by levying a poll tax on every inhabitant. The island had no military defenses, but fortunately the Spanish never attacked. It was divided into six parishes, each with a vestry, but there were not enough clergymen to go round. Governor Hawley had a Council to advise him, and in 1639 he convened the first Barbados Assembly, but in general he ruled as a petty despot.[10]

9. N. Darnell Davis, ed., "Papers relating to the early History of Barbados," *Timehri: The Journal of the Royal Agricultural and Commercial Society of British Guiana*, New Ser., V (1891), 51–60, VI (1892), 328–329. See also Andrews, *Elizabethan Privateering*, chap. 6.

10. For further details see Williamson, *Caribbee Islands*, chaps. 2–3, 5–7; Harlow, *Barbados*, chap. 1; J. Harry Bennett, "Peter Hay, Proprietary Agent in

What sort of people came to Barbados in these early years? To start with, we have the names of a great many colonists who arrived before 1640—four lists totaling nearly 2,000 names.[11] The earliest of these lists records the 74 settlers who came with Capt. John Powell in the ship *Peter* in 1627. There were no women in this party, for Barbados—like Jamestown in 1607 and Providence Island in 1630—was founded exclusively by males. Clearly most of the initial settlers did not tarry long in Barbados, for only 6 out of the 74 in this list can be found among the 764 landholders on the island eleven years later! One reason, certainly, for their short stay was that Sir William Courteen granted them no land. He paid them wages and expected them to return all proceeds to his syndicate. Among the first arrivals in 1627 was Henry Winthrop, the scapegrace second son of the founder of Massachusetts. Young Winthrop says he came to Barbados for a three-year hitch at the "offer" of £100 a year. Whether he was paid this much in wages, or whether he hoped to make this much from his share of the tobacco crop, is unclear. Henry wanted to have some servants of his own in order to make an additional profit, so he asked his father in England to hire and equip ten servants and have them "bound to searve me in the west indyes sum 3 yere or 5 . . . and get them as resonable as you can promysinge them not above 10 pound a yere." The elder Winthrop was highly suspicious of this whole project, especially since the Barbados tobacco Henry sent home proved to be "verye ill conditioned, fowle, full of stalkes and evill coloured." He dispatched Henry two boy servants, for "men I could gett none," but by the

---

Barbados, 1636–1641," *Jam. Hist. Rev.*, V (1965), 9–29. One important effect of Carlisle's proprietorship was that he leased 10,000 acres of what turned out to be the best land in Barbados (St. George's Valley) to a syndicate of London merchants headed by Marmaduke Roydon, William Perkins, and Alexander Bannister. See Ligon's map of the island, fig. 4, p. 63.

11. Seventy-four passengers to Barbados in 1627 are listed in N. Darnell Davis, *Cavaliers and Roundheads of Barbados, 1650–1652* (Georgetown, Br. Guiana, 1887), 42–43; 985 passengers to Barbados in 1635 are listed in John Camden Hotten, ed., *The Original Lists of Persons of Quality . . . and Others Who Went from Great Britain to the American Plantations, 1600–1700* (London, 1874), 33–145; 113 planters who received Barbados land grants from Gov. Hawley, 1637–1639, are listed in Hay of Haystoun Papers relating to Barbados, Scottish Record Office, Edinburgh (microfilm, J. Harry Bennett Collection, University of Texas, Austin). Hereafter cited as Hay Papers; 764 names of persons holding 10 or more acres in Barbados are listed in [William Duke], *Some Memoirs of the First Settlement of the Island of Barbados* (Barbados, 1741), 51–62 (incorrectly totaled as 766). Of course these lists overlap to some extent.

time these youths reached Barbados their master was already back in England, his adventure over.[12]

When Carlisle grabbed control of the island, he reversed Courteen's colonizing policy and distributed land to the settlers, expecting them to pay their own way and set up for themselves. Nearly forty thousand acres were allotted to 250 colonists from 1628 to 1630, and some of these grants were very generous. As immigration continued, Governor Hawley issued rather smaller patents in the 1630s; he seems to have granted each new planter ten acres for himself plus an additional ten acres for each servant. Before the end of the decade all the arable land was parceled out. Land grants in Barbados totaled about eighty-five thousand acres in 1638—practically the same figure as in 1680. This acreage was distributed quite unequally among 764 planters.[13] Some tracts were very sizable, larger than any plantations on the island a half century later. Edward Oistin obtained a thousand acres in 1629 for which he paid £1,000. William Hilliard acquired six hundred acres from Carlisle in 1637.[14] On the other hand, the great majority of patents issued by Governor Hawley from 1637 to 1639 fell into the range of thirty to fifty acres. To an English peasant farmer thirty acres would not seem paltry, for it was a larger tract than most husbandmen enjoyed at home.[15]

The chief initial obstacle for all Barbados farmers, large and small, was that the land was covered with rain forest, which was very hard to clear. The first comers struggled to hack down the massive locust, mastic, cedar, silk-cotton, fiddlewood, poison, and mangrove

12. Allyn B. Forbes *et al.*, eds., *Winthrop Papers, 1498–1649* (Boston, 1929–1947), I, 356–357, 361–362, II, 66–69. Before leaving Barbados, Henry Winthrop switched allegiance from Courteen to Carlisle and became one of the 12 magistrates on the island. *Ibid.*, I, 405–406.

13. [Duke], *Memoirs*, 7–20, 51–62; Pares, *Merchants and Planters*, 2–4, 57–58; list of land grants issued by Gov. Hawley, 1637–1639, Hay Papers. The 764 Barbados landholders listed as of 1638 all held at least 10 acres, which raises the possibility that additional planters held smaller lots. But I doubt that many did. Hawley's grants in 1637–1639 started at 10 acres, and practically all were for at least 20 acres.

14. Edward Oistin to Archibald Hay, May 29, 1638, William Hilliard to Archibald Hay, Dec. 18, 1637, Hay Papers. The fishing village of Oistins in Barbados is named after Edward Oistin. Hilliard still held 500 acres in 1647; he sold a half share of this estate to Thomas Modyford for £7,000, as described in Ligon, *True History of Barbados*, 22.

15. For the size of English husbandmen's farms, see Chalkin, *Seventeenth-Century Kent*, 68–70; Powell, *Puritan Village*, 173–185; and Hoskins, *The Midland Peasant*, 201, 215, 311–313.

trees that towered above them a hundred feet or more. For many years the settlers' fields were encumbered with rotting stumps and logs. Well into the 1640s, if Richard Ligon's map can be believed, the only thoroughly cleared area was along the leeward coast, and the best interior land was still largely unworked.[16]

From the outset, most farm work on Barbados was performed by servile labor. Seventeenth-century Englishmen distinguished between two sorts of servants: temporary, youthful laborers from the middling classes and permanent drudges from the lower orders. For the children of English yeomen, husbandmen, and artisans, there was nothing demeaning about temporary servile status. Indentured labor in a stranger's household was the normal mode of socialization for boys and girls at adolescence. The Essex parson Ralph Josselin, for example, bound out his sons as apprentices when they reached fifteen and his daughters as servants when they reached thirteen. All of his children left home permanently before the age of puberty, and they were expected to work for about ten years until they married.[17] But Josselin also always hired servants to do his own household chores, and here he probably drew upon the large available pool of permanent, cheap, servile labor. About half the population in any English village consisted of the laboring poor, cottagers and wage laborers, who possessed little or no land and worked for wages by the year, day, or piece to eke out a precarious existence. Thus English farmers at home employed a great many servants and day laborers.[18]

Undoubtedly both sorts of English servants—adolescent bondsmen from the middling classes and children of the laboring poor— found their way to Barbados in the 1620s and 1630s. The two points we can be certain about are that they were very numerous and very young. "A plantation in this place," observed Peter Hay, the proprietary rent collector, "is worth nothing unless there be good store of hands upon it." A Barbados planter named Matthew Gibson em-

16. Watts, *Man's Influence on the Vegetation of Barbados,* chap. 3. As late as 1652 Sir Anthony Ashley Cooper's sugar plantation of 205 acres in St. George's Valley contained 95 acres of forest.

17. Alan Macfarlane, *The Family Life of Ralph Josselin, A Seventeenth-Century Clergyman* (Cambridge, Eng., 1970), 46, 92–93, 146–147, 205–210. See also Peter Laslett, *The World We Have Lost* (New York, 1965), chap. 1; Mildred Campbell, "Social Origins of Some Early Americans," in James Morton Smith, ed., *Seventeenth-Century America* (Chapel Hill, N.C., 1959), 69–76.

18. Alan Everitt, "Farm Labourers," in Joan Thirsk, ed., *The Agrarian History of England and Wales, 1500–1640* (Cambridge, Eng., 1967), 397–399; Chalkin, *Seventeenth-Century Kent,* 246–247.

ployed four servants to work his thirty-acre farm. In 1640 James Dering bought a half share in a hundred-acre farm that came equipped with nine servants.[19] Many if not most of the 985 emigrants who embarked for Barbados from London in 1635 were servants; 91 percent of these passengers were single persons in their teens and twenties. An astonishing 29 percent were aged ten to nineteen. An even higher number—47 percent—were aged twenty to twenty-four.[20] These young people bound themselves to four or five years of labor in the tropics for the adventure of it, or in hopes of getting farms of their own. Barbados servants were supposed to receive ten acres apiece when their indentures expired, but there was soon no land for them. Their choice was to try one of the less congested Leeward Islands, or return home, or stay as wage laborers in Barbados.

Thus Barbados developed in the 1630s some of the attributes of a plantation society: agriculture was labor intensive, and land distribution was skewed in favor of the big entrepreneurs. But as long as the colonists raised tobacco and cotton, no one in Barbados was going to be a really big entrepreneur. John Winthrop's low opinion of Barbados tobacco was reiterated throughout the 1630s. When Peter Hay sent his first shipment home in 1637 he was told: "Your tobaco of Barbados of all the tobaco that cometh to England is accompted the worst." Certainly it competed unfavorably with Virginia tobacco, paying a higher duty and fetching a lower price. Between 1637 and 1640 the planters of Barbados and St. Christopher collectively shipped only about one-fifth as much tobacco to England as the Virginia planters.[21] They tried peddling their product on the Continent, in Amsterdam, Middleburg, and Hamburg, but always found bad markets. At the close of the decade, the Barbados planters switched to cotton—with no better results. Peter Hay reported sadly in 1640: "This yeare hath beene so baise a cotton

19. Peter Hay to Sir James and Archibald Hay, Oct. 9, 1638, inventory of Matthew Gibson's estate, Oct. 10, 1635, Hay Papers; James Dering to Sir Edward Dering, July 20, 1640, *Journal of the Barbados Museum and Historical Society*, XXVII (1959–1960), 125.

20. Hotten, ed., *Original Lists*, 33–145. This London port register gives the ages as well as the names of the 4,890 persons who sailed to America in 1635. The tabulation is mine.

21. Archibald Hay to Peter Hay, Oct. 10, 1637, Hay Papers; tabulation of English tobacco imports, 1637–1640, from Additional Manuscripts 35865/247, Br. Museum, cited by Vere Langford Oliver, ed., *Caribbeana: Miscellaneous Papers relating to the History, Genealogy, Topography, and Antiquities of the British West Indies* (London, 1909–1919), III, 197–198.

yeare that the inhabitantes hath not maide so much cotton as will buye necessaries for there servants."[22]

Two inventories of "indifferent good" Barbados estates in 1635 suggest how very crude the early planters' style of life must have been. A Captain Ketteridge had five white servants, a Negro slave, and six hundred acres, yet his total household furnishings consisted of an old chest, six hammocks (the Negro slept on the ground), some empty barrels, a broken kettle, an old sieve, some battered pewter dishes, three napkins, and three books. Matthew Gibson, with four servants, possessed even less: a chest, a cracked kettle, two pots, several barrels, a sieve, a glass bottle, and a pamphlet without covers.[23] For the servants, in particular, life on Barbados must have seemed more discouraging even than servile labor at home. They gained nothing for their toil in the hot sun, and since there were as yet practically no women on the island, the young males must have been thoroughly sex starved. No wonder that when Sir Henry Colt visited Barbados in 1631 he found no one working, everyone drinking, and the servants trying to run away. Yet we need not feel too sorry for these Caribbean pioneers. For people who expected to stay only a few years, life was uncomplicated and relatively easy. They could build simple palm-thatched huts, which provided basic shelter, in a few hours. They had plenty to eat: Barbados was so fertile that corn, cassava, plantains, and yams ripened almost magically, and wild pigs supplied abundant meat. By 1634 the island was being called "a granary of all the rest of the charybbies Isles." And no one complained of the yellow fever that soon would decimate the island population.

The salubrious and easy environment of the Caribbee isles in these tobacco days may explain why so many Englishmen chose to settle there. The population of Barbados grew rapidly in the 1630s, more rapidly indeed than might be expected. The earl of Carlisle deserves no credit for the early popularity of the island, for he did nothing to promote its tropical charms. Almost every other American settlement, even Newfoundland, was better advertised in England. Yet people came by the thousands.

22. Invoices for Barbados tobacco shipments, 1637–1638, Archibald Hay to Peter Hay, May 27, 1639, and Peter Hay to Archibald Hay, Aug. 22, 1640, Hay Papers. See also J. H. Bennett, "The English Caribbees in the Period of the Civil War, 1642–1646," *Wm. and Mary Qtly.*, 3d Ser., XXIV (1967), 360.

23. Inventory of Capt. Ketteridge's estate, 1635, and of Matthew Gibson's estate, Oct. 10, 1635, Hay Papers.

The size of Barbados's population in the tobacco era has, how-ever, been grossly exaggerated. Early visitors to the island were struck by the crowds of people they saw, and their rough guesses have passed down unchallenged over the years. The Barbadian figures cited most frequently are 1,850 inhabitants in 1628, rising to 6,000 in 1636, and to 33,300 in 1643.[24] But these figures are impos-sible. Recently discovered poll-tax returns for Barbados in the 1630s disclose a much less sensational—though still highly impressive—rate of growth. Governor Hawley levied a poll tax on all Barbadians over the age of fourteen. Evidently he was systematic; the colonists grumbled that he distrained beds and hammocks in his effort to collect from everyone. Since few young children lived on the island at this time, the poll-tax returns ought to indicate the total popula-tion pretty closely. The returns are as follows: [25]

Year	Taxpayers
1635	1,227
1636	2,340
1637	3,948
1638	5,705
1639	8,707

These figures suggest that Barbados started slowly, but grew rapidly during the late 1630s, and reached about the same population size as Massachusetts or Virginia by 1640.

During the 1630s Barbados received a huge annual influx of new-comers, particularly servants, who were always the most transient element in the population. The best index to the size of the English migration to Barbados in this decade is the register of all passengers who passed through the port of London to America during 1635,

24. Eugene D. Genovese, *The World the Slaveholders Made* (New York, 1969), 26, credits Barbados with a white population of 37,000 in 1636. Carl Briden-baugh, *Vexed and Troubled Englishmen, 1590–1642* (New York, 1968), 410, 427–428, puts the collective population of the English Caribbees at 4,550 in 1629 and at 20,000 in 1639. In my opinion, this calculation is still too generous.

25. Account of all the goods of tobacco and cotton receaved by Capt. Henrie Hawley . . . which was the halfe of 20 lb. per head granted to him by the country, Hay Papers; Davis, *Cavaliers and Roundheads*, 58–59, 62–63; Bennett, "Peter Hay, Proprietary Agent," *Jam. Hist. Rev.*, V (1965), 12–13. Peter Hay, trying to collect proprietary rents, found 3,250 Barbadians in 1637 and close to 10,000 in 1640. Hay, to Sir James and Archibald Hay, Apr. 13, 1638, Feb. 25, 1640/1, Hay Papers.

summarized in table 1. According to this register, fifty-three ships sailed from London to the various American colonies in this year, carrying a total of 4,890 passengers.

Table 1. London Emigrants to America, 1635

Destination	Ships	Passengers	Percentage
Barbados	8	985	20.1
St. Christopher	5	423	8.6
Bermuda	2	220	4.5
Providence Is.	1	72	1.5
Island colonies	16	1,700	34.7
Virginia	20	2,013	41.2
New England	17	1,177	24.1
Mainland colonies	37	3,190	65.3

NOTE: The register is printed in its entirety in Hotten, ed., *Original Lists*, 33–145. It is interesting to note that the 13 ships bound for Barbados and St. Christopher sailed between Sept. and May, avoiding the three hot summer months when traffic to New England and Virginia was at its peak.

The tabulation is probably not complete, for the number of passengers recorded for the seventeen ships bound for New England is suspiciously low, and it looks as though several hundred additional Puritan emigrants sneaked on board to avoid certifying their conformity to the Church of England. Puritanism was not the only difference between the Caribbean and New England passengers. As noted above, 91 percent of the people bound for Barbados were youngsters between the ages of ten and twenty-nine. Only 6 percent were women. No children under ten and virtually no married couples are to be found. Obviously Barbados was not yet a family-based community. Very much the same pattern emerges among the emigrants to Virginia. But the New Englanders were completely different, being family groups with a much wider age spread and many more women and young children.

London was not the only port of exodus to the islands in the 1630s. Many of the early Barbados settlers sailed from the western outports. And Ireland was already a prime source of supply for servants. Fortunately the business papers have survived of a servant ship that carried fifty-six Irish men and women from Kinsale to Barbados in 1636. In this case, Thomas Anthony, the supercargo, was instructed to sign up Irish servants for Virginia, which he found difficult to do, for the Irish had heard that St. Christopher was the place to go for liberal annual wages. Two other ships at Kinsale in 1636 were busily recruiting servants for that island. In the end, Anthony took his cargo to Barbados. He signed up more women than he wanted, because he could not get enough men, but he assured the ship owners that these women were "from 17 to 35 Eares and very lustye and strong Boddied which I hopp be meyns to sett them of to the best Advantidg." Several of these colleens turned out to be overly lusty. Two became pregnant and one had "the frentche dizeas." These were discharged. Three more servants died en route. The remaining fifty-three were sold in two days at Barbados for five hundred pounds of tobacco apiece.[26] During the Atlantic passage the mortality rate, particularly on servant ships, could run very high. Thomas Rous, arriving in Barbados in 1638, complained bitterly that his ship had been so overcrowded with 350 passengers that it was almost impossible to escape infection. Jammed together below decks during the cold weather, two hundred people became sick at a time, and Rous reported "we have throwen over board two and three in a day for many dayes togeather." Eighty passengers died by the time this ship reached Barbados.[27]

Thomas Rous is of interest because he exemplifies the rising planter class in Barbados. He began operations on a modest scale. In 1645 he sold a 60-acre farm for only £121. But the family fortune rose with the sugar industry, and by 1680 his son John and his grandson Thomas Rous owned 3 sugar works, 658 acres, and 310 slaves. They were members of the planter elite that dominated the island during the late seventeenth century.[28] How many other top sugar-planting families can be traced back to the early tobacco days?

The answer, it turns out, is a substantial nucleus. Thanks to the

26. Abbot E. Smith, *Colonists in Bondage: White Servitude and Convict Labor in America, 1607-1776* (Chapel Hill, N.C., 1947), 62–66. Seven other servant ships which sailed to the islands between 1633 and 1640 are listed by Bridenbaugh, *Vexed and Troubled Englishmen*, 426–427.

27. Rous to Archibald Hay, May 26, 1638, Hay Papers.

28. Though not members in good standing. Thomas and John Rous were active Quakers in the 1670s and were barred from public office. See *Jour. Bar. Mus. Hist. Soc.*, XI (1943–1944), 183; Joseph Besse, *A Collection of the Sufferings of the People called Quakers* (London, 1753), II, chap. 6.

Barbados census of 1680 (to be discussed in the next chapter), we know who the leading families were in the golden days of the sugar industry on the island. In 1680, 175 planters drawn from 159 families constituted the island elite. Some 62 out of these 159 families— or 39 percent—were already Barbados property holders in 1638.[29] The 62 early comers may be called the charter members of the Barbados elite. Among them were such important Barbados names as Allyn, Bulkely, Codrington, Drax, Frere, Guy, Hothersall, Pears, and Yeamans. Many in this core group seem to have had commercial backgrounds in England. The evidence is circumstantial, but it looks as though a high percentage came from English merchant families that had previously invested in overseas trading companies or privateering ventures and were thus particularly attuned to the possibilities of business enterprise in the West Indies.[30] A good many people from this core group were among the early island leaders. In 1639, 14 of the 62 sat on Governor Hawley's Council or in the Assembly. James Drax, founder of the first great Barbados sugar fortune, was a militia captain and assemblyman in the 1630s. From the outset the Council and Assembly were studded with names like Gibbs, Fortescue, Sandiford, Read, Hothersall, and Berringer that would recur repeatedly later in the century.[31]

Yet we must not suppose that Barbados's political and social structure was already taking firm shape in these early years. On the contrary, the island population was highly fluid and transient. The majority of the big sugar-planting families had not yet appeared on the scene, and a great many of the big names in early Barbados history would soon disappear without permanent trace. Sir William Courteen; the earl of Carlisle; Gov. Henry Hawley; John and Henry Powell, who worked for Courteen; Peter Hay and James Holdip,

29. This calculation is reached by correlating the names of the big planters in the 1680 census, C.O. 1/44/142–379, with the list of 764 "Inhabitants of Barbados, in the Year, 1638, who then possessed more than ten Acres of Land." [Duke], *Memoirs*, 51–62. Most of the surnames found on both lists are sufficiently unusual so there can be little doubt that we are dealing with the same families.

30. Rabb, *Enterprise and Empire*, lists over 6,000 persons who invested in overseas commercial ventures during these years. Among our group of 62 Barbadians, 45 have surnames that turn up on Prof. Rabb's list. Since Rabb's list is so large and his time span closes just as West Indian settlement begins, the correlation may prove nothing. However, one would surely expect pre-1630 investors in trade and privateering to interest themselves in post-1630 settlement.

31. List of Barbados Council and Assembly, July 19, 1639, *Jour. Bar. Mus. Hist. Soc.*, X (1942–1943), 173–174. There were 33 councillors and assemblymen in all.

who worked for Carlisle; Marmaduke Roydon, William Perkins, and Alexander Bannister, who headed the merchant syndicate backing Carlisle; Edward Oistin and William Hilliard, with their large plantations—none of these men left descendants in Barbados who were prominent or wealthy two generations later.[32] Barbados began as a raw, crude, roisterous, and unsettled frontier community. "If all whoremasters were taken off the Bench," Captain Futter asked Judge Read in the 1630s, "what would the Governor do for a Council?" Though Captain Futter was an assemblyman with forty servants, Governor Hawley punished his insolence by putting him in the pillory at high noon without a hat.[33] Still, he seems to have asked a fair question.

§•

"There is a greate change on this island of late," reported a Barbadian in 1646, "from the worse to the better, praised be God." The change was great indeed. Between 1640 and 1660 the Barbados planters switched from tobacco and cotton to sugar and from white servants to black slaves. Land changed hands rapidly, population boomed, commerce accelerated, and prices climbed sky high. A five-hundred-acre plantation fetched £16,000 in 1646—more than the earl of Carlisle had been offered for the proprietary rights to the whole island a few years before. A Barbados planter named William Powrey assured his English uncle that, if he spent £1,000 to equip Powrey's estate with slaves and a sugar works, he would receive after three years an annual return of £2,000.

The Barbadians could afford to buy far more luxury goods at the sacrifice of their previous self-sufficiency. Food became scarce on the island, for men were "so intent upon planting sugar that they had rather buy foode at very dear rates than produce it by labour, soe infinite is the profitt of sugar workes after once accomplished." [34] In

32. For a parallel situation in early Virginia, see Bernard Bailyn, "Politics and Social Structure in Virginia," in Smith, ed., *Seventeenth-Century America*, 92–95.

33. Davis, *Cavaliers and Roundheads*, 61; Davis, "Papers relating to the early History of Barbados," *Timehri*, New Ser., VI (1892), 331.

34. William Hay and William Powrey to Archibald Hay, Oct. 8, 1646, Hay Papers; Richard Vine to John Winthrop, July 19, 1647, Forbes *et al.*, eds., *Winthrop Papers*, V, 171. See also Nicholas Foster, *A Briefe Relation of the Late Horrid Rebellion Acted in the Island Barbadas* (London, 1650), 1–3.

this mercurial atmosphere clever and energetic men could get ahead fast. Some of the original settlers invested their money and credit in sugar works and slaves. Others sold out and retired to England. Their places were taken by a sizable group of new planters, pushy and moneyed men who immediately made their mark. Barbados was still a roisterous frontier community, but the planter elite had arrived.

It is surprising, perhaps, that the Barbadians struggled with tobacco and cotton so long before they tried making sugar, for they were keenly aware of its high commercial value. Sugar had always been a scarce, luxury commodity in England, traditionally obtained from the Mediterranean basin and Morocco. The Mediterranean climate is too cool in the winter and too dry all year round for optimum sugar growth, and a seventeenth-century English writer disparaged the "ill" method used in the Mediterranean for planting and curing cane. Nonetheless, it was a Sicilian sugar planter, as long ago as 1449, who invented the three-roller vertical mill that the English planters in the Caribbean used throughout the seventeenth and eighteenth centuries to crush their cane and extract their juice. European cane culture spread westward to the Madeira and Canary islands in the fifteenth century, and Christopher Columbus carried sugarcane from the Canaries to the West Indies. The early Spanish settlers erected sugar works in Hispaniola, Cuba, Jamaica, and Mexico, but the Spanish industry in the Caribbean was limited during the sixteenth and seventeenth centuries, and the English did not learn how to grow or process cane from the Spaniards.[35]

They learned rather from the Portuguese and the Dutch. In the closing decades of the sixteenth century the Portuguese started to make sugar at Pernambuco and Bahia on the northeast coast of Brazil on a scale far surpassing all previous production. By 1600 the Brazilians were virtually the sole suppliers of the European market. Elizabethan privateers made the Brazil sugar trade a prime target during the Anglo-Spanish war. In the three years following the Ar-

35. Ward Barrett, *The Sugar Hacienda of the Marqueses del Valle* (Minneapolis, 1970), analyzes the operations of a large Mexican estate established by Cortés, which flourished in the 16th century, declined in the 17th century, and recovered in the 18th century. Production techniques on Cortés's estate were very similar to those employed by the Barbadians, except that the Spaniards used more Indian than Negro labor. They complained that the Indians were much less efficient sugar workers than African slaves. *Ibid.*, 98–99.

mada they took thirty-four sugar ships with cargoes worth £100,000.[36] Meanwhile the Dutch were also interesting themselves in the Brazilian sugar business; they brought the planters Negro slaves from Africa and carried away their sugar to refine it in Amsterdam; in 1630 they seized control of Pernambuco from the Portuguese. Under Dutch management Brazilian sugar exports rose to their highest level of the seventeenth century, close to thirty thousand tons per year. The Portuguese planters revolted against the Dutch overlords in 1645 and drove them out of Pernambuco in 1654, so the Dutch occupation of Brazil was short. But for the English it was crucial. In the early 1640s, just before the Portuguese rebellion, the Dutch in Brazil taught the English in Barbados how to make sugar.

There are a number of small mysteries about the introduction of sugar culture to Barbados, but the main outline of the story is clear enough. When the English first settled on the island in 1627 they fetched various tropical plants and seeds, including sugarcane, from a Dutch outpost at Surinam. Thirty-two Indians came from Surinam to teach the English how to cultivate these new crops. The Indians planted the canes successfully in Barbados, but did not know how to make sugar; they taught the English "no other use of them than to make refreshing Drink for that hot Climate." In 1639 the colonists heard that the earl of Warwick was "intentive to set up suggar works" on Barbados, a rumor that fizzled out. The following year a planter named Daniel Fletcher complained that Barbados desperately needed a new crop, since both tobacco and cotton had proved to be unprofitable. By 1643, only three years later, the new crop had been found. Barbados, it could now be reported, "is growne the most flourishing Island in all those American parts, and I verily believe in all the world for the producing of sugar. . . . and their sugar works are brought to that maturity that each work for the space of eight moneths in the yeare can and doeth yeild 1500 lb. of sugar each 24 houres."[37] If this was true, Barbadian sugar works could already produce about 150 tons a year, which was a very good rate in the West Indies during the next two cen-

36. Andrews, *Elizabethan Privateering*, 129–133, 207–213. For a comprehensive account of the history of sugar making in Brazil and all over the world, see Deerr's magisterial *History of Sugar*.

37. Dalby Thomas, *An Historical Account of the Rise and Growth of the West-Indian Collonies* (London, 1690), 13; Sir James Hay to Peter Hay, Nov. 11, 1639, Daniel Fletcher to Archibald Hay, June 25, 1640, and Thomas Robinson to Thomas Chappell, Sept. 24, 1643, Hay Papers.

turies. It is evident that sugar production developed with extreme rapidity in Barbados between 1640 and 1643.

There are several reasons why the Barbados sugar boom developed with such explosive force. The island was (and is) far better suited to sugar than tobacco; once the planters discovered the knack, they grew cane of high quality and bountiful yield. The timing was perfect, for no other Caribbean island as yet produced sugar for the European market, and Brazil was a battleground between the Dutch and the Portuguese. The Dutch obligingly showed the English how to process the cane, supplied them with African slaves on easy terms, and sold their product in Amsterdam at generous prices, because sugar was still a very scarce and much desired commodity.

Among the Barbados planters, James Holdip and James Drax are credited with leading roles in starting the new industry. Captain Holdip obtained some canes from a Dutch slave ship or (in another version of the story) directly from Pernambuco. Having planted and harvested them, he helped his neighbors to start cane fields of their own. For example, in March 1644 he gave Thomas Applewait fifty acres of cleared land and "so many good sugar canes to plant upon the bargained premises as shall be expedient and needfull" in exchange for twenty-five of Applewait's men servants.[38] The next, and greater, task was learning how to convert the cane into sugar. According to one account, James Drax, a planter of Anglo-Dutch lineage, brought to Barbados a model of a sugar mill from Holland. Another story is that a Dutchman from Pernambuco visited Barbados and that "this Hollander understanding Sugar, was by one Mr. Drax, and some other Inhabitants there drawn in to make Discovery of the Art he had to make it."

Richard Ligon, who came to Barbados in 1647, says that the first small mill built by the English worked poorly, and for several years their sugar was "bare Muscavadoes," that is, unrefined, coarse brown sugar—too dark, too moist, and full of molasses. This, says Ligon, was because the English had not yet figured out the best way to plant, harvest, grind, boil, and cure. But they kept experimenting, helped "by new directions from Brasil, sometimes by strangers,

38. [Duke], *Memoirs*, app., 1; contract between Holdip and Applewait, Mar. 1, 1643/4, printed by Pares, *Merchants and Planters*, 53. James Holdip, despite his initative in the 1640s, did not prosper in the Indies. His Barbados plantation was ruined by a fire, causing him a loss of £10,000, and thereafter he tried Surinam and Jamaica, but returned to England in 1658. See Deerr, *History of Sugar*, I, 162–163.

FIG. 4. Richard Ligon's map of Barbados, about 1650, at the beginning of the sugar boom. Note that most plantations are still on the leeward coast. (Courtesy of University of Pennsylvania Library, Philadelphia.)

and now and then by their own people" who visited the plantations of Pernambuco and brought back "more Plants, and better Knowledge." By the time Ligon left in 1650—barely a decade after the first crop—he says the planters had learned how to make acceptable white sugar, not so white as Brazilian, but sweeter. In these early days, when the cane fields were new and the land was fresh, the yield per acre in Barbados was extraordinarily high by seventeenth-century standards. Several commentators in the 1640s agree that an acre of Barbados cane should yield upwards of two tons of sugar, twice the yield obtained in most West Indian islands (including Barbados) later in the century.[39]

The Barbados planters learned much from Brazil, but they did not copy the Portuguese style of sugar making in toto. In Brazil the *senhor de engenho,* or lord of the mill, was, as his name implies, a grandiose manor lord. He owned a huge tract, maintained a large force of salaried artisans, tenant farmers, and slaves, lived nobly in his Big House, and presided over a self-sufficient, paternalistic community complete with church, court, police force, and social-welfare agencies. The *senhor* leased his cane fields in small units (ten to fifteen acres) to a number of tenant *lavradores de cana,* or cane growers, who worked on the sharecropping principle; each *lavrador* tilled his small parcel of land with a squad of ten or twenty slaves, sent the cane he raised to the *senhor's* sugar works, and received back considerably less than half of the sugar as his share. This Brazilian plantation organization drew upon Portuguese agricultural traditions of seigneurialism and sharecropping. There was, however, continuous conflict between the *senhor* and his *lavrador* tenants who wished to become land owners and mill owners themselves. As the Brazilian cane fields lost some of their original fertility, the *lavradores* found it harder and harder to make any profit. Some managed to buy land and set up their own mills; others turned to the newly opened gold mines. Overall, Brazilian sugar output sagged perceptibly in the late seventeenth century.[40]

39. Thomas, *Historical Account,* 14; Ligon, *True History of Barbados,* 24, 85–86, 95; James Parker to John Winthrop, June 24, 1646, Forbes *et al.,* eds., *Winthrop Papers,* V, 83.

40. Gilberto Freyre, *The Masters and the Slaves,* trans. Samuel Putnam (New York, 1946) paints a far rosier picture of the Brazilian sugar system than C. R. Boxer's two books, *The Dutch in Brazil, 1624–1654* (New York, 1957) and *The Golden Age of Brazil, 1695–1750* (Berkeley, Calif., 1962). Stuart B. Schwartz, Free Farmers in a Slave Economy: The Lavradores de Cana of Bahia, 1550–1750 (a paper presented at the Newberry Library Conference on Colonial Brazil) focuses interestingly on the sharecropping cane growers.

The English organized their sugar making in a different way, drawing upon their own agricultural habits, which were more clearly capitalistic and less paternalistic than in Portugal. English farmers were used to growing cash crops, paying money rents, and hiring wage labor; they were not used to sharecropping.[41] Rich gentry and humble yeomen alike practiced a species of private enterprise. Accordingly, when the English farmers in the West Indies turned to sugar making, their prime goal was to make money, not to become seigneurs. At first few individual planters had the necessary capital to set up effectively for themselves. The island records show repeated examples of partnerships between two, three, or four men. If two men shared ownership, as most commonly happened, one partner might operate the plantation in Barbados while his colleague marketed the sugar in England or Holland and sent out supplies. Another cost-saving device was for two neighboring planters to build and operate a common sugar works. Barbados plantations might employ one hundred or more laborers and cost thousands of pounds, yet on the average they were considerably smaller establishments than the seigneurial Brazilian plantations. Barbados in 1680 produced rather less sugar than Brazil, but had nearly twice as many sugar works. There were other differences. The English planter combined the roles of mill owner and cane grower. He did not attempt to produce food, clothing, and equipment for his work force on his own estate, but depended on outside suppliers. He offered a minimum of social services. Whatever religious, educational, and charitable institutions there were in the English islands existed outside of the plantation. In short, the English sugar planter was more strictly a businessman than the *senhor de engenho* of Brazil.

Obviously the early English sugar planters received considerable Dutch instruction and assistance. Why were the Dutch so helpful? One argument is that, since they were losing control of Pernambuco in the 1640s, they wanted to promote a rival sugar industry elsewhere. But in fact the Dutch started to subsidize the English in Barbados *before* the Pernambuco revolt of 1645, just at the point when the Brazilian sugar exports of the Dutch West India Company were at their maximum. The Dutch must have reckoned that the European craving for sugar was great enough to warrant ex-

41. The sharecropping principle had been introduced in Bermuda and Providence Island, but in both cases the colonists resisted and rejected it. See Newton, *Colonising Activities of the English Puritans*, 89, 98, 222.

panding the supply by adding Barbados to Brazil.[42] Dutch traders were not strangers in Barbados. Throughout the 1630s they had carried much of the English colonists' tobacco and cotton to Amsterdam. Now they stood to profit much more handsomely by offering a full range of lucrative middleman services to the tyro English sugar planters: credit, slaves, plantation equipment, and shipment to the best sugar refineries and busiest entrepôt in Europe. For the Barbadians this Dutch partnership was especially advantageous in the 1640s when English overseas trade was distracted by the civil war at home.

One measure of the sugar boom is the fantastic rise in Barbados real-estate values during the 1640s. Land that had fetched about 10s. per acre in 1640 sold at £2 or £2 10s. in 1643 and at £5 in 1646 —a tenfold increase in seven years. The price of large, well-sited tracts rose faster than this. Once the industry took root, properties were generally bought and sold fully equipped with sugar works, servants, and slaves. Old Barbados deeds show that five of the choicest plantations on the island changed hands between 1646 and 1648 at prices ranging from £1,800 to £4,500 per hundred acres, which helps explain why few individual planters in these early days could afford to own plantations outright. In the 1650s the Barbados land market slumped temporarily with the opening up of new sugar lands in Jamaica, the exclusion of Dutch traders from the English islands, and a general drop in sugar prices as Caribbean production picked up in volume. Thus we find several Barbados plantations selling for less than £1,000 per hundred acres in the Cromwellian era. But the going rate quickly climbed back to £2,000 or better after the Restoration.[43]

The insoluble problem for Barbadians was that their tight little island contained less than a hundred thousand arable acres. In or-

42. This is the argument of Matthew Edel, "The Brazilian Sugar Cycle of the Seventeenth Century and the Rise of West Indian Competition," *Caribbean Studies,* IX (1969) , 27–31, 40.

43. This paragraph is based on an analysis of 20 Barbados real-estate transactions, large and small, between 1640 and 1681. This sample is regrettably small, but it is all that I have been able to piece together from a variety of sources: five sales, dated 1640, 1646, 1667, 1675, and 1680, in Davis, "Records of Old Barbados," *Timehri,* New Ser., X (1896) , 97–113; ten sales, dated 1643, 1645, 1647, 1648, 1658, 1666, in *Jour. Bar. Mus. Hist. Soc.,* III (1935–1936) , 100–106, X (1942–1943) , 155–156, XI (1943–1944) , 183, XXIII (1955–1956) , 73–77; one sale, dated 1646, in Hay Papers; one sale, dated 1647, in Forbes *et al.,* eds., *Winthrop Papers,* V, 171–172; two sales, dated 1656, 1681, Barbados Deeds, RB 3/3, 3/14, Barbados Archives, Lazaretto, St. Michael; one sale, dated 1655, K. H. D. Haley, *The First Earl of Shaftesbury* (Oxford, 1968) , 230.

der to put as much land as possible into cane fields, they cut down the remaining forests. By the 1650s there was a timber shortage, and by the 1660s Barbados had less woodland than most districts of England.[44] No one wanted to waste valuable cane land on provision crops to feed the island's growing population, so Barbados became dependent on food supplies from England, Ireland, and North America. There was a further problem in converting the old tobacco farms into efficient sugar estates. Many tracts laid out in the 1630s were either too small or too large. A peasant proprietor with twenty or thirty acres had too little land to support a sugar works; his only real choice was to buy his neighbors' property or else sell out. Those fortunate few who started with thousand-acre tracts found it advantageous to sell off some land, for sugar production required close to one laborer for every acre of cane, and no Barbadian in the 1640s or 1650s had the manpower to operate a really large plantation.[45]

Gradually a couple of hundred sugar magnates, with plantation units averaging about two hundred acres in size, acquired all of the choice acreage on the island.[46] The small proprietors were not eliminated, as has been supposed, but their position had certainly deteriorated. Crowded onto tiny plots of marginal land, they eked out a precarious existence by growing a mixture of sugar, cotton, ginger, and provision crops. The gulf between the big and small planters, already perceptible in the 1630s, became a yawning chasm in the sugar age.

The sugar boom created a massive demand for laborers in Barbados. The island planters continued to employ plenty of indentured white servants, but the striking thing is how eagerly they plunged

44. Compare Watts, *Man's Influence on the Vegetation of Barbados*, 44–45, with Chalkin, *Seventeenth-Century Kent*, 12–13, 105–107, and Thirsk, *Agrarian History of England and Wales*, xxix–xxxii.

45. The oft-quoted example of Capt. Humphrey Waterman, who consolidated 40 small farms into an 800-acre tract (John Scott's Description of Barbados, *c.* 1669, Sloan Manuscripts, 3662/59, Br. Museum) is not representative. Very few Barbados sugar plantations were so large, and by 1680 the Watermans had reduced their holdings to 663 acres, divided into two separate production units.

46. The subdivision and consolidation of tobacco farms into sugar plantations produced some oddly fashioned tracts: a plat in the Deeds, RB 3/3, Bar. Archives, dated 1661, shows a 143-acre plantation shaped like a jagged lightning bolt with 21 sides.

into the slaveholding business. "Here are come lately about five hundred Negroes and more dayly expected," was the report in 1642. Three years later a New England visitor claimed that the Barbadians "have bought this year no lesse than a thousand Negroes; and the more they buie, the better able they are to buye. For in a yeare and a halfe they will earne (with gods blessing) as much as they

Table 2. The Labor Force on Fifteen Barbados Plantations, 1640–1667

Year	Planter	Acreage	Servants	Slaves
1640	Lancelot Pace	360	17	0
1643	James Holdip	200	29	0
1646	Sir Anthony Ashley Cooper	205	21	9
1646	?	500	40	50
1647	Thomas Modyford	500	28	102
1648	?	100	11	3
1648	Humphrey Walrond	250	10	29
1649	William Powrey	416	7	23
1650	Gideon Low	150	0	10
1654	Robert Hooper	200	35	66
1656	George Martin	259	0	60
1657	John Read	75	21	25
1658	Thomas Hothersall	140	0	30
1661	?	143	5	20
1667	?	350	5	125

NOTE: Five of these plantations (1643, 1648, 1650, 1654, and 1658) are described in *Jour. Bar. Mus. Hist. Soc.*, VII (1939–1940), 11, 70–71, X (1942–1943), 155, XXII (1954–1955), 116, XXIII (1955–1956), 74; six (1640, 1648, 1656, 1657, 1661, and 1667) are in Barbados Deeds, RB 3/1, 3/3, Bar. Archives; Cooper's plantation is mentioned in Haley, *First Earl of Shaftesbury*, 64, 230; Modyford's plantation is described in Ligon, *True History of Barbados*, 22; and the plantations of 1646 and 1649 are described in Hay Papers.

cost." [47] Naturally it took some years for the planters to acquire as many slaves as they wanted. Table 2, which shows the labor force on fifteen Barbados plantations over a twenty-eight-year span, may not be entirely representative. But it suggests the general trend, a rather gradual switch from servants to slaves.

Several of the planters in table 2 were among the grander entre-

47. James Browne to Sir James and Archibald Hay, Jan. 17, 1641/2, Hay Papers; George Downing to John Winthrop, Jr., Aug. 26, 1645, Forbes *et al.*, eds., *Winthrop Papers*, V, 43.

preneurs on the island. James Drax, with 700 acres and 200 slaves, was the grandest of all. A French visitor in 1654 found it "quite a sight to see 200 slaves working with sugar" at Drax's plantation.[48] Yet Barbados estates were generally underdeveloped compared with the plantations of the next generation. By 1680 seventy Barbadians had larger work gangs than Thomas Modyford's crew of 130 laborers. The norm had become one worker for every two acres, a ratio achieved only by Robert Hooper and John Read among the fifteen listed in table 2. It is more valid, however, to compare the early Barbados sugar planters with their contemporaries in Virginia, who had only 300 Negroes altogether in 1650.[49]

During the initial stage of sugar production, when the white servants found themselves toiling in the same field gangs with black slaves, they became wild and unruly in the extreme. Some of the English and Irish youths shipped over in the 1640s and 1650s had been kidnapped. To be "barbadosed" in the seventeenth century meant the same as to be "shanghaied" in the twentieth. It would be hard to say whether the London thieves and whores rounded up for transportation to "the Barbados Islands" or the Scottish and Irish soldiers captured in Cromwell's campaigns and sent over as military prisoners were any less hostile and rebellious than the Negroes dragged in chains from Africa. Irish Catholics constituted the largest block of servants on the island, and they were cordially loathed by their English masters. One Irishman was given twenty-one lashes for remarking during dinner "that if there was so much English Blood in the tray as there was Meat, he would eat it." In 1647, when Richard Ligon arrived in Barbados, an island-wide servant rebellion had been nipped just in time. Eighteen of the servant conspirators were executed. Small wonder that Ligon found the Barbados planters building their houses "in manner of Fortifications," equipped with bulwarks and bastions from which they could pour scalding water upon the attacking servants and slaves! [50]

It is only fair to add that many, perhaps most, of the Barbados

48. Jerome S. Handler, ed., "Father Antoine Biet's Visit to Barbados in 1654," *Jour. Bar. Mus. Hist. Soc.*, XXXII (1965–1966), 69.

49. As late as 1670, Gov. Berkeley of Virginia reported 2,000 slaves and 6,000 servants in a population of 40,000. Wesley Frank Craven, *The Colonies in Transition, 1660–1713* (New York, 1968), 290.

50. Smith describes the unsavory aspects of the Barbados servant trade and the transport of convicts, rogues, vagabonds, and military prisoners to the island, in *Colonists in Bondage*, chaps. 4–5, 7–8. See also Aubrey Gwynn, S.J., ed., "Documents relating to the Irish in the West Indies," *Analecta Hibernica*, Irish Manuscripts Commission, No. 4 (Dublin, 1932), 233–235; Ligon, *True History of Barbados*, 29, 46.

servants came over voluntarily. Our best information about the servant migration to Barbados at mid-century comes from a register maintained by the city of Bristol from 1654 to 1686. The Bristol city fathers wanted to stop kidnapping at their port, and they required all servants bound for America to register their names, desti-

Table 3. Servants Shipped from Bristol to America, 1654–1686

Destination	1654–1659	1660–1669	1670–1679	1680–1686	Total
Barbados	1,405	948	252	73	2,678
Nevis	43	811	379	14	1,247
Jamaica	0	21	90	357	468
Other islands					133
Total islands	1,448	1,780	721	444	4,526
Virginia	796	2,484	1,477	117	4,874
Maryland	1	20	81	35	137
New England	7	91	59	5	162
Other mainland colonies					34
Total mainland colonies	804	2,595	1,617	157	5,207
Destination not given					661
Total servants					10,394

NOTE: This table is a simplified version of Smith's year-by-year tabulation of the Bristol register in *Colonists in Bondage*, 309. The register has been partially printed, unhappily in an almost unusable format, in William Dodgson Bowman, ed., *Bristol and America* (Baltimore, 1967).

nations, and terms of indenture. This register—the most important surviving colonial emigration list for the seventeenth century—catalogs more than ten thousand servants who sailed to America. As table 3 shows, nearly half of them went to the West Indies. Barbados was the principal destination for Bristol servants in the years of the Cromwellian Protectorate, and doubtless Barbados had drawn more servants than any other colony in the 1640s and early 1650s, before the register was started. But once the Barbados planters fully converted to slave labor in the 1660s, Virginia took over first place.

The Bristol register often gives the servant's home town and oc-cupational status. By surveying the 2,678 who went to Barbados, we discover that 24 percent of them were women—a much higher percentage than in the 1630s. Two-thirds came from the south-western corner of England, from the counties adjacent to Bristol. Two-thirds of those who gave their occupational status called them-selves yeomen or laborers; they were going to have to adapt to a style of agriculture utterly different from anything they knew in England. The others were artisans, some trained as carpenters, coopers, smiths, and masons—crafts very useful in the West Indies —and some as weavers and chandlers, less useful trades.[51]

Why did the Barbados sugar planters turn away from white la-borers such as these Bristol servants and convert so rapidly to black slave labor? Afro-American slavery was of course well established in the 1640s. The Spanish and Portuguese colonies had each acquired at least 150,000 slaves from Africa by this time. Yet the English colonists did not copy everything Spanish, and they roundly con-demned the Spaniards for enslaving the native Caribbean Indians. It is true that the English had dabbled in Negro slavery since the 1560s, when John Hawkins tried to sell African slaves to the Span-ish colonists in the West Indies. The first Englishmen to plant on Barbados in 1627 brought ten Negroes and thirty-two Indians with them. Nevertheless, the English imported few Negroes into Barba-dos during the next dozen years, and they had their reasons for wishing to keep the number small. For one thing, the concept of chattel slavery was still somewhat strange to the English; they lacked the Iberians' long experience in holding Moslem and Negro slaves at home. More to the point, the English were a narrowly ethnocentric people, exceedingly reluctant to live among foreigners of any sort, even Scots or Irish or Dutchmen, let alone really alien peoples such as Jews or Indians or Negroes. Winthrop Jordan has reminded us that the Englishman of 1640 expressed a profound aversion to black-skinned people. He thought the Negro was ugly, barbaric, ape-like, and devilish.[52] What induced the Barbadians to bring thousands of such men onto their small island?

The answer must be sought in the Barbados planters' economic

51. The names of all the Barbados servants in the Bristol register have been published, with full details, in *Jour. Bar. Mus. Hist. Soc.*, XIV (1946–1947) through XIX (1951–1952), *passim*. My comments are based on an examination of this list.

52. Winthrop D. Jordan, *White over Black: American Attitudes Toward the Negro, 1550–1812* (Chapel Hill, N.C., 1968), chap. 1.

needs and social assumptions. They came from a society with no slaves but plenty of servants, domestic drudges, and farm laborers who spent their lives toiling for their betters in exchange for minimum requirements of food, clothing, and shelter. Property owners considered the laboring poor a necessary evil. Subsistence wage laborers were chronically on the edge of pauperism and vagabondage, yet agricultural and industrial production depended on this reservoir of cheap labor. An unprivileged servile class seemed as necessary in seventeenth-century England as refrigerators and washing machines do today, but the Barbados colonists had great difficulty in transporting this English servile class to the West Indies. As we have seen, in the 1630s they commonly employed one white servant for every ten acres. The indentured servant bound himself to his master for a stipulated term of years (generally four or five) in return for free ocean passage, food, clothing, and shelter during his term of service, and certain "freedom dues" when his indenture expired. The planter paid about £12 for a servant and had the right to whip him for his faults. In Barbados one method of punishment was to string servants up by their hands and light matches between their fingers. Richard Ligon was scandalized to see overseers, on the slightest provocation, beat their fellow Christians over the head with canes until the blood ran. It is clear that the Barbados masters were treating their servants more brutally than at home by the 1640s and 1650s, and the servants were behaving more rebelliously than at home. As Barbados gained the reputation of being a hell for the working class, the masters could persuade few laborers whose indentures had expired to stay on as permanent wage workers. Clearly they needed a more settled, more dependable work force.[53]

At this point the example of Brazilian slavery was decisive. The Barbados planters who visited Pernambuco around 1640 in order to learn how to make sugar found that the Brazilian sugar plantations were manned by gangs of African slaves. These black bondsmen had obvious practical advantages over the unstable white labor force in Barbados. An African slave was a better value for the money than an English servant, for while his initial purchase price was £25 or more in the 1640s (the price soon dropped to £15), he cost far less to feed and clothe, and he was a permanent acquisition. Dutch traders could promise a large and regular supply of slaves.

53. Smith, *Colonists in Bondage*, 248, 260–261; Ligon, *True History of Barbados*, 44.

The Brazilian example proved that these black laborers were well qualified to operate a sugar plantation. The Negroes of West and Central Africa were agriculturists, experienced with hoe cropping and easily taught how to use the few hand tools necessary for cane culture. The sugar planter needed a large but unskilled work force; even the more specialized jobs such as boiler, distiller, and potter required only slight training. The West Indian masters soon made a habit of deriding the Negro's intelligence, but they never pretended that any plantation task was beyond their slaves' capacity. The African had another advantage: he was used to living in a hot and humid climate, to tropical food crops, and to tropical insect life. The key factor, however, was that Africans could be forced to submit to slavery. It must have comforted the English visitors at Pernambuco to see a handful of white masters and drivers keeping hundreds of blacks under control. The slaves were deeply rebellious and unwilling, to be sure, but this was no novelty in Barbados. Black slaves performed the required tasks more patiently than white servants, and this consideration more than outweighed the disagreeable prospect of living in close propinquity to a people totally foreign in color, speech, religion, and culture.

So the Barbadians became big slaveholders. The rape's progress was fatally easy: from exploiting the English laboring poor to abusing colonial bondservants to ensnaring kidnaps and convicts to enslaving black Africans. It was, as Winthrop Jordan says, an "unthinking decision." Once the Barbadians took the plunge and began importing Negroes from Africa by the boatload, they never looked back. Nor did they pause to consider whether these black laborers had to be enslaved, whether they might not be organized as indentured servants or wage workers. The African was only attractive to the Englishman as a fixed possession, like a horse or a cow. He was not quite like a horse or cow, to be sure, for it had to be admitted that he was a human being, presumably endowed with a soul, perhaps a child of God—but of a species so obviously inferior in race and culture that the English need not trouble to consider his rights. Besides, the Barbados slave had already been bought and sold several times over, captured in some remote African tribal skirmish, marched in a coffle of fellow prisoners to the sea coast, delivered by an African broker to a European trader who carried him to the Indies and auctioned him yet again. The Barbados planters knew very little about the dark continent from which their new laborers came, and they cared less. They never bothered during the seventeenth century to apologize for their slave system by claiming that the Negroes were better off in the Indies than in Africa. Indeed they seldom talked about their Negroes.

The Barbadians also held Indian slaves, but never very many. The Caribs who inhabited nearby Dominica, St. Lucia, and St. Vincent were far too savage to catch and tame, so the Barbadians procured Indian captives from Surinam or Carolina or even New England during King Philip's War. But they found that Indians made poor slaves. The men in particular would only hunt and fish "and if forced to any labor, eyther hang themselves or Runne away." [54] The red man—standing outside the white man's system in Barbados as elsewhere in English America—had to be categorized as a different sort of barbarous pagan from the black man. His skin color was lighter, he could be considered more European in appearance, he had the sentimental advantage of being a native American, Nature's nobleman. Yet what really mattered was that Indians could not be turned into acceptable agricultural laborers and Negroes could. It was not so much that Indians were more warlike. The rulers of the West African kingdoms were warlike enough to keep the Europeans at arm's length until the nineteenth century. But these kings readily sold their fellows into captivity, and the captive Africans fell into lockstep as menial laborers. The most tragic thing about Afro-American slavery is that all of the black man's admirable human qualities—his sociability, adaptability, endurance, loving kindness, and domesticated, disciplined culture—earned him nothing but debasement in the New World.

§❧

The population of Barbados in the early sugar days is very hard to estimate. As we have seen, poll-tax returns show that the island contained about 10,000 people in 1640, but there are no equivalent statistics for the next three decades. Because of this lacuna, the population estimates of Richard Ligon and John Scott are frequently cited. Both men report exceedingly high totals. Ligon says that he found 11,000 militia on the island in the late 1640s, 50,000

54. Gov. Vaughan of Jamaica to Sec. Coventry, Dec. 17, 1676, Coventry Papers of the marquis of Bath at Longleat (microfilm, American Council of Learned Societies, British Microfilm Project), LXXXV, 111. Hereafter cited as Coventry Papers.

white inhabitants, and 100,000 slaves. Scott, who visited Barbados in the mid-1660s, says he found an old militia roll for 1645 showing that the island then had 18,300 militiamen, 11,200 landed proprietors, and 5,680 slaves. By 1666, according to Scott, the militia had shrunk to 8,300 and the proprietors to 745, but the Negro population had climbed by 1667 to 82,023. Furthermore, he asserts, at least 12,000 white Barbadians—mostly servants and small proprietors—had migrated to the other English colonies between 1645 and 1666.[55]

What are we to make of these figures? Ligon's estimate was made casually, and it may be dismissed. He was a first-rate observer, but an unreliable calculator; for example, he reckoned that Barbados had an area of 292 square miles, whereas the true figure is 166. As for John Scott, he was a notorious trickster, who spent a mottled career as an international spy and counterspy,. peddling dubious maps and military information to the English, Dutch, and French authorities.[56] His story about the old militia roll and his parade of precise-sounding statistics are in my opinion sheer fabrications. Scott's figure of 11,200 landed proprietors in 1645 is at a minimum five times too high. His figure for militiamen in 1645 is three times too high.[57] My hunch—contrary to Scott—is that the white population of Barbados, as well as the black population, rose markedly between 1640 and 1660. The flood of incoming servants during these years more than counterbalanced the exodus to Jamaica and other colonies and the high mortality from yellow fever and other tropical diseases. By the Restoration there seem to have been about 20,-

55. Ligon, *True History of Barbados,* 43, 46; Scott, Description of Barbados, Sloane MSS, 3662/54–59. Another set of Barbados population figures, probably also by Scott, is in *Cal.S.P.Col., 1661–1668,* #1657. Scott's figures are accepted by Williamson, *Caribbee Islands,* 157–158; by Harlow, *Barbados,* 44–45; and by Alfred D. Chandler, "The Expansion of Barbados," *Jour. Bar. Mus. Hist. Soc.,* XIII (1945–1946), 106–110.

56. Scott is best remembered for his effort to stake out a proprietary colony on Long Island, 1660–1665, just before he came to the West Indies, and for his efforts to frame Samuel Pepys during the Popish Plot hysteria of 1679. Wilbur Cortez Abbott paints a very negative portrait of him in *"Colonel" John Scott of Long Island* (New Haven, Conn., 1918), and Lilian T. Mowrer attempts to rehabilitate his reputation in *The Indomitable John Scott: Citizen of Long Island, 1632–1704* (New York, 1960).

57. Gov. Willoughby reported 6,400 militia in 1651, and Gov. Searle reported 5,300 in 1656—after 3,500 fighting men had left for Jamaica. See Harlow, *Barbados,* 70–78; Searle to Oliver Cromwell, June 1, 1655, Searle to Sec. Thurloe, Nov. 6, 1656, in Thomas Birch, ed., *A Collection of the State Papers of John Thurloe* (London, 1742), III, 500, V, 564.

ooo whites and an equal number of blacks in Barbados, **making
this small island by far the most populous and congested English
colony in America.** The population density was higher than in
most regions of England.[58]

One thing is certain. The planters lived more luxuriantly than
they had in the 1630s. All visitors to Barbados during the early
sugar days commented on the rich dress and food of the island gentry. We have no exact description of the houses and furnishings of
such big planters as James Drax and Thomas Modyford. But a few
household inventories of smaller planters, men who had about one
hundred acres and ten laborers, survive for the 1640s and 1650s.
These inventories show a great change in living style from the tobacco days, though still not many frills. The planters lived in two-
or three-storied wooden houses. They slept in four-poster beds, no
longer in hammocks (still used by the servants). Their rooms were
furnished with numerous tables, chairs, benches, cushions, and carpets in lieu of the barrels and chests that served in the 1630s. They
had framed pictures on their walls, linen and pewter (but little or
no silver) in their cupboards, and an occasional looking glass or
clock. One planter in 1649 boasted a library of forty-five volumes.
Another in 1658 had a railed balcony in his dining room and a
polished marble porch floor.[59]

More significant than these tokens of comfort are the signs of
burgeoning family life on the island. The St. Michael parish register (which starts in 1648) records scores of marriages and baptisms
per year in the 1650s. Some of the pioneer wives had been recruited
from the brothels of London and Edinburgh or released from
Bridewell, Newgate, and other prisons. Every young woman who
signed up as a Barbados servant in the early sugar days doubtless
heard that the rich planters on the island were much in need of
wives. On the debit side, the word must have spread that Barbados
was a sickly place. When Richard Ligon landed in 1647, he found
a yellow fever epidemic raging. "The sicknes was an absolute
plague; very infectious and destroying," a Barbadian reported the

58. For other population estimates, see David Lowenthal, "The Population of
Barbados," *Social and Economic Studies,* VI (1957), 445–451; Harlow, *Barbados,*
338–339; Pitman, *Development of the British West Indies,* 369–371; and "The
Population of Barbados," *Jour. Bar. Mus. Hist. Soc.,* XIII (1945–1946), 4–5.

59. This paragraph draws upon nine inventories, dated between 1640 and 1658,
found in Deeds, RB 3/1, 3/3, Bar. Archives; Hay Papers; and *Jour. Bar. Mus.
Hist. Soc.,* XXII (1954–1955), 117. See also Neville Connell, "Furniture and
Furnishings in Barbados during the 17th Century," *ibid.,* XXIV (1956–1957),
102–121.

next year to Governor Winthrop of Massachusetts. "Many who had begun and almost finished greate sugar workes, who dandled themselves in their hopes, but were suddenly laid in the dust, and their estates left unto strangers." Winthrop supposed that the epidemic carried off six thousand colonists, doubtless a greatly inflated figure. Yet the St. Michael parish register consistently lists four times as many deaths as marriages in the 1650s and three times as many deaths as baptisms. If Barbados family structure was healthier than it had been in the 1630s, it was not healthy enough.[60]

Everything about this fast-living, fast-dying tropical community seemed lurid and bizarre to Henry Whistler, who visited Barbados in 1655 as a member of the expedition that later conquered Jamaica. Whistler was particularly fascinated by the Negro slaves, but his overall impression of Barbados is so vivid that it deserves extended quotation:

This island is one of the richest spots of ground in the world and fully inhabited. But were the people suitable to the island, it were not to be compared. . . . The gentry here doth live far better than ours do in England. They have most of them 100 or 2 or 3 of slaves apes who they command as they please. Here they may say what they have is their own. And they have that liberty of conscience which we so long have in England fought for, but they do abuse it. This island is inhabited with all sorts: with English, French, Dutch, Scots, Irish, Spaniards they being Jews, with Indians and miserable Negroes born to perpetual slavery, they and their seed. These Negroes they do allow as many wives as they will have; some will have three or four, according as they find their body able. Our English here doth think a Negro child the first day it is born to be worth £5; they cost them nothing the bringing up, they go always naked. Some planters will have thirty more or less about four or five years old. They sell them from one to the other as we do sheep. This island is the dunghill whereon England doth cast forth its rubbish. Rogues and whores and such like people are those which are generally brought here. A rogue in England will hardly make a cheater here. A bawd brought over puts on a demure comportment, a whore if handsome makes a wife for some rich planter. But in plain, the island of itself is very delightful and pleasant. . . . The people have a very generous fashion that if one come to a house to inquire the way to any place, they will make him drink, and if the traveller does deny to stay to drink they take it very unkindly of him. [61]

60. St. Michael parish register, Vol. 1A, RL 1/1, Bar. Archives; Ligon, *True History of Barbados*, 21; Richard Vines to John Winthrop, Apr. 29, 1648, Forbes et al., eds., *Winthrop Papers*, V, 219–220; Winthrop, *Journal*, ed. Hosmer, II, 328–330.

61. "Extracts from Henry Whistler's Journal of the West India Expedition," in C. H. Firth, ed., *The Narrative of General Venables, with an Appendix of Papers Relating to the Expedition to the West Indies and the Conquest of Jamaica, 1654–1655* (London, 1900), 145–147. I have modernized Whistler's eccentric spelling, capitalization, and punctuation.

The Barbados gentry, whose nouveau riche vulgarity struck Henry Whistler so forcibly, had changed quite a bit in composition since the 1630s. Many of the original colony leaders died or were shouldered aside by newcomers who arrived in the 1640s and 1650s and developed large sugar estates. Among these newcomers were John Colleton, Samuel Farmer, Thomas Kendall, Peter Leare, Thomas Modyford, Daniel Searle, Constantine Silvester, George Stanfast, Timothy Thornhill, Humphrey Walrond, and Francis Lord Willoughby. These were able and aggressive men, more forceful as a group than the leading pre-1640 planters. Some were factors or agents employed by English or Dutch merchants, anxious to get in on the ground floor of the sugar business. Others were English gentry, often younger sons without good prospects at home, who had fought in the civil wars at home and wanted a fresh field of endeavor.[62] With their money and family connections, they contributed decisively to the rapid consolidation of the Barbados aristocracy. As we have seen, sixty-two of the top Barbados families as of 1680—or 39 percent of the total—had already settled on the island by 1638. I have been able to trace another thirty-four of the top families as of 1680—or 21 percent—who made their first appearance between 1640 and 1660.[63] This list is certainly far from complete, but in any case the newcomers were more impressive for their quality than their numbers. By the Restoration they had taken over the political, social, and economic leadership of the island.

62. Note again the parallel with Virginia, as described by Bailyn, "Politics and Social Structure in Virginia," in Smith, ed., *Seventeenth-Century America,* 98: The "struggling [Virginia] planters of the first generation failed to perpetuate their leadership into the second generation. . . . For a new emigration had begun in the forties, continuing for close to thirty years, from which was drawn a new ruling group that . . . absorbed and subordinated the older group, forming the base of the most celebrated oligarchy in American history. Most of Virginia's great eighteenth-century names, such as Bland, Burwell, Byrd, Carter, Digges, Ludwell, and Mason, appear in the colony for the first time within ten years either side of 1655. . . . These immigrants were younger sons of substantial families well connected in London business and governmental circles and long associated with Virginia."

63. My list of 34 is drawn from Davis, *Cavaliers and Roundheads;* Foster, *A Briefe Relation of the Late Horrid Rebellion;* "Some Records of the House of Assembly of Barbados," *Jour. Bar. Mus. Hist. Soc.,* X (1942–1943), 173–185; Harlow, *Barbados; Cal.S.P.Col., 1574–1660;* and Ligon's map, which identifies 285 planters by name. Incautiously supposing that this map identified all of the planters as of 1657, I asserted in "The Barbados Census of 1680: Profile of the Richest Colony in English America," *Wm. and Mary Qtly.,* 3d Ser., XXVI (1969), 18, that the great majority of big planters arrived between 1657 and 1674. This statement is wrong. The majority arrived before 1657.

The rising power and confidence of the Barbados gentry in the 1640s and 1650s is easily demonstrated by a survey of the island politics of the period. The English civil war gave the colonists their chance to cut loose from the absentee proprietor, the earl of Carlisle. In 1643 the Barbados Assembly stopped paying proprietary rents. That same year, James Holdip, one of the first successful sugar planters, went home to ask Charles I for "a grant that noe other Sugars may bee imported into his Majesties Dominions but such as are made upon the Barbadas." The colonists soon concluded, however, that they could do better by a free-trade policy, dealing with traders from Amsterdam as well as London. During the civil war Gov. Philip Bell—originally commissioned by Carlisle—adopted a neutral stance toward king and Parliament and secured effective independence from both. In 1645 the governor and Assembly convened the freeholders in each Barbados parish to secure public approbation for this policy. "It pleased god so to unite all their minds and harts together," Bell explained, "that every parish declared themselves resolutely for the maintenance of their peace and present government; and to admitt of noe alterationes or new commissiones from eyther side, . . . for against the kinge we are resolved never to be, and without the freindshipe of the perliament and free trade of London ships we are not able to subsist."[64]

The Barbadians were too boisterous and volatile to sustain this neutral pose very long. Once the fighting ended in England, the Cavalier and Roundhead soldiers who migrated to Barbados began to contest for control of the island. There ensued a series of plots and counterplots, armed uprisings, fines, and banishments. Of the 115 identifiable colonists who led the rival factions in this mini-civil war, only 55 had lived on Barbados before 1640. Half of the Roundhead leaders and more than half of the leading Cavaliers were newcomers, striking testimony to the changing leadership on the island.[65] The political crisis reached a climax in 1651. On the island the Cavaliers had ousted the Roundheads, but in England the Commonwealth government dispatched a fleet under Sir George Ayscue to reduce Barbados to obedience. Ayscue blockaded the island for

64. Bennett, "The English Caribbees, 1642–1646," *Wm. and Mary Qtly.*, 3d Ser., XXIV (1967) , 367–373.
65. I have culled these 115 names from Davis, *Cavaliers and Roundheads*, and correlated them with the list of 764 landholders as of 1638 in [Duke], *Memoirs*, 51–62. For the 46 leading Cavaliers, see Davis, *Cavaliers and Roundheads*, 72, 81, 98, 101, 139–140, 151–153, 162–163, 218–219, 256. For the 68 leading Roundheads, see *ibid.*, 145, 164–167, 171–178, 190–192.

three months, but he lacked the strength to invade and conquer the Barbados royalist forces. At length in January 1652 the colonists came to terms with Ayscue. They recognized the suzerainty of Parliament and accepted a parliamentary governor, Daniel Searle, in return for guarantees of continued self-government, restoration of all confiscated property, and free trade with the Dutch. The home government did not honor this last proviso and did its best to exclude the Dutch traders. Otherwise, the Barbadians enjoyed practical autonomy for the balance of the decade. Cavaliers and Roundheads settled down to making sugar. The chief planters occupied all of the Council and Assembly seats, while their merchant partners in London lobbied at Whitehall.

At the Restoration the Barbadians had to surrender much of their economic and political independence. Charles II's government was determined to tie the sugar islands to England commercially by means of the navigation acts, so the planters had to abandon their hope of continuing to trade with the Dutch. By the Restoration, also, the London price of sugar had dropped to half what it had been in 1640. Thus the English sugar industry entered a new stage. Henceforth the planters were restricted and protected by the mother country's mercantilist policy. They were required to carry all of their sugar in English ships to English ports, even though a good deal of it was later reexported to the Continent. They were required to buy all of their slaves from a monopolistic English corporation, and to buy any non-English commodities they desired on the English market. In compensation, of course, their sugar enjoyed a protected home market, with prohibitive tariffs set against foreign sugars. But for the Barbados planters, the first golden age of fresh cane fields, friendly Dutch traders, and easy wealth was over.

Nonetheless, the Barbados lobby in London saw to it that West Indian sugar imported to England paid low customs duties, which certainly helped its sale. The Barbados planters asked the king to annul Carlisle's proprietary patent and to confirm their land purchases of the 1640s and 1650s. Charles II did this. He assumed direct control of Barbados and sent out Francis Lord Willoughby as his first royal governor. Willoughby had served previously as governor of Barbados from 1650 to 1652 and was acceptable to most of the leading planters. In 1663 Willoughby persuaded the Barbados Assembly to grant the king a permanent 4.5 percent duty on all commodities exported from the island, in order to cover the costs of crown government. This measure has been interpreted as a surrender to royal power, but the Barbadians had paid a similar tax to Carlisle before 1643, and since Charles II spent the money in England rather than applying it to the governor's salary and other public charges on the island, the Assembly retained control over its purse strings. Though the planters disliked being cheated by the king, they soon recognized that the misappropriation of the 4.5 percent duty preserved their local independence. All in all, the Barbadians struck a pretty good bargain with Charles II.[66]

Five Barbados sugar planters received knighthoods or baronetcies between 1658 and 1665, and a dozen others were knighted later in the century—a good sign that the West Indian planters had reached the status of English gentry.[67] One of these new baronets, Sir Thomas Modyford, had a career in the Caribbean that epitomizes the verve and nerve of the pioneering sugar gentry. The son of the mayor of Exeter, Modyford came to Barbados as a young man in 1647, bringing with him money, connections, and the experience of fighting on the losing side in the civil war. In the Indies, Modyford was seldom a loser. On arrival he bought a half share in a well-equipped, five-hundred-acre Barbados sugar plantation, for which he paid £1,000 down and promised the remaining £6,000 in three installments within two years. He operated this venture in partnership with his brother-in-law Thomas Kendall, a London merchant, who sent "all the supplies to me at the best hand, and I returning him the sugars, and we both thrived on it." Thrive is hardly the word. Modyford told Richard Ligon (who worked for him) that he expected to make £100,000 as a sugar planter.[68] He quickly muscled his way into the center of Barbados politics. He sat on the Council in 1651, was speaker of the Assembly in 1652, and engineered appointment by the Commonwealth authorities at home as governor of the colony in 1660. No sooner had he taken office than Charles II was restored. Undaunted, Modyford reverted to royalism and proclaimed the king. He lost his governorship of Barbados, but with the help

66. For a full account of these developments, see Harlow, *Barbados*, chaps. 2–4. Thornton, *West-India Policy*, 22–39, sees the Restoration settlement as more of a defeat for the Barbadians than I do.

67. The five new knights were Sir Thomas Modyford, Sir James Drax, Sir Peter Leare, Sir John Colleton, and Sir John Yeamans. See E. M. Shilstone, "The Thirteen Baronets," *Jour. Bar. Mus. Hist. Soc.*, II (1934–1935), 89–92.

68. Modyford to William Helyar, July 10, 1677, Helyar MSS; Ligon, *True History of Barbados*, 22, 96. The name Modyford is conspicuously missing from T. K. Rabb's list of 6,000 investors in English overseas ventures, 1575–1630, in *Enterprise and Empire*, 343.

of his kinsman the duke of Albemarle he became royal governor of Jamaica in 1664. Sir Thomas plunged into this new assignment with characteristic brio. Selling off his Barbados property, he staked out more than twenty thousand acres in Jamaica for himself and his relatives and shaped the new colony with a strong hand, as we shall see in a later chapter. When he died in 1679 his Jamaica sugar estate at Sixteen Mile Walk must have been the grandest in the Caribbean, manned by six hundred slaves and servants.[69]

Modyford's transfer from settled Barbados to frontier Jamaica greatly strengthened the new colony without appreciably weakening the old one. By the 1660s large-scale sugar production was reaching full volume in Barbados, and the planters behaved with appropriate freedom and vigor. In 1668 and 1670 the Barbados Assembly petitioned the king for a royal charter making the colony a self-governing corporation like Massachusetts, but the petition was worded so pugnaciously that their London agents dared not deliver it. In 1671, when Charles II asked Parliament to increase the sugar duties, the Barbados Assembly told the king, none too diplomatically, that their impending ruin should be "Obvious to the most Vulgar Capacity." Twelve leading Barbados planters resident in London formed a committee to lobby against the sugar bill. Governor Willoughby testified against it at the bar of the House of Commons and persuaded the Lords to throw it out. The king was reported as "not over well pleased with the loss of his Bill." In 1673 the Barbados lobby tried unsuccessfully to block passage of the plantation duty act and told "several Parliament men how unpracticable it was for them to lay a tax on those that had noe members in theire house," a line of argument that Westminster would not hear again from America until the 1760s.[70]

The best proof, perhaps, that the Barbados planter class had arrived was their constant lamentation in the Restoration era that they were no longer as rich as in the 1640s and 1650s. Having gained their wealth, they now set about trying to conserve it. In the 1660s and 1670s they complained of soil depletion, declining crop yields, rising labor costs, and the need for protection against outside com-

69. Edward Atcherley described Modyford's plantation in a letter to William Helyar, Mar. 2, 1676/7, Helyar MSS. Modyford's Jamaican governorship is discussed in chap. 5 below.

70. Barbados Journal of Assembly, 1670–1683, C.O. 31/2/11–16, 34, 44, 49–76, 81–86, 92–93, 109–115, 123–124. The Assembly sent their London colleagues sugar worth £643 to finance these activities.

petition. They claimed to be squeezed to death between low sugar prices and high taxes. It was harder to complain about lack of manpower, for two thousand slaves arrived on the island from Africa each year. In truth, the Barbados sugar planters no longer made the heady profits they had enjoyed twenty years earlier—but they still did much better than Englishmen anywhere else in America. In an age of slow and uncertain economic growth, the rise of the Barbados planter class was intoxicating. Virginia might be the Old Dominion and Massachusetts the Bible Commonwealth, but Barbados was something more tangible: the richest colony in English America.

3 ❧ Barbados
The Planters in Power

On April 1, 1680, Sir Jonathan Atkins, governor of Barbados, sent a box full of statistics to the Plantation Office at Whitehall. This mass of data, filed away among the Colonial Office papers, constitutes the most comprehensive surviving census of any English colony in the seventeenth century.[1] Indeed, it is a richer store of information than any North American census before the 1770s. The Barbados census of 1680 was ignored at the time by the Lords of Trade, and it has been ignored ever since by historians of Barbados. Nearly a century ago John Camden Hotten discovered Atkins's data in the Public Record Office and published large sections of it, though for some curious reason he omitted half the parish lists.[2] Hotten's interest was genealogical, but the prime value of the census is social. The detailed lists Governor Atkins sent home permit us to reconstruct the style of life in this island at the particular point in time when the sugar industry was at its peak, when the planter class was fully developed, and when Barbados was the richest and most populous colony in English America.

The census of 1680 demonstrates how completely the big sugar planters dominated all aspects of island life and how elaborate their social hierarchy was. The correlation between wealth, privilege, and

1. This chapter is an expansion of my article, "Barbados Census of 1680," *Wm. and Mary Qtly.*, 3d Ser., XXVI (1969), 3–30.
2. This census is filed in C.O. 1/44/142–379. It is calendared inadequately in *Cal.S.R.Col., 1677–1680*, #1336. Hotten, ed., *Original Lists*, 347–508, printed 5 of the 11 parish lists of property holders, 5 of the 11 parish baptismal and burial registers, the list of householders in Bridgetown, and the list of persons ticketed to leave Barbados in 1679.

power is very striking. Something can also be learned about the effect of absenteeism upon the planter class, the role of religion in the colony, the social organization of Bridgetown (the chief port), the stunted character of family life, and the pattern of emigration away from the island. In short, the census of 1680 gives us an exceptionally clear profile of Barbados at the height of its wealth and power.

Unquestionably the Barbados sugar planters were the wealthiest men in English America in 1680. In slaveholding and sugar production they far outdistanced their competitors in Jamaica and the Leeward Islands. They shipped about 60 percent of the annual sugar tonnage to England, and their sugar shipments were more valuable than the total exports to England from all the mainland colonies. "There is not a foot of land in Barbados that is not employed even to the very seaside," said Governor Atkins. The island looked to visitors like one continuous green garden. A pamphleteer of 1676 was much impressed by the "many Costly and Stately Houses" he saw in Bridgetown. What struck him even more was "the Hospitality, or Number of the splendid Planters, who for Sumptuous Houses, Cloaths and Liberal Entertainment cannot be Exceeded by this their Mother Kingdome it self." [3]

Since rich men seldom voluntarily inventory their possessions for government inspection, why did the Barbados planters send home the census of 1680? They did so, or rather Governor Atkins did so, to fend off further pressure from the crown. During the 1670s the Lords of Trade had begun to investigate and overhaul the government of Barbados. Finding this colony—like all the other American colonies—too independent of the king, the home government sent Sir Jonathan Atkins to Barbados in 1674, armed with instructions to make the colonists more obedient. This put Atkins in an awkward spot, for unlike previous governors of Barbados he was an outsider with no estate on the island and only a small salary from the royal treasury. If he wanted to elicit a decent income from the Barbadians he had to cooperate with them. At every opportunity he voiced the planters' objections to the navigation acts, to the 4.5

3. Atkins to Lords of Trade, July 4, 1676, *Cal.S.P.Col., 1675–1676*, #973; *Great Newes from the Barbadoes*, 5–8.

percent duty on commodities exported from the island, to the Royal African Company's monopoly of the slave trade, and to the high freight rates charged by London merchants. He disarmingly told the Lords of Trade that Barbados kept no vital statistics or commercial records and that the annual value of the sugar crop could not be estimated. The Lords began to notice that many of the laws he sent home for royal confirmation had already expired, and in 1679 they discovered that he had silently approved several laws repugnant to the crown. This was too much. Both the king and the Lords of Trade wrote sharp letters to Atkins, accusing him of deliberately deceiving them. The Lords ordered him to send home all laws within three months of passage, together with a precise account of the Barbados judiciary, military defenses, revenue, commerce, slave imports, population, vital records, and a map of the island.[4] Fearful that he might now lose his post, Atkins hastened to assemble as much of this data as he could.

Atkins found various excuses for not transmitting Barbados's complete body of laws or an account of the imports, exports, and public revenue. But he did send a minutely detailed printed map of the island (published in London six years previously), and he packed into a box all the other required information: lists of the judges, councillors, and assemblymen; muster rolls for the 5,588 men in the eight Barbados regiments; an inventory of military stores; a list of 51 ships exporting enumerated commodities between April 1678 and October 1679; a certificate of 1,909 Negroes imported between December 1678 and January 1680; baptismal and burial records for the eleven parishes from March 1678 to September 1679; and an alphabetical list of the 593 persons given tickets to leave Barbados during 1679, showing for each the date of application for departure, the ship and the destination. Most important for our purposes, he sent alphabetical lists, parish by parish, of the 2,639 Barbados property holders as of December 1679, with the number of acres, servants and slaves belonging to each, together with a list of the 405 householders in Bridgetown, showing which were married and the number of children, servants, and slaves for each.

Ironically this box full of data proved to be Atkins's final undoing. When the Lords of Trade received his lists in June 1680 they immediately doubted the honesty and accuracy of his figures.

4. Lords of Trade to Atkins, July 26, 1679, C.O. 29/2/283–285. For further details on Atkins's governorship, see Harlow, *Barbados*, 213–241.

They suspected—no doubt correctly—that many more than 51 ships had carried sugar from Barbados in eighteen months. They refused to believe that the island militia numbered only 5,588, since Atkins himself had reported in 1676 that he had 10,000 men able to bear arms. They blamed him for failing to report the total number of white inhabitants, as well as for failing to transmit import and export statistics.[5] The parish census lists, being of no interest to the

Table 4. Barbados Population Estimates, 1655–1715

Year	White Pop.	White Servants	Men Able to Bear Arms	Militia	Negro Slaves
1655	23,000				20,000
1673	21,309		9,274		33,184
1676	21,725		10,000		32,473
1680		2,317		5,588	38,782
1684	19,568	2,381	6,761	5,911	46,602
1696				2,330	42,000
1712	12,528		3,438		41,970
1715	16,888				

NOTE: The figures for 1655 come from Harlow, *Barbados*, 338; for 1673 from *Cal.S.P.Col., 1669–1674*, #1101; for 1676 and 1696 from C.O. 318/2/115; for 1684 from Sloane MSS, 2441/1–22, Br. Museum; for 1712 from Pitman, *Development of the British West Indies*, 372; and for 1715 from C.O. 28/16. See also Patricia A. Molen, "Population and Social Patterns in Barbados in the Early Eighteenth Century," *Wm. and Mary Qtly.*, 3d Ser., XXVIII (1971), 289.

Lords of Trade, were simply filed away. By late July 1680, Charles II had decided to appoint a new governor of Barbados, Sir Richard Dutton.

The Lords of Trade were unjustly disdainful, for though Atkins's compilation has its faults, it stands up well under close scrutiny. His population figures are incomplete, to be sure, but they are in line with previous and later estimates, as table 4 shows. Atkins's figures for 1680 support the generally accepted demographic picture of a declining white population and a rising Negro slave population on Barbados during the late seventeenth century.

5. Lords of Trade to Atkins, July 6, 1680, C.O. 29/3/7–10.

By 1680 the white depopulation of the island and the shrinkage of the militia was beginning to reach alarming proportions. One reason was high mortality. In eighteen months, according to Atkins's baptism and burial statistics, 506 more whites died than were born on Barbados. Another reason was high emigration. During 1679, 593 white persons left the island, though by no means all of them left permanently. Since the land on Barbados was all long since taken up, there was small incentive for servants whose in-

Table 5. Summary of the Barbados Census, 1680

Parish	Property Holders	Acres	Servants	Slaves
Bridgetown	405		402	1,439
St. Michael	224	7,063	303	3,746
Christchurch	413	12,978	178	4,723
St. James	177	6,742	113	2,895
St. Thomas	193	7,495	226	3,396
St. George	120	9,569	111	4,316
St. Philip	406	12,158	115	4,702
St. John	124	7,658	159	3,303
St. Joseph	195	4,868	170	2,072
St. Peter	248	6,651	375	3,977
St. Andrew	109	5,597	47	2,248
St. Lucy	430	6,800	118	1,965
Totals	3,044	87,579	2,317	38,782

NOTE: The figures in this table and in later tables are based on my calculations and frequently differ from the totals found in *Cal.S.P.Col., 1677–1680*, #1336.

dentures had expired or even for younger sons of established planters to stay. In 1680 the slaves outnumbered the whites by two to one.

Even so, Atkins's census shows that historians have exaggerated the white depopulation of the island during the late seventeenth century. Barbados still had about 20,000 white inhabitants in 1680, more than any English colony in America except Virginia and Massachusetts. The oft-repeated story that by this time the big planters on Barbados had bought up all the land is a myth. As table 5 demonstrates, the census records 2,639 property holders, excluding the 405 householders in Bridgetown. The great majority of these Barbados property holders were small farmers. The mean size of a

Barbados farm was only twenty-nine acres in 1680, and the median size was even smaller, only ten acres. The Barbadians held one slave for every two acres, the standard ratio for effective sugar production throughout the Carribbean in the seventeenth and eighteenth centuries.[6] They employed a minimum number of servants—one servant for every seventeen slaves—and this contributed directly to the shrinkage of the militia.

The totals in table 5 for acreage and slaves are demonstrably deficient, yet not completely distorted. Two other nearly contemporary Barbados documents—a 1680 tax list on Negroes and land and a census taken in 1684—also give parish totals for land and slaveholding. The differences between these three sets of figures, parish by parish, are generally slight, but Atkins's totals are usually the smallest.[7] For example, Atkins reported 87,579 acres, the census taken four years later found 90,517, and the colonists paid taxes in 1680 on 92,717. All three totals are a bit low, for the island actually contains 106,000 acres—though some of this is wasteland and seashore. As for the number of slaves, Atkins reported 38,782 Negroes, the colonists paid taxes in 1680 on 38,352 Negroes, and the census takers four years later (after enlisting the help of five or six "confideing men in every parish") found 46,602. In part the figure of 8,000 additional Negroes reported in the 1684 census reflects the heavy influx of slaves in these years, in part it reflects the colonists' habit of concealing their property from tax collectors and census takers. Actually they paid very light local taxes. The big sugar planter who admitted to owning 200 acres and 100 slaves in 1680 paid a tax of about £10. Even so, we may conclude that Atkins's totals for land and slaves in the census of 1680 are 10 or 15 percent too low.[8]

The really splendid feature of the census is its specific informa-

6. For an excellent survey of this subject, see Ward Barrett, "Caribbean Sugar-Production Standards in the Seventeenth and Eighteenth Centuries," in John Parker, ed., *Merchants and Scholars: Essays in the History of Exploration and Trade* (Minneapolis, 1965), 145–170.

7. The Apr. 15, 1680, tax return (calendared in *Cal.S.P.Col., 1677–1680*, #1336, XXIII) is misfiled with Atkins's census lists. Actually it was sent home six months later. An abstract of the 1684 census (Sloane MSS, 2441/1–22) is printed in *Jour. Bar. Mus. Hist. Soc.*, III (1935–1936), 44–57. Originally, this census consisted of detailed lists, similar to the census of 1680, which have been lost. The St. Michael parish vestry paid three men £13 for "taking a list of persons names and negroes" and "drawing up several lists of the people of this Town and Parish" in 1684. St. Michael vestry records, Mar. 10, 1683/4, Sept. 5, 1685, *Jour. Bar. Mus. Hist. Soc.*, XVI (1948–1949), 197, 201.

8. Edwin Stede to William Blathwayt, May 9, 1682, Dep. Gov. Witham to Blathwayt, Oct. 31, 1683, Blathwayt Papers, XXXIV, XXXV.

tion about individual property holding and officeholding. No doubt the parish lists are riddled with error, but they show unmistakably which of the 2,639 property holders were big planters, which were middling planters, and which were small planters. The only detectable bias in the lists is a persistent tendency to understate the holdings of the big planters. Atkins had the lists certified by the churchwardens and ministers in each parish to prove their accuracy, but since the churchwardens were themselves all substantial planters, they were not impartial witnesses. The big planters did not, however, hide the bulk of their holdings. As table 7 below demonstrates, the Barbados census reports that a small number of planters held a majority of the total property on the island.

To some extent we can test the accuracy of the census returns on individual property holding. We have information from other sources on the acreage held by eighty-two of the biggest Barbados planters to compare with the returns from Atkins's parish lists. Eighteen of these planters have their acreage listed on the muster rolls which Atkins sent home in 1680. According to the muster rolls they averaged 250 acres apiece; according to the parish census lists they averaged only 237 acres. A more important check is provided by a list of the "most eminent planters in Barbados," sent home by the colony government in 1673, which records the names and acreage of seventy-four planters.[9] Though this document is seven years out of date for our purposes, it correlates satisfactorily with Atkins's lists. Sixty-four of the planters from 1673 reappear as big planters in 1680; their holdings averaged 394 acres in 1673 and 349 acres in 1680, a difference of 13 percent. For example, John Pears, the largest landholder on the island, was credited with 1,000 acres in 1673 and 910 acres seven years later. Christopher Codrington had 600 acres in 1673 and 618 in 1680. Sir Peter Colleton had 700 acres in 1673 and 425 in 1680. The glaring conflict in Colleton's case is unusual, yet two-thirds of the planters had higher acreage in 1673. Here again is evidence that Atkins's census figures are 10 or 15 percent too low.

Even with this built-in distortion the Barbados census possesses a unique precision by seventeenth-century statistical standards. This is because Barbados had the most fully developed agricultural-production system in English America. Only in this colony can the

9. The list is printed in *Cal.S.P.Col., 1669–1674*, #1101, II. There are two copies among the Shaftesbury Papers, 30/24, Bundle 49/3, P.R.O. The list records acreage in round numbers and may be exaggerated, but I am inclined to trust it more than the official census.

analyst measure the difference between two planters by comparing their respective land and slave holdings. Anywhere else in seventeenth-century America such quantification would be impossible. A Virginia or Jamaica planter with five hundred acres of fertile land, fully planted, might be worth far more than his neighbor with five

Table 6. Classification of the Barbados Property Holders

Parish	Big Planters (60+ Slaves)	Middling Planters (20–59 Slaves)	Small Planters (10+ Acres, 0–19 Slaves)	Total Freeholders	Freemen (under 10 Acres)
St. Michael	20	23	99	142	82
Christchurch	23	21	169	213	200
St. James	22	12	59	93	84
St. Thomas	19	14	95	128	65
St. George	24	19	50	93	27
St. Philip	19	38	175	232	174
St. John	24	15	47	86	38
St. Joseph	13	13	34	60	135
St. Peter	20	26	86	132	116
St. Andrew	12	18	39	69	40
St. Lucy	7	10	188	205	225
Totals	203	209	1,041	1,453	1,186
Adjusted Totals	175	190	1,041	1,125	1,186

NOTE: Some of the big and middling planters owned land in more than one parish; when these duplicate listings are consolidated, we have 175 big planters and 190 middling planters. The number of freeholders can only be guessed. Ten percent of the property holders were women, and I have assumed that another 10 percent were minors or Quakers in reducing the total estimate to 1,125.

thousand acres of undeveloped or marginal land. But in Barbados all the arable land was under intense cultivation. Though the plantations were small by mainland standards, they were heavily capitalized. Almost every planter with fifty acres, and many smaller ones, invested in sugar mills, boiling-and-curing houses, and a labor force that seldom deviated far from the ratio of one Negro for every two acres.

In table 6 the 2,639 property holders on the parish census lists are classified according to the number of acres and slaves they held. Those with sixty or more slaves are classified as *big planters*. Slave-holding rather than acreage is used as the index here, because the ownership of a labor force of sixty Negroes represents a concrete investment of £1,000, whereas the land of Barbados is of variable quality and planters in the mountainous northern region required more acreage than elsewhere on the island to produce an equivalent sugar crop. Even so, it should be pointed out that the planters with sixty or more slaves were almost all substantial landholders; only seven of them owned less than one hundred acres. Colonists who held between twenty and fifty-nine slaves are classified as *middling planters*. A person in this category had a labor force sufficient to operate a modest sugar plantation. The middling planters held significantly smaller tracts of land than the big planters, ranging from thirty to one hundred acres. Colonists with ten or more acres, but fewer than twenty slaves, are classified as *small planters*. These people had enough property (ten acres) to qualify by Barbados law as freeholders, and therefore unless they were minors, women, or Quakers, they were eligible to vote in the colony elections. Lastly, property holders with less than ten acres are classified as *freemen*, meaning that they were not servants but that they could not vote.

As this table shows, big and small property holders were mixed together in every parish. But the big planters were proportionately most numerous in the parishes with richest soil and heaviest rainfall, St. George and St. John, and proportionately least numerous in the rocky, dry northern tip of the island, St. Lucy. Conversely, the small planters and freemen were relatively sparse in St. George and St. John and especially plentiful in St. Lucy. There were many small planters and freemen also in Christchurch and St. Philip parishes, living along the seacoast where the soil is infertile and the rainfall is light.[10]

The distinction between *freeholder* and *freeman* in Barbados was evidently important. About 250 landholders on the parish lists are credited with exactly ten acres, which suggests that the small Barbados planters valued their voting privileges. Something like 1,125 adult male landholders could qualify as freeholders, as could perhaps an additional two or three hundred householders from the four towns. No firm estimate is possible, but we may guess that 20 or 25 percent of the white adult males on the island could elect or

10. For information on Barbados topography, soil, and climatic conditions, see Starkey, *Economic Geography of Barbados*, especially chaps. 1–2.

be elected assemblymen, vestrymen, and jurors. In the 1690s Gov. Francis Russell wanted to lower the voting qualifications to two acres, arguing that the big planters would then treat the poor whites better "in hopes to gett their votes for 'em att the next Election of the Assembly." But the big planters insisted on keeping the ten-acre minimum so as to guarantee that "men of interest only may share in soe great trusts." [11] Thus, while the Barbadians allowed a considerable measure of popular participation in government, their franchise was more restricted than in the mainland colonies. Several parishes had only a handful of voters.[12]

At this point it is helpful to refer to the printed map that Atkins sent home in 1680. This *New Map of the Island of Barbadoes* was executed by a Quaker surveyor named Richard Ford, who published it in London around 1674 apparently at his own expense.[13] Atkins disparaged Ford's work because the Quaker mapmaker identified the Anglican churches less prominently than the governor thought suitable and because he omitted the island fortifications altogether. But Atkins was unfair, for Ford's minutely detailed map admirably illustrates the Barbados census. Ford identifies 844 plantations by name of owner and shows how many windmills, cattle mills, or water mills each plantation had. Despite the six-year interval between map and census, the two correlate very closely: 164 of the 175 big planters in the Barbados census appear on Ford's map, sometimes with two, three, or four separate plantations attributed to them. A comparison between the census lists for three parishes (St. Michael, St. George, and St. Andrew) and Ford's map yields the following interesting results: 54 of the 56 big planters in these three parishes are to be found on Ford's map; 48 of the 60 middling planters; 59 of the 188 small planters; and 14 of the 149 freemen. In other words, the larger the plantation, the more likely it is to appear on Ford's map. In August 1675, shortly after Ford apparently drew his map, one of the worst hurricanes in Barbados history struck the island

11. Barbados voters had to be 21 years old. Freeholders from the towns had to have dwellings valued at £10 annual rent. Suffrage qualifications are spelled out in An account of His Majesty's Island of Barbados, [*c.* Feb. 1675/6], C.O. 29/2/1–14, and the 1691 act on freeholders, Barbados Manuscript Laws, 1682–1692, C.O. 30/5. Gov. Russell's protest is in C.O. 28/2/234.

12. Thomas Modyford lost an Assembly election in 1655 by a vote of 20 to 19, which suggests the extreme narrowness of the Barbados franchise some years earlier. Birch, ed., *Thurloe State Papers*, III, 622.

13. This map (see fig. 5, p. 94) is in the Blathwayt Atlas. For a fold-out, full-size reproduction of Ford's map, see Dunn, "Barbados Census of 1680," *Wm. and Mary Qtly.*, 3d Ser., XXVI (1969), facing p. 16.

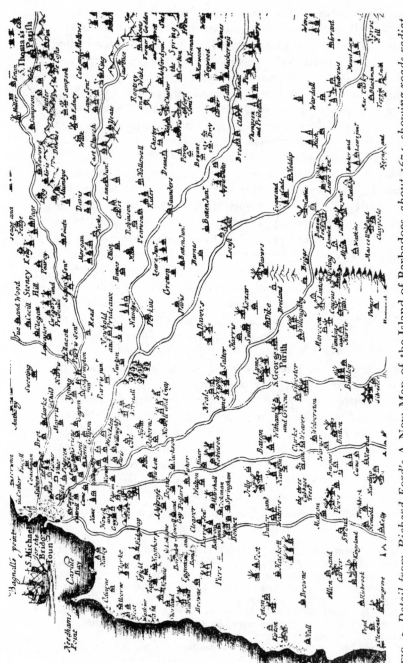

FIG. 5. *Detail from Richard Ford's A New Map of the Island of Barbadoes, about 1674, showing roads radiating from Bridgetown (upper left) to the inland plantations in St. George's Valley. The cattle mills are drawn as houses, and the windmills have sails. (Courtesy of John Carter Brown Library, Brown University, Providence.)*

and wrecked most of the plantations on the leeward coast. Probably some of the smaller planters did not rebuild; a good many names on the map do not turn up on the census. We may safely assume, however, that these persons sold their property between 1674 and 1679 to the big and middling planters who are listed in the census but do not appear on the map.

Barbados, despite its compact size, displayed such wide variations in topography, soil, and rainfall that some districts were much better suited to sugar cultivation than others. Analysis of Ford's map and Atkins's census shows that in the 1670s the biggest planters possessed the best land. St. George's Valley, curving east for about six miles from St. George's church to St. Philip's church on the map, had black, rich, deep soil. Here lived many of the chief planters on the island: Lady Ann Willoughby, Robert Davers, Madam Grace Silvester, Rowland Bulkely, Sir Martin Bently, Robert Haskett, and a dozen others. North of this valley, above a steep escarpment, was the central plateau labeled by Ford "The Topp of the Cliffe," where the rainfall was abundant and the red soil produced excellent cane. Here in the 1670s was the other chief habitat of big planters, among them Sir Peter Colleton, Christopher Codrington, Henry Walrond, John Hallett, John Hothersall, Henry Drax, and Sir Peter Leare. The east and south coasts, where the soil was less fertile and the rainfall lighter, were mostly occupied by small planters and freemen. In the wild Scotland district along the Atlantic coast a number of big planters occupied the sheltered valleys and left the unproductive hilltops to their small neighbors. On the northern tip of the island, labeled "Champaigne Ground" by Ford, was the poorest sugar land. In the 1670s many small planters and freemen lived here and raised cotton, ginger, and ground provisions.

Evidence from map and census indicates that few Barbados planters worked units larger than 200 acres. If a planter owned more land than this, he generally divided it into several separate plantations and divided his labor force accordingly in order to work each unit as efficiently as possible. Some big planters held several widely scattered tracts; for example, Francis Bond owned 445 acres in four parishes and kept three separate slave gangs. More typically a big planter had a single large tract that he divided in two. Richard Seawell split his 550 acres into two contiguous plantations, each with its own sugar mills and presumably its own labor force—occupying land now covered by the jet runways of the Seawell Airport.

Other big planters, including Codrington, Drax, Davers, Frere, Silvester, and Batten, did the same. Evidently a plantation of about 200 acres, equipped with two or three sugar mills and a hundred slaves, was considered the optimum size for efficient production.[14]

Map and census reveal all too little about the small planters and freemen. In the census for St. James parish, thirty-eight of the freemen are described as "pore" or "very pore." These people owned three to five acres apiece and no slaves. But St. James was particularly hard hit by the hurricane of 1675. Elsewhere on the island the freemen seem to have been better off. According to the census 81 percent of the small planters and 65 percent of the freemen owned at least one Negro, and some freemen who held no land at all owned half a dozen Negroes. Every year a good many servants who had worked out their indentures joined the ranks of the Barbados freemen. Some of these ex-servants continued to work for their old masters, living as tenants on the big plantations. Others became wage laborers in Bridgetown. But the more enterprising ones sought better opportunities elsewhere and left Barbados as fast as they could.

§☙

One of the most striking facts to emerge from the Barbados census is the consolidated affluence of the 175 big planters. Table 7 shows how they dominated the island economically as of 1680. Though they constituted only 7 percent of the property holders, they con-

Table 7. The Big Barbados Planters' Share of Property, 1680

	Planters with 60+ Slaves	Percentage	All Other Property Holders	Percentage
Number of planters	175	6.9	2,417	93.1
Acreage	46,775	53.4	40,804	46.6
Servants	1,032	53.9	883	46.1
Slaves	20,289	54.3	17,054	45.7

NOTE: The 405 Bridgetown householders, with their 402 servants and 1,439 slaves, have been excluded from this calculation.

14. In 1681 Andrew Afflick received £1,500 for a Barbados plantation half this size, with 100 acres and 64 Negroes. *Jour. Bar. Mus. Hist. Soc.*, IX (1941–1942), 100.

trolled 54 percent of the property—and it should be remembered that the census understates the holdings of these big planters.

In the other English sugar colonies, as we shall see, there was the same tendency toward a narrow concentration of wealth in the hands of a few planters. But as of 1680 the big planter class in the other sugar colonies was far less fully developed. Only about thirty Jamaica planters at this date owned as many as sixty slaves, and in the Leewards only about twenty men could be reckoned as big planters by Barbados standards. As for the mainland colonies, recent studies of distribution of wealth in Boston, Philadelphia, and Maryland in the 1680s and 1690s demonstrate that the leading merchants and planters in these places were far less affluent and also less numerous than the Barbados plantocracy. The richest colonists in the mainland settlements in the late seventeenth century held a much smaller portion of community wealth than their counterparts in Barbados.[15] Not until the next century did the mainland colonists begin to develop real economic stratification. According to Jackson Turner Main, the richest merchants in Boston, Philadelphia, and Charleston and the richest planters in tidewater Virginia and South Carolina controlled, from 1763 to 1788, about the same percentage of property as the Barbados planters a century before, but elsewhere in mainland America wealth was still distributed very broadly and there was no real economic elite.[16]

The majority of the 175 big Barbados planters in 1680 were second- or third-generation settlers, as has been shown in the previous chapter. Nearly 40 percent of their families had settled on the island in the 1630s. Another 20 percent, at a minimum, had arrived between 1640 and 1660. The very largest Barbados magnates in particular had established themselves in the tobacco era or the early sugar era; among the 44 planters with 150 or more slaves in 1680, at least 33 (75 percent) can be traced to the 1650s or before. The English lineage of these people was more than respectable; Barbados,

15. See James A. Henretta, "Economic Development and Social Structure in Colonial Boston," *Wm. and Mary Qtly.*, 3d Ser., XXII (1965), 75–92; Gary B. Nash, *Quakers and Politics: Pennsylvania, 1681–1726* (Princeton, N.J., 1968), 278–286; Aubrey C. Land, "Economic Base and Social Structure: The Northern Chesapeake in the Eighteenth Century," *Journal of Economic History*, XXV (1965), 641–646.

16. Jackson Turner Main, *The Social Structure of Revolutionary America* (Princeton, N.J., 1965), 23, 31–36, 41–42, 48–60, 63, 57. See also Kenneth A. Lockridge, "Land, Population, and the Evolution of New England Society, 1630–1790," *Past and Present*, no. 39 (Apr. 1968), 62–80; James T. Lemon and Gary B. Nash, "The Distribution of Wealth in Eighteenth-Century America," *Journal of Social History*, II (1968), 1–24.

thought John Oldmixon, could boast "as many good Families as are in any of the Counties of England." And they left a permanent impress upon the island. A Barbados map drawn in the 1790s shows eighty-two plantations carrying the names of big planters from a century before. The Barbados telephone directory of 1969–1970 lists eighteen sugar factories and plantations that still bear the names of their seventeenth-century founders.[17]

To what extent did these 175 big planters dominate the island politically as well as economically? When we check the lists of civil and military officers that Atkins sent home in 1680, it is quickly evident that the big planters played a very active role in public life. As of 1680, 77 of them held at least one civil or military post, and many held three or four important offices simultaneously. During the ten-year span from 1675 to 1685, surviving records indicate that 109 of the 175 big planters held office in Barbados. The total would undoubtedly be higher if we had more complete lists of the vestrymen and militia officers. As for the 66 big planters who are not recorded as holding office between 1675 and 1685, 25 can be identified as women or minors or Quakers, and thus ineligible. A good many of the remainder were absent in England, leaving their estates in the hands of relatives or overseers. Yet enough big planters lived in Barbados in 1680 to fill the top elective and appointive posts on the island.

There was an hierarchical pattern of officeholding in Barbados, as table 8 demonstrates. The most prestigious and powerful positions —councillor, assemblyman, judge, and commander of a militia regiment—were reserved for the colonists of highest economic and social standing. Less important posts—justice of the peace, vestryman, churchwarden, grand juror, and commander of a militia company —were considered suitable for persons of high station, but were also open to smaller planters. Minor offices—petty juror, coroner, lieutenant, and ensign—were reckoned beneath the dignity of the big planters.[18] According to Barbados law a planter had to hold one

---

17. John Oldmixon, *The British Empire in America*, 2d ed. (London, 1741) II, 125; Bryan Edwards, *History of the British West Indies: Maps and Plates* (London, 1818) ; *Barbados Telephone Directory, 1969–1970* (Bridgetown, 1969) . The factories and plantations still carrying 17th-century names are: Alleyndale, Andrews, Applewhaite, Ball, Bentley, Bulkeley, Colleton, Dowding, Drax, Fortescue, Hothersall, Husbands, Kendall, Lambert, Lear, Newton, Pickering, and Searle.

18. The contrast here with the New England colonies is particularly striking. The New England officeholding pattern had to be less snobbish because there

hundred acres to qualify as a field officer in the militia; according to local custom a planter with more than one hundred acres was over qualified for service in the lower ranks of the officer corps. The three big planters who held lieutenant's commissions in 1680 were all very young men. Several sons or brothers of big planters also served as lieutenants—but not as ensigns.

Table 8. Officeholding in Barbados, 1680

Civil Offices	Planters with 60+ Slaves	All Others	Military Offices	Planters with 60+ Slaves	All Others
Councillor	10	2	Colonel	8	0
Assemblyman	20	2	Lt. Colonel	6	1
Judge	19	4	Major	4	4
Justice of the peace	48	16	Captain	19	28
Vestryman	20	14	Lieutenant	3	42
Churchwarden	11	9	Ensign	0	45
Grand juror	6	9			
Petty juror	3	11			
Coroner	1	9			

NOTE: Sons and brothers of the big planters are *not* included in these calculations. All of the officeholders categorized above are listed in Atkins's census material, dated Dec. 1679 or Jan. 1680, except for the justices of the peace, listed in the census of 1684, Sloane MSS, 2441/1–22; the grand jurors, petty jurors, and coroners, listed in an account of a Barbados jail delivery, Nov. 1677, C.O. 1/42/5–6; and the vestrymen for St. Michael and St. John, listed in the records of these two parishes. The vestry records for the other nine parishes have not survived, and Atkins's lists of churchwardens, lieutenants, and ensigns in 1680 are incomplete.

The hierarchical principle worked equally clearly in elective and appointive offices. The small freeholders deferentially elected their betters as assemblymen, vestrymen, and jurors, while Governor Atkins (whose daughters were married to two of the biggest planters, John Pears and Thomas Walrond) distributed practically all the important offices in his gift among members of the Barbados

---

were so many offices. In Boston, for example, the inhabitants in 1685 elected 141 town officials out of a total pool of a thousand adult males. G. B. Warden, *Boston, 1689–1776* (Boston, 1970), 32.

elite. There was little to choose between the appointed Council and the elected Assembly in wealth and dignity. The king had inserted into the Council two royal favorites, Edwin Stede and John Witham, who did not have enough property on the island to qualify as big planters; even so, the twelve councillors in 1680 averaged 420 acres and 190 slaves apiece. The twenty-two assemblymen averaged 340 acres and 153 slaves apiece.[19] When Atkins's successor, Sir Richard Dutton, held his first Barbados jail delivery in 1681, he reported that he had never seen such a wealthy panel of jurors in England. Small wonder, since ten of the nineteen grand jurors were big planters.[20] Indeed, any big planter not personally obnoxious to his peers could join the power structure. In Barbados, unlike some of the mainland colonies during the late seventeenth century, there was no strong challenge from below by smaller planters who wanted a wider distribution of political power.

Instead the challenge came from above, from Whitehall. Already by 1680 Charles II had begun to sap the big planters' political authority by granting eight patent offices in Barbados to English placemen. These patent offices, such as secretary, auditor, provost marshal, and naval officer, were financially remunerative and politically intrusive. The patent officers all resided in England and deputized their posts to persons in Barbados with little or no property on the island, mainly newcomers much despised by the big planters. Far more alarming was the arrival of Governor Dutton, who ruled Barbados in a style all his own from 1680 to 1685. Sir Richard Dutton did everything he could to break up the established political and social structure on the island. He quarreled with his councillors, reshuffled the military and judicial posts, and in general intimidated the big planters. In five years Sir Richard became a rich man. Though he continually complained about his expenses, his enemies reckoned that he spent no more than £3,000 during his stay on the island, and to help meet this burden he extracted nearly £18,000 in salary, perquisites, bribes, and so-called "presents" from the Assembly. Dutton's greed got completely out of hand. In order to

19. Barbados Assembly membership records in *Cal.S.P.Col.* show that big planters won 186 of the 220 seats in the 10 assemblies elected between 1674 and 1685. During this span 42 big planters sat in the Assembly, serving an average of 4.5 terms. The other 17 assemblymen were mostly middling planters as of 1680, but 7 of them first appear in the Assembly in 1684 or 1685, and perhaps they had enough slaves and acreage by that time to qualify also as big planters.

20. Dutton to Sir Leoline Jenkins, Sept. 5, 1681, *Cal.S.P.Col., 1681–1685*, #218. The grand jury is listed in C.O. 1/47/98.

avoid paying Lieutenant Governor Witham's salary he charged
Witham with misconduct and fined him £5,000 pounds! At this
point the home authorities became suspicious, and Dutton was recalled in disgrace.[21]

Dutton was followed by Edwin Stede (1685–1690), another
highly unpopular choice with the big planters. Stede had come to
Barbados as a royal patent officer, and what was worse, he worked
for the Royal African Company as its agent on the island. The Royal
African Company had enough influence at Whitehall so that Stede
was put in charge of Barbados; thereafter he served king and company by prosecuting interloping slave traders. Meanwhile James II
doubled the English tax on sugar and during his short reign added
nineteen persons by royal mandamus to the Barbados Council,
which drastically diluted the power and prestige of that body. It
appears that James sold council seats to anyone willing to pay a high
enough fee. Only ten of his appointees were big planters, and when
a mere overseer named Richard Harwood presented his mandamus
in 1686, the Council loudly—but ineffectually—protested to the
king against Harwood's "servile condition, personall inabillityes,
and other Scandalous Circumstances." [22] Thus the big Barbados
planters, so securely in control of their island in 1680, rapidly lost
control during the next decade. The Glorious Revolution that
drove James II off the throne in 1688 was the planters' salvation. In
the revolutionary settlement under William and Mary they recovered most of their lost privileges and authority. The post-
revolutionary royal governors were much more to their taste than
Dutton and Stede. The Royal African Company no longer had a
monopoly on the slave trade, and in 1693 the home government
even dropped James II's sugar tax of 1685. Nevertheless the crisis
of the 1680s left lasting scars. The planters of Barbados and the
other English islands adopted a new defensive posture of protection-
ism and dependency that they carried into the eighteenth century.
They lost for good the aggressive self-confidence of the master class
in 1680.[23]

The changing political atmosphere in the 1680s helped to persuade many Barbados planters to retire to England as absentee

21. Harlow, *Barbados*, 241–267.
22. Barbados Council to James II, Aug. 3, 1686, Journal of Barbados Governor
and Council, 1680–1686, C.O. 31/1/710–711.
23. This point I hope to develop more fully in a book comparing English
imperial pressures upon the American mainland and island colonies, 1675–1701.

proprietors. The census of 1680 demonstrates that absenteeism was not yet a controlling factor in the 1670s and early 1680s. To be sure, such major proprietors as Sir Peter Leare, John Bawden, Ferdinando Gorges, and Daniel Searle did live in England, where they functioned as sugar merchants and political agents for the colony. But most of their colleagues tended their island plantations, making occasional visits home. As we have seen, three-quarters of the eligible big planters held public office in Barbados during the decade from 1675 to 1685. These men were reelected year after year to posts that could not be relegated to absentees. For example, the twenty big planters who sat as vestrymen in 1680 for the parishes of St. John and St. Michael served an average of nineteen years apiece in this post, with a year's break every now and then for a sabbatical leave in England. Sir Peter Colleton was unusual in being elected to the St. John vestry only nine times between 1661 and 1681, but this reflected his frequent visits home, not his disdain for parochial governance.[24]

During the 1680s, however, the homeward drift picked up. Colleton retired to England for good, joined by such other island luminaries as Henry Drax, Edward Littleton, and the partners Richard Guy and Richard Howell, who between them owned 405 Negroes, the largest slave gang in Barbados. These men left because of the deteriorating economic and political situation on the island. Their sugar fields were showing signs of soil exhaustion, their annual shipments were beginning to decline, and their profits were eroded by the steady drop in sugar prices, which hit bottom in 1685–1686, just when James II imposed his new sugar tax. In island politics the big planters had lost the initiative to the king's creatures —governors Dutton and Stede, the various patent officers, and the flood of new royal appointees to the Council. By 1688 most of the public leaders from the island were to be found in England, desperately lobbying for the restoration of their old privileges. When the Glorious Revolution broke out, Edward Littleton spoke for his fellow planters in a London tract, published in 1689, called *The Groans of the Plantations,* in which he told how the sugar colonies had been ruinously overtaxed and generally mismanaged by Charles II and James II. Littleton's argument had great weight with the new

24. The St. Michael vestry records, 1655–1700, are published in *Jour. Bar. Mus. Hist. Soc.,* XIV (1946–1947) through XVII (1949–1950), *passim.* The St. John parish vestry book, 1649–1699, is in the library of the Barbados Museum and Historical Society, St. Ann's Garrison.

government, thanks to the sugar planters' formation of an effective lobby at Whitehall. They discovered that they could exert more political leverage at home than in the islands. With the onset of the French wars and a yellow-fever epidemic that decimated the Barbados population in the 1690s, many of them delayed returning to the Indies. By the time the long wars ended in 1713 absenteeism had become a permanent way of life for many of the Barbados gentry.

At the time of the Barbados census the island colonists were scarcely noted for their religious zeal. Governor Dutton complained that "God's house and worship . . . was but too much neglected" when he arrived. The clergy found it a hard task to stir the people out of their "wretched Laodicean tepidity."[25] In Barbados eleven Anglican clergymen ministered to twenty thousand colonists, whereas in England there would have been forty parishes for a population group this size. During a six-month span in 1683–1684 seven of the ten councillors on the island (including at least two vestrymen) did not bother to attend church. The Irish Catholic servants were not allowed to have any priests, and a shoemaker named Joseph Salmon was chastised by the governor and Council in 1682 for trying to organize an Anabaptist conventicle.[26] The only religious activists in Barbados were the Quakers.

Quakers first appeared in the Indies in the 1650s, and during the next four decades they recruited many hundred colonists into their fellowship. The Quaker community was probably larger and more active in Barbados than in the other sugar colonies. George Fox spent three months on the island in 1671, and William Edmundson, the Irish Friend, says he addressed a crowd of three thousand at Christopher Lyne's plantation in 1675. The Anglican clergy promptly asked the Barbados government to take action against this "Base Sort of Phanatick People, commonly termed Quakers."[27] In

25. Gov. Dutton to Sec. Jenkins, May 30, 1681, C.O. 29/3/67–68; Francis Crow in Jamaica to Giles Firmin, Mar. 7, 1686/7, *Jam. Hist. Rev.*, III, no. 2 (1959) , 56.
26. Dep. Gov. Witham to William Blathwayt, Feb. 19, 1683/4, Blathwayt Papers, XXXV; Journal of Barbados Governor and Council, Mar. 21, 1682, C.O. 31/1/516.
27. Norman Penney, ed., *The Journal of George Fox* (London, 1924) , 274–281; William Edmundson, *A Journal of the Life, Travels, Sufferings and Labour of Love . . . of . . . William Edmundson* (London, 1774) , 81–85; George Fox, *To*

part they were nettled by the Quaker habit of disrupting Anglican services, and the Friends' derisive comments about the "Periwiggs, Fringes, Paintings, and other wild Attire" that fashionable ladies and gentlemen liked to wear to church. But the Quakers' worst sins were their peace testimony, which depleted the island militia, and their mission work among the slaves. Governor Atkins was determined to stop the Quakers from converting Negroes to Christianity, "of which they can make them understand nothing." The governor evidently feared that the blacks were learning something; "I shall leave to you to consider," he told the Assembly, "whether, Liberty be a fit Doctrine for Slaves." [28] The Barbados Assembly accordingly passed a series of laws that fined the Quakers heavily for non-attendance at militia drill and fined them even more heavily for bringing Negroes to their meetings.[29] The Quaker hagiographer Joseph Besse counted 237 Quaker sufferers who were fined or otherwise punished in Barbados between 1658 and 1695.[30] The high point of persecution came under Atkins and Dutton; these two governors levied about £7,000 in fines during one decade. Dutton found the Barbadian Quakers "very numerous, insolent and rich." He sentenced one Friend to death for blasphemy and ordered the provost marshal to pull down all the seats and stalls in the Quaker Meeting House on Tudor Street, Bridgetown, and nail up the doors and windows.[31]

What does the census of 1680 tell us about this embattled religious community? The Barbados Friends operated six meetings at this date and had a membership of several hundred at least.[32] Richard

the Ministers, Teachers, and Priests, (so called, and Stileing your Selves) in Barbadoes (n.p., 1672), 48–49.

28. Besse, *Collection of Sufferings*, II, 320; Atkins to Barbados Assembly, Mar. 21, 1675/6, C.O. 31/2/207–208.

29. Anti-Quaker legislation of 1676, 1677, and 1678 is in *Acts of Assembly, Passed in . . . Barbadoes, 1648–1718* (London, 1721), 106–107; Journal of Barbados Assembly, 1670–1683, C.O. 31/2/251–252, 261; Barbados Manuscript Laws, 1645–1682, C.O. 30/2/110–111. Barbados Quakers were given some relief by James II in 1688 and by William III in 1697, though they were still barred from officeholding. C.O. 29/3/463–464; *Acts of Assembly, Barbados*, 169–170.

30. See Besse, *Collection of Sufferings*, II, chap. 6. He found about 200 Quaker sufferers during this time span in the five colonies of Nevis, Antigua, Jamaica, Bermuda, and Maryland, and 170 in New England.

31. Gov. Dutton to Sec. Jenkins, May 30, 1681, C.O. 29/3/71; Dutton to William Blathwayt, Aug. 24, 1681, Blathwayt Papers, XXX; Besse, *Collection of Sufferings*, II, 327–328; Dep. Gov. Witham on the Quaker Meeting House in Bridgetown, May 1683, C.O. 1/51/363.

32. See Henry J. Cadbury's two lists of names: "Barbados Quakers, 1683 to 1761," and "186 Barbados Quakeresses in 1677," *Jour. Bar. Mus. Hist. Soc.*, IX (1941–1942), 29–31, 195–197.

Ford, the Quaker mapmaker, shows a group of "Friends Plantations" near Speightstown. Checking the names of known Quakers
against the census lists, I have been able to identify the property
holdings of fifty-eight Barbados Quakers in 1680. These people
came from all walks of Barbadian society. No less than nine of them
were big planters, seven were middling planters, seventeen were
small planters, eight were merchants or shopkeepers in Bridgetown,
three were physicians, and three were craftsmen. The most important point, perhaps, is that all but four of them were slave owners.
Collectively they held 1,626 Negroes. Six of them—Thomas Clark,
Richard Forstall, Thomas Foster, Henry Gallop, John Rous, and
Thomas Rous—owned more than a hundred slaves apiece.

This is worth remembering when we assess the Quakers' role as
agitators for Negro rights in seventeenth-century Barbados. To
George Fox, whites, blacks, and tawnies (Indians) were all God's
creatures, and "is not the Gospel to be preached to all Creatures?"
He urged the Barbados planters to use their slaves gently and to set
them free after a term of servitude. William Edmundson, even more
forthrightly, told Governor Atkins that if the slaves rebelled it was
the masters' fault for "keeping them in Ignorance, and under Op-
pression, giving them Liberty to be common with Women (like
Beasts) and on the other Hand starve them for want of Meat and
Cloaths convenient." This was strong language in the seventeenth
century. But Edmundson was noticeably less upset by the institution
of chattel slavery than by the promiscuous sex habits of the Barbadian blacks, the "Filthiness and Uncleanness committed by the
Negroes and others, one Man having several Women, and one
Woman having several Men."

The Quaker planters in Barbados continued to bring their slaves
to meeting, despite the fines levied by Atkins and Dutton, and
Edmundson could report with satisfaction how "many of the Blacks
are convinced, and several of them confess to Truth." But the
Barbadian Friends by no means repudiated slavery or taught the
Negroes to rebel. As Fox put it, slave rebellion was "a thing we do
utterly *abhor* and detest." The Quaker message to the slaves was
quite similar to John Wesley's message to the English laboring
poor in the next century: they should be sober, fear God, and love
their masters, and then the overseers and masters would love them.[33]
Thus the Quakers were moral radicals in the context of Barbados

33. Fox, *To Ministers, Teachers, and Priests*, 5, 69–70; Penney, ed., *Journal of
George Fox*, 277; Edmundson, *Journal*, 85–86, 329.

society, and they attacked the supine Anglican establishment head on. But even Quakerism offered no serious challenge to the fundamental social institutions of the sugar colonies.

So far little has been said about the inhabitants of the four Barbados towns: Bridgetown, Speightstown, Holetown, and Oistins. They numbered less than 10 percent of the island population, but they paid 14 percent of the taxes in 1680. Bridgetown with a population of nearly three thousand was a community of considerable size and importance. Among the documents that Atkins sent home in 1680 is "A List of the Inhabitants in and about the Towne of St Michaells with their children hired Servants, Prentices, bought Servants and Negroes." This Bridgetown head count contains little information about the wealth of the townspeople, but a good deal about family structure, for it tells which of the 351 householders were married and how many had children. In an appendix the census separately records the 54 Jewish households in Bridgetown, without breaking down the totals to show the number of wives and children (the Jews had no servants). The demographic data in this Bridgetown census are of special interest because John Demos has recently published his analysis of a very similar census for the town of Bristol, in Plymouth Colony, in 1689. No one would expect a small, simple farming community like Bristol to have the same family structure as a large, rich seaport like Bridgetown. But the difference between the two towns, as shown in table 9, is so extreme as to suggest that in the 1680s Englishmen in the Caribbean had radically different living habits from Englishmen in New England.

The Bridgetown households, whether English or Jewish, contained many more servants and slaves than in Bristol and many fewer wives and children. They were scarcely "families" according to the English or New England meaning of the term, for most persons living under one roof in Bridgetown were not kindred. The English households in Bridgetown, however defined, ranged far more widely in size than in Bristol, which undoubtedly reflects a wider range in wealth. Whereas the typical Bristol family contained four to six persons, the most common size in Bridgetown was only three persons, and at the opposite end of the scale there were twenty-seven households with sixteen or more occupants—larger than the

Table 9. Family Structure in Bridgetown (Barbados) and Bristol (Plymouth)

	351 English Households, Bridgetown, 1680	54 Jewish Households, Bridgetown, 1680	70 English Households, Bristol, 1689
Married couples	231		67
Children	330		226
Childless couples	98		7
Widows, widowers	31		1
Single householders	89	5	1
Servants	402		56
Slaves	1,276	163	1
Mean number of persons per family	7.4	6.4	6.0
Mean number of white persons per family	3.7	3.4	6.0
Mean number of children per family	0.9		3.3
Mean number of servants per family	1.2		0.8
Mean number of slaves per family	3.6	3.0	0.01

NOTE: The data for Bristol are drawn from John Demos, "Families in Colonial Bristol, Rhode Island: An Exercise in Historical Demography," *Wm. and Mary Qtly.*, 3d Ser., XXV (1968), 40–57; and Richard LeBaron Bowen, *Early Rehoboth*, I (Rehoboth, Mass., 1945), 75–76. A third community, the English town of Sevenoaks in Kent, analyzed by Gregory King in 1695, occupies something of a middle ground between Bridgetown and Bristol. The 365 households in Sevenoaks averaged 1.8 children and .6 servants, with of course no slaves. The mean number of persons per household in Sevenoaks was 4.3, which appears to be the standard figure in 17th-century England. See Chalkin, *Seventeenth-Century Kent*, 36.

largest Bristol household. Half a dozen Bridgetown residents kept twenty or more servants and slaves; perhaps they operated sugar refineries—the census gives hardly any evidence of occupation. Few of the big planters lived in town; the census lists only thirteen who did so. The two agents of the Royal African Company, Edwin Stede and Stephen Gascoigne, lived next door to each other and employed sixteen black and white laborers between them. Two-thirds of the white servants in Bridgetown were "hired" rather than "bought"; that is, they were wage laborers rather than indentured servants. Forty-eight percent of the English householders had no white servants, but only 9 percent had no slaves, and only 1 percent had no domestics of any sort. John Blake, a newly arrived Bridgetown householder, wrote home in 1675 to explain why he could not discharge his white servant girl, even though she was a slut. His wife was sickly, Blake said, and "washing, starching, making of drinke and keeping the house in good order is no small taske to undergoe here. . . . Untill a neger wench I have be brought to knowledge, I cannot . . . be without a white maid." [34]

The Bridgetown Jews show a rather different family pattern from their English neighbors. They owned almost as many slaves and appear to have had almost as few children, but (as in Bristol) few of their households were particularly large or small. Most contained between four and seven persons, which may reflect a consistent middle range of wealth within the Jewish community. These people were Sephardic Jews who probably came from Portuguese Brazil in the 1650s. The site of their synagogue in Bridgetown is now occupied by the Barbados Turf Club, but the old burial ground, with graves dating back to 1660, still exists. They lived a ghetto existence on Jew Street and Synagogue Street, tolerated for their business skill, but even more ostracized than the Quakers. The Jews were not only listed separately on the census but taxed separately—and very heavily.[35]

Exceedingly few "normal" families—married couples with three or four children—lived in Bridgetown in 1680. One third of the householders were unmarried or widowed, and the majority were childless. As table 10 shows, very few married couples had more than one or two living children. The largest English family in town had seven children. Undoubtedly some of the Bridgetown inhabitants listed in the census as single householders left their wives and children in England. Some of the ninety-eight apparently childless couples had sent their children home to school. But the chief explanation for the stunted family development in this community must be the appallingly high mortality rate. During an eighteen-

34. Blake to his brother in Ireland, Nov. 1, 1675, in Oliver, ed., *Caribbeana,* I, 55–56.
35. E. M. Shilstone, "The Jewish Synagogue, Bridgetown, Barbados," *Jour. Bar. Mus. Hist. Soc.,* XXXII (1966–1967), 3–15; and Shilstone, *Monumental Inscriptions in the Burial Ground of the Jewish Synagogue at Bridgetown, Barbados* (n.p. [1956]) .

month period in 1678–1679, 107 infants were baptized in St. Michael parish, and 82 infants and children were buried. In such a situation it is a miracle that any Bridgetown family had as many as seven living children.

Governor Atkins sent home baptismal and burial records for each of the eleven parishes in Barbados covering the eighteen months from March 31, 1678, to September 30, 1679. These vital statistics cannot be taken very seriously, for they exclude all Negroes (except for a handful of Christian Negroes), Quakers, Baptists, and Jews, and they do not record all burials of servants. For what they are worth, Atkins's figures show that 581 persons were baptized and 1,087 persons were buried in Barbados during this eighteen-month period.[36] They also show that Bridgetown was by far the

Table 10. Children per Family: Bristol versus Bridgetown

| | Number of Children | | | | | | | | | | | Total |
	0	1	2	3	4	5	6	7	8	9	10	Children
Bristol families, 1689	7	10	11	12	9	8	6	4	1	0	1	226
Bridgetown families, 1680	198	58	52	22	7	11	2	1	0	0	0	330

unhealthiest spot on the island. In St. Michael parish four persons were buried for every one baptized; this one parish accounts for most of the island's surplus of deaths over births. Recorded births and deaths are spaced pretty evenly over the year, although rather more people died in the hot summer months. Twenty-one inmates of the Bridgetown almshouse and prison were buried in 1678–1679, as were seventeen sailors from visiting ships. On the other hand, the burial record shows that it was possible to live to a ripe old age in Bridgetown: three persons are listed as being eighty-seven, ninety-two, and ninety-five years old respectively. In three of the country parishes there was a recorded surplus of births over deaths. Probably plantation families had more living children than Bridgetown families. Yet it seems safe to conclude that Englishmen in Barbados were

36. Not all baptized persons were infants; a few were older children and adults. Atkins's vital statistics, however imperfect, are corroborated by Gov. Dutton's census of 1684, which lists 407 baptisms, 285 marriages, and 1,026 burials in Barbados during 1683. An Account of Barbados, Sloane MSS, 2441/17–22.

not maintaining the existing level of population. They were certainly not transferring to the tropics the strong family structure they established in Bristol and everywhere else in mainland America.

§◦

The final document from Governor Atkins's box, and one of the most interesting, is an alphabetical list of the 593 white persons who were granted tickets to leave Barbados in 1679.[37] The Barbados authorities were anxious to prevent servants and debtors from fleeing the island, so they required all persons who wanted to leave to register at the secretary's office three weeks in advance, obtain a ticket, and post security for any dependents left on the island unless they were free from debt and had a competent Barbados estate. Hence the list of 593 ticket holders for 1679. Among them were 11 married couples and 59 single women, the rest being single men. Seventy-three percent of the tickets bore the notation "time out." Many, but not all, of the persons so designated were ex-servants whose indentures had expired, and most—but again not all—of these people were leaving Barbados permanently. Another 20 percent were freemen and freeholders who posted security because they were leaving wives and children behind; these people were likely to return. The remainder were servants accompanying their masters abroad. Seventeen of the 175 big planters were among the departing passengers, 10 of them sailing to London and 4 to Boston, which suggests the high mobility of this group. Table 11 shows where the others went.

They sailed to all the places in commercial contact with Barbados, but it is instructive to note that more of them went to North America than to England and more went to England than to the much closer Caribbean islands. The passengers to England included merchants and planters on business trips and also many young people who, having sampled life in Barbados as indentured servants, had had enough of the New World and wanted to go back home. Those Barbadians who hoped to set themselves up as planters elsewhere in America found Antigua the most attractive of the English

37. Of these ticketholders, 552 were free, the others being servants. Atkins said that he could give no account of those who came to the island and implied that fewer came than left. But this may not be so. During 1683, 710 servants and freemen arrived in Barbados, and only 446 free persons left. *Ibid.*

islands, because it was closer than Jamaica and had more land available than Nevis or St. Christopher. As for the mainland colonies, Virginia and Carolina would seem the most logical places for a Barbadian emigrant to settle, so it is a little surprising to find so many going to New England. Of course Barbados had close economic ties with New England, and many more ships sailed to Boston than to other North American ports. Yet during 1679 twenty ships embarked from Bridgetown for Virginia and Carolina, and there was surely space on these vessels for more than the 100 passengers they carried, even if they brought with them large numbers of slaves. Few ships leaving Barbados for any destination carried more than a hand-

Table 11. Destinations of 593 Persons Leaving Barbados, 1679

Caribbean		North America		England		Other	
Antigua	65	Boston	68	London	151	Holland	1
Nevis	14	Rhode Island	3	Bristol	39	Total	1
Montserrat	1	New England	25	Liverpool	8		
Leeward Is.	15	New York	34	Beaumaris	3		
Jamaica	35	Virginia	62	Topsham	3		
Bahamas	12	Carolina	38	Poole	1		
Tortuga	3	Newfoundland	3	Total	205		
Surinam	5	Total	233				
Bermuda	4						
Total	154						

ful of passengers. The 151 persons who sailed to London traveled on forty-eight different ships.

Did the people who sailed from Barbados to North America come as permanent emigrants, or were they transient visitors? Did those who settled on the mainland bring family and slaves from Barbados, or were they mainly young servants freed from their indentures? A partial answer to these questions can be supplied by following the Barbadians who went to South Carolina in the years just before and after the census of 1680.[38] Everyone who has examined the founding of South Carolina agrees that planters from Barbados played a

38. The following pages draw upon my article, "The English Sugar Islands and the Founding of South Carolina," *The South Carolina Historical Magazine,* LXXII (1971), 81–93.

major role—some would say a decisive role—in shaping this new colony. The most recent historian of colonial South Carolina, Eugene Sirmans, argues that Barbadian immigrants, congregating at Goose Creek a few miles above Charleston, formed the dominant political faction in the first generation of settlement; the years from 1670 to 1712 constituted the age of the Goose Creek men.[39] In Agnes Baldwin's list of 684 settlers who came to Carolina between 1670 and 1680, half the colonists whose place of origin she can identify came from the West Indies.[40] And if we examine the backgrounds of the governors of South Carolina between 1669 and 1737, it turns out that nearly half—eleven out of twenty-three—had lived in the islands or were sons of islanders. Seven of the early Carolina governors had Barbados backgrounds.[41]

Who were these Goose Creek men? Settlers were drawn to Carolina from all the English islands—Bermuda, the Bahamas, the Leewards, and Jamaica—but the principal Caribbean migration came from Barbados. It was a Barbados planter, Sir John Colleton, who first organized the proprietary group that received a royal charter from Charles II in 1663. Three boatloads of colonists from Barbados tried to plant at Cape Fear from 1665 to 1667, and about 20 Barbadians joined the first permanent South Carolina settlement on the Ashley River in 1670. During the decade of the 1670s, 175 Barbadians can be identified as coming to the new colony. They brought with them at least 150 servants and slaves. This migration to Carolina was part of a general exodus from the overcrowded little island, in which something like 10,000 Barbadians moved to other parts of English America during the course of the century.[42] South Carolina

---

39. M. Eugene Sirmans, *Colonial South Carolina, 1663–1763* (Chapel Hill, N.C., 1966), 19–100. See also J. P. Thomas, "The Barbadians in Early South Carolina," *South Carolina Historical and Genealogical Magazine*, XXXI (1930), 75–92.

40. Agnes Leland Baldwin, *First Settlers of South Carolina, 1670–1680* (Columbia, S.C., 1969). She lists 146 settlers who came from the island colonies, 134 from Britain, and 10 from the mainland colonies. The remaining 394 she assigns no place of origin.

41. Jack P. Greene, *The Quest for Power* (Chapel Hill, N.C., 1963), 457–458, 475–488, lists the South Carolina governors and assembly leaders. Governors who came from the islands, or whose fathers came from the islands, were William Sayle (Bermuda), Sir John Yeamans (Barbados), James Colleton (Barbados), James Moore (Barbados), Sir Nathaniel Johnson (Leewards), Robert Gibbes (Barbados), Robert Daniel (Barbados), Robert Johnson (Leewards), James Moore, Jr. (Barbados), Arthur Middleton (Barbados), and Thomas Broughton (Leewards).

42. Alfred D. Chandler, "The Expansion of Barbados," *Jour. Bar. Mus. Hist. Soc.*, XIII (1945–1946), 106, reckons that 30,000 persons left Barbados for other

was by no means the chief destination for these migrants. Governor Atkins's list shows that only 6 percent of the people who obtained tickets to leave Barbados in 1679 sailed to Carolina. The migration to Carolina was important, nonetheless, because the Barbadians who came had exceptional energy, experience, and wealth.

One might suppose that the people who quit Barbados and the other sugar islands were misfits and failures, poor whites unable to compete with black slave labor, squeezed off their little farms by the aggressive big planters. In fact, a great many of these bedraggled poor whites stayed put in Barbados. After thirty years of out-migration, the census of 1680 shows thousands of them still hanging on, with a few acres and a few slaves apiece, repressed and voiceless like the submerged laboring class in England. They had every reason to leave. But relatively few of them found their way to Carolina.

The Barbadians who did move to Carolina in the 1670s and 1680s were a medley of big and middling planters, merchants, artisans, small farmers, sailors, servants, and slaves. The thirty-eight who made the trip in 1679 included two married couples, twenty-five single men, and nine single women. Fifteen persons in this group took out land warrants in Carolina (mostly soon after their arrival in 1679), another three or four were wives or relatives of planters already established in the new colony, and the others left no visible trace in the published Carolina records. Attention therefore focuses on the fifteen who took out land warrants. Arthur Middleton and Richard Quintyne, the latter attended by a servant, were from big planter families, and Robert Daniel, who also brought a servant, was from a middling planter family. Stephen Fox and his wife, Phyllis, arrived in 1679 with the equipage of a small Barbados planter— a maid and twelve Negroes—and obtained 1,350 Carolina acres (more than the largest Barbados plantation) for this party of fifteen. Middleton, Quintyne, Daniel, Christopher Portman, and John Ladson received Carolina tracts of such ample size that we may be sure they also brought Negroes from Barbados. Thirteen of these fifteen Barbadian emigrants received at least 200 acres in Carolina. Only two (one of whom arrived in 1679 as a servant) received the minimum allotment of 70 acres. Possibly these two men were the only emigrants in this group who brought no family or slaves with them from Barbados.[43]

colonies between 1650–1680, but his estimate depends on John Scott's statistics and is greatly inflated.

43. My information on Barbados emigrants to Carolina is drawn principally from the following volumes edited by A. S. Salley, Jr., and published by the

For the small man Carolina opened up possibilities undreamed of in Barbados. John Collins, who arrived in 1679 with a "boy" unidentified in the passenger list, quickly staked out 290 acres. He was probably the same John Collins who served on a Carolina grand jury in 1692 and was commissioned captain of the Charleston militia in 1700—posts well beyond his aspirations in Barbados. John Ladson, another arrival in 1679 of undistinguished Barbados lineage, rose to be a leading member of the Commons House of Assembly in the 1690s. But the scions of substantial Barbados planters did even better. Robert Daniel and Arthur Middleton were not merely leaders in the Carolina Assembly; both eventually became governors of the colony. All in all, four of the six Barbadians who became governors of South Carolina between 1670 and 1730 were from big planter families. Sir John Yeamans (1672–1674), James Colleton (1686–1690), Robert Gibbes (1710–1712), and Arthur Middleton (1725–1730). Robert Daniel (1716–1717) was from a middling planter family. Other Barbadian big planter families—Berringer, Clutterbuck, Davies, Dowden, Elliott, Fenwick, Foster, Hall, Lane, Lake, Merrick, Quintyne, Robinson, and Sandiford—obtained large Carolina land grants between 1672 and 1692.

The striking thing, surely, is the number of Barbadians of wealth and position who chose to come. Planters like the Colletons and Middletons enjoyed privileges in Barbados more tangible than the aristocratic trappings dreamed up by Shaftesbury and Locke in the Fundamental Constitutions of Carolina. But they needed fresh avenues for their younger children. They had no expansion room on Barbados. All of the choice land was long since partitioned into efficiently sized plantations, and the marginal land—which they did not want in any case—was all held by the poor whites. In the case of the Middletons, they tried to start new sugar estates in Antigua and lost heart when the French plundered the island in the 1660s. So Edward and Arthur Middleton came to Carolina. These brothers were younger sons. Their elder brother Benjamin stayed in Barbados and operated the main family estate with its 379 acres and 130 slaves, which doubtless remained more valuable for many years than Edward's new plantation, The Oaks, on Goose Creek.

Historical Commission of South Carolina: *Warrants for Lands in South Carolina, 1672–1711* (Columbia, S.C., 1910–1915); *Journal of the Grand Council of South Carolina, 1671–1692* (Columbia, S.C., 1907); and *Commissions and Instructions from the Lords Proprietors of Carolina to Public Officials of South Carolina, 1685–1715* (Columbia, S.C., 1916).

Not all the leading Barbados families prospered in South Carolina. Ironically the Colletons, prime organizers of the Carolina colonizing scheme, did not fare well in the new settlement. In the 1670s and 1680s Sir Peter Colleton was the head of this family: he was one of the eight lords proprietor of Carolina, a member of the Barbados Council, and owner of a Barbados plantation manned by 180 slaves. When Sir Peter retired to England in 1681, he left the management of his Barbados property to his younger brother Thomas. Though overshadowed by Sir Peter, Thomas Colleton was also a leading figure on the island; he sat in the Assembly, was a colonel of the militia, and a judge on the Barbados bench. A third brother, James Colleton, had no fruitful role in Barbados and could rise to no higher office than vestryman for St. John parish. So he came to Carolina in 1686, took out extensive land grants, and served as governor of the new colony for four years. But the rambunctious Carolinians rose up in rebellion against Governor Colleton in 1690 and banished him from the colony. Poor James retreated back to Barbados. At this juncture brother Thomas conveniently died or retired to England, which opened a slot at last for James in Barbados. In 1692 he assumed management of Colleton plantation and soon took the family seat in the Barbados Assembly, doubtless delighted at having escaped so well from South Carolina.[44]

People like the Middletons and Colletons were drawn to Carolina because of its semitropical setting, which seemed to combine the advantages of Caribbean agriculture with the wholesome environment of the North American mainland. They may have sought escape from the distorted life-style of the West Indian sugar planter, yet surely they carried much of the Caribbean milieu with them. Most basically the Barbadians introduced Negro slavery to South Carolina. Slavery would have developed in colonial Carolina in any case, but certainly the island migrants gave it an early boost. Starting with Sir John Yeamans in 1671, members of the big sugar-planting families brought gangs of Negroes with them. Many of the poor whites also brought a slave or two. In consequence the colony already had a sizable Negro labor force in the 1680s, before the in-

44. The vestry records for St. John parish, Barbados, Bar. Mus. Hist. Soc., show that all three Colleton brothers were elected to the vestry from 1673 to 1681, when Sir Peter left for England. James continued to serve on the vestry until 1686, when he went to Carolina, and Thomas served until 1691. The next year James was back on the vestry and served throughout the decade. James entered the Barbados Assembly in 1694 and sat until at least 1700. *Jour. Bar. Mus. Hist. Soc.*, XI (1943–1944), 171–173.

troduction of rice as a staple crop. Lowland Carolina would soon
have a population ratio of four blacks to every white, not far different from the ratio in Barbados. Carolina rice planters of the eighteenth century had more in common with Barbados sugar planters
of the seventeenth century than large gangs of slaves. They too grew
rich overnight. They too developed a proud and mettlesome school
of politics. They too fashioned an aristocratic elite in which wealth,
privilege, and power were closely correlated. Charleston's brittle,
gay, and showy society, compounded of old-world elegance and
frontier boisterousness, echoed the Barbados atmosphere of a century before. So it was that the Barbadians helped to create in North
America a slave-based plantation society closer in temper to the islands they fled from than to any other mainland English settlement.

Study of the Barbadian emigration pattern to Carolina shows once
again how the big planters in 1680 dominated almost everything.
They not only controlled the island but led the emigration away
from it. Like the terraced cane fields of the island, Barbados society
rose level by level, from the roughly 40,000 slaves occupying the low-
est tier to the 2,300 servants at the next tier, ascending past the
1,200 freemen, the 1,000 small planters, the 400 Bridgetown householders, and the 190 middling planters, to the 175 big planters at the
summit who held the best land, sold the most sugar, and monopolized the best offices. In only one generation these planters had
turned their small island into an amazingly effective sugar-production machine and had built a social structure to rival the tradition-
encrusted hierarchy of old England. But the irony is that in ac-
complishing all this they had made their tropical paradise almost
uninhabitable. By crowding so many black and white laborers onto
a few square miles they had aggravated health hazards and overtaxed the food supply, condemning most inhabitants of the island
to a semistarvation diet. Those who had money squandered it by
overdressing, overeating, and overdrinking and by living in ornate
English-style houses unsuited to the climate. Even the rich were unhappy in Barbados, for they suffered from claustrophobia, heat, and
tropical fevers and longed for the dank, chill weather they were used
to at home. Most of all they hated and feared the hordes of restive
black captives they had surrounded themselves with. The mark of a
successful Barbados planter was his ability to escape from the island and retire grandly to England. Thus sunny Barbados was a
land of paradox in 1680, both parvenu and traditional, both complacent and insecure, the richest and yet in human terms the least
successful colony in English America.

4 ❧ The Leeward Islands

If seventeenth-century Barbados shows us a sugar colony in its prime, the Leeward Islands were sugar colonies still in their infancy. The Englishmen who settled St. Christopher, Nevis, Antigua, and Montserrat were much slower than their Barbadian colleagues to establish a slave-based plantation system. Settlement of these islands started in the 1620s and 1630s, and the planters on St. Christopher were experimenting with sugarcane as early as 1643. But for many years they continued as small tobacco and cotton farmers. Until the 1670s they imported few slaves. Their social structure remained fluid and homespun. The planter class in these four islands was still only half-formed in the closing decades of the century. The heyday of the Leeward gentry came in the eighteenth century, when they finally caught and surpassed their Barbados competitors. By 1750 St. Christopher alone shipped more sugar than Barbados, and Antigua about as much; the four islands collectively exported three times the Barbados total.

Since the Leeward planters eventually flourished, why did they lag so far behind the Barbadians in the seventeenth century? One reason was economic: they were small men without capital or credit who had to pull themselves up by their own bootstraps. Another reason was geographic: they had more arable land at their disposal than the Barbadians, but it was difficult land to clear and work. Everywhere except Antigua the planters had to carve their cane pieces out of steep, jungled hillsides, broken by gullies and mountain streams, and the Antiguan planters suffered from drought. But the biggest problem was political: throughout the century the Leeward settlers found themselves in the center of Anglo-French conflict in the eastern Caribbean. During the French wars of 1666–1667, 1689–1697, and 1702–1713, St. Christopher changed hands seven times. Montserrat and Antigua were sacked twice and Nevis once. Notwithstanding the French menace, the several English islands rejected effective federation because they were so intensely jealous of one another.[1] Within each island there was plenty of local factionalism, especially between the English Protestants and Irish Catholics, who cordially hated each other. In short, the pioneer Leeward planters lived in a state of perpetual crisis.

The early history of the Leeward settlements documents the frustrating problems that could beset sugar makers working in frontier conditions. In some ways the rise of the Leeward planters resembled the rise of the Chesapeake tobacco planters—it was a slow and turbulent process. Yet when the big planters in the Leeward colonies finally surfaced they adopted a code of conduct much different from the noblesse oblige of the Virginia squirearchy. Long years of warfare with the French taught the island planters to flee rather than fight, to accept frequent demolition of their property as a fact of life, and to lobby for compensation from the home authorities. They could run from the French, but not from their own governors. One of the interesting things to watch is the conflict that gradually built up between the Leeward planters and the authoritarian men who tried to manage these insecure outposts. From Gov. Thomas Warner in the 1620s to Gov. Christopher Codrington in the 1690s, the administrators of the Leeward colonies nagged and bullied their people, trying to shape the four islands into effective garrisons, trying to make the settlers cooperate with each other, trying to make them stand up against the French. Always the planters grumbled and prevaricated. And as they gained in wealth and self-confidence during the closing stage of the French wars, they met a governor whose nagging and bullying was too much. In 1710 they gunned down Daniel Parke in cold blood. The murder of Governor Parke, one of the most lurid episodes in English Caribbean history, was not an isolated or accidental event. It summed up many long years of life on the tropical firing line.

There is a paralyzing paucity of information about the first generation of English settlement in St. Christopher, Nevis, Antigua, and Montserrat. Almost no seventeenth-century records survive in the

1. Today rivalry remains intense among these small islands, as witness the recent confrontation between St. Kitts and Anguilla.

government archives on the four islands, and few documents of a date earlier than 1660 have turned up in English public or private archives.[2] In the absence of hard data it is doubtless foolhardy to offer any comment on early developments in the Leeward Islands. Someone may discover a trunkful of papers revealing that the Leeward planters shared fully in the Barbados sugar bonanza of the 1640s and 1650s. It is more likely, however, that the early Leeward colonists will remain forever obscure—for the best of reasons, because they were obscure men at the time. What scraps of information we do have indicate that most of them were still subsistence tobacco farmers at the Restoration.

For the first twenty years St. Christopher was by far the most important of the Leeward settlements. The founding father of St. Christopher was Sir Thomas Warner, a Suffolk man, a friend and neighbor of John Winthrop's. Having tried unsuccessfully to plant in Guiana, Warner decided to try again at St. Christopher and occupied the place with a small party in 1624. For half a dozen years Warner's prospects were touch and go. When a French party arrived at St. Christopher in 1625 he felt so weak that he agreed to share the island with them, the French taking the two ends and the English occupying the middle. In 1627 Warner and the French governor drew up a code of bylaws for living together on St. Christopher, and these articles were confirmed and amplified at least ten times between 1628 and 1663.[3] The two nations "solved" the Indian problem by staging a sneak night attack on the Caribs who inhabited St. Christopher and massacring large numbers of them in their hammocks. In 1629 a large Spanish fleet attacked the island. The invaders quickly overcame Anglo-French resistance, destroyed the planters' buildings and crops, and shipped as many as they could catch home—setting the pattern for many future assaults. But a saving remnant of Englishmen hid out in the mountains, and the French were able to escape by boat to a neighboring island. Within a few months they were rebuilding their ruined plantations. Restor-

2. E. C. Baker, *A Guide to Records in the Leeward Islands* (Oxford, 1965) surveys the early holdings—or lack of them—in the island archives. Higham, *Leeward Islands*, 243–251, surveys the early manuscript and printed materials in English libraries and archives. Not until 1670 did the home authorities begin to keep an entry book of correspondence with the Leeward planters. C.O. 153/1.

3. Articles of peace between the English and French on St. Christopher, Apr. 28, 1627, Egerton MSS, 2395/3. These articles were confirmed and amended in 1628 (twice), 1637, 1638 (twice), 1644, 1649, 1655, 1662, and 1663. See Egerton MSS, 2395/10–13, 30, 34, 37, 62–65, 342, 385.

ing their houses was no great problem, for the planters constructed simple huts framed by four or six forked stakes, walled by reeds, and thatched with palm or plantain leaves.[4]

When the earl of Carlisle secured his title as lord proprietor of the English Caribbees (Barbados and the Leeward Islands), he confirmed Warner as governor of St. Christopher. Surplus English colonists fanned out to occupy Nevis in 1628, Antigua and Montserrat around 1632. The first comers to Nevis had a particularly discouraging start. The Spanish fleet that sacked St. Christopher also attacked Nevis. The planters fired their single great gun from Pelican Point and readied their militia for a fight, but the servants in the militia threw away their arms, crying "Liberty, joyfull Liberty," and other servants swam to the Spanish ships to tell the enemy where the English planters hid their possessions![5] Having weathered the Spanish invasion, the settlers on all four islands made tobacco their staple crop. Tobacco grew rather more successfully in St. Christopher than in Barbados, but not well enough. In 1639 Warner imposed a ban on tobacco production in a vain effort to force up the English price. By 1641 the impoverished Leeward planters were reduced to the "pointe of undoeing, haveing spent their whole Tyme in peddling and chaffering to the multiplying of debt, the infecting them with the love of a long accustomed Idlenes."[6]

The social scene in the 1630s and 1640s was crude to say the least. The governor of Nevis, Anthony Hilton, having narrowly escaped being murdered by his servant as he slept, tried to burn down the house of the deputy governor of St. Christopher, Edward Warner. The governor of Antigua, Henry Ashton, enraged at a woman who resisted his advances, chopped off her long hair, which so shamed the lady that she fled the island. A conspicuous figure among the pioneer planters of St. Christopher was one Phance Beecher—known to his critics as "lyinge Beecher" or "bragging Beecher"—who arrived about 1639 a penniless youth, without servants or luggage, and quickly built what passed for a fortune "by his Cutthroate dealings" in such items as playing cards, pins, needles, and canvas. Beecher was elevated to the island Council because he was a kinsman

4. Davies, *History of Caribby-Islands,* 163–168, 177; Harlow, *Colonising,* 1–4, 18–20.
5. Harlow, *Colonising,* 4–17.
6. According to the tobacco statistics printed in Oliver, ed., *Caribbeana,* III, 197–198, St. Christopher shipped twice as much tobacco to England as Barbados, 1637–1640. For the tobacco cessation of 1639–1641, see Bennett, "The English Caribbees, 1642–1646," *Wm. and Mary Qtly.,* 3d Ser., XXIV (1967), 360.

of the clerk of the Privy Council, and in 1642 "this most arrogant and nowe sawcye proude fellowe" led a rebellion against Governor Warner that convulsed St. Christopher for a year.[7]

Since tobacco was a dead end, why did the Leeward settlers shift so slowly and uncertainly to sugar, from white to black labor, and from small farms to large plantations? The basic reason seems to be that the inhabitants of the 1640s and 1650s were small men who lacked the capital, credit, and confidence to pour thousands of pounds apiece into slaves, land, and sugar works. Many were former servants who set up as subsistence farmers after their indentures expired and built up their estates piecemeal, if at all. Nor were they helped much by the merchants who sold African slaves and European goods in the Lesser Antilles, for these merchants much preferred to deal with Barbados planters, who had more money and sounder credit. The principal new English immigrants to the Indies likewise bypassed the Leewards in favor of Barbados because there sugar production was a proven success. When Thomas Modyford arrived in the Caribbean in 1647 he intended to settle in Antigua and start a new plantation, but he soon decided to settle instead in Barbados, where he could buy a plantation already in working operation. For many years the Leeward planters were overmatched by their Barbados competitors.

St. Christopher remained the most heavily populated island in the Leeward group in the 1640s and 1650s. Governor Warner reported that some sixteen hundred fighting men lived in the English sector of the island in 1642. A few planters on St. Christopher started growing sugar, yet most stuck doggedly to tobacco. "If you go to Christophers," said a visitor to the Lesser Antilles in 1645, "you shal see the ruins of a flourishing place." [8] Ten years later, the island was said to be "almost worne out by reason of the multitudes that live upon it." Over eight hundred men spun off from this multitude to join the Jamaican expedition of 1655, yet the English sector of St. Christopher remained crowded. By the mid-1660s a handful of planters operated large sugar estates manned by slave gangs. Gov. William Watts's plantation returned £1,500 per annum. The great

7. John Jeaffreson to Archibald Hay, Aug. 9, 1641, Hay Papers; Bennett, "The English Caribbees, 1642–1646," *Wm. and Mary Qtly.*, 3d Ser., XXIV (1967), 362–365.

8. Ligon, *True History of Barbados*, 21–22; Bennett, "The English Caribbees, 1642–1646," *Wm. and Mary Qtly.*, 3d Ser., XXIV (1967), 362; Thomas Robinson to Thomas Chapple, Sept. 24, 1643, Hay Papers; George Downing to John Winthrop, Jr., Aug. 26, 1645, Forbes *et al.*, eds., *Winthrop Papers*, V, 43.

majority of the English acreage on St. Christopher, however, was cut up into ten- or twelve-acre tobacco farms belonging to former servants "of an Ordinary and low rank" who did not possess slaves.[9]

Antigua and Montserrat were very thinly settled until the Restoration. In 1646 the population of Antigua totaled 750; it climbed to 1,200 by 1655. Montserrat grew at about the same pace. The Antiguan colonists, according to Gov. Henry Ashton, were so burdened with debts (mostly owed to Ashton) that "it would bee hard to keepe them here if they had meanes to runn off." They were still threatening in 1656 to abandon the island altogether. Montserrat was the favorite retreat for a particularly oppressed group, Irish Catholic servants who had worked out their indentures in the Lesser Antilles and did not want to go back home. As early as 1637 Gov. Anthony Brisket, an Irishman from Wexford, was trying to draw his fellow countrymen to Montserrat. They answered his call and soon heavily outnumbered the English colonists.[10] The home reputation of the Leeward settlements may be gauged by a London guidebook to America, published in 1655. The author of this work was uncertain whether Antigua had yet been settled. Montserrat and Nevis were "of so little consideration, especially to our Nation, that it would seem but tedious to mention them further."[11]

Nevis was the first of the Leeward Islands to convert from tobacco to sugar. This is shown by the following tabulation of debts that Leeward planters, large and small, owed to Dutch merchants in 1655.[12] Despite this sugar production the majority of Nevis colonists were neither prosperous nor content. When Jamaica fell to the Eng-

9. Gregory Butler to Oliver Cromwell, 1655, Birch, ed., *Thurloe State Papers*, III, 754; Margaret Watts to Sir William Darcy, May 13, 1666, *Cal.S.P.Col., 1661–1668*, #1206; Sir Charles Wheler to Council of Plantations, Dec. 7, 10, 1672, C.O. 153/1/60–61.

10. Henry Ashton to Lord Carlisle, Feb. 8, 1641/2, Ashton to Carlisle, *c.* 1646, Hay Papers; Gregory Butler to Oliver Cromwell, 1655, Birch, ed., *Thurloe State Papers*, III, 754; *Cal.S.P.Col., 1574–1660*, 439–440; Anthony Brisket to Charles I, *c.* 1637, *Analecta Hibernica*, No. 4, 185.

11. N. N., *America: or An exact Description of the West-Indies* (London, 1655), 470, 472.

12. Vere Langford Oliver, *The History of the Island of Antigua* (London, 1894–1899), I, xxiii–xxv, xliv; *Analecta Hibernica*, No. 4, 214–219; Williamson, *Caribbee Islands*, 182–183. The Leeward planters also owed trifling debts in indigo and ginger. One hundred Montserrat and 146 Antiguan planters (including Gov. Keynall) were debtors to the Dutch. Among the Montserrat debtors, the Irish owed tobacco and the English owed a mixture of sugar and tobacco, which may indicate that only Englishmen were producing sugar on Montserrat at this date.

	Sugar	Tobacco
Nevis	39,064 lb.	27,516 lb.
St. Christopher	2,444	89,368
Antigua		119,240
Montserrat	1,741	43,278
Totals	43,249 lb.	279,402 lb.

lish, Gov. Luke Stokes led a large contingent from Nevis to settle at Point Morant on the eastern end of Jamaica. The few successful Nevis sugar planters declined to stir, though they held many fewer slaves per capita than their Barbadian rivals. Some 300 Negroes were imported to Nevis between 1665 and 1672; in 1672 the black population stood at 1,739.[13] Because of the slave shortage the Nevis planters relied much longer on white indentured servants than the Barbadians. The register of servants shipped from Bristol to America (see table 3 above) shows that from 1654 through 1660—years in which the Barbados sugar planters were still in the process of converting to black labor—nearly all of the Bristol servants who went to the West Indies signed up for Barbados. Suddenly in 1661 the pattern shifted. From that year until the register closed in 1686 more Bristol servants went to Nevis than to Barbados.[14]

In the 1660s the Leeward planters began to make sugar in earnest and put aside the mutinies and mini-wars that had kept the four islands in turmoil during the preceding two decades. Like the Barbados planters they had long since thrown off their proprietary allegiance to the earl of Carlisle. At the Restoration the Leeward planters made the same bargain with Charles II as the Barbadians: in exchange for royal government and confirmation of land titles, the four island assemblies consented in 1664 to a 4.5 percent duty on commodities exported from the islands. In one important respect, however, it was a poorer bargain. The king appointed Francis Lord Willoughby as commander in chief of the Leeward Islands in addition to Barbados. The Leeward colonists chafed at this arrangement, for the Barbadians were their chief economic competi-

13. For the Nevis migration to Jamaica, see Birch, ed., *Thurloe State Papers*, IV, 603, V, 66, 177; Nevis Islande. . . . A liste of those people that are goinge for Jamecoe, Oct. 21, 1656, Egerton MSS, 2395/83. For the Nevis slave population in 1672, see *Cal.S.P.Col., 1669–1674*, #896.

14. Abbot E. Smith gives a year-by-year, colony-by-colony tabulation of the Bristol register in *Colonists in Bondage*, 309.

tors and they wanted a separate administration. Certainly the union with Barbados soon ended disastrously.

In 1666–1667 war broke out between England and France. Deputy Governor Watts in St. Christopher, when he learned that war was likely, decided that the time was ripe for chasing the French off the island, for the English settlers on St. Christopher outnumbered their rivals by two to one. The anxious French commander got Watts to ratify the Anglo-French articles of peace on St. Christopher once more in March 1666, but less than a month later, when Watts received Charles II's declaration of war, he collected four hundred additional militiamen from Nevis and a party of buccaneers and prepared to attack. Unhappily for Watts, the French attacked first. Sweeping through the unprotected English plantations on the windward side of the island, they stampeded the English in the leeward quarter also. After one day of fighting the panicky English surrendered. The victorious French appropriated the four hundred blacks they found in the English sector and deported upwards of five thousand white settlers. When Lord Willoughby set sail with a relief expedition from Barbados, a hurricane smashed his fleet and drowned the commander in chief. Thereupon the French invaded and ravaged Antigua and Montserrat. They burned the sugar works on these two islands and collected about a thousand more slaves. Only Nevis remained uncaptured. The English counterattacked in 1667, but the French beat off their efforts to recapture St. Christopher. In little more than a year of combat the English had suffered the most humiliating series of defeats they ever experienced in the West Indies.[15]

In 1667 the Treaty of Breda restored the Leeward Islands to their prewar status, though the French delayed handing back the English sector of St. Christopher until 1671 and never returned their war booty. Recognizing belatedly that the Leeward colonists needed their own administration, Charles II commissioned Sir Charles Wheler in 1670 as captain general and governor in chief of His Majesty's Leeward Caribbee Islands, and armed him with two companies of soldiers to be paid out of the 4.5 percent duty. Wheler proved inadequate to the task; he threw up his government less than a year after his arrival. His successor, William

15. The fullest account of the Leeward fighting in 1666–1667 is in du Tertre, *Histoire générale des Antilles,* IV. The best modern accounts are by Higham, *Leeward Islands,* chap. 2, and Crouse, *French Struggle for the West Indies,* chap. 2–3.

Stapleton (1672–1686), worked energetically to build up the sugar industry in the four islands. Stapleton was an Irish Catholic soldier of fortune who came out to the West Indies during the 1666–1667 war, then settled in Montserrat. He married into the Russell family, the biggest planters on Nevis, acquired large properties in all four islands, and received a baronetcy in 1679. Under Stapleton's management the Leeward planters quickly recouped their wartime losses. During the decade of the 1670s at least 4,000 Negroes were imported into the four islands. The slave population more than doubled in six years, from 3,184 in 1672 to 8,449 in 1678.[16]

Life remained unpolished in this frontier territory. The Montserrat authorities found it necessary to fix a fine of five thousand pounds of sugar for cursing a councillor and five hundred pounds for cursing an assemblyman. The Nevis authorities fined freeholders who refused to "subscribe their names to the free Election of Assemblymen." Sugar planters in Montserrat were even fined for distilling all of their cane juice into rum instead of making sugar; this practice was held particularly blameworthy because the colonists, when drunk, called each other names like "English dogg, Scots dogg, Tory, Irish dogg, Cavalier and Roundheade." [17]

Nonetheless, the nucleus of a planter class was beginning to appear. Three examples may suggest the ups and downs of the early Leeward gentry. A Dutchman named Samuel Waad was among the first big planters on Montserrat. His sugar works is described as one of the stateliest in the Caribbees; he lived in a stone house, richly furnished, and possessed seventy cattle, five hundred sheep, fifty slaves, and thirty servants. In 1654 Waad was tried and executed for calling his governor an "Irish Murderer" and an "Irish barbarian." [18] A more fortunate early Leeward sugar planter was Samuel Winthrop of the famous New England family. He arrived in the Caribbees in 1647 at age twenty and after trying various islands settled down at Antigua. By 1670 he was president of the Antigua Council. A New England visitor found Samuel "a reall Winthrop and truely noble to all," unlike the other Antiguans,

16. Higham, *Leeward Islands*, 145, 154.
17. Leeward Islands Manuscript Laws, 1644–1673, C.O. 154/1/76–77; Leeward Islands MSS Laws, 1668–1682, C.O. 154/2/99–100, 294; *Acts of Assembly passed in the Island of Montserrat, 1668–1740* (London, 1740), 32.
18. *Analecta Hibernica*, No. 4, 219–228.

who were "a company of sodomites." The French raid on Antigua in 1666 stripped Winthrop of all but twelve slaves; when he died a dozen years later he left sixty-four Negroes, eleven hundred acres and some £3,000 in debts. His plantation house was called Groaten Hall—a touch of home, since his father had been lord of Groton manor in Suffolk, and the New England Winthrops are commemorated by the towns of Groton, Massachusetts, and Groton, Connecticut.[19]

A third representative of the planter class is Christopher Jeaffreson, who came to St. Christopher in 1676 and found the island still very primitive. Jeaffreson's plantation, which had been started by his father nearly half a century before, was poorly managed, and provisions on the island were so scarce that he wrote home immediately for soap, candles, and a half-dozen barrels of beef. Jeaffreson advised his London commercial correspondents that the planters on St. Christopher were generally too poor to buy English furniture, bedding, hangings, carpets, or the finer grades of cloth. Like the Barbadians of forty years before they slept in hammocks, sat on benches, dressed in coarse linen, and drank vast quantities of Madeira wine. Jeaffreson quickly reorganized his own plantation, switching from indigo to sugar. He had two sugar works in operation by 1681, when a hurricane leveled every building on his property. After repairing this damage, Jeaffreson came home the next year, leaving forty-six working Negroes on his estate—one of the largest slave gangs in St. Christopher. But in the hands of a dishonest steward everything quickly collapsed once more: by 1685 thirteen slaves and almost all of his livestock had died, the mill was inoperable, the fields were unplanted, his household furnishings were gone, and the startled Jeaffreson found himself deeply in debt.[20]

In 1678 Governor Stapleton compiled a detailed census of his four islands that permits for the first time a general appraisal of social

19. Massachusetts Historical Society, *Collections*, 5th Ser., VIII (Boston, 1882), 249–260; Oliver, *History of Antigua*, I, xxx; Antiguan act of Sept. 4, 1678, concerning Samuel Winthrop's estate, C.O. 154/2. Samuel's plantation was near the present Antigua airport; Winthrop (or Winthorp) Bay on the north coast is named after him.

20. Jeaffreson, ed., *Young Squire*, I, 183–186, 190–191, 274–279, II, 77, 236–240, 246–248.

structure in the Leeward Islands.[21] Stapleton's tabulation is a valuable document; though less informative than the Barbados census of 1680, it contains some data not found in those returns. The Nevis and Antigua lists are fuller than those from Montserrat and St. Christopher. Every householder in Nevis and Antigua is enumerated, with the number of white and black men, women, and children attached to his household. The Montserrat return also

Table 12. Population of the Leeward Islands, 1678

	Nevis	Antigua	St. Christopher	Montserrat	Total
White men:					
English	1,050	800	370	346	2,566
Irish	450	360	187	769	1,766
Other	34	76	138	33	281
White women:					
English	700	400	409	175	1,684
Irish	120	130		410	660
Other	8	14	130	6	158
White children:					
English	920	400	543	240	2,103
Irish	230	120		690	1,040
Other	9	8	120	13	150
Total Whites	3,521	2,308	1,897	2,682	10,408
Black men	1,422	805	550	400	3,177
Black women	1,321	868	500	300	2,989
Black children	1,106	499	386	292	2,283
Total Blacks	3,849	2,172	1,436	992	8,449

NOTE: My totals for the Nevis slave population differ slightly from those given by Higham, *Leeward Islands*, 145, 148.

enumerates each householder, but generally does not specify how many women, children, and Negroes belong to individual households. The St. Christopher return enumerates all men able to bear arms and gives parish totals for women, children, and slaves. As table 12 shows, English and Irish colonists were separately counted

21. Stapleton sent the census lists home on June 29, 1678; they are filed in C.O. 1/42/193–243. Oliver has printed the Antigua census in his *History of Antigua*, I, *lviii–lxi*, and the returns for the other three islands in his genealogical magazine, *Caribbeana*, II, 68–77 (St. Christopher), II, 347 (Montserrat), and III, 27–35, 70–81 (Nevis).

in all four islands. Unfortunately Stapleton collected no information on landholding.

The figures in table 12 invite comparison with the Barbados totals in tables 4 and 5. With 10,408 white inhabitants, the Leeward Islands contained about half the white population of Barbados. With 8,449 slaves, they held about one quarter of the Barbadian slave force. They shipped 3,600 tons of sugar per annum, according to Stapleton, which was one-third of the tonnage exported from Barbados at this date. Though their sugar industry was growing rapidly, the Leeward planters still lagged well behind their Barbadian rivals.

Among the four islands Nevis—the only one to escape French invasion in 1666–1667—was by every index the most prosperous in 1678. Stapleton conjectured that the Nevis planters' estates were worth something like £384,000, whereas he valued the property on the other three islands collectively at only £196,500. The governor himself resided in Nevis, and he reported that only Nevis had a large enough planter class to staff its Council and Assembly adequately. Nevis boasted four of the ten churches in the Leeward Islands and the only well-built port in Charlestown.[22] Several Nevis planters were truly large entrepreneurs in 1678: Sir James Russell and Col. Randolph Russell each owned over 150 slaves apiece, and the 8 biggest planters owned 802 Negroes. But the Nevis cane growers more characteristically held smaller slave gangs. There were 45 middling planters on the island in 1678, with 20 to 59 slaves; this group owned nearly half the Negroes in Nevis. The great majority of Nevis householders were subsistence farmers with one or two slaves at most, though some of them had white servants, for servants were more prominent here than in Barbados. In social profile, as table 13 shows, the island of Nevis was roughly equivalent to one of the eleven parishes in Barbados. Only one Barbados parish, St. Lucy, had fewer big sugar magnates than Nevis. On the other hand, Nevis had many more small farmers than any Barbados parish.

Everywhere in the Leewards the planter class was still relatively attenuated in 1678. The Nevis councillors averaged 66 slaves each, a large figure until it is set against the Barbados councillors' 190 slaves in 1680. Only six planters in Antigua and about three apiece

22. On Nov. 22, 1676, Stapleton sent a long, informative report to the Lords of Trade on the state of the Leeward Islands. See C.O. 153/2/139–190; his comments on Nevis are on pp. 139, 161–162, 174, 179–180, 187–189.

in Montserrat and St. Christopher (the exact number cannot be determined from the 1678 census) held as many as 60 slaves, as against the 175 Barbadians who operated on this scale. There were plenty of small gentry in the Leewards: perhaps 200 planters in the four islands commanded enough slaves and servants to operate a sugar works. But the vast majority, about 2,500 householders, cultivated tobacco, cotton, indigo, or provision crops. It is interesting to note that many fewer of these small farmers owned Negroes than their counterparts in Barbados. Whereas 82 percent of the Barbados householders were slaveowners in 1680, the figure for Antigua in 1678 is 47 percent, for Nevis 31 percent, and for Montserrat 26 percent.

On St. Christopher in 1678 the English planters were still trying

Table 13. *Social Structure in Nevis and Barbados, 1678–1680*

	Nevis, 1678	St. Thomas Parish, Barbados, 1680
White population	3,521	c.1,500
Big planters (60+ slaves)	8	19
Middling planters (20–59 slaves)	45	14
Small farmers (0–19 slaves)	c.1,000	160
Servants	c. 500	226
Slaves	3,849	3,396

to untangle the mess left from the French conquest of a dozen years before. "The wars here are more destructive then in any other partes of the world," Christopher Jeaffreson remarked in 1677, "as appeares by this island, where the sad workes of the last unhappy difference, in the yeare sixty-six, are not halfe worne out; nor is the island a quarter so well peopled as it then was." Many of the small tobacco farmers never returned, and French squatters who occupied their land were not easily evicted, since all of the old records were lost and it was hard to prove title to fields, servants, and slaves. The St. Christopher census of 1678 confirms Jeaffreson's testimony that the English sector was underpopulated. About a quarter of the land was planted in sugar and indigo, the rest in provisions and pasture, which argues a shortage of slaves and servants. Four of the six English churches on St. Christopher were still dismantled; during the last war the French had carted the stones and timbers to their quarters. The one English fort was described as a pitiful "durt pye." [23]

As for Antigua and Montserrat, only about half the arable land on either island was patented in 1678, and much of this was undeveloped. Most farms were still peasant plots. When Antigua was resettled after the French invasion of 1666, 53 percent of the planters occupied tracts of less than fifty acres. To protect these small farmers the Antigua Assembly put a ceiling of six hundred acres on individual holdings. Government was cheap as well as simple: the annual Antigua tax levy of one pound of sugar per acre yielded a public revenue of about £400 per annum.[24] In Montserrat the most important social fact was that 69 percent of the white inhabitants were Irish, as compared with 26 percent on Antigua, 23 percent on Nevis, and 10 percent on St. Christopher. Despite this superiority in numbers the Irish on Montserrat were still second-class citizens. They were practically all subsistence farmers, and the few big planters on the island were mainly Englishmen.

The Leeward gentry in 1678 was a diverse and transient group of men. A few families like Warner, Jeaffreson, and Williams had come to the Leewards with the very first settlers. A larger number, among them Russell, Pym, Keynall, Winthrop and Baijer, had arrived in the 1640s and 1650s. But most seem to have come within the last decade or so. Symbolic of the new arrivals were William Byam of Surinam, who proceeded (as he phrased it) to hew a new fortune out of the wild woods in Antigua, or Henry Blake from Ireland, who wrote home shortly after his arrival in Montserrat: "I am sorry you have very hard times, there is nothing sweeter than a good plentifull lieving, which, I thanke God, is not wanting unto Your very loveing Brother." [25] The sweetness of Montserrat did not prevent Blake from returning to Ireland once he had made his fortune.

The constant coming and going on all four islands produced

23. Christopher Jeaffreson to George Gamiell, May 12, 1677, Jeaffreson, ed., *Young Squire*, I, 215; Gov. Stapleton to Council for Trade, Jan. 5, 1673/4, C.O. 1/31/7–16; Higham, *Leeward Islands*, 101.

24. Antigua land patents and surveys, 1667–1669, Oliver, *History of Antigua*, III, 285–300; Leeward Islands Entry Book, 1675–1681, C.O. 153/2/165–169, 180; Leeward Islands MSS Laws, 1644–1673, C.O. 154/1/18; Leeward Islands MSS Laws, 1668–1682, C.O. 154/2/311–313, 324–326.

25. William Byam to Sir Charles Pym, Nov. 8, 1668, Historical Manuscripts Commission, *Tenth Report*, Appendix (London, 1887), Pt. VI, 96; Henry Blake to his brother, July 22, 1673, Oliver, ed., *Caribbeana*, I, 51–52.

great discontinuity in political leadership. None of the ten governors who administered Nevis between 1630 and 1657 left families that were still important on the island in 1678. Few of the Nevis and Antigua councillors and assemblymen of the 1660s were still prominent in 1678. In their turn the big planters of Stapleton's day mostly soon melted away. We can tell this best in the case of Antigua, because Richard B. Sheridan has identified the sixty-five chief Antiguan families of the mid-eighteenth century. Only six of the twenty-nine top Antiguans in 1678 left direct descendants among Professor Sheridan's mid-eighteenth-century plantocracy.[26] And the Antiguan sugar planters of 1678, with their few dozen slaves and servants apiece, were paltry men indeed when compared with their eighteenth-century successors who operated great sugar works manned by hundreds of blacks. In short, the Leeward planter class was still in embryo and by no means fully formed in 1678.

§🙰

In the years between 1678 and 1713 the Leeward sugar planters increasingly followed the Barbados pattern. They grew more affluent and more powerful, consolidated their holdings in the four islands, and controlled the local councils and assemblies. White servants and small farmers began to abandon the Leewards, replaced by black slaves. But as the big planters molded their sugar and slave system in the closing decades of the century, they were harrassed by pressures from every side. These were crisis years for the sugar industry in all the English islands, but the Leeward planters had a particularly troublesome time. Sugar prices fell, sugar taxes rose, commission agents' fees and shipping costs climbed, all of which shaved the planters' profit margin; while the slave supply remained uncertain, the home government's new imperial policy intruded into island politics, and the royally appointed governors, backed by squads of soldiers, behaved more authoritatively than ever. Above all, starting in 1689, came twenty-

26. The early Nevis governors are listed in Harlow, *Colonising*, 17. The Nevis and Antigua councillors and assemblymen of the 1660s are listed in *Cal.S.P.Col., 1661–1668*, 646, 700–701. The 65 leading Antiguan families of the mid-18th century are listed by Sheridan, "Rise of a Colonial Gentry," *Econ. Hist. Rev.*, 2d Ser., XIII (1960–1961), 355–357. I have checked these lists against the surnames of planters with 20 or more slaves in the Nevis and Antigua censuses of 1678.

five years of vicious, plundering Anglo-French war that threatened to erase everything that the Leeward planters had accomplished.

In the 1680s there was still international peace, and the planters behaved accordingly. Sir William Stapleton found his four islands almost unmanageable. He could get answers sooner from London than from Montserrat or Antigua, Stapleton complained, unless he made special inspection trips, "and I am no sooner returned hither [to Nevis] especially from Antego, but all is forgott, in particular the due execution of the Acts of Trade, or repairing of Platforms and Forts." Sir William summoned several general assemblies with representatives drawn from all four island legislatures, but these bodies refused to authorize joint-revenue or defense measures and would not even standardize their laws. The only way Stapleton could secure a salary from the Nevis legislature was by threatening to move his headquarters to one of the other islands.[27] The home government generally stationed a warship in the Lesser Antilles and garrisoned St. Christopher with two companies of redcoats, but it could not be persuaded to equip or pay these soldiers properly. Nor would the Leeward planters pay them. As Stapleton well knew, the French colonists had much stronger naval and military support.

The Leeward gentry made fitful gestures in the 1680s toward beefing up the white manpower in their islands. Christopher Jeaffreson negotiated the transportation of two batches of convicts from the London jails to St. Christopher as indentured servants. The first lot of twenty-eight convicts he sent over in 1684 "threw off their cloathes overboard, and came as bare to the island, as if they had no cloathes," so Jeaffreson economized in equipping the second lot of thirty-eight. As these Leeward immigrants were marched from the prison to their ship, manacled together and guarded by thirty men to prevent their running away, "they committed several thefts, snatching away hats, perrewigs, etc., from several persons, whose curiosity led them into the crowd." Jeaffreson thought it wise not to tell prospective buyers in St. Christopher that some of the felons he was sending over were experienced sailors, "for nobody, I suppose, will be desirous to buy a servant

27. Stapleton to Lords of Trade, Aug. 16, 1682, C.O. 153/3/63; Nevis Council and Assembly Minutes, Apr.–July 1682, C.O. 1/48/122–123, 256–258; Leeward Islands General Assembly Minutes, Nov. 1682, Oct. 1683, C.O. 1/50/29–36, C.O. 155/1/25–27.

that has that convenience of freeing himself, by the first boat he can steal." [28]

When Stapleton died James II shook up the Leeward gentry by appointing a belligerent new governor, Sir Nathaniel Johnson (1686–1689). Stapleton had been an entrenched local magnate primarily interested in promoting Leeward interests, but Johnson— like most colonial appointees of James II—was an outsider, a home-bred royal servant (previously a manager of the hearth tax) sent out to enforce the king's orders in America and break down colonial particularism. He exemplified the overbearing executive style of the 1680s, classification *gubernator tyrannus,* and was a fitting colleague for Sir Edmund Andros in New York and New England, Edward Cranfield in New Hampshire, Lord Culpeper and Lord Howard of Effingham in Virginia, Sir Richard Dutton in Barbados, and the duke of Albemarle in Jamaica.

Johnson moved his seat of power from Nevis to Antigua and established a large sugar estate there. But he did not join the Leeward planter class. On the contrary, like Dutton in Barbados and Albemarle in Jamaica, he invited the discontented small farmers to help topple the large landholders from their accustomed council, assembly, and judicial posts. Taxes were increased. Johnson challenged the validity of existing land titles in the Leeward Islands and proposed to issue new patents that required payment of a quit-rent to the king.[29] One might expect the new governor's religion, at least, to earn him popularity with the Leeward gentry, for Stapleton had been an equivocal Catholic and Johnson was an ardent Anglican. But Sir Nathaniel did his best to carry out James II's pro-Catholic, pro-French policy in the Leewards, and this had a particularly demoralizing effect. With so many Irish Catholic servants and farmers in the local population, the English planters became obsessed with fear of popery and fear of French attack. In fascinated horror they watched Johnson invite French Protes-

28. Jeaffreson to Dep. Gov. Hill of St. Christopher, Sept. 8, 1684, Apr. 18, 1685, Apr. 22, 1685, Jeaffreson, ed., *Young Squire,* II, 123–128, 191–200. Just at this time, Barbados and Jamaica received a larger batch of unwilling white servants, some 600 prisoners from Monmouth's Rebellion. See Smith, *Colonists in Bondage,* 188–197.

29. Antigua revenue acts of Dec. 23, 1687, and Feb. 1, 1688/9, Antigua Manuscript Laws, 1684–1693, C.O. 8/2; Dep. Gov. Powell of Antigua to Lords of Trade, c. Feb. 1687/8, C.O. 153/3/288–289; Leeward Atty. Gen. Archibald Hutcheson to Gov. Johnson, Apr. 19, 1688, C.O. 153/3/324–385; Johnson to Lords of Trade, June 2, 1688, C.O. 153/3/328–341.

tants into his government, grant religious liberty to Catholics, and cultivate cordial relations with the French Governor Blenac at Martinique.

By January 1689 word reached America that William of Orange had invaded England. This news was a tocsin to the colonists in Massachusetts, New York, and Maryland, who quickly overthrew their Jacobite governors. But the Leeward planters felt rudderless and abandoned. "We are Screwed and Taxed up to the height and no manner of Care is taken either of our persons or Estates," the deputy governor of St. Christopher lamented. "I am sure their Majesties Revenue in these Islands is very considerable, which makes me admire we are no more regarded." [30] Sir Nathaniel Johnson was certainly the wrong man for his job in 1689, for he was the stoutest Jacobite in America. He told William III in May 1689 that he could not accept the revolution. The following month in St. Christopher 130 armed Irish servants rose up in the name of King James and sacked the English plantations on the windward side, while the English garrison on the island huddled forlornly inside their fort on the leeward side, too feeble to restore order, their pay six years in arrears. In July, as soon as Governor Blenac learned that war had broken out in Europe between Louis XIV and William III, the French invaded the English sector of St. Christopher. Panic spread to the other three English islands when a letter from Blenac to Johnson was intercepted that seemed to prove that Johnson was plotting to betray his government to the enemy. Yet the Leeward colonists were afraid to do anything drastic. After much debate they asked Johnson to resign. Everyone sighed with relief as Johnson mustered his tattered dignity, commissioned Christopher Codrington as governor in his place, and sailed away to South Carolina. Ten days later, in August 1689, the English garrison on St. Christopher surrendered to the French. Such was the Glorious Revolution in the Leeward Islands. [31]

In 1689 English prospects in the Leewards looked bleak, with St. Christopher lost and the Irish ready to mutiny in Montserrat and Antigua. Yet within a year the English mounted a vigorous

---

30. Dep. Gov. Hill to unknown recipient, Aug. 20, 1689, C.O. 153/3/452.

31. Johnson to Lords of Trade, Apr. 20, 1689, July 15, 1689, C.O. 153/4/101–103, 127–147; Dep. Gov. Netheway of Nevis to William III, June 27, 1689, C.O. 153/3/427–431; Gov. Codrington to Lords of Trade, July 31, 1689, Aug. 15, 1689, C.O. 153/4/148–155, 158–170. Johnson took 100 slaves with him when he left Antigua, and he soon became a leading planter in Carolina. He served as governor of South Carolina, 1703–1709.

counteroffensive and generally outfought the French for the balance of King William's War. What made the difference was naval support and fresh troops from home, a regiment from Barbados, and the spirited leadership of a new commander. Christopher Codrington, commander in chief of the Leeward Islands from 1689 to 1698, was a seasoned planter-politician, an imperious leader, and the owner of huge estates in Barbados and Antigua. Codrington was so rich that he could subsidize campaigns out of his own pocket. In 1690 he gathered a force of twenty-five hundred men, invaded St. Christopher, and retook the island in a three-week campaign. The next year, having assembled another army of the same strength, he attempted to conquer Guadeloupe, but was forced to withdraw from what appeared to be a successful assault when his naval support pulled out. In 1693 a similar invasion of Martinique came to nothing. Codrington was furious, for he saw that the English had a matchless opportunity to chase the French out of the Lesser Antilles. But the Leeward gentry did not share his ambition, fearing that the annexation of Guadeloupe and Martinique would hurt their islands.[32]

Though he was about the most effective English commander in the Caribbean in the seventeenth century, Codrington encountered nearly as much opposition from his own adherents as from the enemy. "The trouble my Lords of Governing a volontary Army is Inexpressible," he told the Lords of Trade. After retaking St. Christopher his soldiers wanted to plunder everything, including property belonging to the dispossessed English settlers. The leading planters on Nevis, Montserrat, and Antigua hoped to see St. Christopher permanently laid waste. Codrington, however, proceeded to resettle both the English and French quarters, reserving fifteen thousand acres for small farms of ten acres apiece so as to ensure an adequate militia. Needless to say, he laid out a splendid plantation for himself, manned by the slaves he had appropriated as his personal share in the French plunder. Unfortunately for Codrington the English diplomats at Ryswick in 1697 returned the French part of the island to Louis XIV. In truth the governor had been too grasping and high-handed for his own good. By the time

32. Vincent T. Harlow sketches Codrington's career in a biography of his son, *Christopher Codrington, 1668–1710* (Oxford, 1928), chap. 2. Codrington's Leeward campaigns in King William's War are described briefly by G. H. Guttridge, *The Colonial Policy of William III in America and the West Indies* (London, 1922), 59–68, and at greater length by Crouse, *French Struggle for the West Indies,* chaps. 6–7.

he died in 1698 the home authorities were barraged with complaints that he had bullied the several island governments, cheated numerous aggrieved planters, and clandestinely traded with the Dutch and French during the late hostilities.[33]

Scarcely had the planters weathered King William's War than Queen Anne's War reopened combat in the Leeward zone from 1702 to 1713. The English resumed hostilities energetically. At the outset of this war the Leeward governor was Christopher Codrington the younger (1699–1704), heretofore an elegant Oxford scholar and London socialite, who continued his father's aggressive policy by driving the French off St. Chistopher once more in 1702, this time almost without firing a shot. The following year he invaded Guadeloupe with thirty-five hundred troops and in a two-month campaign inflicted great damage. But the younger Codrington did not really try, as his father had, to conquer Guadeloupe. His chief objective was to ruin the enemy sugar plantations. The French retaliated by sacking St. Christopher and Nevis in 1706, Montserrat and Antigua in 1712. Fighting between the two combatants had become purely negative. Each side freely looted the other, but neither tried for a knockout blow.

The destructiveness of this style of combat may be gauged by the French raid on St. Christopher in February 1706, for which we have exceptionally full evidence. On this occasion a force of two thousand Frenchmen under the comte de Chavagnac landed along the leeward coast of the island, while the outnumbered English hastily holed up inside Fort Charles. Chavagnac had brought no artillery for a siege; he was only interested in plunder. For a week the French troops systematically stripped and burned every plantation beyond range of the English cannon. When his supplies ran low, Chavagnac quickly pulled out his men, so quickly that he left piles of millwork and boiling-house machinery on the shore. The English did not venture to attack the departing Frenchmen. Only a handful of soldiers were killed or wounded òn either side. But the St. Christopher planters had suffered (or so they claimed) £145,000 in damages.[34]

33. Codrington to Lords of Trade, Nov. 8, 1689, Nov. 26, 1690, Sept. 12, 1691, C.O. 153/4/188–200, 286–306, C.O. 153/5/52–59, 79–95; Codrington to Nevis government, Aug. 18, 1690, C.O. 152/37/374–375; Edward Walrond to Board of Trade, May 6, 1698, C.O. 152/2/205–210. Codrington was also accused of keeping a slave seraglio and fathering four or five mulatto bastards. C.O. 152/2/183.

34. The French raid of 1706 on St. Christopher is described by Crouse, *French Struggle for the West Indies*, 296–299, and in contemporary reports by Lt. Gov.

Showing more energy than they had against the enemy, the St. Christopher planters beseeched the home authorities to compensate them for their terrible losses. Some 334 planters, large and small, filed affidavits with the Plantation Office to substantiate their claims, enumerating as precisely as possible every pennyworth of property taken or wrecked by the French. The Nevis planters, who were raided the following month, claimed far greater damages. Unfortunately the individual affidavits for Nevis are now missing, but the St. Christopher compensation claims are a godsend for the social historian. They document the impact of Caribbean warfare more graphically than any other early island records and incidentally disclose something about the life-style of the Leeward planters in 1706. The claims had practical effect as well, for eventually Parliament in 1711 authorized the distribution of £28,000 among the St. Christopher sufferers and £75,000 among the Nevis sufferers.[35]

According to the St. Christopher compensation claims, the French invaders made no distinction between rich and poor settlers; they plundered them all. The range of wealth among the 334 claimants was very great. One merchant, William Clayton, who lost a ship laden with cargo and a shop stocked with goods, and whose two large sugar plantations were badly smashed, claimed £14,216 in damages. Eight colonists claimed losses of more than £3,000; thirty-seven claimed more than £1,000. But 55 percent of the claims were for less than £100, and many of these little claims were put in by people who had lost everything. For example, July Gardner's claim for £26 included the value of his house, furnishings, livestock, provisions, and the crops in his fields. For most claimants the chief losses were burned cane fields, stolen Negroes, and wrecked houses, which they valued higher than their missing livestock and ruined mills, boiling houses, and distilleries. The French had struck St. Christopher just before harvest time, so the planters lost a year's sugar crop, which they priced at £15 per acre of cane. The French

Johnson of the Leeward Islands, Mar. 13, 1705/6; Dep. Gov. Hamilton of St. Christopher, Mar. 15, 1705/6; and Gov. Parke of the Leeward Islands, Oct. 4, 1706, *Cal.S.P.Col., 1706–1708*, #168, #195, #519.

35. The St. Christopher claims are filed in a fat volume in the P.R.O., C.O. 243/2, entitled Account of Losses sustained by the Proprietors and Inhabitants of the Island of St. Christophers . . . when the French Invaded the said Island and the Island of Nevis in the months of February and March 1705 [i.e., 1706]. A second volume of affidavits, C.O. 243/3, duplicates the information in 243/2. Debentures, or receipts, of compensation money paid to 669 claimants from the two islands, mostly in 1712, are filed in C.O. 243/8.

nabbed some six hundred slaves, valued by and large at around £40 each.[36] Few, if any, of the big planters lost all of their slaves. Some Negroes joined their masters in Fort Charles during the raid, and others hid in the mountains. The French set loose whatever livestock they did not eat; consequently many planters found their unburned fields trampled and devoured by rampaging cattle. The houses, mills, and sugar works on the island were mainly wooden and easily burned, but the French took the trouble to cart off such valuable accessories as mill rollers and boiling coppers. A blacksmith named Edward Barry not only lost his house, shop, and tools, but even his anvils and bars of iron. On the other hand, few of the colonists lost much jewelry, silver, or cash, either because they had none or because they hid it in the fort.

The chief planters on St. Christopher were certainly hard hit by the French attack. The ten members of the Council reported a collective loss of £30,000. One councillor, Michael Lambert, seems to have been pretty well wiped out. On his two plantations Lambert lost 53 Negroes, 85 cattle, 17 horses, 252 sheep and goats, 11 dwellings (including the 2 plantation great houses and a town house), a mill, 2 boiling houses, 2 distilleries, 2 storehouses, 73 acres of cane, £126 in household furnishings, and £999 in specie. Joseph Crisp, president of the Council, was almost as unlucky. He lost few Negroes or livestock, but his stylish £1,500 house with a balconied pavilion at one end was burned down, along with 100 acres of cane and a large sugar works. The chief merchants were particularly vulnerable. Samuel Ball and Company lost a shopful of goods valued at £1,650: such items as 22 chamber pots, two dozen punch bowls, 236 packs of superfine cards, two dozen wig combs, and 8 boxes of patches for the St. Christopher ladies. A London mercantile firm, Robert and William Heysham and Partners, lost an extremely diversified stock of goods ranging from boiling-house furnaces, coppers, ladles, and skimmers to chests of soap, coils of cordage, barrels of hoes, trunks of hats, shoes, lace, fans, masks, gloves, 1,000 yards of linen cloth, 1,000 quill pens, nine dozen earthenware porringers, and 88 custard cups.

The humbler settlers suffered less spectacular damage, of course, but it hurt more. Andrew Patrick, a tavern keeper, lost his house worth £29, his tables, benches, barrels, jugs, and bottles worth £13, a pipe of wine and a barrel of rum worth £35, and his most prized

36. For further discussion of these lost slaves, see tables 28 and 29.

possession, "a Billiard Table 12 feet long and 6 wide covered with fine blew cloth and in very good order" which he valued at £50. Rowland Stathem, a struggling farmer who claimed only £12 for his two-room house, set the same value on three acres of cane "which Capt. John Barriau planted on my land and I to have the fifth pound"— a sharecropping arrangement that may have been fairly common between the big and small planters in the English islands. Another struggling farmer, Nathaniel Higbee, reported the loss of three-quarters of an acre of potatoes "diggable" (£2), two acres of cassava "drawable" (£20), and his tobacco crop (£4). And Joan Lawson, a poor laundress, asked £17 in compensation for her one-room house, her cassava patch, and her bed, table, and laundry bench.

Leafing through these homespun affidavits, nearly half of them sworn to by men and women who could not sign their names and had to scratch their marks, we get some feeling of what it was like to inhabit St. Christopher in 1706. Rich and poor alike lived in long narrow bungalows, designed to withstand the hurricanes. A characteristic three-room house was sixty by sixteen feet. President Crisp's £1,500 mansion was ninety by sixteen feet and contained four rooms. This particular structure was built entirely of timber, though many houses had stone walls, especially facing the windward side. Those who could afford it installed porches or shades at both ends of the house for coolness, bricked or tiled their floors, and shingled their roofs. In houses of any pretension the kitchen and pantry were placed in a separate building to remove the chimney heat and cooking smells from the living quarters. Small farmers and servants lived in houses of wild cane and thatch. The slaves were put in flimsy little huts, generally valued at £2 apiece. Many plantations boasted special hurricane houses to hide in when the wind blew strong.

Fifty years earlier the English churches on St. Christopher had been rather elegantly appointed buildings, trimmed with precious woods,[37] but the churches lost in 1706 were modest affairs, valued at no more than £250 each. Perhaps the colonists had grown tired of refurbishing their churches after every war. The French Huguenots on St. Christopher, particularly vulnerable to attack from both combatants, had a little wooden church, only twenty-four by eighteen feet, worth £60. Even the wealthy planters in 1706 displayed

37. Davies, *History of Caribby-Islands*, 23–24, 177.

relatively few amenities. Councillor John Panton was exceptional in filling his four-room house with expensive walnut and cedar chests and tables, a spinet, an elbow chair, a turkey leather couch, a looking glass, and similar embellishments, altogether worth £306. Philip Verchild said his "new Violin cost £3 at New Yorke," and Jedediah Hutchinson reckoned he lost "a Good Cart Load" of books on divinity, history, law, and medicine that he rated at £80. Otherwise almost no books are mentioned. St. Christopher, after all, was most decidedly a frontier outpost in 1706, by no means firmly occupied. The planters still lived in rude simplicity, much as Christopher Jeaffreson had found them in 1676 or even as Sir Henry Colt had found them in 1631.

In 1708, two years after the French raid on St. Christopher, the governor of the Leeward Islands, Daniel Parke, sent home a new census of his four islands. This enumeration, drawn up according to the same principles as Stapleton's census of 1678, shows how greatly the Leeward settlements had changed in thirty years. Table 14 compares the totals for 1678 and 1708. Overall, the white population had shrunk by two thousand during this time span, and the black population had more than trebled, echoing the Barbados pattern of a half century before. Despite the French wars the Leeward planters imported slaves at the rate of one thousand per year between 1698 and 1707—well below the number shipped to Barbados and Jamaica in these years, but more Negroes than the Leeward planters had ever received in the peace years before 1689. The slaves lost to enemy raiders were probably counterbalanced by the slaves acquired during English raids on Guadeloupe, Martinique, and the French quarters of St. Christopher. With this added labor force the Leeward planters were making more sugar. Production doubled during the war years, from something like five thousand tons annually exported on the eve of the Glorious Revolution to ten thousand tons at the Peace of Utrecht.

The relative strength and wealth of the four islands in the Leeward federation also changed considerably between 1678 and 1708. Nevis, the dominant colony in Stapleton's time, was in a bad way thirty years later, having lost half its slave force in the French raid of 1706. In fact, the Nevis planters owned fewer slaves than in

1678. St. Christopher, potentially the best sugar producer among these islands, had suffered even heavier war damage, yet her planters managed to double their slave force despite the war. Montserrat, always the smallest and most backward settlement, had not been raided since 1666 and stood temporarily on a par with Nevis and St. Christopher in 1708. The most dramatic trans-

Table 14. Population Changes in the Leeward Islands, 1678–1708

	1678	1708
White population		
Nevis	3,521	1,104
Antigua	2,308	2,892
St. Christopher	1,897	1,670
Montserrat	2,682	1,545
Totals	10,408	7,311
Black population		
Nevis	3,849	3,676
Antigua	2,172	12,960
St. Christopher	1,436	3,294
Montserrat	992	3,570
Totals	8,449	23,500

NOTE: The totals for 1708 are drawn from *Cal.S.P.Col.*, *1706–1708*, #1383, #1396, and Oliver, *History of Antigua*, I, lxxviii. Slightly different figures are found in C.O. 318/2/7. The returns from the four islands were compiled between Jan. and Mar. 1707/8. The Nevis and St. Christopher returns are more detailed than those for Montserrat and Antigua. The Nevis figure for the white population probably excludes children; if so, the correct total is more like 1,600 than 1,104.

formation took place in Antigua, a very underdeveloped colony in 1678, where the black population had ballooned sixfold in thirty years, and even the white population had risen. Antigua was clearly the leading member of the federation in 1708, accounting for more than 50 percent of the Leeward slave population and sugar output.

The rising strength of the Antiguan planter class can be measured more precisely if we look at the parish of St. Mary, in the southwestern corner of the island, where the ancient vestry records have survived.[38] Parish tax lists for St. Mary, taken in 1688, 1693, 1696, and 1706, show a remarkable turnover in the population of this Antiguan district within a very few years. Three-quarters of the families who lived in St. Mary in 1688 were gone by 1706. More than half of the parish residents in 1706 had arrived since 1693.[39] One might expect the least successful planters to disappear, but this was by no means always the case. Five of the eleven poorest planters in 1706 had been living in St. Mary since 1688, and four of them can be traced back another ten years to Stapleton's census. Robert Tremills, for example, was a permanent loser, without slaves or land in 1688 and still without slaves or land in 1706. Others among the little people in the parish built up their estates. Robert Shears owned no slaves in 1688 and acquired 26 by 1706. Thomas Horsnale was land-poor in 1688, owning 240 acres with only three slaves to work them; by 1706 he had sold three-quarters of his land and acquired another dozen slaves. Hardly anyone stood still. The biggest planters in the parish were especially active in adding to their slave gangs, while buying and selling land. John Frye, for instance, owned 26 Negroes in 1678, 70 in 1688, 72 in 1696, and 103 in 1706.

Overall, the chief point to emerge from study of these St. Mary tax lists is that the largest planters in the parish dramatically enlarged their holdings during the French wars. In 1688 the biggest planter in St. Mary owned 73 slaves; eighteen years later, four planters held over 100 slaves. It should be added, however, that with three of these four chief planters, the estate rather than the owner was taxed in 1706. This means that Col. Henry Pearne, who owned 665 acres and 150 slaves, Major Martin, who owned 531 acres and 114 slaves, and Capt. John Roe, who owned 410 acres and 101 slaves, were absentees.[40] We can tell from their titles that

38. The St. Mary parish vestry book, the oldest church record in Antigua, with entries starting in 1684, was destroyed sometime between 1938 and 1965. Baker, *Guide to Records in the Leeward Islands*, 18. But fortunately the indefatigable genealogist V. L. Oliver transcribed the parish tax levies for 1688, 1693, 1696, 1706, and 1767 from this manuscript and printed them in his *History of Antigua*, III, 394–397.

39. Compare the situation in Andover, Mass., where 31 families originally settled, 1646–1662; 23 of these families were still living in Andover in 1705, and 21 in 1767. An even better index to the stability of this New England community is that 78% of the second generation and 61% of the third generation Andover sons lived all their lives in the village. See Philip J. Greven, Jr., *Four Generations: Population, Land, and Family in Colonial Andover, Massachusetts* (Ithaca, N.Y., 1970), 48, 140, 212, 216.

40. The alternative possibility is that they were recently deceased, but I rule this out because Capt. John Roe (evidently returned to the island) was elected

these three men had held the top posts in their militia regiment. By 1706 in Antigua, as in Barbados a generation earlier, a power vacuum was beginning to develop within the colony's social and political structure.[41] Yet, as table 15 shows, the plantation system

Table 15. *The Rise of the Planter Class in St. Mary Parish, Antigua, 1688–1767*

	1688	*1706*	*1767*
Taxables	53	36	65
Slaveholders	16	30	65
Planters with 20+ slaves	6	16	46
Planters with 100+ slaves	0	4	22
Slaves	332	1,150	5,610
Acreage	5,811	5,660	12,350

in this Antiguan parish was still far from its full evolution. By 1767 every taxpayer in St. Mary was a slave owner; a third of the taxpayers were very large sugar planters; the planters held an average of 86 Negroes each and one slave for every two acres— the Barbados ratio of 1680.

It was this burgeoning Antiguan planter class, still new, lacking its strongest leaders, harrassed by the endless French war, which confronted Gov. Daniel Parke when he arrived in the Leewards in July 1706, a few months after the French raids on St. Christopher and Nevis, a few weeks after the vestrymen of St. Mary had levied the annual parish tax. Parke found his government on the point of dissolution. The planters on Nevis and St. Christopher had just lost four thousand slaves and suffered damages that they estimated at £500,000, and the planters on Montserrat and Antigua were nearly defenseless against similar attacks. They could not depend upon the royal navy for protection against French privateers, let alone French raiding squadrons. The regiment of redcoats stationed in the Leewards was divided into four small garrisons, riddled by disease, low in morale, and short of arms and ammunition. The

from St. Mary to the Antigua Assembly with Col. John Frye in 1710. See *Antigua and the Antiguans* (London, 1844) , II, 339.

41. Only one of the small planters in St. Mary was apparently an absentee in 1706. Former governor Codrington was an absentee of a different sort; he lived in another part of Antigua, but held 544 acres of undeveloped land in St. Mary, with no slaves.

militia was almost worthless, partly because the small planters and servants who constituted the rank and file were less numerous in the Leewards than they used to be, but mostly because the big planter officials refused to fight. At Nevis in 1706 the commanding officers had hastily surrendered unconditionally, handing over two strong forts without a battle, while their Negroes showed far more courage, keeping up a guerrilla war against the enemy. The Antiguans sat smugly on the sidelines, watching the fires of the burning Nevis plantations, which could be seen forty miles away. It was easy to blame the whole disaster on the acting commander of the four islands, Lt. Gov. John Johnson (1704–1706). Shortly after Parke took over the command, Johnson was killed by a St. Christopher councillor named John Pogson, and the local jury found Pogson not guilty. Though the queen ordered him removed from the Council, Pogson was soon triumphantly elected to the St. Christopher Assembly.

So the Leeward Islanders needed a strong leader in 1706—but Col. Daniel Parke was not their man. He was a Virginian, the father-in-law of the diarist William Byrd. Having sat in the Virginia Assembly and Council in the 1690s, he went to England, stood unsuccessfully for Parliament, and joined Marlborough's army, where he served as the general's aide-de-camp. Parke's great break came in 1704, when he carried the news of Marlborough's victory at Blenheim to Queen Anne and was rewarded with a miniature portrait of the queen, a purse of a thousand guineas, and—some months later—appointment as governor general of the Leeward Islands. As soon as he reached his new post Parke began to question whether this governorship was really a reward. "If I have my brains knokt out," he wrote in August 1706, "the Queen must send some other unfortunate Divel here to be roasted in the sun, without the prospect of getting anything." [42]

Governor Parke challenged the Leeward planters head on. He was quite as domineering as his predecessors, Sir William Stapleton, Sir Nathaniel Johnson, and the two Codringtons, and much more bent on extracting money from his post, since he had no private estate on the islands. Parke tried to remodel the Leeward govern-

42. Harlow, *Christopher Codrington*, 187–192. For other views of Parke's governorship, see Ruth Bourne, *Queen Anne's Navy in the West Indies* (New Haven, Conn., 1939), chap. 7, and John Shy, *Toward Lexington: The Role of the British Army in the Coming of the American Revolution* (Princeton, N.J., 1965), 36–44.

ment by doing all legislative business through the General Assembly and ignoring the four local assemblies. He tried to make the colonists provide living quarters for his regiment. He tried to stop the big planters from buying out the small farmers through forced debtor sales.[43] Seeing former governor Codrington (who still lived in Antigua) as his principal adversary, he confiscated Codrington's 763-acre estate on St. Christopher, permitted a privateering henchman to raid Codrington's island of Barbuda, and brought suit to recover the prize money that the Codrington family had accumulated during the French wars. He accused Codrington and the other leading planters of smuggling, while he himself sent privateers under flags of truce to trade in the French islands. His letters home constantly harped on the Leeward planters' sexual depravity and the "slaveish sooty race" of mulattoes they propagated through their "unnaturall and monstrous lusts." The only way he could make the bawdy Antiguans behave, Parke claimed, was by patrolling the streets of St. John at night in order to set a decorous example.[44] But the Leeward people thought he was spying on them, and even Parke's friends conceded that the governor was hardly a model of morality, since he seduced many of the planters' wives and daughters!

Very quickly the Leeward planters tried to rid themselves of Parke. They drew up a long list of vitriolic charges against him and subscribed £5,000 (or so Parke said) to finance the campaign for his recall at Whitehall. Parke was shot at several times in 1708 and 1709, and one night he received a bullet in his arm. The queen ordered him home in February 1710, but he stalled all summer and fall, sending the Board of Trade a stream of paranoid letters reviling his critics. Growing more reckless, he took the Leeward regiment out of the hands of its colonel and used the soldiers to break up a meeting of the Antigua Assembly at bayonet point. The enraged assemblymen raised a band of three hundred armed insurgents, while Parke garrisoned his house in St. John with seventy

43. The Antiguan Assembly had passed legislation authorizing the forced sale of debtors' lands to meet unpaid taxes. Parke claimed that this was a conspiracy of the big planters to grab the lands of poor men ensnared in debts. When debtors' land was auctioned, he says, the big planters refused to bid against each other in order to keep the bids ridiculously low and acquire as much land as possible as cheaply as possible. It would be interesting to know how much truth there was to this charge. See Parke to Board of Trade, Sept. 9, 1710, *Cal.S.P.Col.*, *1710–1711*, #391.

44. Parke's fullest blast is in his long report to the Board of Trade, Sept. 9, 1710. But see also his letters to the Board on Mar. 21 and May 11, 1710, *Cal.S.P.Col.*, *1710–1711*, #161, #228.

soldiers and placed five cannon in the yard. On December 7, 1710, the rebels surrounded Parke's house and demanded that he depart immediately for Nevis. The governor fired a cannon at them, the rebels charged, and in an exchange of pistol shots Parke killed one of the two rebel leaders, but the other felled him with a bullet in the thigh. According to one witness, "they then broke in upon him, tore off his cloaths, dragged him by the members about his house, bruised his head, and broke his back with the butt end of their pieces." Finally they spat in his face as the dying man asked for water. The rebels not only murdered Parke, but killed or wounded forty-four of his seventy guards. They stole all his belongings, including billets-doux from his island lady loves and the miniature of Queen Anne that hung at his breast.[45]

Even by West Indian standards Parke's assassination was an outrageous act. But none of the participants were punished. When the home authorities endeavored to investigate the governor's death, the Antiguans clammed up, refusing to give incriminating testimony against the ringleaders of the attack. It was scarcely feasible to prosecute the entire island population. Ironically, the only man punished in the wake of Parke's murder was his successor, Gov. Walter Douglas. Sent out in 1711 to restore harmony by pardoning all but the chief assassins, Douglas was soon reported to be accepting bribes, selling pardons, and embezzling the Antigua communion plate! He also proved unable to stop French attacks; in 1712 another enemy squadron raided Montserrat and Antigua, carrying off fifteen hundred slaves and much additional loot. So Douglas was recalled in disgrace in 1713, tried, and sentenced to five years in prison.

Clearly Antigua during Queen Anne's War was a hell for governors, but the war finally ended in 1713. The Peace of Utrecht brought real victory to the Leeward planters. Thanks to Marlborough's successes in the main war theater, the English diplomats could refuse to hand back certain wartime conquests, and one of these was St. Christopher. The French ceded their half of the island in 1713, ending eighty years of troubled joint occupancy. The territorial transfer was small but decisive, for it removed the most

---

45. The reports of Lt. Gen. Hamilton, Mr. Mathews, and Councillor Thomas Morris on Parke's murder are in *Cal.S.P. Col., 1710–1711*, #674, #677, #683. Other witnesses (#783) denied that Parke's assailants broke his back or dragged him around naked; they claimed that the governor died because he thrashed around so much while the humane Antiguans were trying to treat his thigh wound—a likely story!

irritating source of Anglo-French friction in the eastern Caribbean. The Caribbean rivalry between the two nations was, of course, by no means ended. The biggest wars in the West Indies still lay ahead.[46] Anyone who climbs Shirley Heights on the south coast of Antigua, surveys the impressive ranges of gun mounts and barracks that the English installed in the 1780s, and then looks out to sea at the sharply etched silhouette of Guadeloupe only forty miles away, will appreciate how the French menace continued to rule the lives of the Leeward planters throughout the eighteenth century. But fighting stopped for a generation after Utrecht, and the planters could concentrate wholeheartedly on making sugar.

In retrospect the most curious fact about the long Anglo-French war from 1689 to 1713 is that it failed to check the growth rate of the English and French sugar industries in the eastern Caribbean. Despite all the raids and plundering, both the English Leeward planters and the French Windward planters prospered during these war years. In the French Windward colonies of Martinique and Guadeloupe, as in the English Leewards, the slave population doubled between 1689 and 1713. French sugar exports rose more slowly during the war years, probably because the English had better control of the sea and were more successful at keeping their commercial lanes open. But the expanding sugar output in Martinique and Guadeloupe more than compensated for the loss of St. Christopher.[47]

In the English islands the war undoubtedly hurt the peasant farmers and benefited the big planters. Enemy raids accelerated the consolidation of small estates into large ones. On St. Christopher, for example, many of the marginal farmers who were wiped out by the French in 1689 or 1706 gave up in discouragement. But the bigger planters had the resources and the confidence to return and rebuild, and they took over the abandoned small farms. In resettling St. Christopher the two Codringtons tried to create a class of soldier-farmers who would take up the poorest land along the seaside in ten-acre parcels, but they found it much easier to distribute the best land in large units among their rich fellow planters. After the Peace of Utrecht the sugar fields in the former French quarters of the is-

46. The classic study of 18th-century Caribbean warfare is Richard Pares, *War and Trade in the West Indies, 1739–1763* (Oxford, 1936) .

47. For estimates of the French Windward slave population and sugar production in these years, see Deerr, *History of Sugar,* I, 193–202, 233–240, II, 279–280, 412; Philip D. Curtin, *The Atlantic Slave Trade: A Census* (Madison, Wis., 1969) , 59, 62, 78.

land were put up for auction to the highest bidders. It was the big planters who bought this land in large lots at prices that no small man could match. Daniel Parke, when he came to the Leewards, characterized Nevis as "a rich little Island, but there are but few people, the Island was devided amongst a few rich men that had a vast number of slaves, and hardly any common people, but a few that lived in the town." [48] He could have said the same of St. Christopher and Antigua.

By 1713 most of the problems that had slowed the evolution of the Leeward planter class in the seventeenth century were resolved. The Leeward planters were no longer small, obscure men, lacking capital and credit, trying to pull themselves up by their own bootstraps. They had the backing of the home government, the services of home merchants, and a powerful lobby at Whitehall. The difficult job of clearing the land was done, and the destructive French raids were over—for a generation at least. The slave traffic from Africa was booming as never before. The four islands were still intensely jealous of each other, and political behavior within each island was still irresponsible, but these things mattered less than they used to, since no one had to organize for war. The annexation of French St. Christopher eased international tension and gave the big planters additional cane fields. The Leeward planters were thus no longer on the tropical firing line. Their frontier days over, they entered into a new era of ease and opulence.

48. Parke to Sec. Hedges, Oct. 4, 1706, *Cal.S.P.Col., 1706–1708,* #519.

5 ❦ Jamaica

Of all the English Caribbean colonies in the seventeenth century, Jamaica was by far the most boisterous and disorderly. It was founded in blood when an undisciplined gang of soldiers seized the island from Spain in 1655, and it quickly became the chief staging ground for buccaneering expeditions against the Spanish Main. Jamaica, with its strategic position in the center of the Caribbean Sea, was a perfect base for strikes against Spanish shipping and raids on Cuba, Hispaniola, and Central America. The buccaneers could sell their loot to the merchants in Port Royal, refit their ships in the magnificent harbor, and find entertainment in the local brothels and taverns. They could, when necessary, hole up along the many miles of empty coast at the western tip of the island. Thanks to the buccaneers, Port Royal became known as the Sodom of the Indies. The Jamaicans never murdered their governor, but they earned a reputation as England's most lawless colonists. The popular image is suggested by a map of the island, published in London in 1677, which shows a pair of duelers shooting each other. By the turn of the century Jamaica had become a bad joke. The most widely read account of the place, Ned Ward's *A Trip to Jamaica*, which ran through seven editions between 1698 and 1700, lampooned the island as "the Dunghill of the Universe," populated exclusively by prostitutes, convicts, and drunks.[1]

But Jamaica also possessed superb agricultural resources. With far more acreage than Barbados and the Leeward Islands, it offered promise to large and small planters alike. Thousands of poor whites

1. James Moxon, *A New Mapp of Jamaica* (London, 1677), Blathwayt Atlas; Edward Ward, *A Trip to Jamaica: With a True Character of the People and Island* (London, 1700), 13, 15–16.

from the Lesser Antilles migrated to Jamaica between 1655 and 1680 and set up ranches, indigo walks, cotton and cocoa plantations. Planters with the money and ambition staked out grandiose tracts in the coastal plains and the rich interior valleys, imported slaves, and built sugar works. At first there was little conflict between these planters and the buccaneers, but by the 1670s it became evident that farming and freebooting were incompatible. Many of the small planters quit their farms and joined the buccaneers. The large planters found that their indentured servants disappeared in the same direction, that slave vessels from Africa and merchant vessels from England hesitated to trade at the island and charged damagingly high freight rates, and that the nearby Spanish colonies refused to engage in peaceful trade—potentially very valuable—because of the activities of the buccaneers. So the sugar planters tried to quash the buccaneers. For twenty years the two factions staged a bitter internecine struggle for control of the island. At last, with the Glorious Revolution, the planters won out, the buccaneers moved elsewhere, and Jamaica settled into the routine of sugar monoculture.

The brawling, disruptive atmosphere of early Jamaica was in a sense deceptive. Port Royal, home of the buccaneers, was at the same time a thriving business center where industrious artisans plied their crafts and shrewd merchants grew rich and lived elegantly. Out in the countryside the planters likewise accomplished much; they chopped through the wilderness to stake out farms and plantations all over the island and got the sugar industry well started. Yet a sizable proportion of this solid work was undone before the end of the century. A very high percentage of the settlers died of malaria and other tropical diseases. Those who survived soon found themselves victimized by the home authorities, especially Charles II and James II, who pursued such a clumsy and foolish policy toward the colony in the 1670s and 1680s that a good many planters quit in disgust.[2] The disastrous earthquake of 1692, combined with the endless French wars, completed the sense of chronic disorder.

By the close of the century, when the buccaneers had left, most of the small planters were gone also. Jamaica, the one English island

2. This is the theme of my essay, "Imperial Pressures on Massachusetts and Jamaica, 1675–1700," in Alison Gilbert Olson and Richard Maxwell Brown, eds., *Anglo-American Political Relations, 1675–1775* (New Brunswick, N.J., 1970), 52–75. I draw upon this essay to some extent in the following pages.

which seemingly offered good prospects to ex-servants and small freeholders, had been taken over entirely by the large planters, who consolidated the arable land into huge plantations manned by armies of slaves. Even these large planters had withdrawn from the island as much as possible, retiring to England as absentee proprietors. Thus the colorful trappings and lurid events of early Jamaican history mask a social development of considerable significance: the emergence, in England's largest Caribbean island, of the sugar and slave system in its starkest and most exploitive form.

§⧉

"This Isle is a marveilous fertil Isle," cried Sir Anthony Shirley, one of the first Englishmen to see Jamaica, in 1597. "We have not found in the Indies a more pleasant and holsome place." [3] Or, he might have added, a place so lightly held by the Spaniards. By the time the English seized the island in 1655, it had been inhabited by Arawak Indians for some 3,000 years and by Spanish colonists for 150 years, but neither the Arawaks nor the Spaniards had made much of a dent upon the place. In 1655 only about fifteen hundred Spaniards, Portuguese Jews, Negroes, and Arawaks lived in widely scattered cattle ranches along the south coast and at the one town, Villa de la Vega. They were too shorthanded to pen their many thousand head of stock, and so let the cattle, horses, and hogs run wild in the broad savannas. The Spanish colonists operated numerous tanneries in Jamaica, and they had some cocoa groves, a few sugar works, and fields of corn, yuca, cotton, and indigo. But there was no hint of wealth or luxury. On the whole the English started de novo in Jamaica. They rejected everything Spanish from the Catholic church to the plaster and tile bungalow houses. "The Spaniard doth call [Jamaica] the Garden of the Indges," said Henry Whistler when he landed with the English army in 1655. "But this I will say, the Gardeners have bin very bad, for heare is very litell more then that which groweth naterallie." [4]

3. "A true relation of the voyage undertaken by Sir Anthony Sherley," in Hakluyt, *Principal Navigations*, VII, 219.
4. "Whistler's Journal," in Firth, ed., *Narrative of Venables*, 169. See also Frank Cundall and J. L. Pietersz, *Jamaica under the Spaniards* (Kingston, 1919); H. P. Jacobs, "The Spanish Period of Jamaican History," *Jam. Hist. Rev.*, III, no. 1 (1957), 79–93; J. L. Pietersz, "Spanish Documents relating to Jamaica," *ibid.*, I (1945–1948), 106–112.

The conquest of this feeble and marginal Spanish possession was by no means Britannia's finest hour. The English attack was sponsored by Lord Protector Cromwell, who launched his so-called Western Design in the Caribbean by sending in 1654 a large military-naval expedition against the Spanish West Indies. Cromwell's design was in part an old-fashioned, Elizabethan-style freebooting search for Spanish gold, in part a Puritan crusade against the bloody papists. A number of prominent Puritans joined the expedition, among them Edward Winslow, the Pilgrim Father. But most of the manpower came from the non-Puritan West Indian settlements. The two commanders, Gen. Robert Venables and Adm. William Penn, assembled some eighty-two hundred men, of whom thirty-five hundred were recruited in England, thirty-five hundred in Barbados, and twelve hundred in the Leeward Islands. In April 1655 this imposing force attempted to conquer Hispaniola, but in three weeks of futile jungle marches and skirmishes the English never came close to taking the Spanish seat of Santo Domingo. Venables laid much of the blame upon his soldiers from Barbados and the Leewards, "the most prophane debauch'd persons that we ever saw, scorners of Religion, and indeed men kept so loose as not to be kept under discipline, and so cowardly as not to be made to fight." However true this may have been, much else was wrong. The leadership of Venables and Penn was wretched, vital supplies from cannon to water bottles were missing, and the exhausted, disheartened army fell prey to malaria, yellow fever, and dysentery.

Forced to withdraw from Hispaniola with a loss of one thousand men, Venables and Penn decided to try their luck at the adjacent island of Jamaica, which they knew to be almost defenseless. Here the English came ashore virtually unopposed on May 10 and occupied the deserted town of Villa de la Vega, called by the English St. Jago de la Vega or Spanish Town. The Spanish governor, incapacitated by smallpox, surrendered tamely to Venables. But many of his countrymen retired to the mountain fastnesses, where they sniped at the English, obtained reinforcements from Mexico, and kept trying for five years to recover Jamaica. The last Spanish forces were finally driven from Ocho Rios in 1660.

For the English soldiers, victory in Jamaica turned out to be worse than defeat in Hispaniola. It is easy to charge these men with cowardice because they took so long to clear out a few hundred Spaniards and with stupidity because they were so slow in planting the land. But the guerrilla tactics employed by the enemy and by the Maroons, or fugitive Spanish Negroes, were far from easy to combat. The soldiers who came from England were not tropical farmers, and it took time to persuade them that they had to plant enough corn and cassava for bread. They had come for plunder, and when they found none, they sacked and burned Villa de la Vega—a silly stunt, since the town then had to be rebuilt. Having killed all the cattle they could catch in the vicinity of Spanish Town, the soldiers were reduced to eating dogs and snakes. As one observer put it, they starved in a cook's shop. Tropical diseases decimated the army. By November 1655, only eight months after operations began, the eighty-two hundred troops were reduced to thirty-seven hundred! By 1660, despite considerable reinforcements, the garrison had dwindled to twenty-two hundred.[5]

Thus the first Englishmen in Jamaica experienced a harsh initiation rite. It is well to remember that over half of them came from Barbados and the Leewards; they were the first contingent of servants and small planters who migrated from the eastern islands to Jamaica looking for a better chance in a bigger island. But though inured to the tropics, they survived no better than the troopers who came straight from England. In 1656 an additional 1,400 small planters and servants followed from Nevis to plant at Morant Bay —and within a few months two-thirds of these people were also dead! It was been estimated that 12,000 Englishmen came to Jamaica in the first six years, yet the population of the colony in 1661 was only 3,470. Given these circumstances, it is easy to see why so many of the soldiers and early settlers turned to buccaneering. Gov. Edward D'Oyley was anxious for all the help he could get in his campaign against the Spaniards, and in 1657 he invited the English buccaneers at Tortuga to transfer their headquarters to Jamaica. Soon thereafter D'Oyley ejected the last Spaniards from Ocho Rios, but the buccaneers remained. By the mid-1660s a freebooting fleet manned by 1,500 men was operating out of the booming new town of Port Royal.

At the Restoration the West India merchants in London persuaded Charles II to retain Jamaica as a royal colony, and the home authorities set about trying to convert the garrisoned outpost they

5. The most detailed and friendly examination of the conquest is S. A. G. Taylor, *The Western Design: An Account of Cromwell's Expedition to the Caribbean* (Kingston, 1965). Some of the chief sources are assembled by Firth, ed., *Narrative of Venables*, esp. *xxx–xxxii*, 30–40, 135–139, 161–166. For additional discussion, see Arthur P. Watts, *Une histoire des colonies anglaise aux Antilles, 1649–1660* (Paris, 1924), chaps. 12–14; Charles M. Andrews, *The Colonial Period of American History* (New Haven, Conn., 1934–1938), III, chap. 1; and Clinton V. Black, *The Story of Jamaica* (London, 1965), chaps. 1–4.

had inherited from Cromwell into a colony of settlement. The man who did most to accomplish this task was Sir Thomas Modyford, royal governor of Jamaica from 1664 to 1671. Modyford was also as responsible as anyone for the colony's peculiar dual development in the late seventeenth century; he simultaneously promoted agricultural settlement and filibustering attacks upon the Spaniards. Sir Thomas had nearly twenty years' experience as a sugar planter on Barbados and fully appreciated the agricultural potential of this far larger island. He urged Charles II to be prodigal in granting the first million acres of Jamaican land and to issue special tax concessions for Jamaican immigrants. In this way he hoped to persuade many of the leading Barbados planters to join him in moving to Jamaica, for Modyford supposed that Barbados's soil was nearly exhausted and that the English sugar industry must soon decline disastrously unless fresh cane fields were opened. To support Modyford's plans the home government agreed to exempt Jamaica from the 4.5 percent duty levied in Barbados and the Leeward Islands and to excuse Jamaican produce temporarily from customs payments in England.

During his seven years in office Modyford issued approximately 1,800 land patents totaling upwards of 300,000 acres—triple the acreage of Barbados. He allowed 30 acres to each planter plus 30 additional acres for each member of his family, each servant, each slave. Thus an immigrant who arrived in Jamaica with a wife and child could expect a 90-acre grant; a big entrepreneur who imported 100 Negroes could claim a 3,000-acre grant. During Modyford's tenure the finest farm land in the parishes of St. Andrew, St. Catherine, St. John, and Clarendon on the south central coast was laid out, much of it in large allotments. Modyford brought a thousand Barbadians (mainly poor whites) with him in 1664, lured substantial new investors from England, and encouraged those planters already on the scene to buy more Negroes and expand their acreage. The governor particularly encouraged his own family. He and his eldest son, Thomas, patented 9,042 acres; Charles, a younger son, patented 6,330 acres; brother James patented 5,846 acres. Sir Thomas claimed in 1670 that he was being overly scrupulous, since he personally owned 400 slaves, which entitled him to 12,000 acres. All in all, the Modyford clan held twenty-two parcels of land in eight parishes.[6]

6. This paragraph is based on a tabulation of Modyford's land grants as recorded in Index to Jamaica Land Patents, 1661–1826, File 1 B/11, Jamaica Archives, Spanish Town. Hereafter cited as Jam. Land Pat.

During Modyford's administration the Jamaican population rose fairly rapidly—though the number of planters was still disconcertingly thin for such a large island. Wives and children began to make an appearance, as the colonists settled into family life. The figures in table 16, though derived from actual head counts, are probably not very accurate, but they show the trend clearly enough. Obviously the key development in these years was a massive importation of black slaves. By 1673 the Jamaica planters held more Negroes than the Leeward planters, despite the extra thousand miles that the slave traders traveled to do business in Jamaica. As elsewhere in the Indies, slaveholding was concentrated in the hands of relatively few big planters. A planter elite began taking

Table 16. Growth of Jamaica's Population, 1661–1673

Year	White Men	White Women	White Children	Negroes	Total
1661	2,458	454	44	514	3,470
1662	2,600	645	408	552	4,205
1670					15,198
1673	4,050	2,006	1,712	9,504	17,272

NOTE: The estimate of 1661 is in *Cal.S.P.Col.*, *1661–1668*, #204; those of 1662, 1670, and 1673 are in *Journals of the House of Assembly of Jamaica, 1663–1826* (Jamaica, 1811–1829), I, app., 20, 28, 40.

shape during Modyford's governorship. According to Sir Thomas's detailed parish-by-parish survey of 1670, some forty-four planters held one thousand or more acres, and sixteen held two thousand or more acres—larger individual holdings than any in the Lesser Antilles.[7]

Sir Thomas Modyford ruled as an independent potentate. He controlled the island revenue, summoned only one Assembly, disregarded instructions from home, and ruled by proclamation. His Council (which included his brother and two sons) met three or four times a year. The chief military and judicial posts were divided among members of his family. Modyford got away with this

7. Modyford's survey of Jamaica landholding, Sept. 23, 1670, is in *Cal.S.P.Col.*, *1669–1674*, #270. Charles A. Lindley, Jamaica, 1660–1678, or the Rise of an Autonomous Society (unpubl. Ph.D. diss., University of Pennsylvania, 1932), gives a detailed account of the island's internal development. See also R. B. LePage, *Jamaican Creole* (London, 1960), chap. 2.

style of rule because the colony was so young and unformed; no later governor managed affairs with half as much freedom. Even Sir Thomas found the buccaneers unmanageable, so he formed a partnership with them. During the war of 1665–1667 against the Dutch and the French, he commissioned buccaneering ships as privateers to raid enemy commerce. In 1666 and again in 1670 he declared private war between Jamaica and Spain to justify open attacks on Spanish commerce. This arrangement was personally advantageous to the governor; he acknowledged receiving £1,000 a year in fees and kickbacks from the buccaneers, so probably he received a good bit more. Between 1665 and 1671 he sent Henry Morgan on a series of spectacular raids. Morgan's men sacked the Spanish cities of Granada in Nicaragua, Puerto Principe in Cuba, Porto Bello in Panama, Maracaibo in Venezuela, and Panama on the Pacific coast. This last was Morgan's pièce de résistance. The buccaneers marched fourteen hundred strong across the jungled Isthmus, plundered and burned the city of Panama, and returned to Port Royal with a reputed £70,000 in loot. Morgan's extravaganza persuaded Charles II that it was time to recall Modyford and suppress the buccaneers.[8]

With Modyford's recall the colony plunged into factional strife: buccaneers versus planters. Sir Thomas Lynch, who administered Jamaica as lieutenant governor from 1671 to 1675, became the spokesman for the planters. A strong-minded and purposeful man, Lynch tried to chase the buccaneers away and to expand the colony's agricultural output. He encouraged settlers to spread into the far reaches of the island and take up land where the buccaneers had been squatting. Of the twelve hundred patents he issued, over half were in the heretofore empty parish of St. Elizabeth, at the southwestern end of the island, and in the unsettled north coast parishes of St. George, St. Mary, St. Ann, and St. James. Lynch was himself one of the leading landholders in Jamaica, with title to six thousand acres, and he showed a special partiality to his fellow big planters by issuing a flock of very large grants. By the time Lynch left office most of the choicest land throughout the island was

8. Modyford's changing policy toward the buccaneers can be traced in his communications home. *Cal.S.P.Col., 1661–1668,* #629–635, 664, 739, 767, 942, 979, 1264, 1383. A contemporary critique of Modyford's policy is found in William Beeston's Journal, in *Interesting Tracts, Relating to the Island of Jamaica* (St. Jago de la Vega, 1800) , 281–287. See also Thornton, *West-India Policy,* chap. 3; and Haring, *Buccaneers in the West Indies.*

staked out—though very little of it was as yet under cultivation. During the 1670s the island population, white and black, continued to climb. Immigration records for a span of nearly eight years from 1671 to 1679 show that 11,816 blacks were landed on the island, for an average of 1,500 per year, and 5,396 whites, or 700 per year. It is interesting to find that a quarter of these new slaves and a third of the white immigrants came from the Lesser Antilles and Surinam, signifying Jamaica's continuing indebtedness to the older sugar colonies. The large block of new arrivals from Surinam was especially welcome because some of these people were big slaveholders. The Surinam settlers were given quarters on the western and northern coasts.[9]

Unfortunately for Lynch the buccaneers turned out to have better connections at Whitehall than the planters. Henry Morgan, temporarily in disgrace for his raid on Panama, was soon knighted by Charles II for his brave feats against the Spaniards and returned to Jamaica in triumph in 1675. The king had chosen a new governor, Lord Vaughan, an inexperienced outsider, to replace Lynch, and Morgan secured appointment as Vaughan's second in command. Lynch was appalled when he heard the news. "Here's non," he tartly told the secretary of state, "ever thought it possible his Majesty should send the Admirall of the Pryvateers to governe this Island." [10] Lord Vaughan soon shared Lynch's sentiments on Morgan. The new governor thought that Sir Henry's open drinking and gaming, his imprudence and passion, were unbecoming in a public officer. In general Vaughan disliked the raw and unruly atmosphere of Jamaica. The chief planters rode up to greet him in their resplendent coaches drawn by fine horses, but Vaughan could see that only six of the fifteen parishes were equipped with churches and only four were supplied with clergymen, one of whom doubled as the sole schoolmaster on the island. In Vaughan's eyes the colonists were hopelessly obstinate, illiterate, and factious, a compound of unreconstructed Cromwellians, rebellious servants, and convicts "who chose transporting rather than hanging and Jamaica rather than Tyborn." The buccaneers, he complained, connived with the Port Royal merchants, and the planters connived with interloping slave ships in defiance of the Royal African Company monopoly.

9. Lynch's land policy can be traced via the Jam. Land Pat. The immigration statistics, June 25, 1671–Mar. 25, 1679, are in C.O. 1/43/59. The Surinam immigrants are discussed in C.O. 1/35/101–102, 178–185.

10. Lynch to Sec. Arlington, Sept. 23, 1674, Coventry Papers, LXXIV, 19.

The only way he could keep order was "to imploy such of the town [Port Royal] (as were rather inclined to privateering) against Interlopers, and those again of the Country [sugar planters] against the Privateers." [11]

Planters and buccaneers alike saw Governor Vaughan as an intruder. The chief sugar planters took charge of the Jamaica Assembly, and this body, so quiescent under Modyford, began claiming all the legislative and taxing powers enjoyed by the House of Commons at home. The Assembly challenged Vaughan's control over taxation, with the consequence that "my lord and the island were a year without revenue." The Assembly authorized the importation of Negroes from interloping slave ships, launched impeachment proceedings against unpopular crown officials, revised the whole body of colony laws every session, sent home copies of these laws only after they had expired, and ignored all commands from the king. Naturally this behavior vexed the home authorities. In the late 1670s the king's newly created colonial council, the Lords of Trade, concluded that something must be done about the Jamaica Assembly, for the independence of this body bolstered the colonists' roisterous and lawless behavior. "In plain terms," Secretary of State Coventry said, "the King intendeth to make a Plantation of Jamaica and not a Christian Algiers." [12] Therefore the Lords of Trade appointed another governor, the earl of Carlisle, and armed him with a new body of forty permanent laws prepared by the Plantation Office, including a perpetual revenue act. Once Carlisle got the Jamaica Assembly to ratify these laws, he and his successors would need to call few if any further assemblies.

The Jamaicans were not so easily cowed. When Carlisle presented his body of laws in 1678 the Assembly voted down every single one, reserving its sharpest denunciations for the perpetual revenue act. Big sugar planters like Samuel Long and William Beeston led the attack, eloquently insisting that Jamaicans would never surrender their liberties as Englishmen. Long and Beeston protested with special vehemence when they found that Carlisle had allied himself with Sir Henry Morgan and the buccaneering

11. Vaughan to Sec. Coventry, May 28, 1677, *ibid.*, LXX, 181; Lynch's report on the church, 1675, C.O. 1/36/17. Ralph Nevil's "Present State of Jamaica," *Interesting Tracts, Relating to Jamaica,* 105–112, is a contemporary critique of Vaughan's administration.
12. Coventry to Vaughan, June 8, 1676, Add. MSS 25120/74. For a fuller discussion of this constitutional struggle, see Whitson, *Constitutional Development of Jamaica,* chaps. 3–5; and Thornton, *West-India Policy,* chap. 5.

faction. Carlisle soon gave up and returned to England.[13] The Lords
of Trade were furious, but they saw that they had to have some
support from within the island. So in 1681 they reappointed Sir
Thomas Lynch to the governorship and instructed him to press for
a settled revenue. "Arguing with Assemblys is like philosophising
with a Mule," Lynch complained, but in 1683 he wheedled the Assembly into passing a twenty-one-year revenue act that guaranteed
fiscal independence to the royal governor. This measure was bitterly opposed, according to Lynch, by "that little drunken silly
party of Sir H Morgan's." Lynch and his fellow planters had surrendered much of their old independence, but temporarily at least
they had bested the buccaneers.[14]

Unfortunately for the planters Lynch died in 1684. It was a sad
loss, for creative politicians were scarce in seventeenth-century Jamaica. Like Sir Thomas Modyford (who had died five years before), Lynch was an architect of the rising planter class, and in addition he had started to civilize the Jamaicans. Even today, a visitor
who inspects the old tombstones in the unkempt churchyard of the
cathedral at Spanish Town can sense the difference in style between
these two proud founding fathers. Among the weeds on one side of
the church lies Modyford's monument, the epitaph suitably flam-
boyant:

MISTAKE NOT READER, FOR HERE LYES NOT ONELY THE DECEASED BODY
OF THE HONORABLE SIR THOMAS MODYFORD BARRONETT, BUT EVEN THE
SOULE AND LIFE OF ALL JAMAICA, WHO FIRST MADE IT WHAT IT NOW
IS. HERE LYES THE BEST AND LONGEST GOVERNOUR, THE MOST CONSIDER-
ABLE PLANTER, THE ABLEST AND MOST UPRIGHT JUDGE THIS ISLAND
EVER INJOYED.

And on the other side of the church reposes Lynch's tomb, his
epitaph a model of economy:

    HERE LYES SIR THOMAS LYNCH
       IN PEACE AT EASE AND BLEST.
    WOULD YOU KNOW MORE
       THE WORLD WILL SPEAK THE REST.[15]

13. A Breviate of what passed in the Assembly called by his Excellency Charles
Earl of Carlisle, Governor of Jamaica, . . . September 2, 1678, Egerton MSS,
2395/576–583.

14. Lynch to William Blathwayt, June 12, 1682, Blathwayt Papers, XXIII;
Lynch to the Lords of Trade, Nov. 2, 1683, C.O. 138/4/181.

15. J. H. Lawrence-Archer, *Monumental Inscriptions of the British West
Indies* (London, 1875), 58, 60.

With Modyford and Lynch both gone, the Jamaica planters felt leaderless and abused by the home government. The new governor, Hender Molesworth (1684–1687), was another big planter who owned 7,500 acres and worked ten farms, including two sugar plantations. But more to the point, he was the island agent for the Royal African Company, which manipulated Jamaica's supply of slaves. The planters did not appreciate Governor Molesworth's efforts to stop interlopers from importing Negroes in violation of his company's monopoly, and it was useless to complain to Whitehall, because James II, after he came to the throne in 1685, continued as the chief stockholder and president of the Royal African Company. In 1685 Parliament doubled the sugar duty, which drastically cut the planters' profits.[16] Two years later the king challenged the Jamaica planters head on when he replaced Molesworth as governor with Christopher Monck, second duke of Albemarle. James knew that Albemarle was a profligate and irresponsible man who had squandered his fortune in England; he sent him to Jamaica to get rid of him. The duke, for his part, was eager to go because he had an interest in Caribbean treasure hunting. He had recently struck it rich when a ship under his sponsorship salvaged twenty-six tons of silver from a sunken Spanish galleon off the coast of Hispaniola. From an investment of £800 he netted £50,000 and he was looking for another bonanza. Albemarle's appointment thus marked a return to the old freebooting spirit.[17]

Albemarle was a domineering and reckless executive, the counterpart of Sir Nathaniel Johnson in the Leeward Islands and Sir Richard Dutton in Barbados. He proved to be a sort of tory democrat, who challenged the oligarchic power of the local plantocracy and mustered his chief support from the Irish Catholic small planters and servants and the remnants of the buccaneering faction that had lost power a decade before. Albemarle turned out of office the big sugar planters who had held all the chief posts under Lynch and Molesworth. Finding that the big planters also controlled the legis-

16. The voluminous papers of the Royal African Company in the P.R.O. include copies of letters sent to agent Molesworth and abstracts of his replies. Treasury Series, Class 70, Vols. 57, 12. Hereafter cited as T. 70/57, T. 70/12. See K. G. Davis, *Royal African Company*, chap. 7. For the sugar duty of 1685, see Beer, *Old Colonial System*, I, 160–166. Jamaica's reaction to the new tax is in C.O. 138/5/97–105.

17. The negotiations over Albemarle's appointment are in C.O. 138/5/220–335. The Hispaniola treasure salvage is discussed by Sloane, *Voyage*, 1, *lxxix–lxxx*. For background see Estelle Frances Ward, *Christopher Monck, Duke of Albemarle* (London, 1915), 234–270.

lature, Albemarle used an armed gang to secure the election of his own supporters to a new Assembly.[18] As in Barbados, the island gentry began retiring en masse to England in disgust. The buccaneers were naturally pleased to join Albemarle in treasure hunts. Sir Henry Morgan, a prematurely old man, sallow and pot-bellied, became the duke's boon companion. Another confidant was Dr. Thomas Churchill, a Catholic priest who had the ear of the king. Albemarle protected and encouraged Father Churchill and sent him back to England as the colony agent. A rumor spread that the duke was going to demand £50,000 via a poll tax.[19] The disorder and fear rising from Jamaica's political, religious, and social factionalism was papered over in the toadying letters and groveling addresses that the colonists sent to Whitehall. Each notable English event, the king's accession, Monmouth's defeat, the queen's pregnancy, was received with mounting spasms of rapture. When the fateful news arrived in September 1688 that the queen had given birth to a son, Albemarle toasted the infant Prince of Wales so immoderately that he plunged into a fit of jaundice and shortly died.[20]

Soon after Albemarle's demise, during the winter of 1688–1689, rumors filtered into America that William of Orange had invaded England. To the Jamaicans, as to the other sugar islanders, this news was more alarming than stimulating. A revolution at home meant that much of their food, all of their Negro manpower, and all of their manufactured consumer goods might be cut off. In actual fact the revolution proved to be quick and bloodless, but it precipitated a war between William III and Louis XIV—as unwelcome in Jamaica as in the Leeward Islands. Many of the Jamaican buccaneers had transferred to French St. Domingue, from where they could easily strike at their old base, knowing that the Jamaican fortifications were in poor shape. Jamaica's indentured servants, who constituted the island militia such as it was, were few in number and entirely untrustworthy, being mainly Irish Catholic and pro-French. The Negro slaves were even less reliable; the island had seen three major slave revolts between 1675 and 1686. Politically Albemarle's death left the colony torn as usual between two factions, the pro-Albemarle buccaneers and small planters and the anti-

18. Irregularities in the Assembly election of July 1688 are reported in C.O. 1/65/75–90 (Clarendon parish) and C.O. 137/2/142 (Port Royal).

19. Ward, *Duke of Albemarle*, 304, 327–328; C.O. 138/5/334–335; C.O. 138/6/119–120; C.O. 140/4/226–228; *Interesting Tracts, Relating to Jamaica*, 214-215.

20. Sloane's medical report on the duke's fatal drinking bout is in Sloane MSS, 3984/283–284. Sir Henry Morgan had died a few months before.

Albemarle big planters, both now totally bereft of leadership. The duke's supporters kept control of the government, and as tension mounted in the spring of 1689 they ruled by martial law. Everyone waited nervously for orders from England.

Jamaica was close to paralysis in 1689—yet in retrospect the Glorious Revolution marked a decisive turning point in the history of the colony. It signalized the defeat of Stuart autocracy in Jamaica, final repudiation of the buccaneering interest and the small farmers' interest, and victory for the sugar planters. During the revolutionary crisis of 1688–1689 the big Jamaica planters who had fled to England during Albemarle's regime formed a powerful and effective lobby in London. As many as sixty Jamaica merchants and planters could be mustered to sign petitions charging that the duke had subverted the Jamaican constitution. Their essential complaint was that substantial officeholders had been supplanted by "needy and mechanick men such as tapsters, barbers and the like." Both James II and William III needed the Jamaica customs revenue. Accordingly one of James's last orders in November 1688 was that Jamaica be restored to the condition she was in at the duke of Albemarle's arrival. In February 1689 William III confirmed this directive, permitting Albemarle's enemies to reoccupy their former posts in the island. The buccaneers, finally and emphatically excluded from power in Jamaica, moved north to St. Domingue and the Bahamas. The big planters, who wanted and needed a close union with the mother country, henceforth maintained generally cordial relations with the crown. In the 1680s they had felt victimized by Charles II and James II, as they saw all the Caribbean profits and power going to the king and his court friends. The revolutionary settlement restored most of their local control, improved their supply of slaves, their military support, and their protection against foreign competition.[21]

Throughout the long years of Anglo-French war in the Caribbean, from 1689 to 1713, the crown took pains to appease the Jamaica sugar planters. When William III's first choice as governor of Jamaica, Lord Inchiquin, failed to please them, the king gave the post to one of the chief lobbyists, Sir William Beeston, a very big absentee planter who had often served as the colony's agent at

21. The activities of the Jamaica lobby can be followed in C.O. 138/6/144–165, 210–226; C.O. 140/4/261–262, 268, 273–275; *Jours. of Jam. Assembly*, I, 134–136. For background, see L. M. Penson, *The Colonial Agents of the British West Indies* (London, 1924).

Whitehall. Back in the 1670s, when Charles II had tried to remodel the Jamaica Assembly, Beeston had been an Assembly leader and a vigorous spokesman for local self-determination. Now, backed up by his absentee colleagues in London, Beeston epitomized the return of big-planter home rule in the English West Indies. During the decade of his governorship, from 1692 to 1702, Sir William steered Jamaica through a traumatic period. Shortly before his arrival, the earthquake of 1692 did terrible damage throughout the island and wiped out Port Royal. A malaria epidemic as severe as the one of 1655 to 1661 decimated the population. French marauders continually raided the coastline. In 1694 a large French expedition of three thousand men invaded Jamaica and except for Beeston's energetic defense might have captured it. The French laid waste the eastern parishes of St. Thomas and St. David, burned fifty sugar works, and took sixteen hundred slaves, but the English— who could muster only two thousand militiamen—repulsed their efforts to penetrate the richest planting district along the south central coast. The Jamaicans did not win a military victory in 1694, but they certainly resisted the French more stoutly than their countrymen in the Leeward Islands.[22] The home government, answering Beeston's cry for help, dispatched a thousand soldiers to Jamaica at a cost of £50,000. In 1695 a joint English-Spanish expedition invaded St. Domingue, ransacked the towns of Cap François and Port de Paix, and made off with six hundred French slaves—approximate retaliation for the damage done to Jamaica the year before.[23]

Throughout Queen Anne's War the home government stationed a regiment of troops in Jamaica and put military officers in charge of the place. Thomas Handasyd, an army brigadier, was the governor from 1702 to 1711, followed by Lord Archibald Hamilton, a naval captain. Jamaica was once again a garrison colony, as in Cromwell's day, and once again the soldiers quickly fell victim to malaria and died. Ironically, the French left Jamaica alone during this phase of the fighting and concentrated their military efforts in the eastern Caribbean. Thus the Jamaicans suffered less damage from enemy raids than the Leeward planters. Jamaican commerce

22. Beeston described the French attack in letters of June 23, and Aug. 7, 1694, C.O. 138/7/192–196, 402–404; Maj. Richard Lloyd later wrote a detailed, carping critique of Beeston's management of the crisis in An Account of the Invasion of the Island of Jamaica by the French in the Year 1694, C.O. 137/4/324–355.

23. The preparations for the 1695 English counterattack are detailed in C.O. 138/7/197–401. For the French perspective see Crouse, *French Struggle for the West Indies*, chap. 7.

was, however, badly disrupted throughout the long French wars. Since the island lies so deeply within the Caribbean, merchant ships sailing to England or North America had to take the leeward passage west of Cuba to the Florida Channel or take the windward passage between Cuba and St. Domingue through the Bahamas— in either case they were attacked by enemy privateers. During the war Jamaican freight and insurance rates rose exorbitantly, and sugar shipments remained below the Barbados or Leeward Islands level.

The worst effect of the war was demographic. The white population in Jamaica, which had never been large, fell from about ten thousand in 1689 to seven thousand a decade later and made no recovery by 1713, despite the influx of thousands of soldiers and sailors from England. Indeed, the arrival of these unseasoned troops made matters worse, for they became chronically sick and spread their diseases into the civilian population. In essence this population loss pretty well wiped out the small planter class in Jamaica. The ranchers and cotton planters and provision farmers who died in the 1690s and 1700s were not replaced. Their lands were taken over by neighbor planters who expanded their holdings. Thus the process that occurred in Barbados at mid-century repeated itself in Jamaica at the close of the century; all the best land was consolidated into a few large plantations. In Jamaica, of course, the plantations were much larger than in Barbados. Governor Beeston and his successors issued few additional land patents. A million acres, including the choicest tracts on the island, had already been distributed before the Glorious Revolution, and the task of the planters in the next generation was to get this acreage into full production.

By the turn of the century the servant population in Jamaica had also about disappeared. English servants had come to Jamaica in fairly sizable numbers from the 1660s through the 1680s, but they now stopped coming almost altogether. A list of 1,438 servants who sailed from Liverpool to America between 1697 and 1707 indicates that only 41 were headed for Barbados and the Leeward Islands, and none at all for Jamaica.[24] But as the white servants fell away,

24. The Liverpool list is printed in *New England Historical and Genealogical Register*, LXIV–LXV (1910–1911), *passim*. It is very carelessly recorded and not susceptible to precise tabulation, but the slackness of the servant trade to the islands is unmistakable. According to my calculations, 665 Liverpool servants were bound for Virginia or Maryland, 76 for the other mainland colonies, 26 for Barbados, 15 for the Leeward Islands, 7 for "the West Indies," and 649 had no recorded destination.

black slaves arrived in record numbers. After the home government abolished the Royal African Company monopoly in 1698 and opened the African trade to private slavers, blacks were shipped to Jamaica at the rate of 4,500 per year, as compared with 1,500 per year in the 1670s and 2,000 in the 1680s. Between 1689 and 1713 the island's slave population nearly doubled, from about 30,000 to 55,000. By 1713 Jamaica had a larger slave population than Barbados and a far higher ratio of blacks to whites. In Jamaica the slaves outnumbered their masters by eight to one, as against the Barbados and Leeward Island ratio of three to one. The large block of poor whites to be found in all of the eastern Caribbean colonies was missing; in Jamaica a small cadre of white masters was nakedly pitted against their black slaves.

Thus when the Peace of Utrecht closed the French wars, Jamaica emerged at last as a classically proportioned sugar society, totally dominated by the big planters. In the stormy years from 1655 to 1713 these planters had won their contest with the buccaneers, and they had worked out a satisfactory union with the mother country. The peace settlement opened up the lucrative asiento trade with the Spanish colonies, managed by merchants in the rising new port of Kingston, while the planters built up sugar production far beyond the peak seventeenth-century Barbadian volume. Jamaica had finally fulfilled its original promise and was at last England's premier Caribbean colony.

§◆

Pioneer life in seventeenth-century Jamaica was, as we have seen, a harsh winnowing process that separated out the great majority of the early English colonists. The domestication of this island turned out to be a greater challenge than the eastern islands, for Jamaica was wilder, more ruggedly mountainous, more thickly jungled, in every way harder to tame. Like the Spaniards before them, the English learned that it was no easy thing to cultivate this "garden of the Indies," and the first settlers only started the job. Yet, of course, the island had far greater agrarian potential than Barbados or the Leewards. The planters who stuck it out, through luck or skill or strength, founded the greatest sugar fortunes in the English Caribbean. They built a network of plantations that returned good profits in the late seventeenth century and spectacular profits by the mid-eighteenth century, when production reached full swing. Why did these happy few succeed where so many failed? The Jamaican genealogists like to suppose that the founders of the island plantocracy were leaders by birth, sons of English gentry and merchants who had status and connections at home. Others contend that they were people of obscure origins, "a fortunate riff-raff" who scrabbled their way to success in Jamaica.[25] This polemical dispute can perhaps never be resolved, but there is no doubt that a Darwinian struggle took place in early Jamaica and that only the strongest survived.

The Jamaica Archives and the Island Record Office, both in Spanish Town, contain many volumes of patents, plat books, wills, deeds, inventories, and parish registers for the seventeenth century —a huge store of information on early planter life that is unmatched in the other islands. Of special interest for our purposes are the land patents and the inventories of probated estates. The file of land records starts in 1661 and includes some five thousand patents for the seventeenth century alone, all carefully indexed. It is apparently a complete record, from 1661 onward, telling who obtained the original grant for every piece of land in the island. The file of inventories starts in 1674 and includes appraisals of the property held by some eight hundred colonists who died in the late seventeenth century. This file is obviously not complete, but it is of great interest, for the appraisers itemized and valued the belongings of planters, rich and poor, from every parish.[26] Collectively the seventeenth-century land patents and plantation inventories, when supplemented by data from early maps of the island, parish surveys, and export statistics, provide us with a composite portrait of the Jamaican plantation system in its infancy.

The most obvious difference between planting in Jamaica and the eastern islands was the grand scale on which land was dis-

25. W. A. Fuertado, *Official and Other Personages of Jamaica, 1655–1790* (Kingston, 1896), does his best to ennoble the planters. Orlando Patterson, *The Sociology of Slavery: An Analysis of the Origins, Development and Structure of Negro Slave Society in Jamaica* (Rutherford, N.J., 1969), chap. 1, does his best to denigrate them. Patterson's acid exposé of early Jamaica is a healthy corrective to previous writings on the subject, but it is laced with distortions. The two best accounts of pioneer farming on this island are by Craton and Walvin, *A Jamaican Plantation*, chaps. 1–3, and J. Harry Bennett, "Cary Helyar, Merchant and Planter of Seventeenth-Century Jamaica," *Wm. and Mary Qtly.*, 3d Ser., XXI (1964), 53–76.

26. The Index to Patents, 1661–1826 (cited as Jam. Land Pat.) and the 13 volumes of 17th-century land patents, 1662–1704, are in the Jam. Archives. The Jamaica Inventories of Probated Estates, File 1 B/11, Jam. Archives, are discussed more fully in chap. 8. They are hereafter cited as Jam. Inv.

tributed. Each new settler was encouraged to patent as much land as he could conceivably work. After paying a small fee to the land office, he held this acreage in free tenure forever, subject only to a nominal annual quitrent, which was rarely collected in the early days. By 1683, according to Governor Lynch, 3,000 patents had been issued for 1,080,000 acres.[27] This means that the average individual tract was 360 acres, the size of the largest plantations in Barbados or Nevis. During the course of the century 88 Jamaicans patented 2,000 or more acres apiece. Actually the truly land-hungry planters built up much larger allotments than the patent books show, because they bought, sold, and exchanged their lands among themselves at a dizzy rate. Lynch himself, for instance, took out 10 patents for 6,040 acres, but in addition he bought 26,744 acres from other landholders and sold 11,346 acres, so that he ended with 21,438 acres, acquired in 59 separate transactions between 1662 and 1684.[28]

It must be emphasized that very little of this acreage, so freely bandied about, was put under cultivation in the seventeenth century. The most fertile land in Jamaica was heavily forested, generally speaking, and it took the colonists many long years to clear and plant these woodlands. For example, a planter named Francis Price, the founder of one of Jamaica's premier sugar fortunes, patented 3,784 acres in three parishes between 1664 and 1676 and bought another thousand acres in addition. Price may have recognized that the richest land he selected was in Lluidas Vale, future seat of the great Worthy Park sugar plantation, but he did not attempt to grow cane at Worthy Park. Instead he kept a cattle pen in this remote and inaccessible tract and put all of his efforts into building a sugar plantation closer to the coast on 450 acres in Guanaboa Vale.[29]

Initially planters like Francis Price had few servants or slaves to help work their land. In 1662 the Jamaicans collectively owned only 552 slaves, which helps explain why, seven years after the con-

---

27. Lynch to William Blathwayt, Aug. 14, 1683, Blathwayt Papers, XXIV.

28. Oliver untangles Sir Thomas Lynch's real estate transactions in *Caribbeana*, II, 145–151. Lynch himself remarked to William Blathwayt, Apr. 15, 1683, that he owned 20,000 acres in Jamaica. Blathwayt Papers, XXIV.

29. For fuller discussion of Francis Price and the founding of Worthy Park, see Craton and Walvin, *A Jamaican Plantation*, chap. 2. Charles Bochart and Humphrey Knollis's "A New and Exact Mapp of the Island of Jamaica," in *The Laws of Jamaica* (London, 1684), shows Price's sugar plantation at Guanaboa and his cattle pen at Worthy Park. See fig. 6, p. 173.

quest, they had a meager 2,917 acres under cultivation.[30] Most of the first comers had scant capital as well as scant labor, and they farmed accordingly. Some of them set up as ranchers; they rounded up the remnants of the Spanish livestock herds, built cattle pens and hog crawls in the coastal grasslands, sold the meat locally and exported the hides to England. Others planted provision crops such as peas, cassava, plantains, and yams amongst the stumps in their half-cleared fields and cash crops such as ginger, pimento, cotton, and tobacco for export. Indigo was another relatively easy, foolproof commodity that fetched a good price. The indigo farmer needed few laborers to help him crop his dye plants four times a year, soak and beat the stalks to extract the dye, and dry it into shiny blue gummy cakes. By the 1680s indigo was mainly cultivated in two pockets on the south coast: at Yallahs in St. David parish and along the Rio Minho in Vere parish.

Cocoa production offered alluring prospects to the first English planters, particularly since they could take over the existing Spanish cacao groves. But it required a considerable investment of labor, capital, and time to start a new cacao walk. According to Governor Modyford a planter needed sixteen slaves and four servants, working for two years, to plant twenty-one acres of cacao trees. The cost of this was £457, and his trees would not produce their first cacao beans, from which chocolate was extracted, for five years. Once the trees started to bear, however, the planter could expect an annual return of £840—or so Modyford claimed.[31] Actually, a blight in 1670–1671 killed the cacao groves in the south central parishes of St. John, St. Catherine, and Clarendon, and after that the only remaining cacao walks were on the north coast.

So sugarcane remained the most alluring crop of all—but of course a sugar works required considerably more capital and labor than a cacao walk or an indigo works. One can trace through the island records the cases of numerous Jamaica planters who built themselves up to sugar by stages. They started out with provision crops, indigo or ginger, bought a slave or two and cleared an acre or two every year, and when they had assembled a work force of twenty or thirty blacks, converted their fields to cane. In the 1660s

30. Condition of Jamaica, Oct. 28, 1662, *Jours. of Jam. Assembly,* I, app., 20.
31. Richard Blome, *A Description of the Island of Jamaica; With the other Isles and Territories in America, to which the English are related* (London, 1672), 16–21. In 1682 Gov. Lynch urged Aud. Gen. Blathwayt to invest his Jamaican salary of £150 in a cacao walk: "Possibly 4 yeares salary might make yu £500 or more per annum." Blathwayt Papers, XXIII.

Jamaica sugar exports trailed well behind cocoa and indigo in value, but by the 1680s sugar had become the leading island export.

Two early maps of the island document this trend toward large-scale sugar production very plainly. In 1671, at the close of Sir Thomas Modyford's governorship, John Ogilby published a map that identifies 146 plantations by name of owner and principal

Table 17. Jamaican Agriculture in 1671 and 1684

	1671	*1684*
Sugar plantations	57	246
Sugar exports (hhds.)	*c.* 1,000	*c.* 10,000
Cacao plantations	42	32
Cocoa exports (hhds.)	*c.* 20	?
Indigo plantations	19	40
Indigo exports (hhds.)	*c.* 60	*c.* 100
Cotton, provision farms	28	299
Cotton exports (bags)	*c.* 25	1,367
Cattle ranches	?	73
Hides exported	3,230	10,531
Total plantations	146	690
Total planters	115	467
Planters owning 3+ plantations	4	47
Planters owning 6+ plantations	0	10

NOTE: These figures are from John Ogilby, "Jamaicae Descriptio," in Ogilby's *America: being the Latest, and Most Accurate Description of the New World* (London, 1671); Bochart and Knollis, "A New and Exact Mapp of the Island of Jamaica"; and Jamaican trade statistics, Mar. 1680–Dec. 1704, C.O. 390/6/31–38.

crop. Ogilby based his map upon a parish-by-parish survey of the island landholders, which Modyford had taken the year before. In 1684, under the sponsorship of Governor Lynch, Charles Bochart and Humphrey Knollis issued a much larger, exceptionally detailed map that similarly identifies 690 plantations by name and crop. Examination of these two maps, correlated with the colony's export statistics for 1671 and 1684, yields the figures shown in table 17.

Obviously during this thirteen-year span the Jamaica planters expanded their operations in every respect save cocoa production, which declined because the established cacao walks were blighted. The cotton and provision farms that mushroomed along the western and northern coasts during Lynch's administration were small affairs, worked by a handful of slaves apiece, but the new sugar plantations that appeared in every parish except St. George were large and expensive units. Between 1671 and 1684 the Jamaicans imported slaves at the rate of fifteen hundred per year, and it was the sugar planters who snapped up most of these new laborers. Through the Ogilby and Bochart-Knollis maps one can trace forty planters (including a number of the colony leaders) who raised indigo, cacao, or provisions in 1671, but switched to sugar by 1684 as they acquired enough manpower. Only two planters reversed this process, changing from sugar to cotton production.

It is easy to demonstrate, from inspection of Jamaican planters' inventories in the late seventeenth century, that sugar producers were by far the biggest planters—and the only wealthy ones—on the island. Nearly two hundred colonists whose estates were inventoried between 1674 and 1701 can be identified as planters; about half of these itemized lists are sufficiently detailed to make plain the planter's principal crop. Sugar planters are the easiest to spot because of the mill rollers, boiling coppers, sugar pots, and stills that appear among their listed belongings. Among the fifty-four identifiable sugar producers, six owned fewer than twenty slaves, but the great majority had at least forty, and seven of them more than a hundred slaves. Sir Henry Morgan, the buccaneer, was in this select circle: his 122 slaves and his two sugar estates in St. Mary parish were worth far more than his gold rings, emerald drops, and other pirate loot when he died. By contrast, only two of the thirty-five identifiable indigo, cotton, and cattle farmers held as many as thirty slaves, and their property—as table 18 shows—was valued much lower. In Jamaica, as elsewhere in the English islands, the range of wealth among the planters was very great. The top 3.5 percent of the planters in table 18 left estates valued at £3,000 or better, and 8.5 percent were worth at least £2,000, while at the opposite end of the scale 19 percent bequeathed property valued at less than £100, and the bottom 2 percent left a miserable £8 or £10.

It is instructive to take a closer look at one fairly representative district in Jamaica, the parish of St. John, an inland region of craggy mountains and lushly beautiful valleys lying north of Old Harbour and west of Spanish Town. The consolidating process that we observed taking place in the Antiguan parish of St. Mary in the previous chapter also occurred here: with the passage of time the number of white settlers in St. John shrank, the slave population grew, and the gulf between large and small planters became very great. But in Jamaica this social transformation occurred much more rapidly than in Antigua. English settlement in St. John began about 1660, when the surviving soldiers from one of Cromwell's regiments started to plant at Guanaboa Vale. They had only 700 acres under cultivation and 39 slaves in 1662, but by 1670 the St.

Table 18. The Property of 198 Jamaica Planters, 1674–1701

	Average Estate	Average Slaves	Average Servants
54 sugar planters	£1,954	63	3
8 ranchers	£656	16	1
7 cotton farmers	£356	12	0.5
20 indigo planters	£310	13	0.3
109 unidentifiable planters	£306	8	0.6
Median	£375	12	0

NOTE: Several hundred of the other colonists whose estates are inventoried in Jam. Inv. were probably also small planters, but I was unable to identify their occupations clearly enough to include them in this tabulation. Jamaican appraisers generally valued the planter's household goods, stores, tools, livestock, servants, and slaves, but not his land, buildings, or planted crops. For discussion as to how representative these Jamaican inventories are, see pp. 264–265 below.

John planters had 20 cacao walks, 11 sugar works, about 550 slaves, and 25,197 patented acres. The cacao walks were soon ruined by blight, but in 1684 the parish could boast 16 sugar works, 31 provision farms, a number of cattle pens, and over 750 slaves. St. John now ranked third among the fifteen Jamaica parishes in colony tax assessments. Yet the payment in human terms for these accomplishments was very heavy. As in St. Mary, most of the people who came to live in St. John soon quit or died. St. John's white adult male population fell from 390 in 1662 to 246 in 1673, then dipped again to 135 by 1680. Only twenty of the eighty-three families who inhabited the parish in 1670 were still there ten years later, by which time the total number of parish families had dwindled to forty-eight. Jamaica's winnowing process had left a small, seasoned band of survivors in St. John, among them the founders of the planter class in this parish.[32]

By good fortune, a census of the forty-eight families in St. John was taken in 1680—the only surviving early census for any Jamaica country district. This document, when correlated with the Bochart-Knollis map of 1684, permits the same sort of social analysis as the Barbados census of 1680 when correlated with Richard Ford's map of that island. As in Barbados, the inhabitants of this Jamaica parish were ranked in a clear social hierarchy in 1680. The nine biggest planters in St. John completely dominated the scene. They owned 77 percent of the parish slaves, produced most of the sugar, held the chief elective and appointive offices, and occupied the best land under cultivation—the rich bottom land of Guanaboa Vale. The estates of these parish leaders are all identified on the Bochart-Knollis map. Next in the local pecking order came a group of middling planters, with ten to twenty-five laborers apiece. These people owned 16 percent of the parish slaves, operated several small sugar works, held an occasional public post, and planted more modest tracts of land than the big planters. Only four of the middling planters from St. John appear on the Bochart-Knollis map. Below them came the more numerous small planters, with an average of two laborers apiece. Owning only 6 percent of the parish slaves, these people held no public offices and farmed small plots in the hills above Guanaboa, where they apparently raised provisions, cotton, and cattle—though it is impossible to say for sure, since only four of them appear on the map.

Five of the families in this parish were headed by widows in 1680, and one family—the late Philip Vickery's—was headless. There is plenty of evidence here of broken family structure. But it does appear that the big planters in St. John enjoyed, along with their other perquisites, a rather more satisfying family life than their small neighbors. Two-thirds of the big planters seem to have been married in 1680, and they had better than two children apiece living with them, whereas only about half of the middling and small planters were married, and they averaged one child apiece. The St. John census also tells us a little something about the black

32. Condition of Jamaica, Oct. 28, 1662, *Jours. of Jam. Assembly*, I, app., 20; survey of St. John parish, Sept. 23, 1670, *Cal.S.P.Col., 1669–1674*, #270; colony population estimate, Mar. 25, 1673, *Jours. of Jam. Assembly*, I, app., 40; census of St. John parish, c. May 1680, C.O. 1/45/109; colony tax assessment, Oct. 4, 1682, *Jours. of Jam. Assembly*, I, 61.

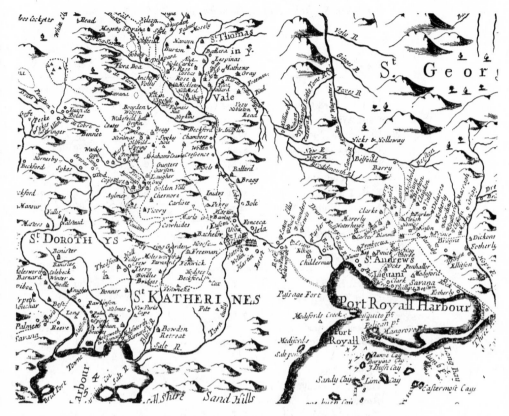

FIG. 6. *Detail from Charles Bochart and Humphrey Knollis's "A New and Exact Mapp of the Island of Jamaica," 1684. Sugar plantations are identified by* houses, *provision farms by* circles, *and cattle pens by* triangles. *St. John parish, discussed in chapter 5, lies inland from St. Dorothy. Bybrook plantation, discussed in chapter 6, in St. Thomas in the Vale, is labeled* Hilliard *on the map. (Courtesy of John Carter Brown Library, Brown University, Providence.)*

Table 19. St. John Parish, Jamaica, in 1680

Big Planters	Crop	White Women	Chil- dren	Ser- vants	Adult Slaves	Slave Chil- dren
Col. John Cope	sugar	2	2	15	100	80
Maj. Richard Guy	sugar	2	3	12	60	10
Capt. William Bragg	sugar	1	0	5	49	13
Lt. Francis Price	sugar	1	4	7	55	3
Philip Vickery (dead)	sugar	0	2	4	38	13
Widow Sams	provisions	0	2	2	31	15
Widow Oldfield	sugar	0	3	5	27	15
Maj. Thomas Ayscough	sugar	1	2	4	35	3
Lt. Col. Whitgift Aylmer	sugar	1	4	1	25	6
9 families		8	22	55	420	158
Middling Planters						
Robert Bates	?	0	0	5	11	8
Qtrm. Stephen Penni- stone	sugar	1	2	3	14	2
Widow Charnock	sugar	0	5	0	6	10
Capt. Reginald Wilson	sugar	0	0	1	8	7
Mr. Elkins	?	0	0	1	7	8
Timothy Dod	sugar	0	0	2	10	3
Gilbert Kennedy	?	1	2	4	6	4
Richard Greene	?	0	0	2	6	2
Teague Mackmarroe	?	0	0	2	5	3
9 families		2	9	20	73	47
Small Planters						
William Thorpe	sugar	0	0	1	2	2
Nicholas Groves	provisions	1	0	0	3	0
Widow Allen	provisions	0	1	0	2	0
Robert Bennett	provisions	1	5	0	1	0
26 remaining small planters	?	20	35	13	27	15
30 families		22	41	15	34	19
Total: 48 families		32	72	90	527	224
5 free Negroes						

NOTE: The Account of the Families both whites and Negroes in the Parish of St. John's, Jamaica, [*c.* May 1680], C.O. 1/45/109. See also fig. 6, p. 173.

population, which outnumbered the whites by three to one. Thirty percent of the slaves were children—the standard ratio throughout the English islands in this period. Slave fecundity appears to have been low in St. John, and slave mortality was certainly high, for during the preceding two years only eleven Negroes were born in the parish and fifty Negroes died. Capt. William Bragg alone lost sixteen slaves. The census taker did not have any slot in his form for the five free Negroes he found living in the parish, and he tabulated them with the white servants.

As in Barbados in 1680, the chief sugar planters of St. John enjoyed a virtual lock on officeholding. The top militia officers were all big slaveholders except for Capt. Reginald Wilson, a royal patent officer who lived in Port Royal. Col. John Cope represented the parish in the Jamaica Council, and Messrs. Guy, Bragg, Price, Ayscough, Aylmer, Wilson, Dod, and the late Captain Oldfield were all elected to the Jamaica Assembly in the 1670s or 1680s— sometimes from other parishes than St. John. Altogether, eleven of the first fifteen planters as ranked in table 19 held parish or colony offices around 1680; the bottom thirty-three planters in the parish were excluded from positions of honor. It would be interesting to know whether this situation changed after the mid-1680s, when many big Jamaican planters retired to England as absentees. Unhappily, during the crisis years of the 1690s and 1700s no one had the leisure to compile a census of St. John or any other parish in the island.

The chief planters of St. John and their fellow gentry in the other Jamaican parishes were a mixed lot, even more so than in Barbados and the Leewards. Some had been soldiers in 1655, others were civilians; some came as Roundheads, others Cavaliers; some migrated directly from Britain, others from the eastern islands; some lived on their estates, some in Port Royal or Spanish Town, and others were absentees in England. Very few of the officers who commanded Cromwell's army when it landed in Jamaica in 1655 lived long enough or stayed long enough to become big planters.[33] But a good many men who arrived with the army in 1655 or joined it during the next five years did end up among the island magnates.

33. A list of 106 officers who held commissions in Gen. Venables's army between Mar. 21 and May 19, 1655 (just before and during the Jamaica campaign) shows only three—Capt. Henry Archbold, Maj. Samuel Barry, and Ens. Thomas Freeman—who became big Jamaica planters. About a dozen of the others acquired smaller tracts. The rest were soon killed or returned to England. See Firth, ed., *Narrative of Venables*, 116–126.

In St. John, for example, John Cope, Francis Price, Thomas Ayscough, and Whitgift Aylmer were all initially Cromwellian soldiers. Such major figures in the early history of the colony as Thomas Lynch, Samuel Long, Henry Archbold, Samuel Barry, and Thomas Freeman came with the conquering army.

It is impossible to tell how many of the successful Jamaica planters were veteran tropical farmers from Barbados or the Leewards. One would expect the number to be large, but it appears that most of the planters who built big estates in the new colony came directly from England and started as novices. Surprisingly few surnames from the Barbados plantocracy turn up in the early Jamaica records. Sir Thomas Modyford was by far the most conspicuous ex-Barbadian, unless one counts Sir Henry Morgan, who is supposed to have started his West Indian career as an indentured servant in Barbados. Richard Guy, Thomas Sutton, and William Drax were prominent Barbadians who became sugar magnates in Jamaica, and perhaps a dozen others could be added to the list.[34] It is quite possible that fewer younger sons and brothers of established Barbados planters transferred their operations to Jamaica than to South Carolina in the 1670s and 1680s.

One point is clear. Most of the planters who succeeded in Jamaica arrived early, within the first decade of settlement. Three-quarters of the eighty-eight biggest patentees (those who acquired two thousand acres during the seventeenth century) took out their first grants by 1670. Richard Beckford, founder of the richest sugar family in the island, started out as a small trader in 1662. William Beeston, a future governor, arrived in 1660. Robert Byndloss, Anthony Collier, Thomas Fuller, Richard Guy, and William Ivey came about the same time. Samuel Bernard, John Bourden, Hender Molesworth (another governor), George Needham, and Andrew Orgill arrived several years later, during Modyford's administration. Among the relative latecomers, after 1670, were William Drax from Barbados and James Bannister from Surinam.[35]

Impressive as this array of big landholders and emerging sugar

34. The only other prominent Barbados surnames that turn up in the early Jamaica land records and lists of officeholders are: Ball, Brown, Burton, Clark, Cox, Davis, Fenwick, Gregory, Hanson, Howell, Kendall, Knight, Lewis, Littleton, Price, Reid, Robinson, Searle, Walrond, and Williams. Some of these names are so common that their appearance in the two colonies is probably unrelated.

35. Using the Jam. Land Pat., I compiled a list of the 88 planters who patented 2,000 acres or more before 1700 and then tracked down, as far as possible, the year in which each of these men first came to Jamaica.

magnates may seem, we must remember that the Jamaican plantocracy was still in embryo in the seventeenth century. The planters
who controlled the best land and the top offices were more numerous and wealthy than the Leeward gentry, but most of them were
fairly small entrepreneurs by Barbados standards, and such they remained until the Peace of Utrecht. Jamaica's sugar industry stopped
expanding about 1685, and thereafter the annual output was
pegged at the relatively modest level of five thousand to seven thousand tons from 1685 to 1713. The combination of English politics,
heavy new taxes, French privateers, the great earthquake, and the
constant ill health of the island arrested Jamaica's economic growth
for a full generation. In St. John, for example, the planters waited
till the next century to open up the best sugar acreage in the parish.
As early as the 1670s Francis Price, Thomas Ayscough, Whitgift
Aylmer, Stephen Pennistone, and other, smaller planters staked out
their claims to the rich lands of Lluidas Vale, fourteen miles further
inland beyond Guanaboa through tortuous mountain trails. But it
took fifty years to develop Lluidas Vale. Eventually Francis Price's
son and grandson would set up a grandiose sugar estate at Worthy
Park in Lluidas, which dwarfed any of the initial Guanaboa plantations and equalled or surpassed the finest Barbados establishments.[36] But this was in a new century and a new era, when the
planters who had stuck it out through fifty years of trouble and
disorder began to reap a rich reward.

ॐ

Between 1655 and 1689 there were two Jamaicas: the agricultural
colony and the buccaneers' rendezvous. Port Royal, seat and symbol
of the buccaneers, perched at the tip of its ten-mile sandspit, was a
separate realm from the cane fields and cattle ranches across the
harbor. Today one can hardly imagine this sleepy and bedraggled
fishing village as the wickedest city in the West, but three centuries
ago, before the earthquake of 1692, Port Royal was indeed a swing-
ing place. More than any other early English settlement in America,

36. The Prices had 257 slaves at Worthy Park in 1731 and 470 slaves in 1796.
At its peak, on the eve of the American Revolution, this one estate grossed
£10,000 annually in sugar and rum sales. Today Worthy Park produces 7,000
tons of sugar per year, more than the entire island of Jamaica in 1680. See
Craton and Walvin, *A Jamaican Plantation*, 3, 35, 55, 89, 130.

this flashy port town breathed a frontier spirit of adventure and bravado. Port Royal was a sailors' dive, but much more besides. It was a handsome, wealthy, and surprisingly cosmopolitan place—altogether a colorful little city.

Fortunately for the historian, surviving evidence about the character of life in Port Royal during the buccaneering era is exceptionally rich. The earthquake of 1692 smashed the town, but in such a way as to preserve a great quantity of memorabilia for posterity. Other island communities, such as Bridgetown, have gradually lost all physical trace of the seventeenth century through the cumulative effect of hurricanes, fires, and systematic rebuilding. But in Port Royal the earthquake simply dumped half the town into the sea, so that manifold relics of the buccaneering community still lie buried under twenty or thirty feet of water in the silt of the harbor floor. Underwater archeologists are now at work exhuming the drowned part of the city; they have already dredged up a great array of artifacts, ranging from onion-shaped liquor bottles to sections of ruined buildings, and they anticipate collecting so much further data that it will be possible to rebuild authentically a considerable section of the preearthquake town. This Port Royal archeological project is of capital importance; it will greatly enlarge our understanding of seventeenth-century social conditions, not merely in Jamaica but throughout the English islands.[37]

One need not be a skindiver to find out something about old Port Royal. The Jamaica Archives contain hundreds of seventeenth-century plats, land patents, and deeds that describe building sites in the town.[38] About a hundred Port Royal inventories, filed for probate purposes, survive for the seventeenth century; like the plantation inventories they describe, often very minutely, the household furnishings of rich and poor inhabitants alike. A parish census taken in 1680, similar to the St. John census, provides interesting demographic information, and a minute description of the town,

---

37. Marion Clayton Link, "Exploring the Drowned City of Port Royal," *National Geographic Magazine,* CXVII (1960), 151–183; Philip Mayes, Jamaica's Port Royal Project (a paper presented at South Carolina Tricentennial Symposium, Columbia, S.C., Mar. 19, 1970). I wish to thank Dr. Mayes, the director of the Port Royal Project in 1968–1970, for giving me a tour of his fascinating site in Jan. 1969.

38. *Real Estate Transactions before 1692 Earthquake, City of Port Royal, Jamaica,* a card-file index prepared by the Institute of Jamaica and distributed by the National Geographic Society, [*c.* 1960]. Hereafter cited as *Port Royal Real Estate Index.*

written by an inquisitive visitor named John Taylor in 1688, gives a vivid picture of living conditions on the eve of the earthquake.[39] All in all, it is possible to learn more about old Port Royal than about any other seventeenth-century town in the English islands.

The Spaniards had used Old Harbour, west of Spanish Town, as their chief port. Point Cagway, the site of Port Royal, was unoccupied during the Spanish regime save for a careenage where ships could be refitted. The English, as soon as they conquered the island, decided to take advantage of the magnificent natural harbor east of Spanish Town, which is shielded from storms and enemy attacks by the ten-mile Palisadoes sand spit terminating at Point Cagway. So they fortified Point Cagway in order to guard the entrance to this harbor and started to plant a town there. By 1664 they had changed the name from Point Cagway to Port Royal and laid out the principal arteries: King Street, fronting on the harbor with its wharves, warehouses, and shops; Queen Street, one block inland, where many of the chief Jamaicans built houses; and High Street, two blocks inland, where the parish church, merchants' exchange, and market bell were placed. The recorded population of the new town rapidly climbed from 690 whites and 50 blacks in 1662 to 1,669 whites and 312 blacks in 1673 and rose again to 2,086 whites and 845 blacks in 1680.[40] In addition several hundred sailors operated out of Port Royal. They kept no residence in town and were gone at sea most of the time, but they belonged to the local militia and spent their earnings in the port. By 1680 one out of every six whites on the island lived in Port Royal, and the town paid about a quarter of the colony taxes.[41] The buccaneers' capital was really a small place, of course, yet it had as many residents as Bridgetown, and only Boston among English towns in America had a larger population. Measured by its bustling commerce, its per capita wealth, and its military strength, Port Royal could claim to be a major port.

In 1680 Port Royal was almost precisely the same size as Bridge-

39. Port Royal census, May 12, 1680, C.O. 1/45/97–109; Taylor MS, chap. 6, 491–507, with a hand-drawn map of the town. I am exceedingly grateful to C. Bernard Lewis, director of the Institute of Jamaica, for letting me examine and quote from this Taylor MS.
40. Port Royal population figures for 1662 and 1673 are in *Jours. of Jam. Assembly*, I, app., 20, 40. The figures for 1680 are in C.O. 1/45/97–109.
41. In 1679 Port Royal was assessed 38% of a colony-wide levy for fortifications. Jamaica Assembly Journal, 1678–1679, 37, Jam. Archives. In 1682 the town paid 20% of another general assessment. *Jours. of Jam. Assembly*, I, 61.

town in Barbados, with 2,931 listed inhabitants as against Bridge-town's 2,927. By a happy accident Sir Henry Morgan sent to the Colonial Office in 1680 a detailed enumeration of all Port Royal householders—a census quite similar in character to the Bridgetown head count that Governor Atkins compiled as part of his Barbados census in the same year. Thus we may easily compare the two chief English Caribbean ports at this particular date (see table 20). If we add to Port Royal's column the several hundred mariners who

Table 20. Port Royal versus Bridgetown, 1680

	Port Royal	Bridgetown
White population	2,086	1,488
Slave population	845	1,439
Total population	2,931	2,927
Households	507	405
Single householders	58	94
Mean number of whites per family	4.11	3.68
Mean number of slaves per family	1.67	3.55
Mean number of persons per family	5.78	7.23

NOTE: Inhabitants both Masters and Servants of Port Royal Parish, May 12, 1680, C.O. 1/45/97–109. The Bridgetown census, discussed above on pp. 106–109, dated "Anno 1680," is filed in C.O. 1/44/142–146 and printed in Hotten, ed., *Original Lists*, 438–450.

sailed out of the port but were not counted among the house-holders,[42] it had a decidedly larger white population than Bridgetown. On the other hand, the Jamaicans owned fewer slaves. The Port Royal sailors and fishermen were generally not slaveholders, and only 52 percent of the Port Royal householders held slaves, as against 91 percent in Bridgetown. Yet plenty of householders in Port Royal employed extraordinarily large staffs of servants and slaves. Sir Henry Morgan had ten whites and fourteen blacks living

42. One third of the 1,181 militiamen, or something like 400 men, were categorized on Port Royal's 1680 muster roll as "Sea-Faring Men," not "Residents." C.O. 1/45/4, 11. Correlation of the muster roll with the census shows that hardly any of these sailors appear among the Port Royal householders.

with him at the Governor's House. A sailmaker named Robert Phillips kept fourteen slaves in and around his nine-room house. John Gale, a carpenter who installed a pair of racks in the courthouse in 1676 for the interrogation of prisoners (billing the authorities £14 for his work), employed a dozen servants and slaves. One John Starr had the most intriguing domestic establishment: twenty-one white women and two black girls. Starr appears to have operated the largest whorehouse in town.

Port Royal was a healthier community than Bridgetown in 1680, probably because it was free from mosquitoes and hence malaria. The census reports that 130 whites had been born the past two years, and only 90 died—quite a contrast to the Bridgetown ratio of four burials for every baptism. Even the Port Royal slaves registered a natural increase: seventy-two births and forty-eight deaths. The sexes were surprisingly equally balanced, with males accounting for 53 percent of the white population and 49 percent of the black. Unhappily, the Port Royal census taker did not identify wives, children, and servants, so we cannot compare family structure in the two towns. Port Royal had fewer listed single householders than Bridgetown, but when we take into account the rootless sailor element, it is doubtful that family life was any stronger here than in the Barbadian capital.

Port Royal must have been the most heavily fortified place in English America. Four forts, armed with ninety-four guns, protected it from sea attack, and a breastwork mounted with sixteen guns guarded the land approach. Two companies of regular soldiers manned these fortifications, and in addition Sir Henry Morgan commanded a militia regiment, which according to the muster rolls of May 1680 consisted of 1,181 officers and men. This is an inflated figure, however, for the mariners who constituted one third of the regiment were generally off fishing or turtle hunting in the Cayman Islands or buccaneering. Night and day one of the Port Royal companies was always on duty, working a twelve-hour shift. On exercise days the regiment drilled on the brick-paved Parade, just inside the town gate, resplendent in their scarlet coats lined with blue.[43]

But Port Royal was not just a soldiers' and sailors' town. It was a thriving business center. Surviving probate records tell us quite a bit about the economic organization of the community. Like

43. Taylor MS, 494–497; Jamaica militia muster rolls, May 1680, C.O. 1/45/2–4. The Parade was laid out in 1675, and its plat appears in the *Port Royal Real Estate Index*, card 671.

every seventeenth-century town of any size, Port Royal supported a wide range of crafts and trades. The inventories of probated estates for the years 1674 to 1701 detail the worldly possessions of some forty-five artisans in twenty-five occupational categories. The most basic semiskilled workers—the porters, watermen, blacksmiths, bricklayers, carpenters, joiners, shoemakers, tailors, and glovers—fared the poorest, compiling estates valued at £50 to £150. This put them on an economic level with the sailors and fishermen, the largest block of workers in town, who seldom collected property worth more than £100. Fancier craftsmen such as cabinetmakers, pewterers, and glaziers, and artisans who produced in volume such as coopers and tanners, earned considerably larger profits and amassed estates worth £250 to £500—about the same as cotton or indigo planters in the Jamaica countryside. Purveyors of food and drink, the bakers, victuallers, and tavernkeepers, who catered to the large floating population of seamen, did better yet and were worth £700 or more. The great majority of these Port Royal artisans— the main exceptions were sailors, smiths, and cloth workers—employed slaves and servants. But the big money in town was made by the merchants who fenced the loot and prize goods carried into town by the buccaneers and privateers and who also serviced the sugar planters, selling them imported English supplies ranging from mill rollers to casks of brandy to cases of silk and marketing their agricultural produce. In the years from 1674 to 1701 twenty-three Port Royal merchants whose probate records survive left estates valued above £1,000. Nine left estates valued above £2,000. Comparison between the probate records of Port Royal and Boston suggests that these Jamaican commercial entrepreneurs did at least as well as their famous counterparts in New England.[44]

The bustling prosperity of the place persuaded a number of the chief sugar planters to spend part or most of the year in Port Royal. These gentry built town houses on High Street or Queen Street and served as officers in the local militia regiment. Other planters elected to live in Spanish Town, the inland seat of government. One cannot always tell from a planter's inventory whether

44. This paragraph is based on an analysis of 93 Port Royal inventories, 1674–1701, found in Jam. Inv., set against a sample of 100 Boston inventories, 1670–1700, from the Suffolk County, Mass., Probate Court Records, Vols. 5, 7–14 (microfilm 689:2–5, University of Pennsylvania Library). Hereafter cited as Suffolk Co. Probate Records. See pp. 269–272 below.

his town house was in Port Royal or Spanish Town, but in either case it was often a larger and more elaborately furnished structure than the great house on his plantation. Certainly the sugar magnates, with their showy life-style, added to the considerable glitter of Port Royal.[45] "The Merchants and Gentry live here to the Hight of Splendor, in full ease and plenty," John Taylor reported, "being sumptuously arrayed, and attended on, and served by their Negroe slaves, which all ways waite on 'em in Livery, or other wise as they pleas to cloath 'em." [46]

Among the Port Royal citizenry was a conspicuously alien element: a small cadre of Sephardic Jews. In the town statistics of 1680, 17 of the 507 householders and 21 of the 1,181 militiamen had Jewish names. Three of these men are identified as mariners, but most of the rest must have been merchants and shopkeepers. Like the Bridgetown Jews these people migrated from Brazil, Surinam, and other sugar colonies. They lived a life apart, congregated in the Middle Precinct of the town, probably in a mini-ghetto on Jew Street, where they had a synagogue.[47] Some were wretchedly poor and others exceedingly prosperous, according to the handful of Jewish inventories in the probate records. Isaac Narvez and Joseph Alvaringa both built up estates of better than £2,000, consisting primarily of cash, bonds, shop goods, and debts, including a few slaves but very little real estate. These two men kept their wealth fluid and shipped much of it to colleagues in London before they died, for they were only grudgingly tolerated by the Jamaican government and forced to pay a special Jew tax.[48]

Port Royal was no ethnic melting pot, but by the standards of the day it was a haven for the persecuted. Most of the Quakers on the island lived here, and even the Quaker hagiographers admitted

45. One indication of the planters' strong presence in Port Royal is that 28 of the 88 biggest landholders on the island—those who patented 2,000 acres—also held town plots in Port Royal. This information is obtained by correlating the Jam. Land Pat. with the *Port Royal Real Estate Index*. Furthermore, in the Port Royal census and muster rolls of 1680, a number of the largest householders and chief militia officers can be identified as big sugar planters.

46. Taylor MS, 500.

47. In the Middle Precinct census the Jewish names are bunched, suggesting that they lived close together. On the other hand, the 21 militiamen were scattered among the 10 companies, suggesting that the English did not trust them! The Jews bought a tract, 63 x 24 feet, for their synagogue in 1677. *Port Royal Real Estate Index*, card 521.

48. Inventories of Isaac Narvez and Joseph Alvaringa, Jam. Inv., Vols. 3, 5.

that they were relatively undisturbed. John Taylor was startled to discover in 1688 that five religious denominations worshiped openly in the town: the Anglicans at St. Paul's church, the Presbyterians and Quakers at their respective meetinghouses, the Catholics at their chapel, and the Jews at their synagogue.[49]

How did this incongruous medley of buccaneers, soldiers, merchants, whores, Negroes, craftsmen, Jews, planters, and Quakers manage to live together? John Taylor, who saw Port Royal during Albemarle's governorship, just four years before the earthquake, has left us a vivid portrait of the place. Taylor tended to exaggerate,[50] but he had an eye for graphic detail. The town as he knew it was crammed into a narrow site at the extreme tip of the Palisadoes peninsula, facing the harbor, surrounded by the sea on three sides, and edged with wharves. Visiting merchant vessels berthed at the wharves along King Street, and the local shallops and sloops berthed at Chocolata Hole, where the turtle pens were kept. There was also a beach for the canoes of the watermen who plied constantly across the harbor to fetch water. Port Royal had no fresh water supply, and the watermen sold it for 2s. 6d. a tun. The crooked streets, narrow lanes, and foot passages were lined by tall wooden or brick houses, commodious shops, and warehouses. Building sites were small, typically only about thirty feet square, even on fashionable Queen and High Streets, as we can tell from the surviving plats in the island archives. Taylor complained that rents were as high in Port Royal as in Cheapside, the business hub of London. House rents started at £60 per annum, and furnished rooms at 30s. per month.

Cramped for space, the townspeople were forced to build up rather than out. Their houses generally had yards and often porches, but there cannot have been much room for gardens or trees. Taylor extolled the fashionable brick mode of construction: four stories high, cellared below, tile roof, glazed sash windows, and the cook room set off by itself in the back yard for coolness. He particularly admired the opulent merchants' Exchange, a stone gallery adjoining the parish church, which was graced by doric pillars and a twisted balustrade. Here, elegantly shaded, the grandees met to transact their affairs. But the raw side of life was also very evident. The town fathers found it necessary to construct two courthouses,

49. Besse, *Collection of Sufferings*, II, 388–391; Taylor MS, 504.
50. He reckoned that 5,000 whites and 5,000 slaves lived in 1,200 houses, with 2,500 men in the militia—all of which figures are at least twice too high.

two prisons, a cage, a ducking stool, and a stocks in order to keep local lawbreakers under some sort of control.[51]

There was plenty of high living in Jamaica according to Taylor. The townspeople were short of water, but they could gorge on rich food and strong drink. The local beef and lamb were not up to English standards, but three daily markets supplied plenty of cheap fresh fish, tortoise, pork (wild or tame), fowl, fruit, and salad greens. The grocers sold imported sweetmeats, sauces, oils, anchovies, capers, olives, and other such delicacies. The pastrycooks vended custards, cheesecakes, and tarts. The taverns and punch houses (which "may be fittly called Brothel Houses") dispensed madeira, canary, brandy, beer, and rum punch. Dinner at a tavern cost 1s. 6d.; a quart of madeira cost a shilling. Businessmen closed their shops from noon till three, and during these hot hours they ate dinner, drank at the taverns, or napped in their hammocks. In the cool of the evening they had the choice of entertainment in a tavern, coffee house, bear garden, cockpit, or music house (another euphemism for brothel). The people took little physical exercise beyond drinking and wenching, though they did shoot at targets and play billiards and shuffleboard. A number of Port Royal houses boasted billiards and shuffleboard rooms.

Taylor castigates the debauched wild blades and vile strumpets who were rounded up nightly and hustled into the cage by the Turtle Market to sober up. There was no way to cage the buccaneers when they came into port. John Esquemeling, who sailed with these rovers, says that a favorite sport in Port Royal was to buy a pipe of wine or a barrel of beer, place it in the street, and force all the onlookers at pistol point to drink—or "throw these liquors about the streets, and wet the cloathes of such as walked by." A buccaneer might spend two or three thousand pieces of eight (£500 to £750) in one wild Port Royal bacchanalia.[52] The town was indeed a gaudy, boozy, uninhibited place, with a history of frequent brawls and riots. Not the wickedest city in the West, perhaps, but undoubtedly the liveliest English community in America.

51. Taylor MS, 492–494, 498–499, 504. For the general layout of Port Royal before and after the earthquake, see the map and aerial photograph in Jack Tyndale-Biscoe and David Buisseret, *Historic Jamaica from the Air* (Barbados, 1969), 10–11. For a conjectural reconstruction of the street plan of the old town, see the map in Link, "Exploring the Drowned City of Port Royal," *Natl. Geog. Mag.,* CXVII (1960), 166–167.

52. Taylor MS, 494, 496, 500–504; Esquemeling, *Bucaniers of America,* Pt. I, 106–107.

In the 1680s the sand spit on which the town perched began to shift ominously. The Assembly, worried by the encroaching sea, warned the people of Port Royal to stop building houses within thirty feet of high tide, and to stop building wharves along the harbor side.[53] These precautions did nothing to prevent the cataclysm of June 7, 1692. The earthquake that shook Jamaica shortly before noon on that day was so powerful that it demolished buildings across the entire island, but it struck Port Royal with the elemental power of Judgment Day. The giant tremors dissolved a huge slice of the Palisadoes peninsula and within three minutes plunged half of the town to the bottom of the harbor. Two of the four forts, all of the wharves, most of the merchants' shops and planters' houses, the three principal thoroughfares—King, Queen, and High Streets—and the chief public buildings, such as St. Paul's church and the Exchange, all vanished from sight and were sucked thirty feet under water. Hundreds of people, trapped in their houses, were drowned or buried alive, and the corpses of these victims soon began to bob to the water's surface. Adding to the macabre scene, the quake ripped apart the Palisadoes graveyard, tumbling further human carcasses and skeletons into the harbor.

At first the streets farthest from the harbor escaped damage, but as the ground continued to roll from repeated aftershocks, the whole town was leveled—all except the humble slave huts, which escaped destruction because of their resilient stick and thatch construction. Symbolically the distraught English survivors ejected the Negroes from these quarters and moved into the slave huts themselves. The death toll was horribly high. Witnesses claimed that two thousand people, two-thirds of the entire town, were killed. A gross exaggeration, no doubt, yet the Quakers listed thirty-eight dead out of their community of sixty or so. Many of the survivors were carried off by a malignant fever that followed the quake and completed the catastrophe.

The Jamaican authorities promptly decided to find a safer site for the island port, and within a few months they laid out the new town of Kingston across the harbor. But many merchants and sailors clung to Port Royal. In the 1690s they rebuilt the town—this time out of wood instead of brick—within the constricted area left after the earthquake. The population of the place was much re-

53. *The Laws of Jamaica . . . Confirmed . . . April 17, 1684* (London, 1684), 49–52.

duced. In 1702 only 580 men could be mustered into the Port Royal regiment, and of these 245 were sailors. The following year another disaster occurred; on January 9, 1703, a fire wiped out the town once again, burning down every single building in town except the two forts. Port Royal never did recover from this second blow. In the eighteenth century it remained a naval station and a fishing port, but Kingston was henceforth the commercial hub of the island.

The symbolic importance of the 1692 earthquake was very clear to people at the time. An angry God had punished the city of sin for its debauchery. "Ah brother!," a Jamaican Quaker wrote home two weeks after the earthquake, "If thou didst see those great persons that are now dead upon the water thou couldst never forget it. Great men who were so swallowed up with pride, that a man could not be admitted to speak with them, and women whose top-knots seemed to reach the clouds, now lie stinking upon the water, and are made meat for fish and fowls of the air." [54] Port Royal became the perfect vehicle for jeremiad sermons, since everyone could agree that the wicked city got what it deserved. The horror of the event inspired at least six London pamphlets, one of which was reprinted in Edinburgh and Glasgow and translated into Dutch for Continental readers.[55] Most of all the earthquake proclaimed the final renunciation of the buccaneers. Just four years before, in 1688, Sir Henry Morgan and his patron, the duke of Albemarle, had both died. Just three years before, in 1689, the Glorious Revolution had removed Morgan's friends once and for all from power in Jamaica. When the buccaneers' playground literally vanished in 1692, no one could doubt that sugar was king.

54. John Pike to his "Loving Brother," June 19, 1692, in *The Widow Witherows Humble Thanksgiving . . . with a Letter from Jamaica concerning the Earthquake that happen'd there* (London, 1694), 39–40, quoted by Henry J. Cadbury in his unpublished essay, Quakers and the Earthquake at Port Royal, 1692.

55. *A Full Account of the late dreadful Earthquake at Port Royal in Jamaica* (London, 1692) was reissued in Edinburgh and Glasgow the same year and translated into Dutch as *Een Ampel en breed verhaal van de jongt-gewesene Aardbevinge tot Port-Royal in Jamaica* (Rotterdam, 1692). Other accounts include *A True and perfect relation of that most sad and terrible Earthquake at Port-Royal in Jamaica* (London, 1692); *The Truest and largest Account of the late Earthquake in Jamaica* (London, 1693); Thomas Doolittle, *Earthquakes explained and practically improved . . . Jamaica's miseries shew London's mercies* (London, 1693); J. Shower, *Practical Reflections on the late Earthquake in Jamaica* (London, 1693); and *Widow Witherow's Humble Thanksgiving*.

6 🔊 *Sugar*

The one outstanding attraction to life in Jamaica, the Lee-wards, or Barbados in the seventeenth century was the opportunity for making a quick fortune. "It is seldome seene," wrote Christopher Jeaffreson, "that the ingenious or industrious men fail of raising their fortunes in any part of the Indies . . . from little or nothing to vast estates." [1] The Caribbean offered many avenues to profit: aside from buccaneering and treasure hunting, there was the Indian trade, the Spanish slave traffic, dyewood lumbering, turtle fishing, cattle ranching, and the cultivation of indigo, cacao, cotton, ginger, limes, pimento, and tobacco. But in all the English islands sugar eclipsed everything else. As soon as Barbados sugar came on the London market in the 1640s, it fetched a far higher and steadier profit than any other American commodity. In particular, Caribbean sugar did better than its chief American rival, Chesapeake tobacco, in the seventeenth century. It commanded a higher price per acre or laborer, paid lower English import duties, and suffered less from a glutted home market. No wonder that when London publicists produced topographical guides to English America, they pointed with pride chiefly to the sugar islands. Richard Blome in his guidebook of 1672 thought Jamaica worth more space than all the continental colonies put together, and in John Oldmixon's two-volume survey, *The British Empire in America,* published in 1708, the favorite plantation was Barbados. [2]

It is proper to emphasize this achievement. The seventeenth-century Caribbean colonists built a truly impressive sugar-produc-

---

1. Jeaffreson, ed., *Young Squire,* I, 256–257.
2. Blome, *Description of Jamaica;* John Oldmixon, *The British Empire in America* (London, 1708; 2d ed., London, 1741).

tion system, especially when one considers the tradition-bound character of English farming at this time. The sugar planters utilized agricultural techniques radically different from those they knew at home and learned how to manipulate men, beasts, and machines on a far grander scale than their cousins in Virginia or Massachusetts.[3] But the story of sugar was not all sweetness. From the beginning sugar makers pegged their production system to black slave labor. Sugar and slavery developed hand in hand in the English islands, two faces of a single phenomenon. Sugar making was also a highly volatile business; with the right combination of skill, drive, and luck, a planter could make a quick fortune, but careless management, a tropical storm, an epidemic disease, a slave revolt, or a French invasion could ruin the most flourishing plantation overnight. Sugar planters were always painfully exposed to external pressures. They depended on English merchants to extend them credit for acquiring slaves and equipment and to take their sugar in exchange for the home commodities they needed. They depended on the royal government for military and naval protection. They depended on the Royal African Company for Negroes. They depended on North American ships for food and transportation.

All of these factors—positive and negative—gave the sugar business in the seventeenth century a peculiarly hectic, frantic character. The boom-and-bust style of sugar making helps to explain why Englishmen in the Caribbean tended to behave differently from Englishmen at home or in mainland America.

৯৯

In the preindustrial world of the seventeenth century, the Caribbean sugar planter was a large-scale entrepreneur. He was a combination farmer-manufacturer. With a work force of one hundred laborers he could plant eighty acres in cane and expect to produce eighty tons of sugar per year. He had to feed, clothe, house, and supervise his labor force year-round. He needed one or two mills to extract juice from the harvested cane, a boiling house to clarify and evaporate the cane juice into sugar crystals, a curing house for drying the sugar and draining out the molasses, a distillery for convert-

3. Richard B. Sheridan has stressed the dynamic character of the English sugar plantation system in several articles, most recently in "The Plantation Revolution and the Industrial Revolution, 1625–1775," *Carib. Studies,* IX (1969), 5–25.

ing the molasses into rum, and a storehouse in the nearest port for keeping his barreled sugar until it could be shipped to England. An operation of this size required a capital investment of thousands of pounds.

The planter's profit margin varied greatly, depending on the fluctuating price of sugar and the fluctuating cost of slaves and supplies. Contemporary statements on this subject are of little help. Writing in 1657, when conditions were exceptionally favorable, Richard Ligon concocted a set of figures to show that the planter who invested £3,000 would soon gross £8,866 and clear £7,517 annually. But Ligon was a propagandist. It is hard to believe that the Barbadians ever did this well, even in the first halcyon days. A generation later, in 1685, when prices were very low and costs climbing high, the Barbados Assembly concocted another set of figures to show that the planter who invested £4,000 was losing £200 annually. But again this was propaganda. Only inept and unlucky planters actually lost money, even in the worst of times. In general the big planters made excellent profits by English agricultural standards. Henry Drax, the second largest entrepreneur in Barbados in 1680, with 705 acres and 332 laborers, was said to ship home £5,000 in sugar annually.[4] Only the landed aristocracy at home enjoyed gross agricultural income of this magnitude, and the English aristocrats leased most of their land to tenants, whereas Drax worked his business himself.[5] But if the Caribbean planters' profits were great, so were their liabilities. Entrepreneurs like Drax accumulated heavy debts to the commission agents and factors who merchandized their produce and serviced their plantations and to the slave traders who supplied them with Negroes. As the planters' gross income rose, so did their debts.

Every stage of the sugar-making process required strenuous labor, close supervision, and careful timing. Unlike any crop the English were familiar with, sugarcane requires more than a year, usually fourteen to eighteen months, to ripen. Thus the Caribbean planters had to work out a much more complicated planting and harvesting

4. Ligon, *True History of Barbados,* 112–116; A Moderate Calculation of the Annuall Charge and produce of a Plantation in Barbados, Sept. 16, 1685, C.O. 31/3/120–121; Gov. Atkins to Lords of Trade, July 4, 1677, C.O. 29/2/181.

5. Lawrence Stone, *The Crisis of the Aristocracy, 1558–1641* (Oxford, 1965), chap. 6. See also Peter Bowden's calculation of the slim profits available to English sheep or grain farmers in the early 17th century: "Agricultural Prices, Farm Profits, and Rents," in Thirsk, ed., *Agrarian History of England and Wales,* 658, 662, 665.

schedule than on an English farm. Cane can be planted any time
of the year in the West Indies, but it grows best during the wet
months from June to November and should be harvested in the
driest months, from January to May, when the sugar content of
mature cane reaches its maximum. Sugar extracted from underripe
or overripe cane is decidedly inferior, and once the cane is harvested,
it spoils unless it is processed within a few hours. Consequently
the planter tried to arrange his fields so that they would ripen between January and May, but not all at once. As early as the 1650s
the English planters divided their land into a number of uniformly
sized cane pieces, each about ten acres, scheduled to mature at
staggered intervals, so that the harvest could be spread over several
months.[6]

The cultivation of sugarcane was a slow and laborious business.
The planter started a new cane piece by digging a series of holes
and inserting cuttings of old cane stalk about two feet in length
(the Barbados method) or by digging a series of trenches and placing the cuttings of old cane end to end (the Jamaica method).
These cuttings, lightly covered with soil, soon sprouted at each
joint into new plants. A field gang of thirty slaves, working with
hoes, could hole or trench two acres in a day. Plows were never
used in the seventeenth century. It was customary to plant between
October and December, months with enough rainfall so that the
cuttings would sprout easily. If all went well, these cane fields
matured some sixteen months later, between January and May.
Cuttings that failed to sprout were replaced at once. When the
rows of young cane reached a foot or two in height, they were
weeded several times and manured with a mixture of cattle dung
and cane trash. Edward Littleton in 1689 claimed that the Barbados
fields required thirty loads of dung per acre.[7] For this reason every
Barbados planter had to keep large numbers of cattle and sheep.
Rats were a greater menace to the young canes than plant diseases
or insect pests during the seventeenth century. Some planters employed Negro rat-catching gangs, but the only really effective de-
terrent was to burn a rodent-infested field from the edges inward,
so as to trap and kill an entire rat population. By the sixth or
seventh month after planting the canes became too tall and thickly

6. For good discussion of sugar making in the English islands during these
early years, see Barrett, "Caribbean Sugar-Production Standards," in Parker, ed.,
Merchants and Scholars, 145–170; Pares, *A West-India Fortune,* esp. chap. 6.
7. Littleton, *Groans of the Plantations,* 18.

sprouting for further cultivation, and during the rainy season from June to November the stalks reached their full height of eight feet —several feet shorter than most modern varieties. In Ligon's words, the ripening cane turned from "grass green" color to "deep Popinjay."

At harvest time field gangs of slaves cut the ripe canes by hand with curved knives called bills. They removed the outer leaves, bundled the stalks, and carted them to the mill for grinding. On the average an acre of plant cane yielded a ton of sugar—only one-fifth the modern rate. Once a field was harvested the cane root would resprout and produce a second crop, known as ratoon cane. This ratoon cane had obvious advantages: it required much less field labor than plant cane and matured more rapidly, in a year or less. On the other hand, it yielded only about half as much sugar. Barbados planters avoided ratooning after the 1680s and grubbed up all their fields at harvest to rest the soil for a few months before replanting in the fall. Jamaica planters often ratooned for two or three crops before replanting their fields with fresh cane.

To Ligon the mill that ground the cane, the "Ingenio" as he called it, was "the *Primum Mobile* of the whole work." Seventeenth-century planters used a three-roller vertical mill, in which the center roller turned against the two outer ones. This enabled a millman to feed the canes through one set of rollers to his colleague who returned them through the second set. The dark brown cane juice flowed down the rollers into a trough and was piped into a cistern in the boiling house. Even with double crushing these "Ingenios" probably extracted no more than half the juice in the cane stalks, compared with an extraction rate of 96 percent or higher in the modern hydraulic sugar mills. Grinding the cane was dangerous work. "If a Mill-feeder be catch't by the finger," says Littleton, "his whole body is drawn in, and he is squeez'd to pieces." Caribbean mills were powered either by water, wind, or cattle. Water mills were popular in Jamaica, where there were abundant mountain streams. Windmills had to be placed so as to catch both land and sea breezes and were chiefly used on the low-lying islands—Barbados and Antigua. Cattle mills were the most common, though they required half a dozen oxen or horses and several men to operate. The plodding teams of oxen turned the rollers more slowly—hence ground the cane more slowly—than windmills in a steady Caribbean breeze. Richard Ford's map of Barbados meticulously identifies the hundreds of sugar mills on the island circa 1674. Ford shows

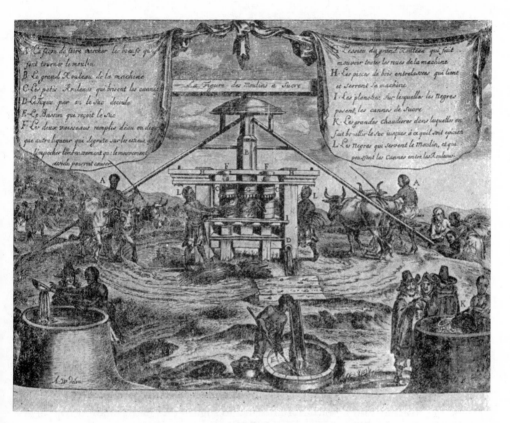

FIG. 7. *Sugar making in the seventeenth century. Slaves are feeding cane into the three-roller mill, powered by cattle. The cane juice pours into a cistern (E) and is ladled into coppers (K) and boiled. Actually the mill and boiling house were enclosed. (From Charles de Rochefort's* Histoire naturelle et morale des Îles Antilles de l'Amérique *[Rotterdam, 1665], facing p. 332; courtesy of the Library Company of Philadelphia.)*

that, although the majority of Barbados planters used cattle mills, the biggest operators, those with two or three mills, relied primarily on windmills. The small man who had only one mill could take no chances with wind failure; he had to have a cattle mill. Sometimes two neighboring planters would economize and build a mill or mills jointly. Ford's map shows fifty-seven mills or sets of mills operated in partnership, often by big planters. The map also shows that hundreds of small planters, some with only a handful of acres and slaves, owned sugar mills. These planters could not have produced enough sugar to keep their mills busy; probably they also ground the cane raised by their even smaller neighbors.[8]

The next step in sugar making was to boil the cane juice so as to clarify and evaporate it into crystallized sugar. The boiling house in seventeenth-century plantations stood adjacent to the sugar mill. Within the boiling house, a battery of four or five great copper kettles hung over a furnace. These coppers were carefully scaled in size. On Bybrook plantation in Jamaica, for instance, the four coppers held 180, 120, 80, and 30 gallons. It was the job of the boiler, the most valued laborer on the plantation staff, to ladle freshly extracted juice from a cistern into the first copper, skim off the impurities that rose to the surface, and ladle the remaining liquid into the second copper. As the juice passed into progressively smaller, hotter coppers, with constant skimming and evaporation it began to turn thick, ropey, and dark brown in color. A gallon of juice contracted into a pound of muscovado sugar. The final, smallest copper had the thickest bottom and hottest fire. The boiler "tempered" the bubbling syrup with lime to promote granulation, and when he thought it on the point of crystallization he made his "strike"— dampened the fire and ladled the sugar into a cooling cistern. The boiler had to be something of an artist, for there was no sure way of telling whether the sugar had been tempered enough or too much, or when it was ready to strike. He had to endure suffocating heat and stench, and his work was more hazardous than milling. "If a Boyler get any part into the scalding sugar," says Littleton, "it sticks like Glew, or Birdlime, and 'tis hard to save either Limb or Life."[9]

8. Ligon, *True History of Barbados*, 56, 87, 90; Littleton, *Groans of the Plantations*, 19–20; Ford, *New Map of the Island of Barbadoes* (see fig. 5, p. 94). In St. Christopher at mid-century, the small planter used a little sugar press, worked by two or three men, or a horse. See Davies, *History of Caribby-Islands*, 196.

9. Littleton, *Groans of the Plantations*, 20; Ligon, *True History of Barbados*, 90–91; Taylor MS, 521–522. An 18th-century Nevis planter, John Pinney, made

Harvesting, milling, and boiling required close synchronization. The cane, once cut, had to be crushed within a few hours before its sugar content deteriorated. The cane juice, once extracted, had to be boiled within a few hours before it fermented. For these reasons a sugar works often operated around the clock at harvest time, with the millmen and boilers toiling in shifts. Three of the oldest surviving windmills in Barbados (one of them dating to 1688) are equipped with interior fireplaces where straw fires were once lit to provide illumination for night work.[10] The overseers had to watch the slave gangs particularly closely during the night shift to forestall accidents and negligence.

Once the sugar was boiled there were two ways of curing it to make it fit for sale. The most common method in the English islands was to make muscovado, golden brown sugar, which needed further refining in England before it could be offered to the general public. In Barbados the planters also made clayed sugar, white and semi-refined, which brought a considerably higher price. Even when making muscovado the early English planters took considerable trouble with their curing and followed a more complex procedure than their successors in the eighteenth century. When the sugar had granulated and cooled for about twelve hours after boiling, they packed it into earthenware pots and placed the pots in the curing house on earthenware pans called drips. The curing house was kept as hot and close as possible in order to dry out the sugar; some planters set a fire in the center aisle. Even a small planter needed several hundred sugar pots. These vessels, shaped like large flower pots with holes in the bottom, were designed to drain the molasses from the sugar. Each pot had its bottom hole plugged for forty-eight hours, then unplugged, and the molasses that poured out was collected and taken to the distillery to make into rum. The planters kept their potted sugar drying and draining in the curing house for about a month. When they finally knocked it out of the pots, it had hardened into cone-shaped loaves. They cut away the frothy top end and the molasses-saturated bottom end from each loaf and reboiled them. The central two-thirds of the loaf—well-drained muscovado —was spread in the sun, packed into hogsheads, and stored in a

---

his boiler test the sugar before striking by dipping thumb and forefinger into the scalding brew to see whether the sugar that stuck between two fingers spun into a thread of the right consistency! Pares, *A West-India Fortune*, 117.

10. J. Sydney Dash, "The Windmills and Copper Walls of Barbados," *Jour. Bar. Mus. Hist. Soc.*, XXXI (1963–1964), 43–60.

warehouse for shipment to England.[11] In the 1660s a fifteen-hundred-pound hogshead of muscovado might fetch £15 in the islands; the price dropped to £8 or £9 in the 1680s, then rose considerably by the turn of the century.

To make white sugar the planters followed the same procedure as with muscovado except that they sealed the top of each pot with a well-moistened clay cap, several inches thick. Water from the clay gradually seeped through the pot and dissolved so much of the molasses that the sugar turned white and soft. It took the early English planters four months to cure clayed sugar. On the French islands this was the common way of curing, but only Barbados among the English islands had a good local supply of clay. Barbados export statistics indicate that very little white sugar was shipped even from this island—only 3 percent of the crop, for example, in the years 1698 to 1700. But such figures are deceptive. White sugar carried a much higher English duty, and the Barbadians habitually entered their clayed sugar with the customs officers as muscovado in order to evade this tax.[12]

The final component in the sugar works was a distillery for manufacturing rum, the staple Caribbean liquor and a valuable export commodity. The English planters in the West Indies were apparently the first sugar makers to discover how to distill molasses and other sugar by-products into a potent alcoholic drink with a sweetly burnished taste. Finding a profitable vent for molasses was a great boon to the sugar planters, for great quantities of this thick syrup were removed from the sugar during the curing process. A hogshead of muscovado might yield one hundred gallons of molasses. Some of this could be fed to the slaves and livestock, and some could be sold to the North American colonists as a cheap sweetener. But molasses acquired a greater allure and earned a higher price when distilled into rum. Nearly every planter had a still house equipped with a pot still, worm, and receiver. The planter mixed a solution of molasses, inferior cane juice, and skimmings from the boiling

11. Labat, *Nouveau voyage aux isles de l'Amérique*, IV, 406–407; Ligon, *True History of Barbados*, 91–92; Barrett, "Caribbean Sugar-Production Standards," in Parker, ed., *Merchants and Scholars*, 159–163. When the French planters made muscovado, they dispensed with pots and packed the boiled sugar directly into hogsheads with pierced bottoms. This much simpler (and cruder) method was adopted by the English in the 18th century.

12. Barbados exports to England and plantations, 1698–1700, Rawlinson Manuscripts, B 250/61, 64, Bodleian Library, Oxford; Starkey, *Economic Geography of Barbados*, 86–87. John Taylor (MS, 523) reported in 1688 that only two Jamaica planters made white sugar, both for local consumption.

coppers in a large vat and let it ferment for about a week. If we can believe John Taylor, unorthodox ingredients were sometimes tossed into the vat: "Perhaps the overseer will empt his camberpot into it," says Taylor, "to keep the Negroes from Drincking it." Once fermented, the liquid was heated and vaporized in the still and recondensed into rum. From the 1640s rum was the cheapest and most popular strong drink in the English islands. In Barbados it was also a major export item. The Leeward and Jamaica planters, lagging as usual, exported relatively little rum or molasses until the next century.

A mill, boiling house, curing house, and still did not cost much to build or equip. In the Jamaica inventories of 1674 to 1701 and the St. Christopher compensation claims of 1706 the planter generally placed about the same value on his sugar works as on his livestock. His cane fields and Negroes were worth far more to him. For example, a Jamaica planter named William Gent had a mill appraised at £65, a boiling house at £100, and a still at £55. His 26 horses, 35 cattle, 27 sheep, and 7 goats totaled £204, while his 45 Negroes and 3 white servants were priced at £637. Even a great planter like Samuel Long had only £37 worth of coppers, skimmers, and ladles in his boiling house, and his 1,200 sugar pots brought £90, whereas he held nearly £1,000 in livestock and 288 Negroes valued at £4,629.[13]

However low the valuation of a sugar works, it had to be in good operating condition at harvest time. Should the frame of the millhouse give way, or a mill roller break, or the furnace hearth crack, or a boiling copper burn out, or the lead pipe feeding a cistern snap—all common accidents—a year's output might be spoiled. Every part had to be imported from England, and the planter was always ordering replacements. In 1693, for example, one John Underwood, the manager of a Barbados plantation, directed the absentee owner in England to ship by next year's fleet (along with the usual supplies of food and clothing) the following items needed for refurbishing his sugar works:[14]

> 50,000 nails in assorted sizes
> 10 brass fittings for the mill frame
> 12 ladles and 6 skimmers

13. Jam. Inv., Vol. 2.
14. John Underwood to Sir Robert Davers in Richard Pares, ed., "Barbados History from the Records of the Prize Courts: The *Six Friends* of London, 1693," *Jour. Bar. Mus. Hist. Soc.*, VI (1938–1939), 16–17.

3 sheets of lead
600 hogshead and barrel hoops
a 70 gallon copper, the last one sent being too big

Every well-run plantation needed a carpenter and a smith (they might be either white servants or black slaves) to make necessary repairs, a potter to make sugar pots and drips, and a cooper to assemble barrels and hogsheads.

The sugar planter thus combined agriculture with industry. His industrial operations required little manpower; the great majority of his laborers were engaged in field work. The distribution of labor on a seventeenth-century plantation is hard to estimate because of the paucity of early estate records, but we can learn something from the compensation claims that the planters on St. Christopher filed after the French raid of 1706. The planters identified 450 of the slaves lost to the French by occupation: 64 percent were field hands, 10 percent worked in the sugar factory, 14 percent were domestics, and the remaining 12 percent were overseers, craftsmen, carters, shepherds, and fishermen.[15] This is about the same labor pattern that we find in the plantation accounts of three eighteenth-century estates: Codrington plantation in Barbados, Pinney plantation in Nevis, and Worthy Park in Jamaica.[16] As might be expected, the most highly valued laborers were the drivers of the field gangs and the specialists who operated and maintained the sugar works: millmen, boilers, clarifiers, clayers, distillers, potters, coopers, carpenters, and smiths. It should be added that about a fifth of the slaves on any large plantation were nonworkers, too young, too old, or too sick for useful employment.

The most instructive difference, perhaps, between a Caribbean sugar plantation and an English farm was the huge, unskilled force of field workers employed in the Indies—nearly one laborer per acre of cane on an average seventeenth-century Barbados plantation. Men did the work of animals. Such tasks as planting and cultivating, performed on English or North American farms by horse-driven plows and harrows, were carried out in the Indies entirely by hand. Caribbean farm implements were few and simple. A Negro field laborer had three tools; an ax, a hoe, and a bill. The planter could equip a gang of fifty field laborers for about £5, whereas the average

15. See table 29.
16. Bennett, *Bondsmen and Bishops*, 11–18; Pares, *A West-India Fortune*, 129–130; Craton and Walvin, *A Jamaican Plantation*, 101–102; Ulrich B. Phillips, "A Jamaican Slave Plantation," *American Historical Review*, XIX (1914), 543–547.

FIG. 8. *Another early view of sugar making, showing the mill* (1), *the boiling house* (2), *and the distillery* (4). *In the background slaves are cutting ripe cane. (From Jean-Baptiste Du Tertre, Histoire générale des Antilles habitées par les François [Paris, 1667–1671], II, 122; courtesy of William L. Clements Library, University of Michigan, Ann Arbor.)*

Moulin 2. Fourneaux 3. Formes. 4. Vinaigrerie 5 Cannes 6. Gros 7. Latanir 8 Pajomiroba 9. Choux 10. Cafes 11 Figur. 12.
et Chaudieres.   de Jura Cocos, pic. p. iii. p. 32. Carinbes de Negres
                                                                                              G. Clerc. f.

English day laborer owned a diversified set of some two dozen hand tools worth £1.[17]

The reason for all the inefficient hand tillage in the Indies was to keep the slaves busy year-round. Cane cultivation, like most farming, is really seasonal. The planter needs a large labor force at crop time, but not during the slow six months of the year from July through December. Yet the seventeenth-century slave-owning planter had to keep his laborers fully occupied in the slow months, as well as in crop time, to forestall mischief and rebellion. So he put them to work in the fields with hoes instead of horse-drawn plows. The slave's appointed tasks were exceedingly monotonous and degrading, and he executed them unwillingly, unskillfully, and inefficiently. Manual labor in the islands became a badge of dishonor. Once the slave labor system was well entrenched, no white man cared to soil his hands if he could possibly avoid doing so.

By the closing decades of the century absentee ownership was becoming a major problem in the English sugar industry. Most planters who retired to England left their estates in the hands of salaried overseers, but this arrangement seldom worked well. The owner, anxious for all the profits, rarely offered his overseer a generous cut, so the overseer either cheated on his master or simply let things slide. A carelessly managed sugar plantation deteriorated rapidly, as is shown by the example of the Long family's properties in Jamaica. Samuel Long had been one of the most successful pioneer planters, and when he died in 1683 he left two of the choicest estates on the island, Seven Plantations and Lucky Valley, to his son Charles. About the turn of the century Charles Long retired to England to enjoy his wealth in more polished surroundings. In 1707 he asked his friend Peter Heywood, the chief justice of Jamaica, to check up on his property. Heywood reported that he found "all things in disorder, the whole [sugar] works a Pott of nastiness and in General out of repair." The millhouse at Seven Plantations was literally knee deep in cattle dung, the boiling-house floor swimming in molasses, the coppers burned and filthy, the curing-house pots overflowing with wasted sugar. The plantation house needed re-shingling, the cane fields were choked with weeds, and so little corn was planted, says Heywood, "that I heartily pity the poor slaves, the mules and the stock the next year. The slaves in general rejoyced to see us, for we call'd them all before us and inquir'd into their

17. William Gent's inventory, Jam. Inv., Vol. 2; Everitt, "Farm Labourers," in Thirsk, ed., *Agrarian History of England and Wales*, 431–432.

useiages." The slaves told Heywood that the overseer had confiscated their hogs and fowl and given them no salt for their food
or any new clothes. So Heywood dismissed the overseer and appointed a new one. But if Colonel Long hoped to restore his plantation, he would have to return to Jamaica himself.[18]

Even when the owner managed his plantation carefully, his
method of making sugar had obvious economic defects. The cane
fields returned a relatively low yield, the sugar mills left half the
juice in the cane stalks, the boiling process was haphazard, the curing process cumbersome, and much of the sugar shipped to England
was still full of molasses. Nevertheless, by the technological standards of the day, the English sugar-production system was well organized and efficient. It worked well enough so that the Caribbean
planters saw no need to make technical improvements for a full
century after 1700. Richard Ligon boasted in 1657 that "the right
and best way of sugar making used in Barbados will admit of no
greater or farther improvement." Dalby Thomas bragged in 1690
that "we at present exceed all the Nations in the world in the true
Improvement of that Noble Juice of the Cane." [19]

How large was English Caribbean sugar production in the early
days? This question cannot be answered with much confidence, for
seventeenth-century commercial statistics are notoriously unreliable.
The island planters never recorded annual sales or exports, for they
had no wish to reveal their wealth. Before 1660 much or most of the
sugar crop went to the Dutch, and for many years after 1660 the
English government kept spotty, confused, and in some cases contradictory records of sugar shipments imported into England. When
customs officials did record annual totals, they sometimes reckoned
in years running from Christmas to Christmas, sometimes March to
March. Sugar could be packed in hogsheads, butts, tierces, or barrels,
and all of these casks varied greatly in size and weight. A sugar
hogshead usually held about a thousand pounds in the seventeenth

18. Heywood to Long, Oct. 16, 1707, Deerr, *History of Sugar*, II, 338–342. See
also Robert Mowbray Howard, *Records and Letters of the Family of the Longs of
Longville, Jamaica, and Hampton Lodge, Surrey* (London, 1925), I, 36–71.

19. Ligon, *True History of Barbados*, 86; Thomas, *Historical Account*, 14;
Barrett, "Caribbean Sugar-Production Standards," in Parker, ed., *Merchants and
Scholars*, 148–149, 159, 168.

century, but might weigh anywhere from eight hundred to sixteen hundred pounds.[20] Not even the ton was standardized; the Jamaican naval officer in 1679 explained that a ton of sugar from that island weighed at least three thousand pounds. Obviously, therefore, the statistics presented in table 21 are exceedingly rough and untrustworthy. They are drawn mainly from data collected at the time by the clerks in the Plantation Office and represent the best information available to the home authorities. Unfortunately the totals for Barbados are especially deficient. In standardizing these figures I have translated all weights into tons and made the dangerous assumption that a hogshead equals half a ton, or a thousand pounds.

There is no reason to question the general thrust of these figures that English Caribbean sugar production doubled or trebled between the Restoration and the turn of the century. The only counter evidence is the very low figure for 1688, and 1688 was an exceptional year, for English shipping was paralyzed by the revolutionary crisis at home. After 1700 commercial statistics become more complete and somewhat more reliable and show a steady continuation of the same upward trend. The English sugar planters achieved an annual output of fifty thousand tons before 1750 and seventy-five thousand tons by the American Revolution. Obviously the industry in our period was not yet fully developed.

The totals in table 21 give only a poor idea of Barbados's dominant role in the early sugar business. Contemporary writers assure us that the Barbadians exported fifteen thousand tons in good years from the 1650s to the 1680s. Governor Stede thought the crop of 1686 was the largest ever harvested on the island. In the banner years of the Restoration era, Barbados drew more than two hundred ships annually from England, Ireland, and North America, far more than the other islands.[21] In 1676–1677, for example, eighty-five ships sailed from Barbados to London, thirty-five ships from Jamaica to London, and thirty-three ships from the Leewards to London.[22] During the decade of the 1670s Barbados probably produced 60 or 70 percent of the sugar exported to England from the Carib-

20. Sugar hogsheads in the 18th century seem to have been considerably larger, close to a ton. See A. P. Thornton, "Some Statistics of West Indian Produce, Shipping and Revenue, 1660–1685," *Caribbean Historical Review*, IV (1954), 251–252; Craton and Walvin, *A Jamaican Plantation*, 111–112, 121–122.

21. Gov. Stede to Lords of Trade, Apr. 27, 1686, C.O. 29/3/375; Thomas Tryon, *The Merchant, Citizen and Country-man's Instructor* (London, 1701), 188, 218.

22. C.O. 1/42/121–123. The 85 ships from Barbados were larger than the others, so that the Barbados tonnage to London in this year was 63% of the total from the sugar islands.

Table 21. Estimated Sugar Imports (in Tons) to England, 1651–1706

Year	Barbados	Jamaica	Leeward Islands	Total
1651	c. 3,750			
1655	7,787			
1663	c. 7,176		c. 1,000	8,176
1669	9,525	c. 500	c. 1,679	11,704
1672		522		
1676		1,154	3,600	
1678		2,259	1,505[Nevis]	
1680		3,563		
1681		2,082		
1682		5,278		
1683	c. 10,000	4,902	c. 3,300	18,202
1686		7,739	2,054[Nevis]	
1687		5,585	2,134[Nevis]	
1688	757?	6,032	255?	7,044?
1690		4,810		
1691	9,191	7,099		
1696	7,613			
1697	5,154			
1698	15,587	6,004	c. 5,060	c. 26,651
1699	9,140	5,276	c. 8,015	c. 22,431
1700	12,170	4,474	c. 6,812	c. 23,456
1704		6,056	1,630[Nevis]	
1705	9,419			
1706	10,236			

NOTE: Many of these figures are derived from Thornton, "Some Statistics of West Indian Produce," Carib. Hist. Rev., IV (1954), 251–280. I have extracted additional Jamaica totals from C.O. 1/43/59 and C.O. 390/6/31–38; additional Barbados totals from Cal.S.P.Col., 1574–1660, 388, 434, from Pares, Yankees and Creoles, 98, and from C.O. 390/6/51–56; and additional Nevis totals from C.O. 390/6/87–89. Deerr, History of Sugar, I, 193–203, offers a less complete and slightly different set of figures from mine.

bean. Gradually the Barbadians lost this primacy. In the 1680s and 1690s they complained endlessly of declining crop yields, insect and vermin plagues, drought, barren soil, and rising costs. To meet the worsening agricultural conditions, they fertilized the soil heavily with cattle dung, planted the cane in holes rather than trenches, grubbed and replanted their fields freshly every year instead of letting the old cane resprout into a second ratoon crop. These strategies all required added labor.[23] By the turn of the century Barbados was still the island leader, with exports to England in 1698–1700 averaging £316,000 per annum as against Jamaican exports of £201,400 and Leeward exports of £192,000. Shipping statistics for the years from 1698 to 1704 indicate much the same thing, that Barbados's share of the island commerce with England had fallen to about 45 percent.[24] And it kept on dropping. After Utrecht, Barbados's sugar output was rapidly surpassed by the Leewards and Jamaica.

The rather full run of early Jamaican sugar export figures in table 21 shows very nicely the slow beginnings of production on this island in the 1670s and 1680s, with a leveling off during the long French wars. It was in Jamaica, of course, that the eighteenth-century spurt in production was most pronounced. By the 1750s Jamaica was making more sugar than all of the English islands put together in 1700. Even so, it can be argued that the most dynamic stage in the English sugar industry came early, before 1713. Certainly the early planters enjoyed a larger piece of the European market than their successors. It so happened that the English entered production just when the Brazilian industry began to slump, and before the French on St. Domingue, Martinique, and Guadeloupe hit their stride. The Brazilian slump was apparently quite dramatic. An English observer in 1668 claimed that Brazilian shipments to Europe had dropped from seventy thousand to twenty thousand chests since the English had entered into competition. It was reported in 1670 that English exports had cut the price of Brazilian white sugar by two-thirds and beaten Brazilian muscovado off the market. Thus the English had become "the Sole Merchants, almost of all that Sugar that is Manufactured into loafe or hard Suger either in Holland, France, or Hambrough as being all made out of our Muscovadoes." This claim was rather too boastful, for it disguised the fact that Brazilian white sugar did not need to be re-

23. Gov. Stede to Lords of Trade, Oct. 19, 1687, C.O. 1/63/211. A pamphleteer of about 1689 claimed that 100 Negroes in Barbados could accomplish no more than 25 in the Leewards. *A State of the Present Condition of the Island of Barbadoes* (n.p., c. 1689), 3.

24. Calculation of England's trade with the sugar islands, 1698–1702, C.O. 318/1/27, 31. See also the shipping figures for Barbados in C.O. 390/6/51–56; for Jamaica in C.O. 390/6/31–38; and for Nevis in C.O. 390/6/87–89.

fined in Holland, France, or Hamburg, being of a higher quality and more expensive than English muscovado. But the English did sell a great deal of sugar on the Continent until they were supplanted by the French. The French sugar industry in the Caribbean started slowly in the seventeenth century, but after 1713 St. Domingue developed at an even faster clip than Jamaica, and by about 1735 French sugar was not only more plentiful, but cheaper, and probably better. Thus the English were only briefly in command. They could claim to be the leading sugar makers in America from roughly 1680 to 1720. The very crude estimates available suggest that in 1700, when the English West Indian planters sold about twenty-five thousand tons a year, Brazilian output was under twenty thousand tons, the French West Indies produced about ten thousand tons, and the Dutch in Surinam about four thousand tons.[25] Never again were the English in such a favorable competitive position.

As production rose, the market price of sugar fell. The English price of muscovado dropped from £4 per hundredweight in the 1640s to £2 at the Restoration, slid again to 25s. in the 1670s, and reached a low of 16s. in 1686–1687. The price in the islands dipped accordingly. The planter who had sold his muscovado to a factor in Barbados for 28s. per hundredweight in the 1650s could only get 10s. in the 1680s. The planters complained of being tied to the English entrepôt by the navigation acts, but actually they would have fared no better in an open market. Amsterdam sugar prices correlated very closely with London prices in the late seventeenth century, sinking to the equivalent of 16s. in 1686–1687. During the war years prices in London and Amsterdam recovered strongly, but wartime freight and insurance rates climbed steeply also, so that the American producer never regained his early profit margin.[26]

The planters also thought that their product was being taxed too stiffly by the home government. From 1663 on, all commodities exported from Barbados and the Leewards were subject to a 4.5 per-

25. Pitman, *Development of the British West Indies*, chaps. 7–8; Beer, *Old Colonial System*, II, 5–6; Deerr, *History of Sugar*, I, 101–112, 123–132, 193–203, 212–218, 233–240.
26. K. G. Davies's table of London sugar sales by the Royal African Company, *Royal African Company*, 356–366, matches neatly with Noel Deerr's sugar price index for Amsterdam in the same years. By contrast, Deerr shows a sharp differential between the two sugar markets in the 18th century, after the English gave up competing for the European trade. Between 1728 and 1789 muscovado averaged £33 5s. per cwt. in London and only £23 3s. per cwt. in Amsterdam. Deerr, *History of Sugar*, II, 529–531.

cent duty, paid in the islands. This duty, collected in the early years by tax farmers, funneled over £81,000 into the royal exchequer between 1670 and 1688.[27] But the principal sugar tax was levied when the hogsheads were unladed in an English or mainland colonial port. Starting in 1651 the English duty was 1s. 6d. per hundredweight on muscovado and 5s. on clayed or semirefined sugar; foreign sugars were taxed much more stiffly. The tax differential between muscovado and clayed sugar was introduced to discourage the planters from refining their own, so that the sugar bakers at home could process the West Indian muscovado. As with tobacco the duty on sugar reexported to the Continent was rebated. The planters persuaded Parliament not to increase the sugar duties in 1671, but James II's Parliament doubled the duties. The colonists petitioned the king that it was "utterly impossible" for them to bear this "fatall tax," but bear it they did until the act expired in 1693.[28]

The combination of James II's high tax and the low prices of 1686–1687 put the sugar planters in a real squeeze, but they were at least better off than the tobacco farmers of Virginia and Maryland. The customs duty on tobacco in the seventeenth century was always far higher than on sugar. Between 1660 and 1685 the king generally received more from each pound of imported Virginia leaf than the planter who grew it. Clearly the sugar planters had organized a more effective lobby at Whitehall than the tobacco interests. English tobacco prices fell so low in the 1660s and again in the 1680s that the Chesapeake planters found their product selling below cost and had to cut back production, which never happened in the sugar islands. In 1668–1669, one of the very few years for which we have comparative tobacco and sugar figures, it appears that the West Indian planters sold their sugar crop for about £180,000 and that this sugar paid customs duty of about £18,000 on arrival in England. By contrast, the Chesapeake planters sold their tobacco for only about £50,000, and it paid customs duty of £75,000 in England.[29]

This discrimination in favor of sugar continued for the balance of the century. In the late 1670s Chesapeake tobacco was paying over £100,000 in customs and Caribbean sugar less than £25,000. In

27. Thornton, *West-India Policy*, 258–259, has compiled the 4.5% duty returns.
28. Beer, *Old Colonial System*, I, 82–83, 130, 133, 148–167; Barbados Council and Assembly to James II, Sept. 15, 1685, C.O. 31/1/648–649; John Gibbes to William Blathwayt, June 15, 1687, Blathwayt Papers, XXXI.
29. Sugar and tobacco imports for 1662–1663 and 1668–1669, C.O. 388/2/6, 12.

1685 James II levied an additional tax on tobacco as well as on sugar, and by 1700 the home tobacco tax was six times the market value of leaf in Virginia.[30] West Indian sugar maintained its wide competitive edge; from 1698 to 1700 the island colonies shipped to England commodities valued at £710,000 per annum, while Virginia and Maryland exported only £230,000 to England. Thanks to sugar the island planters could and did buy more English imports than the Chesapeake colonists, despite their far smaller numbers.[31]

In one vital respect, however, the tobacco planters fared better. They did not depend, as the sugar planters had to, upon merchant ships from Britain and New England for their very survival. Traders to the English Caribbean kept the colonists alive by bringing them food and clothing, as well as all other needed supplies, and carrying off their sugar. The West India trade was a major branch of English commerce in the late seventeenth century. Normally, about two hundred ships called each year at Barbados, and one hundred each at Jamaica and the Leeward Islands. Ralph Davis, the historian of the English shipping industry in this period, reckons that the West India trade accounted for 7 percent of English merchant tonnage and 11 percent of the value of English overseas commerce in 1700. To the merchants of London and the English outports this trade was certainly inviting. To the New England merchants it was essential.[32] But the sugar planters felt exploited and manipulated by these commercial middlemen.

No matter how they marketed their sugar, the planters found that a great part of their profits was siphoned off by island factors, ship captains, and English merchants. At first such planters as James Drax doubled as merchants, sailing their own ships, marketing their own sugar, even fetching their own slaves from Africa. More commonly partners like Thomas Modyford and Thomas Kendall divided the work between them, one serving as planter and the other as merchant. But as the sugar business grew larger, it grew more

30. Lewis C. Gray, *History of Agriculture in the Southern United States to 1860* (Washington, D.C., 1933), I, chap. 12; sugar duties collected, 1677–1678, C.O. 1/42/123; *Cal.S.P.Col., 1675–1676,* #1106. See also Jacob M. Price, "The Economic Growth of the Chesapeake and the European Market, 1697–1775," *Jour. Econ. Hist.,* XXIV (1964), 496–511.

31. West Indian exports to and imports from England, 1698–1700, are tabulated in C.O. 318/1/27. Chesapeake exports and imports for the same years are tabulated in U.S. Bureau of the Census, *Historical Statistics of the United States, Colonial Times to 1957* (Washington, D.C., 1960), 757.

32. Ralph Davis, *The Rise of the English Shipping Industry in the Seventeenth and Eighteenth Centuries* (London, 1962); Pares, *Yankees and Creoles,* chap. 1.

specialized. By the 1670s few planters took shares in ships or sold their own produce in England. Small planters generally sold their crops to factors or ship captains in the islands. This method eliminated risk and bother, but of course the middleman who bought the small planter's produce tried to keep the price of sugar in the islands as low as possible. In 1682, for example, all of the Jamaican factors entered into a combination and agreed to delay buying sugar until they could force down the price.

To avoid this predicament and to reduce middleman costs, the big planters—particularly the big Barbados planters—dealt directly with commission agents in England. In this arrangement the planter shipped his own sugar, consigning it to a particular agent who sold it for him (at a 3 percent commission), placing the net proceeds in his account where it was drawn upon for bills of credit or used to pay for goods the planter ordered from England. The largest firms, Bawden and Company and Eyles and Company, maintained very lucrative accounts with dozens of big planters. For the planter this mode of merchandizing entailed great risks during wartime, when sugar cargoes were frequently lost at sea to the enemy. At such times the London agents were likely to reject the planters' bills of exchange.[33] For Jamaican planters the Heathcote brothers combined the roles of English agent and island factor. Gilbert Heathcote operated as a commission agent in London and also served as the colony agent. His brothers, George and Joshua, were factors in Port Royal. Joshua Heathcote was a big man in Jamaica in the 1690s, an assemblyman and councillor, who made more money from supervising the estates of planters living in England than the absentee owners.[34]

The pattern of trade between the islands and the mother country is well illustrated by a pair of Jamaica documents. A freight book for the ship *Samuel,* sailing from Jamaica to Bristol about 1685, shows us a typical outgoing cargo. On this voyage the *Samuel* carried 120 hogsheads of sugar, 13 bags of cotton, 5 small casks of indigo, and 18 tons of logwood. Freight charges totaled £215, or about £3 per ton. Eighteen planters and merchants consigned goods on this particular voyage. Three planters loaded 32, 31, and 23 hogsheads

33. K. G. Davies, "Origins of the Commission System," Royal Hist. Soc., *Trans.,* 5th Ser., II, 89–107.

34. The powerful role of the Heathcotes in the affairs of Jamaican planters can be traced through the Bybrook plantation records, Helyar MSS, discussed **below.**

of sugar, the others only a few hogsheads apiece. It was standard practice to ship home sugar in small lots, not only to spread the risk but to bolster the price. Merchant John Napper explained to William Helyar that, when a planter loaded 100 hogsheads in one ship, "if five should be sould, the rest will be accompted Refuse." [35]

The other end of the Caribbean trade, the incoming traffic from England to the islands, is well illustrated by an invoice, preserved in the Jamaica Archives, that details the cargo carried by the *Friendship* when she sailed from London to Port Royal in 1671. The goods are itemized as follows: [36]

> 40 barrels of beer
> 6 barrels of rum
> 2 pipes, 22 barrels and 1 hogshead of brandy
> 1,160 stone bottles of Passada wine
> 73 pipes of St. George's wine
> 2 pipes of Pico wine
> 100 doz. stone bottles
> 10 doz. stone jugs
> 1 cask of corks
> 32 barrels and 2 hogsheads of flour
> 6 jars and 1 rundlet of oil
> 1 pack of wearing apparel
> 1 butt of tinware
> 5 caldrons and 1 vat of sea coals
> 11 coils of cordage
> 7 chests of earthenware, glasses, soap and guns
> 10 barrels of powder
> 8 barrels of shot
> 2 casks of brimstone
> 24 barrels of pitch and tar
> 1 hogshead of rosin
> 3,970 pantiles
> 2 casks of tobacco pipes
> 2 parcels of paper
>
> 14 men servants, aged 18 to 41 years
> 4 women servants, aged 24 to 28 years

Most of these commodities reached Port Royal safe and sound. To be sure, the sailors on the *Friendship* drank up two barrels of beer during the voyage, the casks of St. George's wine (picked up en

35. A freight Booke for the ship Samuel of Bristole from Jamaca, [*c.* 1685]; John Napper to William Helyar, Oct. 18, 1682, Helyar MSS.
36. Powers of Attorney, I (1674–1676), File 1 B/11, Jam. Archives.

route in the Azores) leaked badly in transit, two barrels of pitch had "leakt quite out by default of the hoopes," and many stone bottles of Passada wine (likewise from the Azores) were smashed when the ship was unladed. One servant was also missing, having either run away or died during the voyage. The other servants proved hard to sell; it took the Port Royal merchant a full month to find a master for the last of them.

The most noticeable thing about this Jamaica cargo of 1671 is its wide-ranging variety, a characteristic of the Caribbean trade, for shippers tried to avoid glutting the small island markets with any one commodity by mixing their wares as adroitly as possible. The enormous quantity of liquor, bottles, and corks carried by the *Friendship* was not unusual. Jamaica deserved its reputation as a hard-drinking place. During a six-month period in 1683–1684 incoming ships delivered 719 tons of spirits and wine at Port Royal, as against 756 tons of meat and fish and 315 tons of wheat, bread, and other provisions. The *Friendship* carried no meat, no fish, and only a little flour, which again is not surprising, because such foodstuffs were normally shipped from North America or Ireland. What *is* unusual about this particular cargo is the near absence of cloth, stockings, shoes, and haberdashery, for most ships from England carried an assortment of dry goods as well as household furnishings. The island planters imported almost everything, even (as in this example) pantiles to roof their houses. Jamaica at least had plenty of local timber for building purposes, but the Barbadians found it necessary in the 1680s to import housing timber from St. Lucia.

The Caribbean trade was pretty evenly divided between English and New England ships in the closing decades of the century. Scattered shipping returns for Nevis, St. Christopher, and Montserrat in the years between 1678 and 1684 identify 290 vessels by port of origin. Nearly half of these, 139 in all, came from English ports, another 25 came from Ireland, 107 from New England, 2 from other mainland colonies, and 19 from Barbados and the Leeward Islands. The three leading home ports were Boston (77), London (64), and Bristol (28). The New England ships were generally smaller than the English ones, and—more important to the sugar planters—they carried a different line of cargo. The New England ships brought cheap, low-quality goods for the slaves; the English ships brought goods for the master class, the fancier the better. From New England came dried fish, corn, barreled meat, staves for the sugar hogsheads, and horses to work the mills. From

England came luxury wares: silks, furniture, expensive groceries, and wines.[37] As a Port Royal merchant explained in 1674, such wares must be "fresh and good and fashionable, for there is a proud generation in this Countrey, although people in England thinke any thing will serve here." [38]

Freight rates to England were normally £1 or £2 higher per ton in Jamaica than in Barbados or the Leewards, because of the greater distance and risk. This explains why merchants in London consistently asked a higher price for Jamaican sugar than for eastern Caribbean sugar; the price differential undoubtedly helped to maintain Barbados's favored position in the English sugar market. In wartime freight rates quickly trebled in all the island ports. Wartime insurance was extremely costly. In 1694 William Helyar paid 18 guineas to obtain £85 worth of coverage on £100 worth of sugar. But the most serious consequence of the French wars at the close of the century was the scarcity of shipping, especially from England. For example, during the crisis years from 1688 to 1697, Barbados received an average of 152 ships per year, a significant drop from prewar levels, and since the great majority were small New England ships, her supplies were seriously reduced. With the return of peace, in the years 1698 to 1700 an average of 266 ships, including many more big London vessels, crowded into the Bridgetown wharves.[39]

The long French wars did more than disrupt normal commerce between the islands and the mother country. The wartime losses, combined with uncertain sugar prices and rising costs, sapped the planters' old aggressive independence. The Barbadians, who had cried out loudest against English controls from 1660 to 1668, now

37. Shipping returns for Nevis, C.O. 1/42/270, C.O. 1/47/67–72; St. Christopher, C.O. 1/46/85–89, C.O. 1/54/230–235; and Montserrat, C.O. 1/49/66, C.O. 1/55/26–27. See also Thornton, "Some Statistics of West Indian Produce," *Carib. Hist. Rev.*, IV (1954), 265–266, 269–272.

38. Thomas Bolton at Port Royal to Gilbert Allenson in London, Sept. 20, 1674, Powers of Attorney, I (1674–1676), 1 B/11. Bolton found Allenson's silks too shoddy to sell in Jamaica. Thirty years later, a Kingston merchant, William Parke, had the same complaint about linen and silk he received on consignment in 1705–1708 from the London firm of John and Thomas Eyre. The Parke-Eyre correspondence is in the Institute of Jamaica, Kingston, and in Jamaica Commercial Papers, 1662–1788, Manuscript Division, New York Public Library.

39. Abstract of Barbados shipping to England and colonies, 1687–1700, C.O. 390/6/51–56; abstract of Jamaica shipping to England and colonies, 1682–1704, C.O. 390/6/31–38; Gilbert Heathcote to William Helyar, Nov. 10, 1691, Helyar MSS; Pares, *Yankees and Creoles*, 92–100; K. G. Davies, *Royal African Company*, 201–203, 366. Barbados sugar was not only cheaper than the Jamaican but better in quality: more sweet and full-bodied. Jamaican sugar was the lightest in color; Antiguan muscovado was the blackest and coarsest.

felt most acutely the need for such controls. The Jamaica and Leeward planters had come to depend on the home government for
military aid, and once the war was over, they wanted home protection against French sugar competition. With so many of the chief
planters withdrawing to England, the sugar interest became centered more and more in London, where a small clique of complacent,
rich, absentee planters—unable or unwilling to compete any longer
with foreign sugar producers—preserved their favored status by
strenuous political lobbying. As the eighteenth century progressed,
the sugar lobby assumed a dominating voice in American affairs out
of all proportion to its real strength. Such an essentially parasitic
role had not seemed necessary to the seventeenth-century pioneer
sugar planters, less rich but more self-confident.

The best way by far to grasp the character of seventeenth-century
plantation life is to study the records of individual planters. Unhappily, such documents are exceedingly scarce. For the eighteenth
century, when the sugar industry was fully established, there are
indeed several splendid surviving collections of planter's correspondence, accounts, inventories, and invoices. Utilizing these sources,
Richard Pares composed a first-class business history of the Pinney
plantations in Nevis from 1685 to 1808, Michael Craton and James
Walvin have done the same for Worthy Park in Jamaica from the
1720s to the present day, and J. Harry Bennett has reconstituted in
rich detail the day-by-day operations of the Codrington plantations
in Barbados from 1710 to 1808.[40] Professor Bennett also discovered
another set of documents illuminating the early years of Bybrook
plantation in Jamaica; he set to work on this collection, but died
before he could complete his analysis. The Bybrook records are
more fragmentary than the Pinney, Worthy Park, and Codrington
papers, but they have special value because they document an earlier
time span, from 1669 when Cary Helyar laid out this plantation to
1713 when his nephews William and John Helyar sold it.[41]

40. Pares, *A West-India Fortune*, based upon the Pinney Papers in Bristol
University; Craton and Walvin, *A Jamaican Plantation*, based chiefly upon the
estate records at Worthy Park; Bennett, *Bondsmen and Bishops*, based upon
manuscripts in the London archives of the Society for the Propagation of the
Gospel in Foreign Parts.
41. The Bybrook records are among the Helyar MSS. Prof. Bennett discussed
the earliest years of Bybrook, 1669–1676, in three articles: "Cary Helyar," *Wm.*

The Bybrook plantation documents give us a fascinating view of the problems faced by a pioneer planter during the formative years of the English sugar industry. Bybrook, situated in the lush interior valley of Sixteen Mile Walk, later known as St. Thomas in the Vale, has been an operating sugar estate for three hundred years. One of the principal sugar factories in Jamaica today is called Bybrook; it stands on or near Cary Helyar's original tract. But Cary Helyar, his brother, and his nephews had a terrible time starting Bybrook and extracting a profit from it. During most of the years of Helyar ownership, from 1669 to 1713, the family tried to operate their plantation while living in England. The story of Bybrook reveals above all the insoluble problems of absentee ownership.

Cary Helyar felt sure that he was going to make a quick fortune when he started his Jamaica plantation. He was one of those hungry young Englishmen of good family, slender purse, and buoyant expectations who flocked to the West Indies in the middle years of the century looking for a bonanza. Being a younger son, Cary had only a small annuity in England, but his elder brother William, a Cavalier colonel in the English civil war, was a substantial Somerset squire who could help finance profitable-looking ventures. Cary Helyar arrived in Jamaica at age thirty in 1664, made some money peddling Negroes to the colonists, and became an intimate of such big planters as Sir Thomas Modyford, Sir Thomas Lynch, and Hender Molesworth. He was appointed the island treasurer and elected to the Jamaica Assembly. On the advice of Modyford and Molesworth he began in March 1669 to patent land adjacent to theirs in the interior valley of Sixteen Mile Walk.

This valley was (and is) a prime sugar-planting region, with ample rainfall and rich, red soil. Helyar called his tract Bybrook because it bordered the Rio Cobre and a smaller stream cut through it; he had plenty of water power for a sugar mill. Bybrook lay near the present town of Bog Walk, some ten miles north of Spanish Town. Helyar quickly acquired six hundred acres at Bybrook and a thousand acres on the north coast of the island. "If you did but see," he explained airily to brother William, "what brave estates are gotten by very much meaner principals than wee begin upon, you would say it is a brave thing to have elbow room enough and that

---

and Mary Qtly., 3d Ser., XXI (1964), 53–76; "William Dampier, Buccaneer and Planter," *History Today,* XIV (1964), 469–477; and "William Whaley, Planter of Seventeenth-Century Jamaica," *Agricultural History,* XL (1966), 113–123. My discussion draws upon these articles and uses the Helyar MSS microfilm to carry the story of Bybrook to 1713.

planting is a happy and innocent way of thriving." The Helyars never developed their north-coast tract, but by 1674 Bybrook plantation contained 1,236 acres "almost square, of as good land and as well watered as any in the island." [42]

Cary Helyar talked his brother into taking half a share in Bybrook. The partners agreed in 1669 to divide costs and profits equally, with Cary managing the plantation while William shipped the necessary supplies and laborers from England. Squire William accepted this arrangement on the understanding that Bybrook was going to be a cacao plantation. Cacao was a good crop to start on, Cary explained, even though the trees took about five years to produce their first cacao pods, for they required little investment in labor or capital and yielded fat returns. Cary spent £346 during his opening year at Bybrook to get a cacao grove started. Too impatient to wait for his brother to send laborers from England, he bought twelve Negroes and hired several white servants. With this work force he planted six acres of cacao trees and enough plantain trees to feed his men. Then came the first blow. A blight killed practically all the Bybrook cacao trees in 1670–1671, long before they bore any fruit.

Buoyant as ever, Cary immediately began to convert Bybrook into a sugar plantation. Sugar required a considerably larger capital investment than cacao, to be sure, yet Cary told his brother in April 1671 that they could get by with eighteen more Negroes, for a total of thirty, and that all the necessary added outlay—including equipment for a sugar works—would cost only £846. A bargain, surely, since Bybrook would earn £30 per acre in sugar and rum once production started. William Helyar was persuaded and soon shipped over the fittings for a water mill, four coppers with ladles and skimmers for a boiling house, and pewter worms, tubs, and stills for a distillery. At Cary's urging he recruited a carpenter and other artisans for Bybrook from the local village of East Coker, though Cary quickly protested against the "ugly weavers" who arrived, bred to the Somerset cloth trade and totally unsuited for Jamaica plantation craft work. To keep some sort of check on his ebullient brother, William Helyar sent over his young godson, William Whaley, in 1671 to assist Cary at Bybrook. Whaley's initial impression was heartening indeed. "Every time I goe up to the plantation,"

---

42. Cary Helyar to William Helyar, Apr. 15, 1671, Helyar MSS; Bennett, "Cary Helyar," *Wm. and Mary Qtly.*, 3d Ser., XXI (1964), 61.

he reported in January 1672, "it makes mee more and more to love the Countrey for to see how bravely the canes grow and how the negroes goe tumbling down the trees." [43]

By June 1672 Cary was almost ready to make sugar. He had twenty-four acres planted in cane, sixteen in provisions and twenty cleared for pasture. Though the boiling house was not yet set up, he was framing the water mill and had the distillery in place. So far, he reckoned, the Helyar brothers had spent as follows to outfit their plantation:

Negroes (55)	£1,205
White servants and hired labor (14)	160
Millwork, ironwork, and tools	223
Horses, hogs, and poultry	35
Food and drink	128
Cloth and clothing	21
Furniture for the plantation house	26
Land	21
Taxes and rewards for runaway servants	7
Miscellaneous	32
	£1,858

Thus Bybrook, still unfinished, already cost twice as much as Cary told William it would, mainly because he bought so many slaves. Most of the money came out of William's pocket; Cary had drawn £1,298 on his brother and by his own calculation owed him £389. If the squire was dismayed at this news, worse soon followed. In July 1672, before Bybrook had returned any income at all, Cary Helyar suddenly died. He was thirty-eight years old. [44]

On his deathbed Cary Helyar willed his half share of Bybrook to his young assistant, William Whaley. When Whaley discovered, however, that Cary's obligations were larger than his assets, he conveyed his claim on Bybrook to William Helyar, on condition that William pay off Cary's Jamaica debts. Thus in 1673 William Helyar found himself the sole owner of a remote and costly sugar plantation. Doubtless the Somerset squire wanted to sell the place, but everyone in Jamaica assured him that he could never recover his

43. Bennett, "Cary Helyar," *Wm. and Mary Qtly.*, 3d Ser., XXI (1964), 62–72; William Whaley to William Helyar, Jan. 20, 1672, Helyar MSS.

44. Bennett, "Cary Helyar," *Wm. and Mary Qtly.*, 3d Ser., XXI (1964), 73–76; Cary Helyar to William Helyar, June 4, 1672, Helyar MSS. Cary Helyar's tombstone, embellished with his coat of arms, is in the cathedral at Spanish Town; he is identified on his tomb as a "merchant," not a planter.

investment by selling an unfinished plantation, whereas if he laid out an additional £200 he could start to receive a handsome yearly return. So Helyar hung on. From 1672 to 1676 Whaley managed the plantation. He built a boiling house and curing house and began to make sugar. Whaley complained constantly to Helyar about his manifold difficulties: he needed more skilled workmen, more provisions, and more tools; his curing house (forty feet by thirty-two feet) was far too small; Bybrook rum was a drug on the market; and the rats devoured much of his ripe cane even after he ordered a dozen "large Wyer Ratt Trapps." By April 1676 all of Whaley's initial enthusiasm had evaporated, and he spoke sourly of "slaveing it here a yeare or two the more which I have been ever since I knew Jamaica." [45]

Squire William for his part believed that his manager was cheating him, for though Whaley produced at least £400 of sugar annually, he sold it all in Jamaica and drew further bills of exchange on Helyar. In 1674 Helyar sent William Dampier, the young son of one of his East Coker tenants, to keep Whaley's books. This infuriated Whaley, who refused to accept Dampier as a bookkeeper or to pay him wages unless he worked as a sugar boiler. When Whaley slapped his new assistant in the face, Dampier punched him back, said he had "not cum heither to slave it," and took his leave. (It is interesting how ready the colonists were, whenever they felt abused, to identify themselves as slaves.) So William Dampier headed off for the Bay of Campeachy and the start of a celebrated career as buccaneer, explorer, and adventure writer.[46] Meanwhile, the much-maligned William Whaley continued Cary Helyar's policy of building up Bybrook's productive capacity as fast as possible. In four years Whaley acquired at least 59 Negroes, which brought the Bybrook slave force to 104—one of the largest in Jamaica. All owner Helyar knew was that he had yet to receive a pennyworth of income. At this juncture Whaley fell ill and died in July 1676.

Bybrook in 1676 must have been worth close to £4,000. After William Whaley's death the Jamaica authorities inventoried the Negroes, livestock, servants, and household goods on the plantation and valued them at £2,737. The appraisers did not value the land or sugar works at Bybrook "in regard they are fixed to the freehold," but noted that Whaley had eighty acres planted in cane and an ex-

45. Bennett, "William Whaley," *Ag. Hist.*, XL (1966), 113–123; Whaley to William Helyar, Apr. 30, 1676, Helyar MSS.
46. Bennett, "William Dampier," *Hist. Today*, XIV (1964), 470–476.

ceptionally large sugar works with a water mill, six coppers in the boiling house, three stills in the distillery, and five hundred sugar pots in the curing house.[47] No other Jamaican estate inventoried between 1674 and 1678 possessed so many slaves and servants. On the other hand, Whaley kept surprisingly little in the way of live-stock, which explains why he was always sending for provisions. And Bybrook was not yet producing sugar efficiently. A plantation of this strength, with fresh cane fields, should have turned out far more than the forty-six hogsheads Whaley says he made in 1675.

How could William Helyar extract some profit from the place? He had no wish to come over and manage the plantation himself, especially considering how quickly brother Cary and godson Whaley had gone to their graves in Jamaica. Nor were his sons old enough to manage Bybrook for him. So he tried a makeshift expedient and articled three agents in 1677 to operate the plantation jointly. Only one of these, Edward Atcherley, had previous experience in sugar making. But Atcherley lost the use of his arms from a disease known as the dry bellyache. The cogwheel of the Bybrook mill broke during harvest season, spoiling production for 1677, and Helyar had to send the ironwork for a new water mill from England. The follow-ing year a major slave revolt broke out at a plantation near Bybrook. One of Helyar's slaves—a man named Quashee Eddoo, the most intelligent and trusted Negro at Bybrook—was implicated in this revolt, turned state's evidence in order to save his life, and accused twelve other Bybrook Negroes of complicity in the plot. The ac-cused Bybrook slaves were court-martialed; four were burned alive, eight hanged, and Quashee Eddoo transported. Thus the Bybrook work force abruptly shriveled in size and in morale. Atcherley did ship Squire William his first consignment of sugar, eight hogsheads, in 1677, but like Whaley he sold the bulk of the sugar in Jamaica and drew bills of exchange on Helyar for further supplies. Very quickly the squire became convinced that Atcherley was an ir-responsible drunkard who idled away his time at Port Royal while the neglected slaves and servants at Bybrook starved, stole, plotted, or ran away.[48]

In 1677 the greatest planter in Jamaica, Sir Thomas Modyford, wrote to his old friend William Helyar (they had been comrades

47. William Whaley's inventory, Jan. Inv., Vol. 1.
48. Edward Atcherley to William Helyar, Mar. 2, 1676/7, May 20, 1677, Joseph Bryan to William Helyar, July 23, 1677, June 8, 1678, William Helyar to Thomas Hillyard, Aug. 26, 1678, Helyar MSS.

in Charles I's army) and told him that his method of depending on salaried employees like Atcherley was all wrong. According to Modyford an absentee proprietor had three basic choices. He could rent out his plantation for a fixed term of years, stipulating that the tenant maintain the stock of slaves and animals. This was trouble free, but the tenant got most of the profits. Or the proprietor could employ three Jamaica planters to supervise his estate, granting them a 5 percent commission on returns. This would stimulate greater productivity than Helyar's present method, but—as Modyford freely admitted—any Jamaica planter would naturally take greater care of his own affairs than of Helyar's. Thus Modyford thought the best bet was to find "an honest partner and, if possible a neare relation that may live on [Bybrook], and make home all the goods on the partable account." Modyford and his brother-in-law, Thomas Kendall, had followed this method in Barbados, with Modyford managing the plantation while Kendall supervised the English end of the business. Sir Thomas urged Helyar to send over a member of his own family, "no drinker, pretty well stricken in years and of honest principles." Allow this man one-third of the Bybrook profits, and "you will receive more yearly, than by keeping the whole as now you doe." With better management Modyford thought Helyar could clear £1,000 per annum from Bybrook.[49] Persuaded by this line of reasoning, Helyar cashiered Atcherley in 1678 and entered into a new agreement with a kinsman named Thomas Hillyard, poor but seemingly honest, who agreed to manage Bybrook, ship home the sugar, and receive one third of all profits.

Thomas Hillyard managed Bybrook for about a decade, from 1678 to 1687. At first the squire was well pleased, for Hillyard stopped drawing bills upon him, cleared the plantation expenses, and shipped home fifteen or twenty hogsheads of surplus sugar a year to Bristol.[50] William Helyar also enjoyed receiving parcels of tamarind and chocolate from Bybrook. But by 1683 the squire was getting very nervous. Hillyard, like his predecessors, sent such vague accounts that it was hard to tell just what he was up to, but he seemed to be buying every scrap of food for the slaves and servants

49. Sir Thomas Modyford to William Helyar, July 10, 1677, Helyar MSS. Modyford operated a large sugar plantation adjoining Bybrook.

50. Squire Helyar expected to market the Bybrook sugar in England, and in 1678 he directed Thomas Hillyard to consign the sugar shipments to him at Bristol, the nearest port. He soon discovered, however, that not being a freeman of Bristol he must pay an exorbitant duty. So he had to hand over the English end of his business to a Bristol commission agent named John Napper.

instead of growing it, and he began to order annual shipments of provisions from Bristol without returning enough sugar to cover these costs, let alone meet the interest payments on William Helyar's Bybrook debt. Furthermore, what sugar Hillyard did send was noticeably coarser than the general run of Jamaica sugar and fetched a lower price. In 1684 Helyar reckoned that Hillyard owed him £744. Now thoroughly alarmed, he sent his young son, John, out to Jamaica to discover what was going on. When John Helyar arrived in March 1686, he found Hillyard "mighty civill unto me" and Bybrook in good working order, but within three months the two men quarreled so violently that Hillyard threw John off the plantation. In 1687 John had to accept a humiliating settlement worked out by Chief Justice Samuel Bernard. The only way he could break Hillyard's contract and regain control of Bybrook was to pay his father's ex-partner an alleged debt of £786. John told Squire William that during the past decade Hillyard had taken one-third of Bybrook's gross proceeds rather than net proceeds. Thus the squire bore all the expenses while Hillyard did so well that he was able to buy his own well-stocked plantation of fifteen hundred acres! [51]

Once John Helyar took personal charge, Bybrook at last began to return considerable profit to its owner. John, being a younger son with limited prospects in England, asked his father to give him Bybrook, but Squire William was so mired in Jamaican debts by this time that he was only willing to allow John half the net profits for managing the plantation. John had to weigh his probable gain from these Bybrook profits against the risk of living long in Jamaica, for he was constantly ill with fevers and bouts of dry bellyache. He came home for his health in 1688, tried Jamaica again in 1690–1691, then returned to England for good. So John Helyar's management was short. But the years from 1687 to 1691 constituted the brightest period in Bybrook's checkered early history.

Under John Helyar's management Bybrook produced 692 hogsheads of muscovado sugar and 11,050 gallons of rum in four and a half years and earned gross receipts of £7,513. Though Thomas Hillyard had never sent home more than 40 hogsheads of sugar in any one year, Bybrook produced 241 hogsheads in 1689 alone. Plantation charges during this period totaled £5,072, leaving a hefty

51. William Helyar to Thomas Hillyard, Aug. 26, 1678, Sept. 5, 1681, Aug. 28, 1682, Feb. 19, 1682/3, Oct. 8, 1683, Sept. 1, 1684, n.d. [1686]; John Helyar to William Helyar, Mar. 27, 1686, Nov. 30, 1686, Oct. 3, 1687, Helyar MSS.

profit. John sold enough of his sugar in Port Royal to meet running
expenses and shipped the remainder to Bristol or London. He dealt
in particular with a Port Royal merchant named Joshua Bright, who
supervised Bybrook during his absence from 1688 to 1690 and sold
him £2,442 worth of goods, including 20 slaves, 3 servants, 20 mules,
a parcel of wrought plate and a dozen cane chairs for the plantation
house, 177 yards of duck cloth and 34 Spanish hats for the work
force, provisions of all kinds, and even "three hue and cryes for a
white servant runn away." John Helyar built up the Bybrook labor
force to its peak strength. He bought at least 33 Negroes between
1687 and 1691 and left the plantation with 144 slaves. He employed
14 white servants in 1687 and paid annual salaries totaling £200 in
1691, including £35 for the slave doctor and £10 for the seam-
stress who made linen breeches, drawers, and stockings. He hired
sawyers, carpenters, smiths, and masons and paid the cooper £334
for making hundreds of sugar and molasses casks. He maintained a
plantain walk for slave food, but (like his predecessors) also bought
a lot of corn and salt fish. At Christmas he killed two cows for the
Negroes. The white workers at Bybrook consumed a barrel of salt
meat per week and a good bit of fresh beef and pork as well. Helyar's
records indicate that he paid minimal local taxes—£18 per annum
to the parish and £4 for quitrents. When he left in 1691 John had
reason to brag: "I have managed the plantation better than ever it
was before." [52]

Trouble was brewing again, however. The closing decade of the
century was a rough one for Jamaica sugar planters, and Bybrook
shared in the general misfortune. A hurricane in 1690 wrecked the
Helyars's plantain walk, and the earthquake of 1692 shook down
many of their plantation buildings. The French war was a constant
source of tension. During invasion scares the Bybrook Negroes were
requisitioned to help build fortifications, while the Bybrook servants
drilled in the militia. French privateers captured 102 hogsheads of
Bybrook sugar in the first two years of the war alone. The price of
a new slave rose quickly from £20 to £30. But Bybrook's biggest
problem was its reversion to absentee management. When John
Helyar departed he placed the plantation in the hands of two
prominent Port Royal merchants, George and Joshua Heathcote,

52. Bybrooke Plantations accompt Charges and Product commencing the 12th
March 1686/7 to the 8th August 1691, *ibid.;* account between John Helyar and
Joshua Bright, Apr. 1687–Mar. 1690, William Helyar to John Helyar, Jan. 20,
1686/7, Richard Smith to John Helyar, Mar. 18, 1689/90, John Helyar to William
Helyar, Oct. 3, 1687, Aug. 15, 1691, n.d. [1691], *ibid.*

who soon had him £2,000 in debt. Worse than this, Bybrook sugar output fell from 178 to 89 hogsheads in three years. John thereupon persuaded his father to let John Austin, a family servant, manage the place. But Austin did no better. By 1696 production was down to 69 hogsheads. In five years 80 Bybrook slaves died of dropsy and dysentery, which was almost certainly induced by malnutrition and filth. Despite costly new purchases the total Bybrook slave force shrank to 103 in 1698.[53]

When Squire William Helyar died in 1697 Jamaican correspondents told his sons William, Jr., and John that Bybrook—not yet thirty years under cultivation—was nearly worn out and worth very little. The Helyar brothers squabbled in England over how to manage the property, while a succession of overseers tried fitfully to keep Bybrook in running order. In 1700 the overseer, one Robert Hall, told the Helyars that almost everything needed overhauling. The water mill must be completely rebuilt, the boiling house repaired, the sugar pots replaced, the curing house moved to a drier place, the Negro houses moved to a healthier place. The Helyars's storehouse in town was so rickety that sugar and rum casks were stolen from it. Bybrook plantation house was sound enough, but almost empty of furnishings: it contained a few broken beds, a table, chest, chairs, a few pieces of pewter, and one silver spoon. The slaves were so sickly that they could cultivate only twenty-five acres a year, and this small acreage required heavy dunging. Annual sugar production was now down to fifty hogsheads. All this was discouraging enough, but the insoluble problem was finding an honest, careful Jamaica factor who would keep tabs on the overseer, supply Bybrook with needed provisions, and convey whatever modest profits the plantation earned to the absentee owners in England. In 1698 the Helyar brothers dissolved their arrangement with George and Joshua Heathcote and entered into contract with another Port Royal merchant, Thomas Whitson. In six years Whitson shipped them only ten hogsheads of sugar, yet insisted that they owed him money. In 1704 he took possession of Bybrook and prevented the Helyars from planting any cane that year. "I wish," said William Helyar, Jr., bitterly "that [Whitson] may not goe from one hot countrey into a hotter." [54]

The only solution was to sell out. The Helyars conveyed a half

53. John Helyar to William Helyar, n.d. [1691], Oct. 18, 1695, John Austin to William Helyar, Aug. 7, 1690, July 19, 1695, July 6, 1696, Aug. 16, 1696, John Austin to John Helyar, Aug. 23, 1695, *ibid.*

54. Robert Hall to William and John Helyar, Apr. 16, 1700, Nov. 16, 1700, n.d. [1702], William Helyar, Jr., to Joshua and George Heathcote, Nov. 1698, William Helyar, Jr., to John Walters, Dec. 2, 1704, *ibid.*

share in Bybrook about 1705 to John Halstead, a Jamaica planter, probably to raise enough money to settle with Whitson. For the next eight years Halstead managed the whole plantation. He got it into better working order and shipped a little sugar to the Helyars. But it was another uneasy partnership, and Halstead kept begging the brothers to rent him their half share for £200 per annum. As it was, they drew scarcely any money from Bybrook; in the three years between 1710 and 1713 Halstead sent them a grand total of £174. Beaten down at last, the Helyars sold their remaining interest in the plantation to Halstead's son-in-law William Gibbons for £2,350 in 1713. Everyone seemed to agree that it was good riddance. John Austin, the Helyars's old servant who handled the sale, reported: "The Land is quite wore in out soe that every body Blowed on it. I am very glad tis gon." Gibbons seemed to feel sorry he had bought Bybrook, for he told the Helyars that even with a further investment of £2,000 he would have "but an old Estate new Vampt up for my money." And a Bristol merchant reminded William Helyar, Jr., that Bybrook was scarcely "worth your minding in respect to the great Estate you have in England under your own carefull Eye." [55]

The Helyars's estate of East Coker in Somersetshire had been farmed for a thousand years, their estate of Bybrook in Jamaica for forty. Yet Bybrook was worn out. Perhaps Bybrook was not quite so worthless after all, for William Gibbons paid almost as much for a half share in 1713 as the valuation of the full property in 1676. If Gibbons and his successors worked the place intelligently, they could be assured of good returns. The point, of course, is that a West Indian sugar plantation required close, careful management to yield a profit, and Bybrook received this sort of management only in the years from 1669 to 1672 and 1687 to 1691, when the Helyars were personally in charge. Bybrook was not a typical seventeenth-century sugar plantation. It was a dreadful example of absentee ownership, of a property constantly abused by lazy owners, underpaid overseers, irresponsible short-term partners, and dishonest Jamaica factors.

Yet the story of Bybrook does illustrate in an extreme way the generally wasteful, exploitive character of English husbandry in the New World. The pioneer farmers in Plymouth Colony, according

55. Bybrook plantation accounts, Dec. 1704–Dec. 1706, Dec. 1710–May 1713, John Halstead to William and John Helyar, Nov. 16, 1705, Feb. 9, 1710, June 13, 1710, John Austin to the Helyars, Apr. 30, 1713, William Gibbons to the Helyars, Dec. 12, 1713, Abraham Birkin to William Helyar, Jr., June 4, 1712, *ibid.*

to the latest authority, discarded the more arduous English farming techniques and refused to adopt the more arduous Indian practices; in consequence their crop yields dropped to the level of thirteenth-century England. It has been said of the Virginia tobacco planters that they "bought land as they might buy a wagon—with the expectation of wearing it out." [56] From New England to Virginia to Jamaica, the English planters in seventeenth-century America developed the habit of murdering the soil for a few quick crops and then moving along. On the sugar plantations, unhappily, they also murdered the slaves.

56. Darrett B. Rutman, *Husbandmen of Plymouth: Farms and Villages in the Old Colony, 1620–1692* (Boston, 1967), 52–62; Gray, *History of Agriculture*, I, 446.

7 ❧ *Slaves*

The sugar planters of Barbados, Jamaica, and the Leeward Islands were the first Englishmen to practice slavery on a large scale. Before the close of the seventeenth century they brought a quarter of a million Negroes from Africa to these six islands and branded them as perpetual bondsmen. Without English precedents to draw upon, the colonists worked up a law code and a set of customs that divided island society starkly into two classes: white masters and black slaves. The Negro was defined as a chattel and treated as a piece of conveyable property, without rights and without redress. To be sure, as in all slave systems, the Negroes in the English sugar colonies exerted certain countervailing pressures against their masters. As David Brion Davis puts it, "Even the most authoritarian master, supported by the most oppressive laws, was to some extent limited by the will of his slaves, who had the power to appeal, flatter, humiliate, disobey, sabotage, or rebel." [1] Yet the thrust of the system was all the other way. Slavery in the English islands was ruthlessly exploitive from the outset, a device to maximize sugar production as cheaply as possible. And it was nakedly racial, for only Africans and Indians were enslaved. The seventeenth-century English sugar planters created one of the harshest systems of servitude in Western history.

No aspect of our subject is more relevant to present concerns than the origins of black slavery in the English islands. Slavery in one form or another is the essence of West Indian history: the black

1. David Brion Davis, *The Problem of Slavery in Western Culture* (Ithaca, N.Y., 1966) , 251.

people of Barbados, Jamaica, and the Leeward Islands are still exploited today, even though they are technically independent. Slavery is a crucial theme in the history of the thirteen English mainland colonies, and investigation into the early slave system in the sugar islands helps to explain how and why Negro bondage spread to North America, for the mainland colonists borrowed heavily from their island cousins even as they worked out a distinctly different formula. Finally, the comparative history of slavery is currently fashionable, and here again it is instructive to compare the early slave system in the English islands with the rise of Negro bondage in the French, Dutch, Portuguese, and Spanish sugar colonies.

The origin and character of Afro-American slavery is a highly tendentious topic, of course; it has inspired a richly provocative and controversial literature. I think it wise to warn the reader in advance where I stand on some of the currently controverted points. Most fundamental is the question as to whether New World slavery differed essentially from older forms of bondage in classical antiquity, medieval Europe, and the Arabic world. It seems to me that there *was* an essential difference, that American Negro slavery of the seventeenth, eighteenth, and nineteenth centuries, because of its starkly racial character, was more profoundly oppressive and more socially divisive than Graeco-Roman slavery or medieval serfdom. Some historians think the Europeans in the New World enslaved Negroes primarily because they were racists: white over black. Here I incline toward the alternate view, that whites enslaved blacks because they discovered this sort of labor system worked very well. Economic exploitation seems to me the prime motive; racism conveniently justified and bolstered the use of forced black labor. Another major bone of contention is the argument as to whether Protestant English slavery was more vicious and traumatic than Catholic Spanish or Portuguese slavery. In my opinion this sort of sweeping national contrast is misleading, for the English, Spanish, and Portuguese all handled the color problem in various ways at various times and places. Certainly English slavery was often far less brutal than Portuguese slavery at its worst. The real point here, I think, is that the Protestant English sugar planters of Barbados handled their Negroes in a manner strikingly different from the Protestant English tobacco planters of Virginia or the Protestant English rice planters of Carolina. From the beginning English West Indian slavery had a style of its own. It was physically more cruel

and debilitating than Negro bondage in the English mainland settlements, yet psychologically perhaps less traumatic.[2]

ॐ

The initial difference between slavery in the two sectors of English
America is that the island colonists plunged into the slaveholding
business and the mainland colonists inched into it. The first Barbados settlers brought ten Negroes with them in 1627. The English
on Tortuga and Providence acquired their first slaves in 1633, and
five years later the blacks on Providence Island staged the first slave
revolt in English America. When the Spaniards captured this island
in 1641 they found four hundred Englishmen and six hundred
slaves.[3] The colonists in the eastern Caribbees owned fewer slaves
than this during the tobacco years, but with the beginnings of sugar
production, five hundred Negroes reportedly arrived at Barbados in
1642 and a thousand in 1645. By 1660, as we have seen, there were
about twenty thousand blacks in Barbados, two thousand in the
Leewards, and five hundred in Jamaica—as against a thousand in
Virginia.

In their well-known essay on the origins of slavery in English
America, Oscar and Mary Handlin discount the above facts and
argue that both the island and mainland colonists took many long
years to develop a concept of chattel slavery. "The term, slave, in the
West Indies was at the start as vague as in Virginia and Maryland,"
say the Handlins. According to their view the English did not at first
distinguish in any meaningful way between white indentured servants and the Negroes who arrived from Africa. The English were
not innately prejudiced against blacks. White and black laborers

2. In addition to Davis's book, *ibid.*, provocative interpretations of New World
slavery include—in order of publication—Melville J. Herskovits, *The Myth of
the Negro Past* (New York, 1941) ; Eric Williams, *Capitalism and Slavery* (Chapel
Hill, N.C., 1944) ; Frank Tannenbaum, *Slave and Citizen: The Negro in the
Americas* (New York, 1947) ; Oscar Handlin, *Race and Nationality in American
Life* (New York, 1957) ; Stanley M. Elkins, *Slavery: A Problem in American Institutional and Intellectual Life* (Chicago, 1959) ; Patterson, *Sociology of Slavery;*
Herbert S. Klein, *Slavery in the Americas: A Comparative Study of Virginia and
Cuba* (Chicago, 1967) ; Jordan, *White over Black;* and Genovese, *The World the
Slaveholders Made.* Of these books, Patterson's *Sociology of Slavery* focuses most
particularly on slavery in the English sugar islands, though he deals exclusively
with Jamaica and concentrates on a later time period.
3. Newton, *Colonising Activities of the English Puritans,* 110, 149, 258, 261,
301–302.

were equally unfree, equally slavish servants, the only real difference being that whites served for specified terms of years and blacks sometimes served indefinitely. Though the Negroes in the mid-century Barbados sugar fields were called slaves, this "comprehended [no] more than the presumption of indefinite service." [4] But the Handlins are surely mistaken. However valid their interpretation may be for the mainland colonies, it does not hold for the West Indies. On the contrary, the Englishmen who planted in the islands immediately categorized the Negroes and Indians who worked for them as heathen brutes and very quickly treated them as chattels.

The testimony of Capt. Henry Powell, who brought the first shipload of English settlers to Barbados in 1627, is pertinent here. Powell says he proceeded from Barbados to Surinam, where he persuaded thirty-two Indians to accompany him to Barbados "as free people" to plant tropical produce. The Indians asked "that I should allow them a piece of land, the which I did, and they would manure those fruits, and bring up their children to Christianite, and that we might drive a constant trade between the Island and the Mayne." But after Powell left Barbados his countrymen "hath taken [the Indians] by force and made them slaves" and kept them "long in Bondage." The ten Negroes who were brought to Barbados in 1627 were also called slaves, like the Indians. Henry Winthrop, who arrived with Powell, wrote home that the infant colony contained only "Inglishe men save a matter of 50 slaves of Indyenes and blacks." He varied his language slightly in a second letter: the Barbados population "is but 3 score of christyanes and fortye slaves of negeres and Indyenes." Winthrop was hazy about the exact number of slaves, but keenly aware of their difference from Christian Europeans. In a couple of artless phrases he managed to discriminate between Englishmen and Africans on the basis of race, color, religion, and class.[5]

The Handlins quite rightly point out that the English colonists avoided defining the nature of slavery. The early Barbadians could get no help at all from English precedents in trying to spell out the social relations between slave and master or the race relations between black and white. But this does not mean that they saw no

4. Oscar and Mary F. Handlin, "Origins of the Southern Labor System," *Wm. and Mary Qtly.*, 3d Ser., VII (1950), 221.

5. Henry Powell's testimony [c. 1648], Davis, ed., "Papers relating to the early History of Barbados," *Timehri*, New Ser., V (1891), 53–55; Henry Winthrop to Emmanuel Downing, Aug. 22, 1627, Henry Winthrop to John Winthrop, Oct. 15, 1627, Forbes *et al.*, eds., *Winthrop Papers*, I, 357, 361.

distinction between servant and slave. Rather, they worked out the problem pragmatically and built up piecemeal a regulatory structure governing their relations with Negroes.[6] The most striking feature of these early regulations is their roundabout, negative character. Every time a black man did something objectionable the English drew up a rule against it, until in a few years they had erected a wall of taboos around the slave. Thus, when some Negro or Indian asked for his release, the Barbados governor and Council decreed in 1636 that "Negroes and Indians, that came here to be sold, should serve for Life, unless a Contract was before made to the contrary." Such contracts were sometimes made with Indians. In 1648 a New England Indian named Hope was sold to a Barbados master for a term of ten years "according to the Orders and Customs of English servants in the said Iland." However, I have not seen any such contract for a Negro servant. In the few surviving Barbados inventories of the 1630s white servants are valued according to their remaining time of service, whereas Negroes are valued higher, without any suggestion that their servitude will ever expire.[7]

It took a few years for the problem of interracial sex to develop, since practically all of the first inhabitants—black and white—were males. But in 1644 the Antigua Assembly composed a law against miscegenation, doubtless after the discovery of a mulatto baby. In forbidding "Carnall Coppullation between Christian and Heathen," the Antiguans defined "heathens" as Negroes and Indians and devised a sliding scale of punishments. A freeman or freewoman who fornicated with a black was fined, a servant had his or her term of indenture extended, and the offending heathen was branded and whipped. But to sleep with a black woman was at least held preferable to sleeping with your sister; in this same year the Antiguans passed another law punishing incest with death.[8]

By 1650 certainly, and probably a good bit earlier, slavery in Barbados had become more than a lifetime condition. It extended through the slave's children to posterity. Richard Ligon, who

6. Wesley Frank Craven makes the same point about the mainland colonists in *Colonies in Transition*, 290–300.

7. Jordan, *White over Black*, 64–65; bill of sale for Indian named Hope, Forbes *et al.*, eds., *Winthrop Papers*, V, 196–197; inventory of Capt. Ketteridge's estate, 1635, Hay Papers.

8. Leeward Islands MSS Laws, 1644–1673, C.O. 154/1/49–51. The Antiguans decided in 1644 that a mulatto child produced by a mixed union should be enslaved until age 18 or 21, then freed. But in 1672 they decided to enslave the child for life. *Ibid.*, 41.

thought the Negroes were treated better than white servants, sharply distinguished between the two categories of servitude: "The Iland is divided into three sorts of men, viz. Masters, Servants, and slaves. The slaves and their posterity, being subject to their Masters for ever, are kept and preserv'd with greater care than the servants, who are theirs but for five years, according to the law of the Iland." [9] The blacks in these early days of sugar production probably did receive better treatment than later. But they were already clearly construed as articles of private property.

§

How many slaves were imported from Africa into the English sugar islands during the seventeenth century? Philip D. Curtin is the latest and best authority on this subject. Estimating that some 9.5 million Africans were landed in America during the entire four hundred years of the trade, he figures that about 42 percent of the cargoes went to the Caribbean Islands and 38 percent to Brazil. Jamaica, Barbados, and the Leeward Islands were among the major Caribbean importers; they received roughly 1,480,000 slaves during the seventeenth and eighteenth centuries, or 15 percent of the grand total. The English planters, like their French rivals in St. Domingue, Martinique, and Guadeloupe, bought the bulk of their slaves in the eighteenth century when English and French sugar production reached maximum proportions. Yet the seventeenth-century English slave trade was very sizable. Curtin estimates that a quarter of a million slaves were landed in the English islands at an ever-accelerating rate between 1640 and 1700.

Professor Curtin has extrapolated ingeniously from the spotty surviving evidence in order to work out the conjectural totals in table 22. His estimate is the best we can expect to have. The volume of the trade to the English islands before 1673 can only be guessed, since we have almost no hard data. But the Royal African Company, which handled much of the English business between 1673 and 1711, kept extensive records of its shipments and deliveries. Something is also known about the interloping traders who competed against the Royal African Company. In sum, though the English slave trade is difficult to assess quantitatively, it is about as

9. Ligon, *True History of Barbados*, 43.

well documented as the English trade in the next century and better documented than the French or Spanish trades in almost any period.

The Atlantic slave trade was already a booming business in the seventeenth century. According to Curtin's projections some 1,340,-000 slaves were brought to America from Africa during the course of the century, with the volume rising sharply in the closing decades. Sugar planters were the hungriest for slave labor and the best able to pay for it, hence three-quarters of the shipments in the seventeenth century went to sugar colonies. Brazil was the leading slave market,

Table 22. Estimated English Slave Imports, 1640–1700

Years	Barbados	Jamaica	Leeward Islands	Total
1640–1650	18,700		2,000	20,700
1651–1675	51,100	8,000	10,100	69,200
1676–1700	64,700	77,100	32,000	173,800
Total	134,500	85,100	44,100	263,700

NOTE: Curtin, *Atlantic Slave Trade*, 52–64, 88–89, 119. Curtin's estimate for the English islands in the 17th century is substantially higher than the totals arrived at by Noel Deerr, the only other systematic investigator of the subject. Deerr reckoned that 76,400 slaves were imported into Barbados and 63,000 into Jamaica during the 17th century. See Deerr, *History of Sugar*, II, 278.

as it would continue to be until the 1840s. The sugar-producing northeast coast of Brazil was of course particularly convenient to the West and Central African slave stations. The English mainland colonies were virtually excluded from the African trade; systematic importation to the Chesapeake and the Carolinas only began around 1700. But the English sugar islands absorbed a steadily rising share. Between 1675 and 1700, the planters of Barbados, Jamaica, and the Leewards matched the Brazilian imports; they bought an average of 7,000 Negroes per year—and wanted still more. They got more during the next century. By 1740 these six English islands were taking 10,000 slaves a year; by 1770 the annual import figure had climbed to 13,000.

Who were the traders who supplied this swelling English appetite for slaves? The seventeenth-century traffic to the islands passed through three distinct phases. From 1640 to 1672 a medley of Dutch and English private traders handled the business. Then between

1673 and 1688 the Royal African Company, a joint-stock enterprise sponsored by Charles II and James II, tried with indifferent success to corner the English market. After 1689 interlopers broke the company's monopoly, and Parliament opened the trade to all Englishmen. No matter who supplied the slaves, the planters always cried for more and cheaper Negroes, and the traders always struggled to collect overdue planter debts.

The opening stage of the traffic to the English islands is veiled in obscurity. Before 1660 only the Barbadians bought many slaves, and they must have bought most of them from Dutch slavers already experienced in the Brazilian and Spanish trades.[10] But English slavers were also active from the start. In 1647, for example, Thomas Modyford and Richard Ligon sailed from England to Barbados by way of the Cape Verde Islands so as to pick up Negroes, horses, and cattle. They carried trading goods such as broad-brimmed hats designed specially for the Portuguese taste, which they exchanged in the Cape Verde Islands for slaves. Once Modyford and Ligon reached Barbados their ship went on to Africa, carrying goods to barter with the tribal kings and merchants for more slaves.[11] By the 1660s the Dutch slavers were pretty well excluded from the English islands; nonetheless, the traffic seems to have picked up steadily in volume. During the four years from 1667 to 1671 some 135 English ships reportedly embarked for Africa. This number of ships could probably deliver twenty thousand Negroes to the islands, or five thousand a year.[12]

London merchants and Westminster officials agreed that such a major and vital trade needed promotion and protection. They knew that the slaving business was exceptionally risky and dangerous, that traders from every Atlantic state were scrambling for cargoes along the coasts of West and Central Africa. They believed that the English slavers needed forts and factories (warehouses) in Africa, and this required large capitalization, joint-stock incorporation and

10. The Dutch slave trade in the 17th century has not yet been systematically investigated. Records in the Netherlands may tell how many Africans were carried to Barbados in Dutch ships before enforcement of the English navigation acts shut off this source of supply.

11. Ligon, *True History of Barbados*, 1–2, 8, 21. In 1654 the Barbados planter James Drax owned shares in two slave ships. *Jour. Bar. Mus. Hist. Soc.*, VII (1939–1940), 69–70.

12. Between 1680 and 1688 the Royal African Company dispatched 249 ships to Africa and delivered 46,396 slaves in the West Indies, for an average of 186 slaves per ship. See K. G. Davies, *Royal African Company*, 106, 192; Negroes shipped and delivered by the Royal African Company, 1680–1688, C.O. 318/2/11.

backing by the king. Accordingly in 1663 Charles II chartered a Company of Royal Adventurers into Africa, with a monopoly on the slave trade, and when this enterprise shortly foundered, he chartered in 1672 a new and better-organized corporation, the Royal African Company. The shareholders were chiefly merchants active in overseas trade. A number of Barbados planters, resident in London, decided to take shares in order to influence the counsels of the company.[13] The Royal African Company operated ambitiously in the fifteen years prior to the Glorious Revolution, yet never could provide as many slaves as the West Indian colonists wanted. Its ventures were always undercapitalized; hence the company sent insufficient trade goods to Africa. The peak performance came in 1685–1686, when company ships delivered 13,116 slaves to the Caribbean islands in two years.[14] Over a forty-year span the company bought roughly 150,000 Negroes in Africa, lost 20 percent of them through mortality on the middle passage, and delivered some 120,000 in the West Indies.[15]

The island planters perennially remonstrated against the "foul monopoly" of the Royal African Company, asserting that they had been better supplied, at lower prices, before 1672. The Barbados Assembly in 1693 even stigmatized the quality of the Negroes shipped over by the company: "People Nurst up in Luxury and Ease, and wholly Unaccustomed to worke, which in shorte time Dye upon our handes to our Irrepairable Loss." The planters could scarcely complain about the company's credit policy. By 1690, according to the company's books, the West Indian colonists owed a collective debt of £170,000—equivalent to the price of ten thousand Negroes! [16] Nevertheless the planters heartily patronized interloping slave ships. Even during the years of peak company delivery, from 1673 to 1688, the interloping trade was very large. Such major Barbados planters as Henry Drax, Christopher Codrington, John Pears, John Hallett, and William Sharpe were said to own the interloping vessels that smuggled Negroes ashore at night or on the unfrequented back side

13. Committee of Barbados planters in London, Nov. 22, 1671, C.O. 31/2/104–105.

14. K. G. Davies, *Royal African Company*, 65–70, 74–76; Negroes shipped and delivered by the Royal African Company, 1680–1688, C.O. 318/2/11.

15. Davies estimated that the company delivered only 100,000 slaves in the West Indies, but his totals are less complete than those presented in table 23 below. *Royal African Company*, 299, 361–363.

16. Barbados Assembly remonstrance, Nov. 14, 1693, C.O. 31/3/358–360; K. G. Davies, *Royal African Company*, 319.

of the island. When company agents did manage to catch interlopers, they had trouble getting the island courts to condemn them. For example, the captain of a New England slave ship seized at St. Christopher in 1685 explained to the local admiralty court that the cruel Portuguese had forced him to buy Negroes in Africa and carry them to the West Indies. The judge (who was also the governor of the island) accepted this piteous tale and set the vessel free.[17]

The Royal African Company countered planter hostility as best it could by appointing some of the chief sugar magnates in the islands as company factors to handle sales and collect debts for a handsome 7 percent commission. These posts were so highly profitable that the company was able to engage three governors—Edwin Stede of Barbados, Hender Molesworth of Jamaica, and William Beeston of Jamaica—as factors. In the mid-1680s, when Stede and Molesworth simultaneously administered the two chief sugar colonies, the company came closest to enforcing its monopoly.

The Revolution of 1688–1689 was a shattering blow to the Royal African Company. Monopolistic privileges bestowed by royal prerogative were reckoned null and void after the downfall of James II, and the company dropped its efforts to seize interlopers. The French wars of 1689–1697 and 1702–1713 also hit very hard: the company lost several of its African posts to the enemy and a quarter of its fleet. The English slave trade sagged particularly badly during King William's War; the few cargoes were mainly carried by private traders. In 1698 Parliament responded to the pleas of the sugar lobby by letting private slave ships enter the African trade on payment of a 10 percent duty. When this duty expired in 1712 all English slave ships were henceforth on an equal footing. The trade zoomed fantastically at the turn of the century, as the private slavers rushed in. For the first time sizable shipments reached Virginia. By 1713 the Royal African Company had virtually retired from business, defeated as much as anything by the slave-hungry sugar planters who had lobbied against it so long.

Table 23 shows how the company's performance declined in the years after the Glorious Revolution. In the decade from 1698 to 1707 private traders outmatched the company by a margin of better than three to one. The company served Barbados more solicitously than

17. Testimony by Royal African Company agents in Barbados, May 19, 1677, June 16, 1677, Coventry Papers, LXXVIII, 60; Barbados agents, July 2, 1681, Nov. 9, 1681, C.O. 1/47/231; St. Christopher Admiralty Court, Sept. 30, 1685, C.O. 155/1/43–51.

234 / Sugar and Slaves

the other islands, because it was the closest to Africa and because the big Barbados planters could buy Negroes in large lots and pay well for them. Sometimes, according to agent Edwin Stede, the company supply actually outpaced Barbados's demand, and Stede then had to spend as much as ten days in selling a cargo or he had to re-ship the Negroes elsewhere. There was no such problem in Jamaica.

Table 23. Slaves Delivered by the Royal African Company, 1673–1711, and by Private Traders, 1698–1707

Years	Barbados	Jamaica	Leeward Islands	North America	Annual Average
Royal African Company					
1673–1679	8,642	5,477	3,722		2,549
1680–1688	21,521	18,802	6,073		5,155
1689–1697	7,359	5,146	1,274		1,531
1698–1707	14,988	6,854	2,777	679	2,530
1708–1711	2,144	1,709	849		1,175
Total	54,654	37,988	14,695	679	2,843
Private traders					
1698–1707	34,157	37,522	6,729	9,100	8,751

NOTE: The figures for 1673–1679, 1689–1697, and 1708–1711 represent auction sales by the Royal African Company as tabulated in K. G. Davies, *Royal African Company*, 363. The figures for 1680–1688 are from C.O. 318/2/11 and are more complete than Davies's totals for these years. The company and private traders' totals for 1698–1707 are from Customs House Accounts, T. 70/1205/A43, and are likewise more complete than the totals in Davies, *Royal African Company*, 143. I am indebted to Jacob M. Price for pointing out these last figures. To the company's totals of 108,016 deliveries, shown in this table, should be added another 10,000 or so Negroes sold in the Indies by contract or delivered to Virginia before 1698.

The Jamaica planters held many fewer slaves than the Barbadians when the company started operations, and they were very anxious for more. But Jamaica, being a thousand miles further from Africa, encircled by buccaneers, with fewer rich sugar entrepreneurs than Barbados, offered a less tempting market to the company. The Jamaicans never got as many Negroes as they wanted before 1698, and the Royal African Company's clear preference for Barbados probably retarded Jamaica's economic growth in the late seventeenth

century. Jamaica was the chief staging ground for the asiento or
Spanish trade, and if we believe Jamaican protests, the company
factors diverted some of the best incoming Negroes to the Spanish
colonies.

The Leeward planters felt specially neglected. The company
seems to have shipped its least salable cargoes to these four islands.
Leeward consignments were regularly described as a "very meane
parcel" or "refuse" from Barbados or "the worst that came here."
The sole company agent was stationed at Nevis, which vexed the
planters on the other three islands. Of forty-five company shipments to the Leewards between 1674 and 1686, St. Christopher and
Montserrat received two apiece, and Antigua, one. From the company's point of view, however, the Leeward planters were poorer
risks than the bigger operators in Barbados and Jamaica. In 1681
they had paid for only half the slaves received since 1674.[18]

English slaving records from the late seventeenth century enable
us to tell pretty well what regions of Africa the traders drew upon.
Over 70 percent of the slaves imported by the Royal African Company from 1673 to 1689 came from the Guinea coast, with the rest
fairly equally divided between the Senegambia region further north
and Angola further south. Thus the first forced black migrants to
the English islands were chiefly inhabitants of the Windward Coast
(modern Liberia), the Gold Coast (Ghana), and the Slave Coast
(Togoland, Dahomey, and western Nigeria).[19] These people lived
in small and shifting political units and spoke a hundred different
languages. They came from the part of Africa that most closely resembles the Caribbean islands in climate and ecology. The Guinea
coast is a region of steaming coastal rain forest and interior grass-
land. The weather is always hot and humid, with the temperature

18. For fuller discussion of the supply to each island, see K. G. Davies, *Royal
African Company*, 300–312. On Barbados, Edwin Stede to Royal African Company, Feb. 28, 1693/4, Harleian Manuscripts, 7310/149, Br. Museum; on Jamaica,
address to James II from Council and Assembly, Sept. 18, 1688, *Jours. of Jam.
Assembly*, I, 130–132; on the Leeward Islands, Higham, *Leeward Islands*, 151–161

19. K. G. Davies, *Royal African Company*, 213–233; Curtin, *Atlantic Slave
Trade*, 122–123, 128–130, 150, 160, 207, 211. Patterson, *Sociology of Slavery*, 135,
argues that Jamaica, supplied mainly by interlopers in the late 17th century,
obtained only 50% of its slaves from the Guinea coast and 40% from Angola.
The great bulk of Africans shipped to Brazil and Mexico in the 17th century
were Bantu peoples of the Congo and Angola. In the 18th century all of the
English islands received a rising proportion of new slaves from Central Africa,
as the English slavers shifted their focus from the Guinea coast further south
to the Niger delta and the Congo basin.

averaging close to eighty degrees year-round and very heavy rainfall and violent storms, especially on the jungled coast. Plant growth is rapid and insect life is teeming. The West African people in the seventeenth century practiced settled, intensive agriculture. They grew food crops much like the Caribbean staples: plantains, yams, beans, cassava, and corn—the latter two borrowed from America. They ate little meat, a special merit from the English slave master's viewpoint. They were used to hand labor in the fields, cultivating their crops with iron hoes, but not draft animals, for horses and cattle in West Africa were destroyed by sleeping sickness carried by the tsetse fly. Above all West African kinship and tribal structure inculcated the values of community cooperation and community discipline.

The English supposed, probably correctly, that the great variety of languages and intense tribal rivalries among the Guinea-coast peoples hindered these blacks, once enslaved, from combining against their masters. A writer of 1694 remarked that "the safety of the Plantations depends upon having Negroes from all parts of *Guiny,* who not understanding each others languages and Customs, do not, and cannot agree to Rebel, as they would do . . . when there are too many Negroes from one Country." The West Indian planters were always profoundly ignorant of and indifferent to the cultural attributes of the West Africans. They contented themselves with a simple set of prejudices, such as that Papaws from the Slave Coast made the most docile and agreeable slaves, the Cormantins from the Gold Coast were proud, brave, and rebellious, and the Ibos from the Niger delta were timorous and despondent. All of these West African Negroes were considered preferable to the Bantu-speaking Angolans, who had the reputation of being not merely rebellious but—unforgivable sin—lazy as well.[20]

The black cargoes assembled on the Guinea coast by the English slave traders in the seventeenth century were, on the whole, selected more carefully than the shiploads of white servants sent out to the West Indies from Britain. When the English traders dealt with African kings and merchants for slaves, they tried to buy as many healthy, young adult males as possible; young women, boys, and girls over the age of twelve were considered acceptable; adults over

20. *Some Considerations Humbly Offered, against Granting the Sole Trade to Guiny . . . to a Company with a Joint Stock* [n.p., c. 1694], Harleian MSS, 7310/240; parliamentary hearing on the slave trade, Feb. 13, 1693/4, Harleian MSS, 7310/222–228; LePage, *Jamaican Creole,* 74–79.

forty, infants, and sickly persons were rejected when possible. The price of slaves in West Africa rose steadily with the demand. In the 1670s and 1680s the Royal African Company typically paid about £3 in trade goods for a slave. By 1710 the purchase rate had quadrupled. This increase was of course transferred to the West Indies. Before the Glorious Revolution the company policy, broadly adhered to, was to charge £15 for slaves in Barbados, £16 in the Leewards, £17 in Jamaica, and £18 in Virginia. Interlopers sold their slaves rather more cheaply. But the rising African costs, coupled with the risks of the French wars, led the English traders, both company and private, to double their prices in the Indies. After 1700 a newly arrived African slave fetched £25 or £30 in the English islands. This increased market value of the slave had one beneficial effect: it persuaded the slave trader to take better care of his human cargo during the sea passage to America. Mortality on the middle passage was always frightfully high, but it did drop very considerably between 1680 and 1734. In the nine years between 1680 and 1688 the Royal African Company shipped 60,783 Negroes to the West Indies and delivered only 46,396—a loss of 23.5 percent! By 1734 company ships had reduced the loss of slaves in transit to 10 percent, and this seems to be about the average level of loss throughout the eighteenth century.[21]

Thanks to the volume of the slave trade, the sugar planters were soon heavily outnumbered by their slaves. The black population surpassed the white population in Barbados around 1660, in Jamaica soon after 1670, and in the Leeward Islands soon after 1680. By 1713 there were four Negroes for every white man in the English sugar islands. The ratio in the mainland colonies was of course quite the reverse: six whites for every Negro in 1713. Even when the North American slave trade became large in the eighteenth century, South Carolina was the only mainland colony with more black than white inhabitants. A slave system in which the slaves greatly outnumber their masters naturally differs in many respects from a system in which the slaves constitute a minority. The West Indian slave masters could not expect to assimilate or acculturate such a huge alien population. If they wished to preserve their own identity, they had to segregate themselves socially and culturally from the blacks. And if they wished to preserve control, they had to de-

21. K. G. Davies, *Royal African Company*, 292, 299–300, 313–314; Negroes shipped and delivered by the Royal African Company, 1680–1688, C.O. 318/2/11; Curtin, *Atlantic Slave Trade*, 276–278.

vise a plantation regimen to make the slaves docile and dull and a policing system to keep them disciplined and intimidated.

The slave laws enacted by the island legislatures in the seventeenth century tell us a good deal about the treatment of Negroes and the character of slavery in the Caribbean colonies. These laws set formal standards, to be sure, which were not necessarily enforced. But it was the big planters on the islands who sat in the assemblies and composed these laws, which is to say that in the statute books the chief slaveholders articulated their views on how to handle Negroes. Unfortunately seventeenth-century West Indian legislation on slavery is hard to piece together. The main body of surviving island statutes for this early period is still in manuscript in the Public Record Office.[22] Only a handful of acts passed by the island assemblies was printed contemporaneously,[23] and the compilations of West Indian acts of assembly published by the home government early in the eighteenth century omit most obsolete seventeenth-century legislation.[24] When the scattered manuscript and printed laws of the seventeenth century are scrutinized, it turns out that very few predate the Restoration. Thus the big problem with the island slave laws is that the earliest ones are mostly missing. Tantalizingly the Barbados slave act of 1661 speaks of the "many good Lawes and Ordinances" already issued by the Barbadians on this subject. We do not know what these good laws said.

By 1661, at any rate, Barbados had a comprehensive slave code.

22. The most useful manuscript volumes of 17th-century West Indian statutes in the P.R.O. are C.O. 30/2 (Barbados laws, 1645–1682); C.O. 30/5 (Barbados, 1682–1692); C.O. 139/1 (Jamaica, 1662–1674); C.O. 154/1 (Leeward Islands, 1644–1673); C.O. 154/2 (Leeward Islands, 1668–1682); C.O. 154/5 (Nevis, 1680–1703); and C.O. 8/2 (Antigua, 1684–1693).

23. These include: *Acts and Statutes of the Island of Barbados, 1651–1654* (London, 1656); *The Laws of Jamaica . . . Confirmed . . . Feb. 23, 1683* (London, 1684); *The Laws of Jamaica . . . Confirmed . . . April 17, 1684* (London, 1684); *The Continuation of the Laws of Jamaica . . . Confirmed . . . Dec. 26, 1696* (London, 1698).

24. *Acts of Assembly, Barbadoes, 1648–1718; Acts of Assembly, Passed in the Island of Jamaica, 1681–1737* (London, 1738); *Acts of Assembly, Passed in the Charibee Leeward Islands, 1690–1730* (London, 1734); *Acts of Assembly, Passed in the Island of Nevis, 1664–1739* (London, 1740); *Acts of Assembly, Montserrat, 1668–1740.*

The act passed in 1661 by the Barbados Assembly "for the better ordering and governing of Negroes" is the most important surviving piece of legislation issued in the English islands during the seventeenth century. It was reenacted with slight modifications by later Barbados assemblies in 1676, 1682, and 1688, was copied by the assemblies of Jamaica, in 1664, South Carolina, in 1696, and Antigua, in 1702. The preamble to this document implies that Negro slaves are chattels, for it undertakes "to protect them as wee doe men's other goods and Chattles." It explicitly characterizes Negroes as "an heathenish, brutish and an uncertaine, dangerous kinde of people," unfit to be governed by English law. Yet "the right rule of reason and order" tells the Barbadians that slaves cannot be left "to the Arbitrary, cruell and outragious wills of every evill disposed person." They require somewhat fuller protection than other forms of property, "as being created Men, though without the knowledge of God in the world." [25] Thus the Barbados code aimed to protect the masters from the brutish slaves and the slaves from their bloody-minded masters. But in fact the masters were offered far fuller protection than the slaves.

The Barbados code of 1661 accorded masters, servants, and slaves carefully differentiated rights and obligations. The master had almost total authority over his slaves and markedly less power over his servants. He was obliged to give his Negroes new clothing once a year—a pair of drawers and a cap for every male, a petticoat and cap for every female—but no rules were laid down about slave food or slave working conditions. The master could correct his slaves in any way he liked, and if while beating a Negro for a misdemeanor he happened to maim or kill him ("which seldom happens"), he suffered no penalty. To be sure, the master could be stiffly fined (three thousand pounds of sugar or about £25) for wantonly killing his slave; the fine was a good deal stiffer for wantonly killing someone else's slave. But since the master could always claim to be correcting a slave for a misdemeanor, this fine was easy to evade. By contrast, in legislating for servants, the colony government fixed minimum food allotments as well as clothing allotments and permitted servants to sue in court or appeal to the magistrates if mistreated. The master could be fined for failing to take proper care of a sick servant, and he could be charged with

25. Barbados Act for the better ordering and governing of Negroes, Sept. 27, 1661, Barbados MSS Laws, 1645–1682, C.O. 30/2/16–26.

murder should a servant die at his hands. Servants' corpses were routinely checked for signs of lash marks or starvation.[26]

Slave crimes were judged and punished by a different standard than servant crimes. The guilty servant was given an extended term of indenture: one year of extra servitude for laying violent hands on his master, two years for theft, three years for running away or getting a female servant pregnant, seven years for entertaining a fugitive slave. A Negro found guilty of these same offenses was whipped, branded, or had his nose slit. Though castration appears to have been a favorite slave punishment, it was not officially incorporated into the Barbados code. Murder, rape, arson, assault, and theft of anything beyond a shilling in value were all capital crimes for Negroes. A key difference between servant and slave justice is that servants were entitled to jury trial, whereas "brutish slaves deserve not for the baseness of their Conditions to bee tryed by the legall tryall of twelve Men of their appeares [i.e., peers] or Neighborhood." So the Negro was tried by his master for petty offences and by two justices of the peace and three freeholders for major crimes. The most heinous Negro crime was rebellion or conspiracy against the white ruling order, tried by court-martial. The master of a rebel slave received compensation from the island treasury when his Negro was executed. But should a black man fight and hurt a fellow black, he might be merely whipped while his master paid compensation to the owner of the injured slave.

The Barbados slave act of 1661 was in large part a policing measure, designed to control the restive black population on the island. Within each plantation the overseers were expected to keep the Negro cabins under close surveillance, searching twice a month for stolen goods, clubs, and wooden swords. Six days a week the overseers kept the slaves busy at their tasks, but Sundays were free and therefore worrisome days for the whites. The Negroes tended to wander to neighboring plantations and hold markets. The act of 1661 stipulated that a slave who left his plantation on Sunday must carry a ticket stating the hour his master expected him back. The white man who found an unticketed Negro wandering loose was encouraged to give him a "moderate whipping." A French visitor to Barbados in 1654 saw slaves given fifty lashes for walking off

26. See the Barbados act for the good governing of servants, Sept. 27, 1661, passed at the same session as the slave act, *Acts of Assembly, Barbadoes,* 23–28.

limits on Sunday, which shows what "moderate" could mean. To punish a more serious offence, he says, the master sometimes applied a firebrand all over the slave's body, "which makes them shriek with despair." [27] The Barbadians were particularly concerned about stolen and fugitive slaves in 1661. They established a registry of runaway slaves and organized a posse of twenty men to scout the island fastnesses and capture them dead or alive. Evidently some whites in Barbados were suspected of entertaining fugitive slaves, for the colony government promised immediate freedom to any servant who revealed that his master was keeping a runaway and fined the guilty master £80. Note that the fine for adopting a fugitive was much heavier than for murdering a slave. The Negro who caught a fugitive slave was rewarded with a fancy new set of clothes adorned "with a Badge of a Red crosse on his right Arme, whereby hee may be knowne and cherished by all good people"—the archetype of Uncle Tom.

The Barbados slave code was modified in one important respect in 1668, when the Assembly decided to classify Negroes as real estate instead of chattels, so that a slave could be legally tied to a given plantation. The purpose of this measure was to prevent executors from dismantling plantations in probate settlements. Sometimes creditors attached and sold all the slaves on an estate, leaving the heirs with "bare land without Negroes to manure the same," and the Assembly wanted to keep the island plantations as viable working units. What effect, if any, this legislation had upon the slave himself is a moot point. Eugene Sirmans has argued that the Barbados Negro, enjoying the status of freehold property, became a species of serf, and that his master, bereft of absolute ownership, had a right only to his services, not to his person. In practice, however, the Barbados slave certainly enjoyed no new freedom. If anything, the slave laws of the later seventeenth century further restricted his opportunities.[28]

The Barbados Assembly betrayed a growing sense of alarm as the

27. Handler, ed., "Biet's Visit to Barbados," *Jour. Bar. Mus. Hist. Soc.*, XXXII (1965–1966), 66–67.
28. Sirmans, not knowing about the Barbados act of 1661, supposed that the statute of 1668 was the earliest formal statement on the slave's status. See his article, "The Legal Status of the Slave in South Carolina, 1670–1740," *Journal of Southern History*, XXVIII (1962), 462–466. Barbados slaves, despite their freehold status, continued after 1668 to be valued in inventories along with the rest of the master's personal property.

black population rose and the white population fell. In 1676 Barbados Negroes were prohibited from entering such skilled crafts as cooper, smith, carpenter, tailor, or boatman, so as to reserve these occupations for Christian artisans, which might encourage freed servants to remain on the island. An act of 1682 berated the Negroes for driving the small white planters away by their insolent carriage. Policing measures to deal with slaves who prowled and stole at night were tightened up. Another measure of 1685 tried to shut down the Sunday markets by prohibiting white persons from trading with Negroes for pots of sugar and jars of molasses filched from their masters. The last major Barbados slave act of the century, in 1688, mainly echoed the provisions and language of 1661, with greater emphasis than before on the wickedness of Negro "Disorder, Rapines and Inhumanities to which they are naturally prone and inclined." For the first time, however, the Assembly admitted that some Negroes stole food because they were starving. The master who failed to provide his slaves with enough to live on was "in some measure guilty of their Crimes" and could not expect compensation from the island treasury when his Negroes were executed.[29]

In Jamaica the chief Negro problem during the initial decade of settlement was how to handle the fugitive Spanish slaves, or Maroons as they became called, who hid in the remote northwestern mountains and raided the English colonists. The English could neither conquer nor tame the Maroons. Some of the Spanish Negroes came to terms; in 1663 Gov. Charles Lyttelton granted them "the same state and freedom as the English enjoy," with full power to manage their own affairs—as long as they stayed well away from the English.[30] But other Maroons refused to join this treaty, and they remained totally independent, a state within a state in Jamaica. Trouble broke out sporadically whenever the Maroons killed English hunters who penetrated into their territory, but generally these people isolated themselves and caused little trouble after 1670. Sometimes they even helped the English track down fugitive plantation slaves.

Meanwhile in January 1664 the Jamaica Assembly drew up its

29. The slave laws of 1668 and 1688 are in *Acts of Assembly, Barbadoes*, 63–64, 137–144. The law of 1676 is in Barbados MSS Laws, 1645–1682, C.O. 30/2/114–125. The laws of 1682 and 1685 are in *ibid.*, 1682–1692, C.O. 30/5.
30. Gov. Lyttelton's declaration on the Spanish Negroes, Feb. 1, 1662/3, C.O. 140/1/75–77.

first statute for governing plantation slaves. Finding that it was too expensive and inconvenient to try Negro crimes by due process, the Assembly directed any master "whose slave has committed any offense worthy of Death" to bring the culprit before a justice of the peace and two neighbors for formal sentencing. No other English statute of the century stated quite so nakedly the white man's arbitrary determination of black crime. But this legislation was quickly superseded. A new governor, Sir Thomas Modyford, arrived from Barbados in June 1664, bringing with him a copy of the Barbados slave law of 1661. Modyford's first Assembly in the fall of 1664 issued a new "Act for the better ordering and Governing of Negro Slaves," which copied the language and all major provisions of the Barbados statute almost exactly. Thanks to Governor Modyford, Jamaica adopted the Barbados slave code, lock, stock, and barrel.[31]

The Jamaican legislation of 1664 was revised a number of times, but the final statement of the century, the Jamaica slave act of 1696, remained very similar to the Barbados slave act of 1688. In minor respects the Jamaicans did deviate from the Barbados model. For one thing, since they were always short of slaves in the seventeenth century, they were reluctant to execute too many troublesome Negroes. In 1683 the Assembly decreed that whenever a black gang committed a crime short of murder, only one member of the group should be executed as an example to the rest. Another special Jamaica problem was that runaways could easily join the Maroons or hole up in the unoccupied sectors of the island. If a planter had a slave who was always running away, he fitted him with an iron yoke that had three long hooks projecting from it to hinder his future escapes. The Assembly directed that any plantation deserted by its owner for six months should be "ruinated" lest it become "a Receptacle for Fugitives." A Jamaican master could be fined five shillings for failing to clothe a Negro properly. More surprisingly, Jamaican masters were urged in 1696 to instruct their bondsmen in Christianity and "cause to be baptized all such as they can make sensible of a Deity and the Christian Faith." This seems to have been the first official endorsement of religious instruction for Negroes in the English sugar islands, and it suggests—what was undoubtedly the case—that Jamaican slaves were generally better

31. The two Jamaican slave laws of 1664 are in C.O. 139/1/42, 55–58.

off than their brothers in Barbados. The two colony governments, however, expressed very much the same alarm about slave revolts in the closing years of the century. Echoing Barbados's complaint in 1688 of Negro "Disorder, Rapines and Inhumanities," the Jamaica Assembly in 1696 worried over their slaves' "bloody and inhuman Practices" and their "often Insurrections and Rebellions." [32] And indeed, as we shall see, the Jamaica slaves did often rebel.

The Leeward colonists defined the legal status of their slaves quite loosely in the seventeenth century. The assemblies in these four islands enacted plenty of policing measures, but they did not adopt comprehensive slave codes—or at least I have discovered none until the Antigua slave act of 1702. Probably the Leeward slaves enjoyed rather more freedom than in Barbados or Jamaica. There was enough interracial fraternization to upset the Nevis Assembly, which in 1675 forbade "the unchristianlike association of white people with Negroes: their drinking together in common upon Sabbaoth dayes," or other days for that matter.[33] On Antigua and Montserrat slaves were customarily whipped rather than killed for stealing horses and cattle. On Montserrat and Nevis the master was expected to plant an acre of provisions for every eight slaves. If, however, the master discovered any meat in his slave's cabin, he was directed to cut off the culprit's ear! This is by no means the only sign of extreme brutality in the Leeward Islands. A Nevis law of 1675 tried to make "severall evill minded persons" pay compensation for the "many" Negroes they had "frivolously" killed. In Montserrat during the 1690s one black was hanged for stealing two turkeys and five yards of fustian; another was hanged, drawn, and quartered for running away, with "his quarters put up in Publicque places as usual." And when Antigua finally passed a comprehensive slave law in 1702, modeled on the Barbados and Jamaica codes, it was for the better government "of Slaves and free Negroes." Antiguan blacks, once freed, could enter craft apprentice-

32. Important Jamaican slave legislation includes the acts of 1671, 1673, 1675, 1683, and 1696. See, for 1671, Council Records, 1662–1671, C.O. 140/1/219–220; for 1673, Council Records, 1672–1678, C.O. 140/3/335–336; for 1675, Miscellany Entry Book, 1667–1677, C.O. 138/2/138–139; for 1683, *Laws of Jamaica Confirmed, 1684*, 140–148; and for 1696, *Acts of Assembly, Jamaica*, 73–82.

33. Nevis act of May 26, 1675, Leeward Islands Laws, 1668–1682, C.O. 154/2/107–108. This statute was reissued in 1697, when whites "found with any negroes at play or assisting them with light, liquor or otherwise, shall be seized and publickly whipt." Nevis act of May 4, 1697, Leeward Islands Assembly Records, 1692–1699, C.O. 155/2/412.

ships, work as wage laborers, or own up to eight acres of land. But they were subject to the same criminal code as the slaves.[34]

When Governor Atkins sent home some Barbados laws for review, he feared that the slave legislation "may seem to shock." He need not have worried. The legal counsel to the Plantation Office approved of Barbados's severe code of justice for slaves. Since Negroes are "a brutish sort of People and reckoned as goods and chattels in that Island, it is of necessity or at least convenient" to enact separate laws for them.[35] The Lords of Trade did boggle at one feature of the West Indian slave code. They thought the penalty for wantonly killing a Negro was too light; a murderer should be more than fined. The Jamaica Assembly added a three-month prison term, but the home authorities were still not satisfied. So in 1696 Jamaica reluctantly stipulated that the bloody-minded Negro killer would get benefit of clergy for his first offense, but would be charged with murder, punishable according to English law, for a second offense.[36] The Barbados and Leeward governments, however, continued to fine Negro murderers.

Thus the English sugar planters rapidly evolved a legal system of chattel slavery. By the 1660s, if not before, they erected a comprehensive slave code that became the basic social and economic law of the islands. Not surprisingly the island colonists worked out their slave laws more quickly than the mainland planters. Virginia, for example, did not draw up a code comparable to the Barbados statute of 1661 until 1705. The seventeenth-century island laws proved to be remarkably durable; they continued in force with only minor modifications for 150 years.[37] As in any slave-based society, the West Indian laws disciplined and regimented the masters as well as the slaves. The chief planters, speaking through the island assemblies, required each slave owner to act as a policeman, to

34. Important Leeward slave legislation includes the Nevis acts of 1675, 1682, and 1688, C.O. 154/2/100–101, 122, 161–162, C.O. 155/1/172–175; the Montserrat acts of 1660, 1679, 1680, and 1693, C.O. 154/1/94, C.O. 154/2/237, 244–245, *Acts of Assembly, Montserrat*, 43–45, C.O. 155/2/525, 536, 543; the Antigua acts of 1669, 1672, 1681, 1694, and 1702, C.O. 154/1/38, 47, C.O. 154/2/349, *Acts of Assembly, Leeward Islands*, 84, 135–139.

35. Gov. Atkins to Lords of Trade, Jan. 31, 1677/78, C.O. 29/2/226; Serg. Samuel Baldwin to Lords of Trade, [c. 1680], C.O. 29/3/6.

36. Instructions for Gov. Howard of Jamaica, Nov. 25, 1685, C.O. 138/4/334–335; *Acts of Assembly, Jamaica*, 80.

37. Goveia discusses the 18th-century West Indian slave code in *Slave Society*, chap. 3. Patterson surveys the Jamaican legislation to 1834 in *Sociology of Slavery*, chap. 3.

suppress his humanitarian instincts, and to deal with his Negroes lash in hand. The slave laws legitimized a state of war between blacks and whites, sanctified rigid segregation, and institutionalized an early warning system against slave revolts. After all, the price of tyranny is eternal vigilance.

The corrosive effect of slavery is well demonstrated by the bland and disingenuous descriptions we have of Negro life in the English sugar islands. The blacks themselves of course left no chronicles. Some of the traditional folk tales and songs still recited in the remote Jamaican villages probably go all the way back to the earliest slave rituals and entertainments. For example, a principal hero in Jamaican folk lore is a cunning spider man named Anancy, who seems to be a spin-off from Ananse, a similar trickster hero in Gold Coast mythology.[38] But for firsthand accounts of slave conditions in the seventeenth century we have to depend upon white witnesses. Few of the early white writers took any interest in African culture or the slave's adaptation to captivity. A resident of St. Christopher in the 1650s who wrote an elaborate natural and moral history of the Indies spent only four pages on the African slaves and 150 pages on the Carib Indians! The Africans were ugly and the Caribs handsome, the Africans impressionable and easily subdued, the Caribs independent and self-reliant. "We are now going to dip our Pen in Blood," he proclaimed enthusiastically, as he launched into a lurid chapter on Carib cannibalism—similar to the titillating accounts of buccaneers' atrocities that were so popular in the seventeenth century—but he had nothing to say about slave punishments. Bondage was really a blessing for the Africans, who had suffered so much neglect and warfare in their native habitat that they "prefer their present slavery before their former liberty, the loss whereof they never afterwards regret." [39]

The three white witnesses who have most to say about early slave life in the English islands are Richard Ligon, John Taylor, and Hans Sloane. These three men were all decent, sensitive people, yet they were profoundly ethnocentric reporters and their conde-

---

38. Patterson, *Sociology of Slavery*, 249–253. See the four Jamaican creole stories transcribed by David De Camp in LePage, ed., *Jamaican Creole*, 127–179.
39. Davies, *History of Caribby-Islands*, 200–202, 251, 326.

scending remarks about the Negro betray instinctive though un-
conscious racism. Richard Ligon, who saw slavery in its early form
in Barbados, had an eye for feminine beauty, and he extravagantly
admired the lovely smiles and graceful, softly muscled bodies of the
black girls he met in the Cape Verde Islands and Barbados, not to
mention the young maids' breasts, which "stand strutting out so
hard and firm, as no leaping, jumping, or stirring will cause them
to shake any more, than the brawn of their arms." Ligon also
praised the male Negroes' athletic prowess and their richly resonant
voices. But though he encountered several highly intelligent black
men, he likened Negroes to cows passing through a gate, "as near
beasts as may be, setting their souls aside." At best the black man
displayed dog-like devotion and obedience; more often he was
cruel, fearful, and false. Ligon contended that the Barbados sugar
planters treated their slaves better than their servants, though his
own evidence demonstrates that the servants were far more carefully fed, clothed, and housed than the slaves. It upset Ligon to see
servants performing the same sort of plantation jobs as slaves,
subject to the same sort of discipline by overseers. The white servants were more harshly treated because they were given brute tasks
beneath their dignity but appropriate to Africans.[40]

John Taylor was even more patronizing about the Jamaican
blacks he saw in 1688, "these Ignorant pore souls" as he called
them. He thought the slaves were suitably costumed in loincloth or
petticoat, "for they deserve noe better since they differ only from
Bruite beast, only by their shape and speach." He justified the
harshness of slave punishments on the grounds that Negroes do not
respond to kindness. Black men would sooner cut your throat than
obey you. Dr. Sloane, who visited Jamaica at about the same time,
was inclined to agree on this last point with Taylor. After catalog-
ing such slave punishments as castration, rubbing lash wounds with
melted wax, lopping off half of a Negro's foot with an ax, or im-
paling his body with stakes and slowly burning him alive, the good
doctor commented: "These Punishments are sometimes merited by
the Blacks, who are a very perverse Generation of People, and

40. Ligon, *True History of Barbados*, 13, 15, 43, 46–53. An anonymous writer
of 1667, probably John Scott, reports disapprovingly that he often saw 30 or 40
white servants laboring in the Barbados fields under the parching sun while the
Negroes were given pleasant craft jobs. *Cal.S.P.Col., 1661–1668*, #1657. The story
sounds dubious, but the most interesting thing is the author's assumption that
black men should do the dirty work.

though they appear harsh, yet are scarce equal to some of their Crimes." [41]

Even Sloane, Taylor, and Ligon, with their warped vision of the Negro, portrayed the West Indian slave regime as a dehumanizing mechanism. They told how, when a slave ship docked, the blacks were greased with palm oil to improve their appearance and paraded naked into the auction hall so that prospective buyers could look into their mouths and test their joints, paying top prices for "the strongest, youthfullest, and most beautiful." New slaves, says Taylor, lamented their captivity and sang mournful songs about their loss of freedom. Carried to the plantation, the new arrivals were branded with their owner's mark (a silver branding iron for the Negroes is a common artifact in seventeenth-century Jamaican inventories). If they tried to run away they were tracked down by dogs (John Helyar ordered two bloodhounds for Bybrook in 1686). Generally the planter housed his slaves in a row of little oblong huts, built out of sticks and cane trash, facing onto a Negro yard. Each hut was furnished with a mat for sleeping, a pot for cooking, and a calabash gourd or two, cut open to make cups and spoons. One Barbados planter in the 1680s installed his Negroes and his cattle in two sheds of the same size and valuation.[42] The slaves ate a monotonous, meager, and starchy diet of corn, plantains, beans, and yams, supplemented by rum on Saturdays and meat whenever a bullock died of disease on the plantation. The manager of Bybrook claimed unusual benevolence in giving his one hundred slaves a barrel of herring per month. Most planters spent considerably less than £2 per annum to feed and clothe a slave.

The slave's work schedule was long and monotonous. Six days a week the Negroes were roused before daylight when the overseer sounded his conch-shell horn. They labored from about six o'clock to noon and, after an hour's recess for dinner, returned to their jobs until dark. The standard work day was ten or eleven hours. At crop time the Negroes labored in shifts around the clock, sometimes seven days a week. Plantation labor was purposely made more debilitating than difficult. The slave was locked into a week-long routine that kept him out of mischief (on the same principle as the

41. Taylor MS, 539–541; Sloane, *Voyage*, I, lvii.
42. Inventories of Thomas Morris (1681) and Nicholas Usher (1686), Barbados Deeds, RB 3/14.

modern boarding school), was underfed to break his resistance, was given childish tasks to numb his intelligence. The deadening round of simple, repetitive plantation chores, totally bereft of challenge or responsibility, promoted what Stanley Elkins calls the "Sambo" and Orlando Patterson calls the "Quashee" slave personality: docile, stultified, and infantile.[43]

A striking characteristic of Negro slavery in the sugar islands, at least initially, was the planters' determination to keep their blacks at arm's length. Ligon tells us that in his day very few Negroes were permitted inside their masters' houses. Before the close of the century this changed, as the wealthy islanders employed large retinues of house slaves dressed in livery. But even in Bridgetown and Port Royal these domestics lived segregated in huts behind their masters' houses. The humble field hands continued to dwell apart, work apart, dress and eat differently from white men, and of course they remained heathens. Only the Quakers tried to convert their slaves to Christianity, and as we have seen, this activity profoundly upset the colony leaders in Barbados, who fined the Quakers thousands of pounds for bringing their Negroes to meeting.

In refusing to admit slaves into their churches the English planters differed markedly from contemporary French, Spanish, and Portuguese slave owners. The difference can largely be explained by Protestant versus Catholic conversion techniques. The Catholics could baptize their slaves into the church without requiring extensive preparation from the initiates. The Quakers, likewise, in their mystical quest for the Inner Light, could work with the blacks without worrying about book learning and catechizing. But for other forms of English Protestantism, mission work was valueless without some modicum of formal religious instruction, and here was the sticking point for the English planters. Ligon and Taylor both remarked on the planters' adamant refusal to instruct or educate the most intelligent slaves in anything beyond plantation crafts. In 1681 the Barbados Assembly declared that the Negroes' "Savage Brutishness renders them wholly uncapable" of conversion to Christianity. When the Jamaica Assembly reversed this position in 1696 and called upon the slave masters to instruct and baptize "all such as they can make sensible of a Deity and the

43. Elkins, *Slavery*, chap. 3; Patterson, *Sociology of Slavery*, 174–181.

Christian Faith," the lawmakers added reassuringly that no slave should become free by becoming Christian.[44] But the planters knew better. They sensed the danger of "civilizing" the Negro to the point where he might have to be reckoned with as a man with human rights.

The West Indian slave, barred from the essentials of European civility, was free to retain as much as he wished of his West African cultural heritage. Here he differed from the Negro in Virginia or New England, who was not only uprooted from his familiar tropical environment but thrown into close association with white people and their European ways. It is not surprising, therefore, that blacks in the sugar islands preserved more of their native culture than blacks in North America. The West Indian slaves learned enough broken English to communicate with their overlords, but they were always bilingual and retained their tribal dialects. The large number of West African languages prevented easy communication among the slaves, so they evolved a common creole patois, compounded of English and African elements, which was unintelligible to their masters. At night and on weekends they sang and danced. The English disliked the racket they made with trumpets and African hollow-log drums and banned the drums for another reason, because they could be used to signal island-wide revolts. So the slaves made music with calabash gourds fitted out with twine or horsehair strings. The dancers tied rattles to their legs and wrists and cow tails to their rumps, while the onlookers clapped hands rhythmically and chanted "Alla, Alla." Sloane, who recorded the words and music of several African songs, says their content was always bawdy. Taylor says they howled and bellowed "in an Antique manner, as if they were all madd."

Neither Sloane, Taylor, nor Ligon showed any understanding of West African religion. Unable to fathom their slaves' mode of invoking and propitiating the gods through magical practices, the English put them down simply as devil worshippers. Sloane and Taylor did notice that the blacks staged elaborate and mournful funeral rites at slave burials. The peoples of West Africa believed that their ancestors would help and protect them from the other world; hence it was essential to honor the dead in the best way possible. For African tribesmen the funeral was the true climax

44. Ligon, *True History of Barbados*, 48–49; Taylor MS, 540; Barbados Assembly to Gov. Dutton, Mar. 30, 1681, C.O. 31/1/336; Jamaica Act for the better Order and Government of Slaves, 1696, *Acts of Asssembly, Jamaica*, 80–81.

to life.[45] At a Caribbean slave funeral the mourners placed cassava bread, roast fowl (if they could get any), sugar, rum, tobacco, and lighted pipes into the grave to sustain the dead man on his journey to the pleasant mountains in Africa where he would dwell after life. This belief in a happy afterlife in Africa tempted many slaves to suicide. Ligon tells a grizzly tale of how Colonel Walrond in Barbados checked a rash of suicides on his plantation. He had one of his Negroes decapitated and stuck his head on a pole to show the other slaves that their companion's body had not traveled home after all and that they could not escape back to their own country through death.[46]

The island slaves retained some semblance of the family structure they knew in West Africa. Customary kinship patterns were dissolved, of course, by the forced migration to America, but the male slaves insisted on having wives, and the slave couples produced children. Unmarried males would wander off to neighboring plantations in search of women or refuse to work, so the planters did their best to keep a pretty even sex ratio within their slave gangs. Among the large Jamaica slaveholders, for example, Robert Freemen had 33 men and 32 women, James Bannister had 36 men and 39 women, Samuel Long had 80 men and 90 women, Edmund Duck had 32 men and 33 women, John Banfield had 36 men and 42 women, and Sir Henry Morgan had 44 men and 45 women.[47] It was desirable for matrimonial purposes to have rather more women than men, for the West African males practiced polygamy, and in the sugar plantations the slave gang leaders were often permitted two or three wives apiece. The small slaveholders naturally had more trouble in marrying their Negroes and providing for black family life. In the slave quarters each couple normally occupied a separate hut. When a slave wife became pregnant, she was exempted from flogging until after delivery of her child. But two weeks after childbirth, she was expected to return to field work, the newborn infant strapped to her back. Dr. Sloane salaciously observed how the mothers' breasts lost their firm shape during

45. Herskovits, *Myth of the Negro Past*, 63; Patterson, *Sociology of Slavery*, 195–198.

46. Sloane, *Voyage*, I, xlviii-lvi; Taylor MS, 540–547; Ligon, *True History of Barbados*, 47–53.

47. These figures are drawn from Jam. Inv. By the 18th century men heavily outnumbered women in the big Jamaican slave gangs. On four of the Price estates, for example, there were 791 male and only 356 female slaves. Craton and Walvin, *A Jamaican Plantation*, 127, 151.

suckling and "hang very lank ever after, like those of Goats." Ligon and Taylor noticed the same thing. To look at the slave mothers as they stoop over their work while weeding the fields, says Ligon charitably, "you would think they had six legs."

The island slaves bore a strange medley of names in the seventeenth century. Some blacks imported into the Caribbean kept their native names; others were given new names by their masters. Newborn infants were generally named by the plantation overseers. The Jamaican inventories, the St. Christopher compensation claims, and the Bybrook plantation records list many hundred slaves by name. Inspection of these lists suggests a fairly even distribution between African and English slave names. In a large gang three or four blacks often had the same name. They might be distinguished from each other as Ebo Jack, Coromantee Jack, and Congo Jack. Already in the seventeenth century the most favorite name was Sambo. Other popular African names included Mingo, Cuffee, Samboth, and Yambo for males, and Quasha, Adjaba, and Affrah for females. Quashee Eddoo, a Bybrook slave, had a name that proclaimed that he was born on Sunday. English nicknames were especially popular, such as Jack, Robin, Tom, Will, Harry, and Dick for the males, or Doll, Maria, Bess, and Betty for the females. The planters often used pretty much the same names for their slaves and their cows. As the century wore on, planters enjoyed giving their slaves funny names: Monkey, Baboon, Hard Times, Trouble, Oxford, Cambridge, or London, among many others. Cromwell was a popular slave name among Cavalier planters. And classical tags were also thought amusing: Dido and Venus for the women, Pompey, Nero, and Scipio for the men. All of this suggests the ambiguous status assigned the black man in the English sugar islands. Torn from Africa, excluded from European culture, he was placed in limbo somewhere between the dumb beasts and rational men.

Keeping the Negroes at arm's length did not mean keeping hands off. The English sugar planters, like slave masters everywhere in America, slept with their slave women and sired mulatto children. At least occasionally, white women in the islands cohabited with black men. How much interracial sex play occurred we can only guess, but it is certain that the English planters in the West Indies

sanctioned the practice more frankly than their cousins in the mainland colonies. As far as I can discover, Antigua was the only Caribbean colony to legislate against miscegenation in the seventeenth
century.[48] The Barbados and Jamaica slave codes, savage in their
punishment of every other black peccadillo, are silent on the subject of blacks who fornicate with whites. For obvious reasons. The
planters who drafted these codes had no desire to prohibit their
extramarital liaisons with black prostitutes and mistresses. Many
of the planters, merchants, managers, and overseers who operated
the sugar industry were young bachelors or married men who left
their wives and children in England. There were always fewer
white women than white men living in the islands in the seventeenth century. But this was perhaps not the key consideration.
The master enjoyed commandeering his prettiest slave girl and
exacting his presumed rights from her. Many planters whose wives
and children lived with them in the islands openly kept black
concubines.

Illicit sex relations between blacks and whites were tolerated,
yet not fully approved. Hence concrete evidence of miscegenation
is hard to furrow out of the early island records. The Bybrook
plantation manuscripts reveal two (possibly three) cases of interracial union. Cary Helyar lived for some time with a mulatto
mistress who bore him two sons; Cary shelved her with an annuity
of £32 when he decided to marry a white woman. Later a Bybrook
overseer named Abraham Wilson married "a holy sister," evidently a Christian mulatto girl who "hath the name of an overseer" and a dowry of £1,000. Wilson's colleague at Bybrook reported all this rather snidely to William Helyar, concluding: "But
gods lambs must play." Another Bybrook overseer was dismissed
because "he got one of the creeholding wenches with child," but
this creole wench was probably a white servant rather than a black
slave.[49] Incidents such as these were doubtless very common in the
islands.

48. Antigua law "against Carnall Coppullation between Christian and Heathen," 1644, reissued in 1672, Leeward Islands MSS Laws, 1644–1673, C.O. 154/1/
49–50. North American slave laws, such as the Virginia code of 1705, severely
punished miscegenation. For fuller discussion of this contrast between the mainland and island sex attitudes, see Winthrop D. Jordan, "American Chiaroscuro:
The Status and Definition of Mulattoes in the British Colonies," *Wm. and Mary
Qtly.*, 3d Ser., XIX (1962), 183–200.
49. Bennett, "Cary Helyar," *Wm. and Mary Qtly.*, 3d Ser., XXI (1964), 75;
John Austin to William Helyar, Aug. 7, 1690, July 6, 1696, Helyar MSS.

The earliest baptismal registers record a few mulatto births, but certainly only a small portion of the total number. In St. Andrew parish, Jamaica, several illegitimate children were baptized almost every year from 1675 on. They were a mixed lot: the white bastards of servant girls, mulattoes born of white mothers, mulattoes born of black mothers. Charles Hudson, a lieutenant in the Jamaica militia, accepted the paternity of three mulattoes in this baptismal register. Maria, a mulatto woman at Fulker's plantation, was the mother of three other illegitimate babies.[50] In the wills of early island colonists, mulatto children figure rather more prominently. For example, a Jamaica planter named William Bonner (d. 1714), having fathered four mulatto children, freed their mothers when he died and bequeathed the children one hundred acres of his best land together with twenty of his Negro slaves. The most curious test of paternity I have seen occurs in the mid-eighteenth-century will of Jacob Ricketts. This Jamaica gentleman, after granting £200 to a mulatto son, considered what to do about "the Child my Negro Ancilla is now big with" and decided that this baby, if it turned out to be a mulatto, should be freed and given £100 at age twenty-one![51]

As these examples show, the island colonist who took a Negro mistress and fathered mulatto children was likely to display some measure of love and responsibility toward his illicit black family. Moralists have condemned the slave master's lustful abuse of black women as roundly as his sadistic abuse of black men, but it can be said in the master's behalf that his sexual vices forced him to accept some blacks—his own offspring—as real human beings. I have seen no seventeenth-century will in which a West Indian planter gave the major part of his estate to his black mistress or bastards, but the planter sometimes baptized them into the Church of England, released them from slavery, articled them as apprentices, or set them up as small farmers and craftsmen. The great majority of West Indian mulattoes remained slaves, but they were accorded a social rank distinctly superior to pure-blooded Negroes and assigned the favored inside jobs as domestics and artisans. Here again the Caribbean racial pattern diverged from the mainland English colonies, where mulattoes were lumped together legally and socially with Negroes and treated no better. In the sugar islands

50. St. Andrew Parish Register: Baptisms, Marriages, Burials, I, Island Registry Office, Spanish Town.
51. Abstracts of Wills Proved in Jamaica, 1625–1792, Add. MSS 34181/252, 334.

it was possible to pass from black to white in three generations. In North America black blood was like original sin and stained a man and his heirs for ever.

The early sugar planters occasionally granted freedom to slaves who were neither their concubines nor their children. Thomas Wardall, a Barbados councillor who owned ninety slaves, set some of his favorites free when he retired to England in 1683 and arranged in his will that all of the others born after 1673 should be manumitted at age thirty-four, provided they had received baptism as Christians. Wardall was not being completely altruistic here; by the age of thirty-four a sugar worker was already past his prime. Some West Indian slaveholders released their most aged and decrepit Negroes in order to get rid of them. But kindly masters rewarded their most faithful black workers with manumission. Matthew Crew of Jamaica set free four Negroes when he drew up his will in 1704, among them "Bess the Cook" and "Toby the Driver." The Jamaica Assembly manumitted at least two Negroes in 1699 for their valorous service during the recent French war.[52]

All told, the number of free mulattoes and Negroes in the English islands was very small in the seventeenth century. The 600 Jamaica colonists whose inventories I have inspected employed a total of six free Negroes and three free mulattoes as indentured servants, a miniscule number compared with their 6,937 Negro slaves. In Bridgetown, Barbados, the community of Christian Negroes was tiny. During an eighteen-year span from 1670 to 1687 only thirty-four mulattoes and Negroes were baptized, married, or buried in St. Michael's church, Bridgetown. Twelve of these blacks belonged to two families of free Negroes. John Cornsoe was a free Negro who entered the church when already an adult in 1676. Nine years later he married a free Negro woman, Anne Williams, and baptized his two daughters, aged about nine and four, who were probably not Anne's children. Seven months after their nuptials, John and Anne presented a new infant daughter for baptism.[53] The most intriguing early entry in the St. Michael parish register is a marriage celebrated on December 4, 1685, between

52. Thomas Wardall's will, *Jour. Bar. Mus. Hist. Soc.*, I (1933–1934), 94–95; Matthew Crew's will, Abstracts of Wills Proved in Jamaica, 1625–1792, Add. MSS 34181/298; *Acts of Assembly, Jamaica*, 86.

53. St. Michael Parish Register: Baptisms, Marriages and Burials, Vol. 1A, RL 1/1, Bar. Archives. One free Negro, baptized in the 1690s in Bridgetown, was called William Sambo.

"Peter Perkins, a negro, and Jane Long, a white woman." I have seen no other evidence that the island colonists tolerated mixed marriages, especially between black men and white women. In general any black man was stigmatized in the English colonies unless he could pass for white. Free Negroes and mulattoes could neither vote, hold office, occupy profitable jobs, nor own much land. They were governed by slave law, not English law. As of 1700 the white planters were light-years away from accepting blacks as their equals.

§❦

The acid test of any slave system is the frequency and ferocity of resistance by the slaves. How many major Negro uprisings took place in the English sugar islands during the course of the seventeenth century? The planters hated to talk about this subject, but it is possible to identify seven separate slave revolts in the English islands between 1640 and 1713 in which fifty or more Negroes participated and in which blacks and whites were killed. Another half-dozen major slave conspiracies were nipped in the bud. These early revolts followed a curious pattern. The Negroes took many years to gear themselves for combat with the white man; no major black revolt occurred, no serious black plot was uncovered, in any of the English islands until 1673, a full generation after the start of the slave trade. Then, during the closing quarter of the century, black risings or rumored risings were frequent. When trouble did come nearly all of it was confined to Jamaica. There were several plots in Barbados and the Leewards, but only one small rising; the black slaves on these islands were by every standard more constrained than the white servants.[54]

One might expect Barbados to be the center of slave revolts. The island was compact, the plantations close together, and the slaves heavily outnumbered their masters from 1660 onwards. But the big problem in Barbados was that the island offered no opportunity for halfway measures; black rebels could not simply seize a few guns, kill a few whites, burn a plantation or two, and disappear into the woods. Since the island was fully settled, their

54. Throughout the 18th century, the pattern continued the same; the Jamaican blacks rebelled frequently, and their brothers in the eastern islands did so very little. See Patterson, *Sociology of Slavery*, 266–283.

only chance for success was to stage a colony-wide conspiracy and take over the entire island. The white servants on Barbados had tried to do this in 1649 and failed. The slave masters, alerted by this past experience, kept guard inside their fortified houses as though they lived under a state of siege. Through the Barbados slave law of 1661 they policed the blacks as systematically as possible. Each planter took care to buy new slaves a few at a time, from a variety of West African regions, on the theory that tribal animosities and linguistic barriers would keep the blacks divided and confused. Perhaps this theory was correct. It would help explain why the Barbados Negroes did not mount a conspiracy against the English until 1675, by which time many blacks had lived long enough on the island to forget African animosities and to speak in creole patois with Negroes from alien tribes. Gov. William Willoughby in 1668 feared that the "Creolian generation" of young slaves then growing up in Barbados would soon strike against their masters. It is likely also that slave conditions deteriorated on the island between 1650 and 1675. At first, when the blacks worked side by side with large numbers of white servants, they were protected by the whites' refusal to work too long or hard. By the 1670s, with the white field laborers gone and sugar profits narrowing, the Barbados planters were more tempted to take shortcuts by feeding their slaves less and working them harder. Finally, the slave masters grew a bit overconfident and careless. In 1673 they even armed some of their Negroes in order to bolster the militia. All this set the stage for Barbados's biggest fright of the century.[55]

In June 1675 a house slave named Fortuna heard that a ring of Cormantin Negroes from the Gold Coast was plotting a general rising. The aim was to murder all of the whites (except for the fairest white women) and install an ancient Cormantin named Cuffee as king of Barbados. The rising was scheduled for two weeks hence. Fortuna dutifully warned her master, Capt. Giles Hall, a leading planter, who alerted Governor Atkins, who hastily commissioned a dozen militia officers to examine the alleged ringleaders secretly. This court-martial sentenced six Negroes to be burned alive and eleven others to be beheaded and dragged through the streets of Speightstown, the rebel center. One brave black named Tony, who was condemned to be burned, stoutly refused to tell all

55. Gov. Willoughby to Council for Foreign Plantations, July 9, 1668, *Cal.S.P.Col., 1661–1668*, #1788; Barbados Council to Council for Trade and Plantations, May 28, 1673, *Cal.S.P.Col., 1669–1674*, #1098.

he knew about the plot. "If you Roast me today," he taunted the provost marshal, "you cannot Roast me tomorrow." The Barbados authorities executed thirty-five Negroes before they felt satisfied that they had snuffed out the conspiracy. They rewarded the faithful Fortuna by granting her freedom.[56]

Barbados had further scares in 1683, 1686, 1692, and 1702. The alarm of 1683 was patently phoney: a broadside was found distributed around the island, urging the slaves to rebel ("Brothers, . . . lett us begin the next Sunday about Midnight"), but since the slaves could neither read nor write, this inflammatory message was obviously the work of a white sadist who wanted to enjoy some more Negro executions. In 1692 another full-blown slave conspiracy was uncovered, a replay of 1675. Governor Kendall commissioned a court-martial to investigate the "Devilish but cunningly managed Designes" of the blacks. Two suspects were strung up in chains for four days until they "confessed" that the Barbados Negroes had secretly formed six regiments of troops and were planning to seize horses, arms, and cannon, burn Bridgetown, murder the planters, and share out their wives and daughters as cooks, chambermaids, and concubines. The purported leaders of this scheme were mainly black overseers, craftsmen, house slaves, "and such others that have more favour showne them by their Masters, which adds aboundantly to their crimes." These leaders were all promptly executed. It is impossible to judge from this distance whether the Barbados plots of 1675 and 1692 were real or imagined, but it is evident that their exposure kept the slave masters on their toes and that the savage punishment meted out to the rebels helped to intimidate the rest of the slaves.[57]

In the Leeward Islands rebel slaves had a better chance of hiding in the mountains than in Barbados or running away to the French. Here the white servants gave a model for action; disloyal servants betrayed Nevis to the Spaniards in 1629 and St. Christopher to the French in 1689. In fact, however, the Leeward slaves were not rebel-

56. The best account of this conspiracy is an anonymous pamphlet, *Great Newes from the Barbadoes*. Other details are in Atkins's letter to Sec. Williamson, Oct. 3, 1675, C.O. 1/35/231; Barbados Assembly Minutes, Nov. 24–25, 1675, *Cal.S.P.Col., 1675–1676*, #712. The Jamaica Council refused entry to Barbados Negroes implicated in the conspiracy, least they spread the rebel virus to Jamaica. *Ibid.*, #661.

57. The rumor of 1683 is described in C.O. 1/53/264–265; of 1686 in C.O. 31/1/675; of 1692 in C.O. 28/1/200–205; C.O. 28/37/175; and of 1702 in Robert H. Schomburgk, *The History of Barbados* (London, 1848), 309.

lious. When the French attacked St. Christopher and Nevis in 1706, the slaves fought more stoutly than their masters did, doubtless because they knew that the French would not liberate them, but carry them off to work in another, strange settlement. Only Antigua, the most secluded island in this group, seems to have experienced a genuine slave uprising in the seventeenth century. Runaway slaves habitually hid in the jungled hills around Boggy Peak in the southwest corner of the island. In 1684 the colony government posted bounties for hunting the "great body" of black fugitives: £2 10s. for a live Negro and £1 for a dead one. By 1687 fifty armed fugitives maintained a fortified camp in the hills and were slipping into the sugar plantations "to Exite and stirr up the Negroes to forsake their masters, and . . . to make them selves masters of the Country." Spurred on by the promise of doubled bounties, the Antigua militia stormed the rebels' camp, captured or killed most of them, and dispersed the remainder. One ringleader was "Burned to ashes." Others were executed. A slave of Governor Powell's, implicated in the revolt, had his tongue cut out and a leg chopped off "as a Living Example to the rest." After that life returned to normal on Antigua.[58]

In Jamaica black unrest was a far more serious matter. During the first dozen years of English occupation, the colonists were constantly fighting the fugitive Spanish Maroons, and once plantation slavery took hold on the island, they had to cope with six sizable slave revolts between 1673 and 1694 and smaller ones thereafter. The first two rebellions, in 1673 and 1675, took place on the remote north coast; in both cases slaves on isolated plantations seized arms and killed their masters. A St. Mary planter named Charles Atkinson reported privately in 1675 that the rebels had been made desperate "by the ill government of their Master." Atkinson's own slaves, though tempted to join, remained faithful to him and disclosed the plot to their overseer. A posse of twenty militiamen, which chased the rebels for three months, caught and killed only eight or nine of them. The others vanished into the wilds or joined the Maroons.[59]

58. D. Grosse to Sec. Williamson, Aug. 21, 1666, *Cal.S.P.Col., 1661–1668*, #1270; Antigua Council Minutes, July 14, 1684, Feb.14–Apr. 7, 1787, C.O. 1/50/21–22, C.O. 155/1/95–96, 99–109, 115.

59. Patterson, *Sociology of Slavery*, 267; Charles Atkinson to Sir Thomas Lynch, Dec. 13, 1675, Coventry Papers, LXXIV, 146; Jamaica Council Minutes, Dec. 15, 1675–Feb. 17, 1676, *Cal.S.P.Col., 1675–1676*, #741, 793, 820, 822.

The next Jamaican revolt broke out within five miles of Spanish Town in 1678. Slaves from various plantations plotted this rising when they were brought together to build a fort. Some of the conspirators, interestingly enough, had known each other in Barbados. The revolt started on Capt. Edmund Duck's plantation, where the slaves killed their mistress and several other whites. Martha Duck's weathered tombstone in the yard of Spanish Town cathedral tells the story: "UNDER THIS STONE LYETH THE BODYS OF EDMON DUCKE ESQ. AND MARTHA HIS WIFE, SHE BEING MOST BARBAROUSLY MURTHERED BY SOME OF THEIR OWNE NEGRO SLAVES DEPARTED THIS LIFE THE 28 DAY OF APRIL 1678." Some of Duck's slaves were quickly caught and executed, but thirty of them slipped into Sixteen Mile Walk in the vicinity of Bybrook plantation and gathered fresh recruits from Sir Thomas Modyford's and William Helyar's Negroes. A loyal slave of Modyford's spied the rebels tossing water into the air from bowls "to see by their witchcraft whither they should be fortunate in their proceedings or not." Some twenty Negroes from Helyar's and Modyford's plantations were implicated and executed. The Jamaica records do not reveal how many Negroes were killed altogether in the process of stamping out this rebellion. The overseer at Bybrook witnessed one execution, and his description amply details the sadistic torture employed upon this unfortunate man: "His leggs and armes was first brocken in peeces with stakes, after which he was fasten'd upon his back to the Ground—a fire was made first to his feete and burn'd uppe by degrees; I heard him speake severall words when the fire consum'd all his lower parts as far as his Navill. The fire was upon his breast (he was burning neere 3 houres) before he dy'd." [60]

Worse was still to come. In 1685–1686 Jamaica suffered a year-long slave revolt. About 150 Negroes started the rebellion on the north side in July 1685, when they obtained twenty-five guns, killed eleven whites, and hid out in the mountains. Governor Molesworth proclaimed martial law and sent out patrols of militiamen and dogs, but the rebels eluded capture for many months while inflicting a great deal of damage to the north-coast settlements. The rebellion spread south in March 1686 when 105 slaves at Madam Guy's plantation seized arms in the night "through the faults of the

60. Joseph Bryan to Matthew Bryan, July 12, 1677; Bryan to William Helyar, June 8, 1678, Helyar MSS; Gov. Carlisle to Sec. Coventry, July 31, 1678, C.O. 138/3/253.

white servants, who were gotten drunk and therefore unable to Quell them." Madam Guy herself leaped out of a window and was hidden by a loyal house slave, but fifteen of the seventeen whites on this plantation were murdered. As the Negroes continued to burn and plunder, John Helyar braced himself for an attack on Bybrook. "Wee will give them such reception," he wrote his father, "as the strength of the house will afford." Every Negro caught during this rebellion was killed—burned alive, torn by dogs, or drawn and quartered. Eventually the colony government restored order, at a total cost of £3,203.[61] Five years later the 400 slaves of Thomas Sutton, the speaker of the Assembly, rose en masse. Sutton's plantation had been considered the largest and finest in Jamaica, but 200 of his Negroes were killed within three weeks in this revolt.[62] Further, smaller revolts occurred in 1694, 1702, and 1704, mainly on the north coast, with the rebels slipping off to join the other slave fugitives hiding in the mountains, setting the stage for the Maroon Wars of 1720 to 1739.

Why were the Jamaica Negroes so much more rebellious than in the other islands? Slave conditions were no worse here. On the contrary, Jamaican slaves had more to eat than in Barbados, for the planters had enough land to spare so that they could give each Negro couple a half acre for provision ground and often a pig, cock, and hen. The Jamaica slave laws, as we have seen, were slightly less repressive than the Barbados code. The plantations that blew up—Edmund Duck's, Madam Guy's, Thomas Sutton's— were not absentee operations. These owners lived on the premises and probably treated their Negroes more humanely than a salaried overseer or manager would tend to. Surely the explanation is that the Jamaican Negroes saw they had a better chance for successful rebellion than in the other islands. The Jamaican revolts started in the largest plantations because the slaves felt safety in numbers. Action centered on the north coast because the plantations were widely scattered there and escape to the mountains and the Maroons was relatively easy. It was not necessary in Jamaica to try to take

61. Taylor MS, 548–552; John Helyar to William Helyar, Mar. 27, 1686, Helyar MSS; Gov. Molesworth to William Blathwayt, Aug. 29, 1685, C.O. 138/5/87–92; Jamaica Council Minutes, Aug. 1, 1685–July 21, 1686, C.O. 140/4/88, 105–108, 126.

62. Gov. Inchiquin to Lords of Trade, Aug. 31, 1690, C.O. 138/7/3–4; John Helyar to William Helyar, Aug. 10, 1691, Helyar MSS; Jamaica Council Minutes, Dec. 10, 1694, C.O. 140/5/298.

262 / Sugar and Slaves

over the entire island, as in Barbados; all the rebels had to do was cut and run.[63]

The Jamaican slaves rebelled more vigorously and frequently than the blacks in most other American colonies; their uprisings were decidedly bigger affairs than the slave revolts in colonial North America. The Jamaican slaves put the lie to the planters' contention that Africans were really happy in their bondage; on the only island where rebellion had a chance of success, it happened often. Yet even in Jamaica the blacks were rather ineffectual rebels, a key reason being that in nearly every conspiracy some loyal slave betrayed the secret to his master. Here is the supreme irony. The English planters, who treated their slaves with such contemptuous inhumanity, were rescued time and again from disaster by the compassionate generosity of the Negroes. In consequence the slave uprisings—even in Jamaica—caused less damage to the planters than hurricanes, earthquakes, malaria epidemics, and French raids. It turned out to be true that a small number of Englishmen could manage a horde of black slaves more easily than white servants. The most telling point about the black protest movement in the seventeenth century is that it never began to challenge the vicious slave system in the English islands head on.

63. Patterson, *Sociology of Slavery*, 273–278, suggests other reasons for Jamaican rebelliousness: the unusually high ratio of blacks to whites, the unusually high proportion of native Africans among the Jamaican slaves, and the unusual ineptitude of the white masters in this colony. None of these factors seems to me as important as Jamaican geography.

8 ⁊ *Life in the Tropics*

The early West Indian colonists, who discarded so many traditional English habits and values when they erected their plantation society, tried their best to transfer English modes of diet, dress, and housing to the tropics. Scorning to imitate the Spaniards, the Indians, or the Negroes, who were all experienced at living in hot countries, they clung determinedly to their own North European styles and standards. One can see in these seventeenth-century settlers the archetypal Englishman dressing for dinner in Rhodesia or wearing the old school tie in Bengal.

Why did the colonists try to retain English fashions in food, clothing, and shelter in the eighty-degree heat and humidity of Barbados and Jamaica? First and foremost, they felt threatened by the alien characteristics of their island settlements: the hordes of black slaves, the stultifying plantation regimen of sugar monoculture, the irresponsible antics of buccaneers and enemy raiders, the deadly tropical fevers and explosive storms. Imperiled by the volatile Caribbean atmosphere, they needed the reassurance of English beef and beer, English waistcoats and periwigs, and English brick houses. Furthermore, the Caribbean planters, like all Europeans in the seventeenth century, conceived of food and clothing in hierarchical terms. Each rank in the social order, from aristocrats at the top to beggars at the bottom, had its own distinct style of dress, diet, and habitation. By the late seventeenth century, as we have seen, the island colonists had erected a graded social system in which the big planters, small planters, servants, and slaves were meticulously ranked and segregated. Naturally the masters wished to distinguish themselves from their slaves by the clothes they wore and the food they ate. So the masters dressed and ate like the gentry in England, while the slaves—several notches lower in the social order than the laboring poor at home—went seminaked and ate tropical produce. But the English planters did not exactly imitate the habits of gentry at home. Having plenty of easy money to spend, they freely indulged in conspicuous consumption, living in a more showy fashion than persons of their station would do in England. And because of the year-round humid heat, they drank more and slept less than Englishmen at home.

The planters quickly decided that Englishmen were not designed by providence for physical toil in the tropics. After a little more experience they concluded that Englishmen could not even live comfortably in the tropics. Naturally they blamed the Caribbean environment for the debilitating diseases and early deaths they suffered, but for some of their problems they had only themselves to blame. In their basic domestic arrangements—food, clothing, shelter—the early settlers stubbornly resisted accommodation to the tropical facts of life. They retained English habits ill suited to the Caribbean climate and developed new habits ill suited to any climate.

§∾

Our best information about the living arrangements of the early island colonists comes from inventories of probated estates. Only scattered inventories for Barbados and the Leewards have survived, but the four volumes of inventories from 1674 to 1701 in the Jamaica Archives contain a mass of information about the colonists' eating habits, wardrobes, furniture, and housing.[1] When a Jamaican property owner died, two or three appraisers surveyed his possessions to determine the value of his estate. Some estates are valued at less than £10, others at more than £10,000. Some of the appraisals are sketchy and brief, others are room-by-room schedules with each possession precisely identified and valued to the half-penny. There are several methodological problems in working with inventories. Few of the Jamaican assessments are complete, for

1. Jam. Inv., Vols. 1–3, 5. Vol. 4 (1694–1699) is missing. The series continues into the 18th century. The four volumes from the 17th century contain approximately 800 inventories, of which I have examined 600. Of these 584 record the value of the deceased person's estate and the number of his servants and slaves (if any). His place of residence is listed in 260 inventories, and 232 give his occupation.

while the appraisers generally listed clothing and other household goods, livestock, servants, and slaves, they seldom included land, planted fields, houses, and other buildings in the valuation.[2] Nor did they always list outstanding debts. The Jamaicans lived on credit to a great extent, and the assets of an apparently wealthy colonist might be entirely offset by his debts. Nathaniel Hickes, for example, had an estate appraised at £6,313, but he also owed £6,745 to 132 creditors. By the time Hickes's administrator paid £155 for the funeral and £376 in legal fees and collected a £635 commission for himself, many of the dead man's creditors could not be paid off.

But the chief problem with inventories is that one cannot be sure how representative they are. The inventories I have examined in the Jamaica Archives describe six hundred estates, but what about the others? The presumption is that poor men are less likely to have their estates probated, hence my sample is skewed in favor of the rich. However, plenty of very poor men are to be found in this collection, and only a small fraction of the colony leaders appear. It may be significant that the distribution of slave owner-ship in the Jamaica inventories is strikingly similar to the dis-tribution of slave ownership in the Barbados cencus of 1680. In the Jamaica inventories 5 percent of the colonists held sixty or more slaves, compared with 7 percent in the Barbados census. In Jamaica 9 percent held between twenty and fifty-nine slaves, com-pared with 7 percent in Barbados. In Jamaica 57 percent held be-tween one and nineteen slaves, compared with 62 percent in Bar-bados. In Jamaica 29 percent held no slaves, compared with 24 percent in Barbados. These figures suggest that the Jamaica in-ventories present a fairly accurate cross section of the island popula-tion. The collection includes estates from every parish and a wide range of occupational categories.

If, as we assume, these inventories are roughly representative, they indicate that Jamaica in the late seventeenth century had a much more stratified social structure than such mainland colonies as Maryland, Pennsylvania, and Massachusetts.[3] Comparing the Ja-

2. Only 14 out of the 600 inventories I examined include real estate and build-ings; in these 14 cases real estate and buildings account for 53% of the total value of the estates.

3. My remarks on Pennsylvania are based on Nash's discussion of 162 inven-tories, 1683–1702, in *Quakers and Politics*, 281–285. My remarks on Massachu-setts are based on analysis of 250 inventories in the Suffolk Co. Probate Records.

maica inventories with probate records from the mainland colonies is a tricky business, since each government had its own system of evaluation. But Jamaica's inventories can be set against those of Maryland, for the appraisers in both places used pretty much the same standards.[4] The qualitative difference between the two sets of estate records, as set forth in table 34, is very striking. The Jamaica inventories display a great deal more concentrated wealth at the top of the scale and a wide spread in wealth from rich to poor.

Table 24. Distribution of Wealth in Jamaica and Maryland

Appraised Value	Jamaica Estates, 1674–1701	Maryland Estates, 1690–1699
£1–99	34.4	74.6
£100–499	37.9	21.7
£500–999	12.8	2.2
£1,000–1,999	9.4	1.5
£2,000+	5.5	0.0
	100.0	100.0

NOTE: The Maryland percentages are drawn from Land, "Economic Base and Social Structure," *Jour. of Econ. His.*, XXV (1965), 641–646.

The Maryland inventories show that sixty years after its founding the colony was still a community of subsistence farmers, sharing a life of rude simplicity. Obviously the Jamaicans could spend a great deal more on food, clothing, and housing than the Marylanders.

In many respects the Jamaica inventories confirm impressions obtained from other sources. The successful Jamaicans were growing rich on sugar and slaves. The fifty-four sugar planters in this group had estates averaging nearly £2,000 in value. The six hundred colonists in the sample owned nearly seven thousand slaves. And

4. Maryland and Jamaica appraisers both only declared movables and valued items like silver and books at the same rate. But in the Massachusetts and Pennsylvania inventories, appraisers generally included land and buildings as well as movables and valued all property at a 50% higher rate than the Jamaican appraisers. Thus a £500 estate in Jamaica or Maryland was worth two or three times as much as a £500 estate in Massachusetts or Pennsylvania.

as the slave population of the colony climbed, the value of inventoried property also climbed. Table 25 shows how the average number of inventoried slaves and the average value of inventoried estates doubled in twenty-seven years.

But the Jamaica inventories also show—better than any other early evidence—the wide contrast in living habits between the richest and poorest members of the community. This was the most distinctive feature of the island life-style. Those colonists who had a great deal of money to spend displayed it ostentatiously. Those who had none lived in grinding poverty.

Among the poorest inhabitants were the schoolteachers, booksellers, physicians, and clergy—the intelligentsia of the island. Ebenezer Hicks was a schoolmaster who owned a horse worth £2,

Table 25. Summary of the Jamaica Inventories, 1674–1701

Years	Total Inventories	Total Value	Average Value	Total Negroes	Average Negroes
1674–1678	195	£75,853	£389	1,847	9
1679–1686	182	£84,785	£461	2,101	12
1686–1694	139	£95,318	£686	1,943	14
1699–1701	68	£54,066	£825	1,055	16

furniture worth £1, and a parcel of books worth £1 when he died. He left no clothes, for he was buried in them. The parish owed him two years' back salary. Dr. Michael Davies, a surgeon, had an estate appraised at £18, mainly medicines and a box filled with "great instruments." He left few clothes and no furniture. Of the nine other surgeons and physicians in this sample, four were very poor, and all had estates of less than average value. William Shermore, a bookseller, had few assets beyond his stock of books valued at £70 and his maps, atlases, and globes valued at £10. His clothing—all worn and worth about £4—is itemized in exceptional detail: he had a cloth suit and a stuff suit, five shirts, two hats, two pairs of shoes, one pair of silk stockings, four pairs of wash leather gloves, a parcel of wearing linen, and a bengal gown. Two of the three clergymen left estates of around £150. The third, the Reverend James Zeller, was also a sugar planter with thirty-nine slaves, and he was worth £3,152.

In Port Royal and Spanish Town there was a considerable contrast in living standards between the small craftsmen and the big shopkeepers and merchants. The craftsmen lived in modest comfort, but far from extravagantly. For example, John Waller, a shoemaker and tanner in Port Royal, had an estate of £158. He employed four servants and an aged slave. His house had six rooms for living quarters, besides the shop, workroom, and tanning house. His furniture, all described as "old," was appraised at £18 and consisted of three beds, a hammock, ten chairs, four stools, four tables, one desk, four chests, two carpets used to cover the tables, two pictures, two mirrors, two dozen pewter and earthen plates, cooking utensils, table linen, eleven candlesticks, and six silver spoons. In the cellar he kept a quarter cask of madeira and four gallons of brandy. In his yard among the tanning vats he kept twenty-seven goats. A far more dashing style was maintained by Henry Wastell, a dry-goods shopkeeper with an estate six times the value of Waller's. Wastell employed eight Negroes and a servant. His house had nine rooms, among them a billiard room and a shuffleboard room, in addition to his shop and stable. His household furnishings were valued at £108, which again is six times the value of Waller's furniture. He possessed only twelve books, but he had £31 in plate—the equivalent of 120 silver spoons.

The sharpest contrast in living styles was in the countryside, between the peasant farmers and the big planters. Struggling small farmers had little to spend on housing, clothes, and furniture. For instance, William Valet owned 86 acres worth £110 and eight Negroes worth £86—and scarcely anything else. His household goods, appraised at £6, were skimpier than the modest furnishings of John Waller, the Port Royal tanner. Valet owned a bed, two hammocks, three tables, a parcel of old books, four cooking pots and pans, a chamber pot, two pewter plates, three silver spoons, two silver cups, and a gold ring. At the opposite end of the spectrum, a rich sugar planter like Samuel Long lived grandly indeed. Samuel Long served as councillor, chief justice, and colonel, among other offices. He took out land patents for 11,183 acres in six parishes,[5] and when he died at the age of forty-five he owned 288 slaves. His estate was valued at £12,000, not including his land, plantation buildings, and two mansion houses. Long lived in a style befitting his wealth. His house in Spanish Town, more expensively fitted than his

5. Long's land grants are itemized in Jam. Land Pat.

plantation house, had a hall—the principal room—large enough to hold sixty chairs and seven tables. In his dining room Long had a dozen table cloths, twelve dozen napkins, and £76 worth of silver to dress his table. In the bed chambers he had four costly looking glasses and a best bed with hangings (valued at £100), which he bought on a trip to England. In his plantation house Long had another fifty-eight chairs, seven tables, and three looking glasses. All of the big planters kept dozens of chairs in their houses, suitable for large-scale entertainments.

Not surprisingly, the most lavish inventory in this sample is that of Sir Thomas Lynch, the governor of Jamaica. Lynch's mansion house had thirteen rooms, and its furnishings were appraised at £1,236. Sir Thomas's silver service (£361) consisted of forty-two dishes and plates, forty-four spoons and forks, four candlesticks, a basin, beaker, salt cellars, mustard pots, sugar and pepper boxes. In his stable Lynch had a coach, a chariot, and thirteen horses. His library of about a hundred books included handsomely bound volumes in French, Spanish, Italian, and Latin, and his wardrobe contained such costly garments as a £9 scarlet embroidered coat—more valuable than William Valet's entire household furnishings.

Since so much has recently been written about the living arrangements of the early New England colonists, it is instructive to compare our sample of Jamaican estates with an equivalent sample of Suffolk County, Massachusetts, estates for the years from 1670 to 1700.[6] This one Massachusetts county, with the commercial town of Boston and twelve surrounding agricultural villages, had about the same white population as Jamaica at this time, and the two sets of inventories offer plentiful examples of rich and poor householders, of town and country social conditions. Needless to say, the most glaring difference between the two sets of inventories is that the Jamaicans employed so much more servile labor. Among the 600 householders in our Jamaica sample, 421 owned black slaves, 145 had white servants, and 51 had Indian servants or slaves, some of whom had come from New England, captured in King Philip's

6. The Suffolk Co. Probate Records, Vols. 5, 7–14, contain roughly twice as many inventories as the Jamaica series for the late 17th century. I have examined 250 of these Massachusetts inventories, sampling all 9 volumes. The best way to see what they are like is to consult Abbott Lowell Cummings, *Rural Household Inventories, 1675–1775* (Boston, 1964), 3–84, where 40 room-by-room inventories of rural Suffolk Co. households for the years 1675–1700 are reproduced.

War. By contrast, a sample of 250 Massachusetts householders includes only 13 with black slaves, 5 with white servants, and 1 with an Indian servant. The Massachusetts appraisers held that white servants were not chattels and so omitted them from most inventories. We know from other evidence that there were plenty of servants in New England, but nothing like the thirteen servants or slaves per household in Jamaica. Not only could most white Jamaicans avoid onerous physical labor, but the wealthiest colonists could keep some slaves for show, dressing them in livery and assigning them ceremonial tasks. In New England almost everyone habitually worked with his hands.

One might suppose that the Jamaicans, with so many slaves and servants, had much larger houses than in Massachusetts. The inventories suggest that such was not the case. In both colonies, houses ranged in size from one-room cottages to four-storied mansions of a dozen or more rooms. Overall, however, the Massachusetts houses had more rooms, especially bedchambers, to accommodate the very large families characteristic of this colony. Jamaican houses rarely had more than three bedchambers, whereas Massachusetts houses often had five. The inventories also show that Massachusetts servants and slaves generally had their own quarters inside the master's house. One finds several examples of beds, bedding, chairs, and chests "which belong to the Negro's." Sir William Phips, governor of Massachusetts, kept three Negroes and four servants at his Boston mansion house—a large retinue by New England standards. The Negroes occupied a bedchamber and the servants were relegated to the garret. No such arrangement can be found among the Jamaica inventories. In Port Royal as well as in the country plantations, Jamaican Negroes usually lived in small thatched huts situated behind the master's house, and the white servants strung up hammocks in the hall or kitchen.

The inventories show, not surprisingly, a marked difference in intellectual tone between these two colonies. In Jamaica there was a Bible in most households, but few planters owned more than a small parcel of books. One excellent collection of about 135 books and pamphlets was kept by Thomas Craddock, a Port Royal glazier, in his upstairs closet.[7] Craddock's taste was exemplary. He owned

7. Jam. Inv., Vol. 2. Craddock probably kept these books for sale, since he had several duplicates, such as four new gilt Bibles and six new Common Prayers. Other volumes are described as old or damaged.

volumes of English poetry by Edmund Spenser, George Herbert, Francis Quarles, Abraham Cowley, John Cleveland, Nahum Tate, and Thomas Flatman, classical works by Plutarch, Tacitus, Ovid, Terence, and Seneca, and the chief books of Erasmus, Grotius, Francis Bacon, John Foxe, Richard Hooker, and Joseph Glanvill. Craddock showed his Anglican, royalist colors in the choice of such books as *Hudibras* and *The Portraiture of Charles I*. More characteristic, perhaps, of the Jamaican literary temper was John Kent, a merchant who collected Restoration farces and erotic poetry. Among Kent's books were the earl of Rochester's *Poems,* Ovid's *Epistles, The Lover's Watch, The Double Cuckold,* and other plays.

In contrast, the Suffolk County inventories disclose a good many sizable libraries, generally of a very sober taste. The Boston bookseller Michael Perry left a large stock of such titles as *Conscience the Best Friend,* Increase Mather's *Folly of Sinning, Remarkable Judgments,* Richard Baxter's *Call to the Unconverted, The Duty of Parents and Children,* and John Flavel's *Saint Indeed*. In Massachusetts, unlike Jamaica, clergymen were among the most affluent members of the community. In our sample of Suffolk County inventories three of the four clergymen left estates valued at more than £1,000.

The most telling difference, perhaps, between the two sets of documents is that the Massachusetts inventories exhibit a greater equality and frugality in living conditions. To be sure, there was a considerable range of wealth within late seventeenth-century New England society. The Boston merchant with a shop, a warehouse, and shares in a half-dozen ships and cargoes was five or ten times as wealthy as the Medfield farmer with one hundred acres and two dozen horses, cows, sheep, and pigs. But the Boston merchant did not parade his wealth ostentatiously. His clothes and furniture were twice as costly as the Medfield farmer's, but not five or ten times as costly, and after he filled his warehouse, cellar, and garret with goods, he made room in his bedchambers for hogsheads of fur, bales of cloth, and barrels of fish and meal. Accepting the social teachings of their favorite preachers and authors, the Massachusetts colonists—both rich and poor—saved money more purposefully than the Jamaica colonists and avoided running up tremendous debts. Whereas the rich Jamaica planter mortgaged next year's sugar crop on imported furniture, clothing, and plate and left an estate hopelessly entangled in debts, the rich Boston merchant lived carefully within his income, contracted few debts, and passed on to his heirs a strongbox full of cash. In every respect Jamaican living habits differed radically from those in New England.

&

The provision of food and drink posed a major problem for seventeenth-century Englishmen in the West Indies. The food crops they were used to in England could not be grown in the Caribbean, for the most part, and those food crops that flourished in the Caribbean were generally unappealing to the English palate. At first the early planters in Barbados and the Leeward Islands made do with local produce, though they bought salt fish, meat, and dairy products from Dutch or English traders whenever they could afford to. Once the planters in these small islands converted their prime acreage to sugar cultivation, they no longer had enough land left for provision crops to feed themselves and their slaves. After 1650 or 1660 the Barbadians and Leeward Islanders were forced to import most of their food from England, Ireland, and North America. In Jamaica there was plenty of land for provision crops, yet the monied planters in this colony also imported a great deal of their food from abroad, since they would rather eat salted English beef and salted New England mackerel than fresh tropical produce.

The English diet these people were accustomed to was basically quite simple. English farmers in the seventeenth century concentrated heavily on cereals and legumes such as wheat, barley, rye, oats, peas, and beans. They raised a great many sheep, for wool more than mutton, and a good many cattle for beef, milk, butter, cheese, and hides. Swine and poultry were less popular; the typical English farmer kept twice as many cows as pigs. Vegetables were mainly roots such as carrots, parsnips, and turnips, and the most common English fruits—apples, cherries, and pears—were not yet widely cultivated commercially. Fish was a major element in the seventeenth-century Englishman's diet, especially smoked or salt herring and cod. Since much of the English countryside was wild and wooded, it was easy to hunt for deer, rabbits, and other game, and the poor scavenged for nuts and berries. The laboring classes subsisted chiefly on bread, variegated by puddings, pies and cheese, with beer to wash it down. The middling classes added meat to their menu; "bread, beer and beef, yeoman's fare," as the farmer poet Thomas Tusser put it. Englishmen boasted of their good roast beef, unspoiled by French sauces and salads, and the upper classes consumed prodigious quantities of beef and mutton. It has been calculated that a member of a noble household in seventeenth-century England ate well over a pound of meat and drank a half-dozen pints of beer daily.[8]

This diet of bread, beer, and beef was not easily transplanted to the Caribbean. The colonists were unable to grow wheat and barley in the islands, so they could not reproduce English bread and beer. Nor were they satisfied by the Caribbean substitutes for wheat and barley—cassava and corn. The native Indians extracted the poisonous juice from cassava roots, grated them, and baked them into cakes. The Indians also made cornmeal bread and a cornmeal mush known as loblolly. Bread could also be made from the plantain, a starchy fruit akin to the banana. "Their Bread groweth upon trees," said one reporter, "or the roots of trees." The great advantage of these Caribbean provision crops was that they grew rapidly and year-round. A plantain walk ripened in two months, a cornfield in three or four months. Sweet potatoes and yams also grew plentifully, and could be boiled or roasted. But the English relished none of this food. "Casader," said a Barbados clergyman, is "a bread I approve not off." Other commentators agreed that cassava bread was dry and tasteless, though Richard Ligon learned how to make acceptable cassava pie crusts. Flour imported from England or North America was often spoiled by weevils and too stale for making soft English bread.[9] Nevertheless, the islanders bought vast quantities of imported flour, especially when the Pennsylvania flour and bread trade opened at the end of the century. Jonathan Dickinson, a Quaker merchant who traded between Jamaica and Pennsylvania, sold 83 casks, 174 half barrels, 66 quarter barrels, and 9 barrels of flour to some 100 customers in Port Royal during a six-month period in 1699. This was enough flour to bake bread for

8. For fuller discussion of these points, see Thirsk, *Agrarian History of England and Wales*, chap. 1, 3, 7–8; Charles Wilson, *England's Apprenticeship, 1603–1763* (London, 1965) , chaps. 2, 7; Bridenbaugh, *Vexed and Troubled Englishmen*, 91–98, 146–148, 202–208; Mildred Campbell, *The English Yeoman under Elizabeth and the Early Stuarts* (New Haven, Conn., 1942) , chap. 6; and Stone, *Crisis of the Aristocracy*, 555–562, app. 24.

9. T. Walduck to James Petiver, 1710, *Jour. Bar. Mus. Hist. Soc.*, XV (1947–1948) , 31; James Parker to John Winthrop, June 24, 1646, Forbes *et al.*, eds., *Winthrop Papers*, V, 84; Ligon, *True History of Barbados*, 30; Sloane, *Voyage*, I, *xviii–xx;* Taylor MS, 501.

FIG. 9. *Slaves preparing cassava flour (left) and tobacco (right). (From Du Terte, Histoire générale des Antilles, II, 419; courtesy of William L. Clements Library, University of Michigan, Ann Arbor.)*

the entire population of the island. According to his ledger Dickinson also supplied his customers with 47 barrels of bread and 33 hogsheads, 5 barrels, and 3 tuns of Pennsylvania beer.[10]

The English raised cattle and sheep in the islands, but found their beef and mutton to be far less fat and tasty than at home. In Barbados and the Leewards most planters kept a few cows for milk, but rarely slaughtered them. In Jamaica the cattle ranchers bred their animals more for hides than meat. By far the most popular fresh meat in Jamaica, as elsewhere in the islands, was pork. Not only the native hogs, which ran wild in the woods, but the domesticated swine brought from England had sweeter, more succulent flesh than pork at home. The term "buccaneer" means someone who "boucans" or barbecues meat—which is how the West Indian buccaneers cooked the wild hogs they killed. Island turkeys, ducks, and chickens were also reckoned to be tastier than English poultry and among the Jamaican delicacies were sugar-fed rats trapped in the cane fields. But the colonists could not be satisfied with pork, turkey, and rodent meat. "Our poultrey and swines flesh exceed any you have in England," a Barbadian planter wrote home, "But yor sirloyne of Biefe wou'd better relish our palats than all the vians in the Indies." [11]

Fresh meat of any sort in the Caribbean had to be cooked quickly before it spoiled. In Nevis no meat sold in the Charlestown Saturday market could be slaughtered before sunset on Friday. Furthermore, fresh meat was very expensive. Late in the century fresh beef and pork ranged as high as ninepence a pound in Barbados and Nevis, as against one or twopence a pound in Virginia.[12] Consequently the islanders bought a great deal of salt beef and pork from England, Ireland, and North America. Surviving records of goods shipped into the islands during the 1680s indicate that barreled beef and pork were consistently the principal imports, with salt fish

10. Jonathan Dickinson Ledger, 1699–1701, Logan Papers, Historical Society of Pennsylvania, Philadelphia. Dickinson's barrels, half barrels and quarter barrels varied greatly in weight, but the average half barrel of flour weighed about 250 lb. and the average barrel of bread about 200 lb.

11. T. Walduck to James Petiver, 1710, *Jour. Bar. Mus. Hist. Soc.*, XV (1947–1948), 32. See also "A Brief Discription of the Ilande of Barbados," Harlow, *Colonising*, 46–47; Ligon, *True History of Barbados*, 34–35; Taylor MS, 500; and Sloane, *Voyage*, I, xx.

12. *Acts of Assembly, Nevis*, 15; Sir Richard Dutton to William Blathwayt, Aug. 24, 1681, Blathwayt Papers, XXX; Robert Beverley, *The History and Present State of Virginia*, ed. Louis B. Wright (Chapel Hill, N.C., 1947), 292.

coming next.[13] At Bybrook Plantation in Jamaica the manager and his white servants slaughtered an ox on special occasions such as Christmas, but otherwise they ate fresh local pork and dried imported beef. In 1674, when the overseer was away, three white servants at Bybrook consumed fifty pounds of pork in one week. In 1691, when a dozen whites lived on the plantation, they ate a barrel of beef per week. Even cattle ranchers bought imported meat. A Jamaica rancher named William Vincent, with 125 head of cattle and only one white servant to feed, left among his household goods a quarter barrel of New England pork.[14]

Fishing was excellent around the English islands, but the colonists did not relish the local varieties. Fresh fish spoiled quickly in the heat, and few planters bothered to fetch them inland. At Port Royal one could buy excellent fresh fish in the market very cheaply each morning, but a few miles inland at Spanish Town it was much harder to get. According to Ligon, the only place to eat fresh fish in Barbados was at the Bridgetown taverns. Ligon could get very little green sea turtle, except for pickled turtle, shipped down from the Leeward Islands and so crudely prepared that it was mixed with sand. The turtle capital was the Cayman Islands, west of Jamaica. Late in the century a fleet of 180 sloops brought these beasts into the turtle market at Port Royal, and turtle meat became the staple food for poor whites in Jamaica. Dr. Hans Sloane disapproved of this; he claimed that turtle eaters had pronouncedly yellow complexions and that the armpits of their shirts were "stained prodigiously." The slaves were given salt fish. The local fish, when salted, turned mealy, and rather than bother to prepare and pack it, the islanders found it cheaper and easier to buy the poorest grade of New England cod and English herring for slave food. The planters themselves, when they ate fish, preferred salt mackerel or salmon, imported from New England or Ireland.[15]

Englishmen tended to drink heavily in the seventeenth century, and those who came out to the Caribbean drank especially heavily,

13. Thornton, "Some Statistics of West Indian Produce," *Carib. Hist. Rev.,* IV (1954), 265–266, 270–272.

14. Bybrook Plantation accounts, Mar. 12, 1686/7–Aug. 8, 1691, Helyar MSS; Bennett, "William Dampier," *Hist. Today,* XIV (1964), 476; inventory of William Vincent, Jam. Inv., Vol. 1.

15. Ligon, *True History of Barbados,* 35–37; Sloane, *Voyage,* I, xviii; Taylor MS, 494, 510; Alexander Gunkel and Jerome S. Handler, eds., "A Swiss Medical Doctor's Description of Barbados in 1661: The Account of Felix Christian Spoeri," *Jour. Bar. Mus. Hist. Soc.,* XXXIII (1966–1967), 10.

for the humid heat made them thirsty. But they were not satisfied by the native fermented drinks—mobby distilled from sweet potatoes, perino distilled from cassava, or plantain drink. None of these potions kept long, and they had to be drunk up within a few weeks after bottling or barreling. Once the planters turned to sugar production, rum (popularly known as kill-devil) became the staple local liquor. It was most commonly served up in a punch mixed with water, lime juice, sugar and nutmeg. According to Ligon a gallon of rum cost only half a crown. "The people drink much of it, indeed too much; for it often layes them asleep on the ground, and that is accounted a very unwholsome lodging." John Taylor describes the common people of Port Royal walking about town barefoot, satin hats jammed over their eyes, tobacco pipes clenched in their teeth, "and thus they trampouse about their streets, in this their warlike posture," ready to booze a cup of punch with anyone. Taylor says that nearly every Jamaica planter kept a lusty bowl of cold rum punch ready on his table to accommodate friends and visitors.[16]

Nevertheless, those planters who could afford the extra price served imported European wines and liquors. Rum, they held, was a common and coarse drink, fit to fuddle the servants and Negroes. Madeira and brandy were proper drinks for the island gentry. Many English ships picked up cargoes of madeira or canary en route to the Indies. The planters drank these wines diluted with water or mixed them with lime juice in a punch. They also drank plenty of French wine and brandy, which was more expensive. English beer and cider were also very popular in the islands, even though they spoiled quickly.[17] John Helyar, newly arrived at Jamaica, wrote home for Somerset cider well corked and "some beere alsoe will doe mighty well," particularly if it be Temple Street beer from Bristol. Until he could get some English beer or cider, Helyar was making do with Adam's ale—that is, water. The Jamaicans cultivated a good deal of cocoa, and abstemious planters could drink chocolate

16. Ligon, *True History of Barbados*, 27, 31–33; Taylor MS, 501–504. The price of rum in the islands was scarely more than a shilling per gallon by the close of the century.

17. Sloane, *Voyage*, I, *xxvii–xxix*; Jeaffreson, ed., *Young Squire*, I, 185, 191; Gunkel and Handler, eds., "A Swiss Medical Doctor's Description of Barbados," *Jour. Bar. Mus. Hist. Soc.*, XXXIII (1966–1967), 9–10. In the taverns of Montserrat in 1669, beer was priced at a shilling a gallon, madeira at 4s., French brandy at 6s., and a bowl of punch made with a quart of rum at 2s. See *Acts of Assembly, Montserrat*, 15.

as well as water. "They feed all their children with it here instead of milk," reported Cary Helyar from Jamaica, "and there are no clearer children in England." [18]

The only West Indian foods that the English admired extravagantly were the tropical fruits—oranges, lemons, limes, watermelons, muskmelons, guavas, papayas, mangos, and pineapples above all. Pineapple juice, declared Richard Ligon, "is certainly the Nectar which the Gods drunk." The islanders pickled and preserved these fruits and made candied sweetmeats that were always gratefully received by friends and relatives back home. West Indian officials anxious to curry the favor of William Blathwayt, the influential secretary of the Colonial Office, shipped him presents of oranges, casks of preserved ginger and citrus, and once "a Pott of pickled peppers." But despite these exotic fruits and preserves the English planters hankered after the desserts and confections they were used to at home. In the cool of the evening at Port Royal the merchants gathered at the taverns to eat cheese cake, tarts, creams, custards, and sillabub, made as precisely as possible after the recipes of London pastrycooks. [19]

The contrast between the eating habits of the upper and lower classes in the English islands was tremendous. The slaves ate decidedly less well than agricultural laborers in England. Their diet consisted of meager rations of corn, plantains, sweet potatoes, peas, and beans, supplemented by a little salt fish. Jamaican slaves fared better, since they were given land to grow their own corn and yams, whereas the slaves in the smaller islands depended on weekly food doles from their masters. The custom in all the English islands was to give the carcasses of diseased cattle and horses to the Negroes. On Saturdays slave masters generally gave each Negro family a quart of rum and a quart of molasses for weekend carousing. The white servants ate much better, though they complained constantly about their food. The basic menu for servants included a good deal of salt beef, salt fish, and pork, as well as cassava bread, plantains roasted or fried, and cold cornmeal mush. This last dish, known as loblolly, was disliked by the Negroes, who according to Ligon would cry out "O! O! no more Lob-lob." The blacks preferred to roast

18. John Helyar to William Helyar, Mar. 27, 1686, Cary Helyar to William Helyar, Nov. 7, 1670, Helyar MSS.

19. Ligon, *True History of Barbados*, 33, 36; William Blathwayt to John Witham, May 5, 1681, Reginald Wilson to Blathwayt, Apr. 16, 1688, Blathwayt Papers, XXXV, XXXVI; Taylor MS, 501, 503.

corn and eat it on the cob, which was cattle food in English eyes. For the white servants—as for the slaves—the high point of the week came on Saturday, when they got a dole of rum and sugar for making punch.[20]

Members of the master class enjoyed a very different culinary style. The chief planters in the English islands dined richly, drank copiously, and entertained lavishly. Breakfast and supper were minor meals; the main repast was dinner, which began between noon and two o'clock, as in England, though this was a very hot time of day for heavy eating in the Indies. Dinner and after-dinner drinking lasted four or five hours if company was present. Roast meats, pies, and custards dominated the planter's menu, but plenty of imported condiments were available to add variety and spice. A Jamaica grocer named Robert Scott, who evidently catered to the planters and merchants, stocked his shop with many bottles of sauces, olives, capers, and gherkins, jars of sweet oil, casks of anchovies, and barrels of figs, prunes, raisins, and currants.[21]

On special occasions the planters devised elaborate feasts. In the middle years of the century Richard Ligon (who relished good cookery) attended banquets given by two of the early Barbados sugar magnates, the Roundhead James Drax and the Cavalier Henry Walrond. Colonel Drax served his guests fourteen distinct dishes of beef, eight of fowl, three of pork, three of goat, a suckling pig, mutton, and veal. Most of these meats were elaborately garnished with herbs, spices, and citrus. There were accompanying dishes of potato pudding, bacon, oysters, caviar, anchovies, olives, custards, creams, puffs, and fruit and a dozen varieties of strong drink to wash it all down. Colonel Walrond offered fewer meat dishes at his feast, but since he lived by the sea he served his guests fresh mullet, parrot fish, coney fish, snapper, cavalla, turbot, crabs, and lobster.[22]

After the meal the planter and his guests settled down to some heavy drinking. A French priest named Father Antoine Biet, who visited Barbados a few years after Ligon, was particularly struck by the mode of after-dinner entertainment. When the cloth was re-

20. Ligon, *True History of Barbados*, 3, 37; Taylor MS, 536–540; Handler, ed., "Biet's Visit to Barbados," *Jour. Bar. Mus. Hist. Soc.*, XXXII (1965–1966) , 66.

21. Scott's inventory is in Jam. Inv., Vol. 3. There are interesting descriptions of planters' dining habits in Taylor MS, 500–503, and Labat, *Nouveau voyage aux isles de l'Amérique*, IV, 394–395, 411–412.

22. Ligon, *True History of Barbados*, 38–39.

moved, a trencher of pipes, a trencher of tobacco, and a bowl of brandy laced with sugar were set upon the table. The brandy was set aflame and burned one-third down, whereupon the company passed the rest of the afternoon smoking and toasting until they eventually emptied the bowl. Whenever a guest needed more tobacco, an attendant slave refilled his pipe and presented it to him on bended knee. Around 1700 a Barbados planter named Walduck attended the annual Cockney feast, celebrated by all the island gentry born within the sound of Bow Bell in London. The company breakfasted on plumb broth, marched to church for a sermon, and repaired to an elaborately decorated hall, where they were summoned to dinner by twelve trumpeters. Each course of the banquet was punctuated by a toast and a volley of twenty-five guns! After dinner everyone continued to drink for another four to six hours, and the more tenacious members of the party were still toasting and firing guns at midnight.[23]

Perhaps the most magnificent feast of the century took place in Barbados in August 1688 to celebrate the birth of James II's son, the warming-pan baby. On this occasion Gov. Edwin Stede, "splendidly arrayed," led a triumphal procession of officers and gentlemen into Bridgetown, where they were met by twelve hundred militiamen. As the governor drank the health of each member of the royal family, the soldiers fired their muskets, cannon from the forts and ships around the harbor boomed, and the loyal citizenry huzzahed. Stede ordered wine casks opened in the Bridgetown streets and wine casks distributed among the militia companies for mass toasting. He provided meat and bread for two thousand persons and set up a 250-foot table at his mansion house, where the five hundred chief gentlemen of the island dined while their ladies were entertained at a separate banquet of sweetmeats.[24]

Dr. Thomas Trapham, a Jamaica physician, disapproved of his fellow colonists' dietary habits. In his *Discourse of the State of Health in the Island of Jamaica*, Trapham argued that it was foolish to transplant English menus and English hours of dining to the tropics. He proposed a new schedule so as to avoid eating in the hottest hours: chocolate at six in the morning, dinner at ten, choco-

23. Handler, ed., "Biet's Visit to Barbados," *Jour. Bar. Mus. Hist. Soc.*, XXXII (1965–1966), 62; T. Walduck to James Petiver, 1710, *ibid.*, XV (1947–1948), 45–47.

24. Account of the Barbados celebration, Aug. 19, 1688, C.O. 1/65/122; Stede to Lords of Trade, Aug. 30, 1688, C.O. 29/4/7–8.

late again at four, and supper at seven or eight at night. His most surprising proposal was that half of the planters' food should be chocolate. Trapham was a great believer in the humoral theory of disease, and he supposed that tropical fevers were caused by an excess of choler in the system. Chocolate had great therapeutic powers, he thought, because it regulated the humors by dampening choler in the stomach. Trapham wanted the planters to try eating more local fruits, yams, rice, fish, and turtle in lieu of English meats, and he urged them to eat as sparingly as possible. But his own menus called for large and heavy dinners and suppers. Only a hearty trencherman could do justice at 10:00 A.M. to Trapham's recommended spread of a dozen varieties of fruit, followed by broth, goat cooked with lettuce, yams with red peppers, rice with okra, legumes with salt pork, a choice of local fish, and the baked belly of Cayman turtle. And Trapham also permitted between-meal snacks of candied fruits washed down with madeira.[25]

However foolish or inadequate some of Trapham's notions, he was surely on the right track in criticizing the planters' eating habits. The essence of the problem was that the sugar planters ate too much heavy food for their own good, their servants and slaves ate too little, and everyone tended to drink too hard. The English clung to their North European dietary habits, even when such habits were ill suited to a tropical climate. Most of the food and drink they valued had to be imported and was expensive. Even slave food had to be brought into the smaller islands and was doled out sparingly. Since food and drink were important status symbols in the seventeenth century, the rich islanders glutted themselves as much or more than the gentry at home, and the poor lived on the edge of starvation.

§❧

The provision of suitable clothing posed another problem for the island colonists in the seventeenth century. Unfortunately they came to the West Indies during a period when extreme overdressing was fashionable at home. Styles changed greatly in England between the 1620s and 1713, but throughout this period those who

25. Thomas Trapham, *A Discourse of the State of Health in the Island of Jamaica* (London, 1679), chap. 4. Trapham lived in St. Mary parish on the north coast and sat in the Jamaica Assembly four times.

could afford to do so lavished their money on gorgeously ornate and uncomfortable costumes. Ladies always wore skirts that trailed the ground and always favored luxurious fabrics, richly patterned, embroidered, braided, and bejeweled. The starched ruffs, stiff bodices, and swollen farthingales characteristic of female fashion in the reign of James I gave way to softer bustles, layers of petticoats, and yards of ribbons and lace, but the well-dressed lady in the time of Queen Anne can scarcely have been at ease in her wired head-dress and boned corset. Through most of the century the gentlemen were more flamboyantly and awkwardly costumed than the ladies, if such was possible. The quilted doublets, slashed sleeves, stiff ruffs, and bombastic breeches of the Jacobean period were gradually dis-carded in favor of long, full-skirted coats, embroidered waistcoats, flowing cravats, and beribboned knee breeches, which were just as showy and impractical in a new way. At the Restoration gentlemen gave up wearing ungainly boots, but adopted even more ungainly periwigs. Both sexes favored long hair, long cloaks, long leather gloves, and hats of every conceivable size and shape, trimmed with feathers and gems. Both male and female costumes had to be in-tricately pinned, tied, or hooked together and scented to conceal the smell of unwashed bodies underneath. The total effect was more romantic from a distance than close up.

The clothes a man wore in the status-conscious seventeenth cen-tury identified his social position more readily than the food he ate. Every occupation had its own designated wardrobe. The rich took care to dress richly, and the poor were expected to dress poorly. An English nobleman who spent £1,000 per annum on his personal wardrobe could further magnify his public image by outfitting his chief household retainers in gorgeous livery, but he dressed his more menial servants in gray or russet brown. Apprentices tradi-tionally wore blue, the symbolic color of constancy. The clothing of the English laboring classes in the seventeenth century was crudely made, shapeless, baggy, and ill fitting. A typical farm woman, for example, wore a coarse linen shift or smock next to her skin (no Englishwomen wore underpants in this period) and over the shift a full, ground-length skirt and bodice and shoes or pattens. Indoors or out, she had some sort of headgear, most likely a coif, and when working she wore an apron. Her husband wore a shirt and drawers next to the skin and over them breeches, stockings, shoes or boots, and a doublet or coat. High-crowned, sugar-loaf hats were popular with seventeenth-century English workingmen, despite the ease with which they blew off the head. In hot weather male laborers stripped down to breeches, shirt, and cap. The humble laborer was even smellier than the fine gentleman; he rarely bathed, and his clothes (which were mainly woolen) were seldom or never washed.[26]

How could these English habits of costume be transferred to the torrid zone? The seventeenth-century colonists did make some concessions to the climate. They immediately saw the need for lighter, more washable clothing than the standard woolen garments used at home. Since cotton cloth was not yet in practical use, they relied heavily on linen. Slaves and servants wore shirts, breeches, smocks, and skirts made of canvas or osnaburg, coarse grades of linen. Their masters and mistresses wore finer linens such as holland. Those islanders who could afford it also bought flowered silks and taffetas and fabrics made from mixtures of silk and cotton (bengal), or silk and wool (drugget and farrenden), or silk and mohair (camlet), or linen and cotton (calico). But much of their clothing was woolen and worsted. The Jamaica inventories show that dry-goods shops stocked large quantities of woolen cloth, used especially for making suits, cloaks, and blankets. When Richard Ligon advised a prospective Barbados planter to spend £400 on clothing for his family, servants, and slaves, he allotted £100 of this for linen cloth, £100 for woolen cloth, £25 for knitted Monmouth caps, £40 for rugs and stockings, £50 for boots and shoes, £15 for leather gloves, £30 for hats and bands, and £40 for ribbons.[27]

The slaves in the English islands wore little clothing. Up to the age of puberty, black children went naked. Adult black males put on loincloths or drawers and sometimes shirts on Sundays or canvas jackets in the cooler months. Adult black females wore loincloths, smocks, or skirts. Very rarely did field Negroes wear hats or shoes. The master of one hundred slaves, according to Ligon, need spend only £35 per annum on clothing; this would buy three pairs of coarse canvas drawers for each man and two cheap skirts for each

26. For fuller discussion of these points, see Virginia A. La Mar, *English Dress in the Age of Shakespeare* (Washington, D.C., 1958); Iris Brooke, *English Costume of the Seventeenth Century* (London, 1934); Phillis Cunnington and Catherine Lucas, *Occupational Costume in England* (London, 1967), chaps. 1, 4–7; C. Willett Cunnington and Phillis Cunnington, *The History of Underclothes* (London, 1951), chap. 2–3; and C. Willett Cunnington, Phillis Cunnington, and Charles Beard, *A Dictionary of English Costume* (London, 1960).

27. Inventories of Charles Jessop, Joshua Spencer, and Samuel Allen, Jam. Inv., Vol. 2; Ligon, *True History of Barbados*, 109–110.

woman. Negro garments were usually made of blue cloth, the same color as apprentices' costumes at home. Unencumbered by layers of sweat-drenched clothing, the slaves probably kept cleaner than the white servants, and since they liked to wash more than Englishmen thought necessary in the seventeenth century, they very likely kept cleaner than their white masters. Dr. Sloane remarked on their odd habit of bathing "in fair water every day, as often as conveniently they can." House slaves, quite contrary to the field hands, were often decked out in livery, in emulation of English noblemen's retainers. In 1678 Christopher Jeaffreson of St. Christopher ordered fifteen yards of green serge to make into several suits of livery for his slaves.[28]

Servants and poor whites in the islands wore less clothing than laborers at home, though much more than the Negroes. The yearly wardrobe for thirty servants, in Ligon's estimate, would cost £170, or sixteen times the per capita expenditure for slaves' clothes. Male servants wore canvas doublets and breeches in addition to smocks and skirts. Servants of both sexes generally used shoes and stockings to protect their feet against the chiggers, and they wore out their shoes so fast that they needed a new pair every month. They always put on headgear, but being socially inferior, they were expected to wear caps and coifs rather than hats or hoods. The brimless Monmouth cap worn by most island servants in the seventeenth century cannot have provided much protection against the fierce sun. When servants were given enough linen by their masters, they changed out of their sweaty clothes on coming in from the fields and wrapped themselves in "rug Gownes, such as poor people wear in Hospitalls." [29] For military drills the male servants and poor whites, who constituted the island infantry, were garbed in red coats and black hats. Military uniforms were much the same in the Indies as at home. When a squad of fifty-seven English soldiers sailed to the Leeward Islands in 1677, each man was issued a red coat, a hat, a pair of breeches, two pairs of shoes, and—in case he ever needed to change his linen—two shirts, two pairs of stockings, and two neck cloths.[30]

28. Handler, ed., "Biet's Visit to Barbados," *Jour. Bar. Mus. Hist. Soc.*, XXXII (1965–1966), 66; Ligon, *True History of Barbados*, 116; Sloane, *Voyage*, I, xlvii, liv; Jeaffreson, ed., *Young Squire*, I, 233–236.

29. Ligon, *True History of Barbados*, 44–45, 115; Taylor MS, 536; invoice of Barbados servants' clothing, 1649, Hay Papers; invoice of clothing for Sir Thomas Lynch's servants and slaves in Jamaica, *c.* 1680, Egerton MSS, 2395/599.

30. Invoice for soldiers' clothes, Aug. 11, 1677, C.O. 1/41/45–46; Barbados militia law, Nov. 16, 1681, C.O. 30/2/169–70; Taylor MS, 496.

Those colonists with money to spend enjoyed displaying their prosperity in fancy clothes. Snobs often complained that the Caribbean colonists tended to dress above their proper station. "For a cooper's wife," said the Reverend Francis Crow of Port Royal, "shall go forth in the best flowered silk and richest silver and gold lace that England can afford, with a couple of Negroes at her tail."[31] Coopers' wives, not to mention planters' wives, wished to keep their complexions as white as possible, in contrast to their black-skinned slaves and red-necked servants. Consequently the island ladies shaded their faces from the sun with hoods and covered their hands in gloves. For the same reason the gentlemen took care to wear broad-brimmed hats, neckcloths, stockings and gloves.

Just how elaborately an island gentleman dressed is suggested by the unusually detailed inventory of Capt. George Green, a successful Barbados sugar planter who died in 1676. Captain Green left two trunks full of clothes, itemized as follows:[32]

1 black farrenden suit lined with sarcenet, trimmed with blue ribbon
1 black silk coat and drawers, the coat lined with black sarcenet and trimmed with black ribbon
1 camlet coat and pantaloons lined with persian silk, and a silk jacket
1 stuff coat and drawers, lined with silk
1 brown holland suit trimmed with scarlet ribbon
1 worsted gauntlet coat and plush drawers
1 frizzle [frieze?] coat, flannel waistcoat, and duff pair of drawers
1 cloak
2 dimity jackets
7 other jackets
7 shirts
7 cravats, lace and plain
4 plain neck cloths
5 pairs of plain shirt cuffs
5 pairs of lace shirt cuffs
4 lace bands
1 lace bosom piece
2 pocket handkerchiefs
5 pairs of stockings
6 pairs of shoes
2 pairs of gloves
2 night gowns and night caps
4 periwigs

31. Francis Crow to Giles Firmin, Mar. 7, 1686/7, *Jam. Hist. Rev.*, III, no. 2 (1959), 54.
32. Barbados Deeds, RB 3/19/134–137. Capt. Green had 51 slaves when he died.

Captain Green must also have owned several hats, for well-dressed gentlemen of this period perched hats on top of their periwigs. Three of his seven suits were made of silk or a silk mixture, one was linen, and three were wool. His nightgowns were a status symbol; we find in the inventories that important personages such as Sir Henry Morgan owned silk nightgowns, but most colonists slept in street clothes, simply loosening their breeches or girdles before going to bed.[33]

The shops of Port Royal were amply stocked with luxury apparel in the late seventeenth century. One merchant carried among his wares a case of flowered silk valued at £263, ten boxes of lace valued at £635, three trunks of haberdashery and buttons worth £403, sixty dozen white kid gloves, and fifty beaver hats. Another merchant offered eight varieties of silk and linen hose, some two thousand pairs in all, worth £333. A third merchant sold richly embroidered sleeves to gentlemen, leather fans and lutestring hoods to ladies, and laced pumps to children.[34] In the Leeward Islands, where shopping was more difficult, the planters were also fashion conscious. Christopher Jeaffreson complained that the gallants on St. Christopher dressed "beyond their abilities, or at least their qualities." Nevertheless every year he instructed his sister in Westminster to send him a new outfit: cloth for a suit, a periwig, embroidered waistbelt, cravat and cuffs, hat, silk stockings, and a dozen pairs of shoes—everything to be "modest and creditable," but in the latest mode.[35]

Dr. Hans Sloane saw the irony in this situation. "It seems to me," he mused, "the Europeans do not well, who coming from a cold Country, continue here to Cloth themselves after the same manner as in England, whereas all Inhabitants between the Tropics go even almost naked, and Negros and Indians live almost so here," in the English islands. In clothing style as in dietary habits, the English refused to accept tropical realities. But there was one important difference. All of the island colonists, rich and poor alike, ate unbalanced meals and drank too freely, but only the rich and ambitious colonists overdressed. Consequently the island elite probably suffered more from the humid heat than their servants and slaves.

33. Inventory of Sir Henry Morgan, Jam. Inv., Vol. 3; Sloane, *Voyage*, I, xlvii.
34. Inventories of Henry Coward, Samuel Allan, and Joshua Spencer, Jam. Inv., Vols. 2–3.
35. Jeaffreson, ed., *Young Squire*, I, 233–236, 248, 269–70.

ᔓ

Housing was also something of a problem, since once again the English fashion in building and design was not easily transferred to the West Indies. Discussion on this point is necessarily conjectural; nearly all of the early houses in the islands have long since disappeared, victims of storms, fires, and tropical rot. Buildings had short life spans in the English islands during the seventeenth century. For example, the parish records of St. Michael and St. John in Barbados show the vestry continually repairing or rebuilding these two churches.[36] Today St. Michael and St. John look as picturesquely antiquated and weatherbeaten as any medieval parish church in England, but in actual fact they are both Victorian structures. As for old plantation houses, Fontabelle in Barbados, a house possibly designed by Richard Ligon and certainly occupied by governors of the island in the late seventeenth century, was recently torn down. Warrens House, Drax Hall, and Nicholas Abbey still survive in Barbados, all probably dating back to the seventeenth century, though extensively altered since. In Jamaica, Colbeck Castle and Stokes Hall (both in ruins) may possibly predate 1713. These few surviving houses were built by big planters. The cottages occupied by small planters in the seventeenth century and the huts lived in by slaves have disappeared entirely or at any rate have not yet been identified. Fortunately several detailed plans and pictures of seventeenth-century island houses, large and small, do exist, and we can tell from inventories how the colonists laid out their houses as well as how they furnished them.[37]

Because so few early buildings survive in the English islands, it has been argued that the seventeenth-century colonists were too

36. St. Michael's church, built of stone between 1661 and 1664, was repaired in 1666, 1675, and 1684, yet in 1685 the roof was near collapse. The church bell, donated in 1668, was cracked and unserviceable by 1677. The parish almshouse, built in 1666, was partially rebuilt in the 1670s and completely so in the 1680s. St. Michael vestry records, *Jour. Bar. Mus. Hist. Soc.*, XIV (1946–1947) through XVII (1949–1950), *passim*. In St. John a new stone church was built in 1660 and repaired in 1667. After the hurricane of 1675 the chancel was dismantled and rebuilt, and the following year the body of the church and porch was similarly pulled down and "new built." St. John vestry book, 1649–1699, Bar. Mus. Hist. Soc.

37. List of ancient Barbados buildings, *Jour. Bar. Mus. Hist. Soc.*, I (1933–1934), 28–32; Thomas T. Waterman, "Some Early Buildings of Barbados," *ibid.*, XIII (1945–1946), 140–148; and A. C. Acworth, *Treasure in the Caribbean: A First Study of Georgian Buildings in the British West Indies* (London, 1949).

poor to build grandly and that their houses, churches, and public buildings were crudely and cheaply constructed.[38] This proposition applies well enough to the first generation of settlers, but it does not fit the sugar planters of the late seventeenth century. Initially, from the 1620s to the 1640s, when the Barbados and Leeward Islands colonists were small tobacco farmers, they lived in simple wooden cottages, furnished with the barest essentials. Roger Mills, whose forty acres made him an average Barbados planter for this period, had a two-storied house in 1642, with only two rooms, a hall below and a chamber above. His lower room was equipped with a long table and two forms to sit on. His upper room contained a bed, brass lamp, table, and form. Probably he cooked outdoors and ate his meals off wooden trenchers with pewter spoons.[39] But this situation changed as soon as the colonists converted from tobacco to sugar. The successful sugar planters quickly built much larger houses, furnished with such luxury items as leather chairs, carpets, gilded leather wall hangings, pictures, table linen, and silver.

Father Biet, who visited Barbados in 1654, found the planters' dwellings to be handsome, many-roomed, sumptuously furnished houses, though still built entirely of wood. His contemporary Richard Ligon was more critical. Barbados houses, he complained, have roofs "so low, as for the most part of them, I could hardly stand upright with my hat on." The planters made no use of cool cellars, according to Ligon, because they found them too dank and moldy. Nor did they let the constant eastern breezes play through their rooms, because they were afraid of being drenched by sudden showers. So they closed up the eastern walls of their houses and installed all their windows to the west, "that in the afternoons, when the Sun came to the West, those little low roofed rooms were like Stoves or heated Ovens"—ready to ignite from the combination of hot timber, rum fumes, and tobacco smoke.[40]

Ligon contrived an ingenious design for tropical houses, fitting the windows with shutters instead of glass and providing plenty

38. A. C. Acworth, *Buildings of Architectural or Historic Interest in the British West Indies,* Colonial Office Research Studies, No. 2 (London, 1951).

39. Barbados Deeds, RB 3/1. The inventories of Capt. Lancelot Pace (1640), Ens. George Bulkley (1640), and Ens. Michael Cooke (1643) in this volume of Barbados deeds give similar details, as do the Barbados inventories of Capt. Ketteridge (1635), Matthew Gibson (1635), and William Powrey (1649) in Hay Papers.

40. Handler, ed., "Biet's Visit to Barbados," *Jour. Bar. Mus. Hist. Soc.,* XXXII (1965–1966), 65, 68; Ligon, *True History of Barbados,* 40–43.

of shade and ventilation. Only two Barbados planters took up his design. The others, says Ligon, insisted on putting all their labor and money into sugar making. But they had other reasons for rejecting Ligon's architectural plans. Many Englishmen in the tropics believed that too much ventilation was unhealthy. They wished particularly to shield themselves from the night air, which they held to be corrupt and putrefying. Dr. Thomas Trapham, the Jamaica physician, felt that the sea breezes that blew during the daytime were very refreshing, but the land breezes at night were very bad. The land breezes enveloped the planters in "stagnated Air, harbouring in mountainous Caverns and woody confinements," which caused dangerous chills and "hot paroxysm." [41] This explains why the island colonists not only shut out the night breezes from their houses but slept in beds enveloped by curtains, as at home.

Another problem with Ligon's design for tropical houses was that it was not in the familiar English architectural tradition. The colonists were not easily persuaded to abandon the forms they knew at home. In 1668, for instance, the Montserrat Assembly laid down instructions for building a new courthouse. The carpenters were "to cause good and substantial Cratches to be erected . . . for the making of a good, substantial, and firm Cratched-house." This was the favorite building technique in northern and western England, in which the house was framed by large curved posts called crucks or cratches. Furthermore, the Montserrat courthouse was to be thatched, wattled, and daubed with "good Palmetto Thatch and Wattles," meaning a thatched roof and mud walls.[42] This courthouse must have been a hot and stuffy building, for cruck-built houses have low walls and little fenestration, and the low-sloping thatched roof would not only heat up the interior but be highly inflammable. In the very year this Montserrat courthouse was built, a fire in the garret of a Bridgetown house quickly spread to the island magazine next door, touching off 170 barrels of powder. This holocaust consumed most of the wooden, thatched buildings in Bridgetown. The Barbados people learned something from this sad experience and rebuilt their town in stone and tile. Out in the countryside the Barbados planters also gradually replaced their

41. Trapham, *Discourse of the State of Health in Jamaica*, 6–7, 10–11.
42. *Acts of Assembly, Montserrat*, 7–8. For a discussion of cruck construction and cob (mud) walling, see M. W. Barley, *The English Farmhouse and Cottage* (London, 1961), 22–25, 35–36; Thirsk, *Agrarian History of England and Wales, 1500–1640*, 725–726, 770–788.

wooden houses with stone ones. In Jamaica brick became the favorite building material. In the 1680s at least half the houses in Port Royal sported brick walls, tile roofs and glazed windows. By 1700 the Montserrat and Nevis assemblies were ordering all thatched houses in Plymouth and Charlestown to be shingled or pulled down.[43]

Visitors to Barbados and Jamaica at the close of the seventeenth century described the islanders' houses as built "in the English style" or "after the English manner." What did this mean? The seventeenth century was a major building age in England; architectural historians speak of the "great rebuilding" or the "housing revolution" in England between 1575 and 1690. All classes were remodeling their houses or building anew: the aristocrats their great houses, the gentry their manor houses, the yeomen and husbandmen their farmhouses, the Londoners their town houses. On all social levels the trend was toward a national stylistic uniformity in place of the old vernacular tradition in which builders from each region used local materials and local methods (such as cruck construction) to create a distinctive local style. This new uniform English style included greater use of brick, stone, and tile in lieu of timber and thatch; greater emphasis upon symmetry of design; and a tendency to build houses taller, with more stories, more rooms in each story, more staircases, more fireplaces, more chimneys, and more windows. Traditionally the focal point in all English houses, large and small, had been the hall, an all-purpose room where one might cook, eat, sleep, or entertain company. In a small cottage the hall had been the only room, and in larger houses the hall had generally been two stories high with open rafters above and often an open hearth at one end of the room for heat and cooking. The chief effect of the "housing revolution" of the years 1575 to 1690 in England was to introduce more specialty rooms into the typical house. Even fairly small dwellings now had a kitchen and one or more parlors, as well as the hall, on the ground floor and sleeping chambers above. Rooms were often smaller than they had been before, but better heated and lighted, less drafty, and more cozy. Many an

---

43. *A true and perfect Narrative of the late dreadful fire . . . at Bridge-Town in the Barbadoes, April 18, 1668* (London, n.d.) ; Taylor MS, 492; *Acts of Assembly, Montserrat*, 61, 70; *Acts of Assembly, Nevis*, 24. In St. Christopher, according to the compensation claims of 1706, the house walls were of wood or stone by this date, but cruck frames and thatch roofs were still common on this island.

old house was modernized by installing a floor over the upper half of the hall in order to make a second-story chamber and by inserting enough chimney stacks to provide heat for every room.[44]

It must be emphasized that this "housing revolution" was geared to the English climate, not to the Caribbean. The island planter did not need fireplaces in every room. He only needed one fireplace for cooking, and generally he placed his kitchen with its chimney some distance to the rear of the main house. Otherwise, however, he blindly followed the new English style in building up rather than out, making his house several stories high, with low-ceilinged rooms on each story. The contrast in Jamaica between the new English houses and the old Spanish houses was evidently very striking in the 1680s. The Spanish houses, mostly to be found in Spanish Town, were bungalows constructed of wood and plaster, with tile floors, shuttered windows, tile or thatched roofs, and great double doors opening from the street into interior courtyards. John Taylor ridiculed this Spanish affectation of making doorways wide enough so that three horsemen could enter abreast; he much preferred the lofty English houses, four stories high in Port Royal, with their trim brick walls and glazed sash windows. But Dr. Hans Sloane had a different response. The Spanish houses, he noted, were designed for maximum coolness and to withstand tropical storms, whereas the English houses "are neither cool, nor able to endure the shocks of Earthquakes." [45] No wonder the English found it necessary to install great fans in their parlors and lounged prostrate much of the time in hammocks. As in Ligon's day, they seem to have ventilated their houses inadequately. In England large windows were a status symbol; the facades of some seventeenth-century great houses were veritable walls of glass, whereas humble people hesitated to insert too many windows because of the cost of glass and the window tax, levied after 1696 on all householders with more than ten windows. In the West Indies glass was not only expensive but leaded casement fittings were easily bent or smashed in stormy weather. Nevertheless, because it was in the English style, the planters fitted their windows with glass rather than with wooden louvers, jalousies, or shutters.

44. For discussion of various aspects of the 17th-century English building boom, see J. Summerson, *Architecture in Britain, 1530–1830* (London, 1953) ; Barley, *English Farmhouse and Cottage;* Thirsk, *Agrarian History of England and Wales,* chaps. 10–11; and J. Alfred Gotch, *The Growth of the English House* (London, 1909) , chaps. 9–12.

45. Taylor MS, 492, 509; Sloane, *Voyage,* I, x, xlvii.

Samuel Copen's closely detailed panoramic view of Bridgetown in 1695 makes this Caribbean entrepôt look almost indistinguishable from a commercial town in England or Holland. The houses press as close as possible to the wharves along the waterside, tall and narrow, ranging from three to five stories, with gabled fronts and fireplace chimneys. The building lots are small, with no room for shade trees or gardens. Some of the houses have small porches, but none has balconies or verandas. Except for the gables, they look very similar to London row houses built after the great fire of 1666.[46] A structure with large windows in the center of town is possibly an exchange or market house. There was no courthouse or town hall in Bridgetown at this date. Like all English colonists, the Barbadians were exceedingly reluctant to spend money on public buildings. The Council, Assembly, and courts met in various Bridgetown taverns. We learn from the parish records that the town did boast a stocks, pillory, whipping post, and ducking stool, also "a cuple of Water Enjuns" for putting out fires, a pesthouse for the sick, an almshouse for the poor, and a cramped, heavily barred cage for keeping runaway slaves and servants.[47] Unhappily, the parish records also indicate that Copen's vista of the town may not be very accurate. In Copen's picture the parish church has no tower, but in fact a tower was built for St. Michael's in 1664, fitted with a bell in 1668, and with a clock and chimes in 1697.

However Bridgetown looked exactly, it impressed an enthusiastic French visitor in 1700. "The town is fine and noble," Father Jean-Baptiste Labat wrote, "its streets are straight, long, clean and well intersected. The houses are well built in the English style with many glass windows; they are magnificently furnished. The shops and the merchants' warehouses are filled with all one could wish from all parts of the world." Father Labat did not share Ligon's and Sloane's low opinion of English buildings in the West Indies. He found the planters' mansions in the Barbados countryside to be even better

46. Samuel Copen, "A Prospect of Bridgetown in Barbados," copper-plate engraving by J. Kip (London, 1695), Cunard Gallery, Bar. Mus. Hist. Soc. In London, the Rebuilding Act of 1667 imposed a standardized code for new houses: facades were to be aligned and of uniform height, ranging from three to five stories depending on the street; exterior woodwork, bows, and jetties were banned; rooms were to range in height from 8½ to 10½ feet; and walls from 1 to 2½ bricks in thickness. See T. F. Reddaway, *The Rebuilding of London after the Great Fire* (London, 1940), 79–82.

47. E. M. Shilstone, "Old Days and Old Ways in Bridgetown," *Jour. Bar. Mus. Hist. Soc.*, V (1937–1938), 169–179; also the St. Michael vestry records, *ibid.*, XIV (1946–1947) through XVII (1949–1950), *passim*.

fashioned than the Bridgetown houses. "They are large with good fenestration, completely glazed; the arrangement of the rooms is commodious and comfort is well understood." He admired the avenues of handsome shade trees leading up to these country seats and the "magnificent" furniture and silver within.[48] Labat was perhaps too easily impressed. But his testimony fits with other evidence we have that the English planters at the turn of the century were beginning to adopt a style better suited to the climate.

The few surviving island "great houses" of the late seventeenth century more closely resemble a small English manor house in scale than an English nobleman's great house. Drax Hall, built by one of the richest families in early Barbados, has been much altered. Originally it probably had three full stories, with five rooms on the ground floor. Its principal architectural feature is a stately staircase, Jacobean in appearance, with a handsomely carved balustrade. Nicholas Abbey, another old Barbados house with a gabled front and four chimneys at the corners of the building, was also built three stories high, with four or five rooms on the ground floor.[49] According to the Jamaica inventories the early plantation houses on that island were generally smaller than Drax Hall or Nicholas Abbey, having two stories and a garret. There was likely to be a hall, one or more parlors, a dining room, several service rooms, and sometimes the master's chamber on the ground floor, with the remaining chambers upstairs and the kitchen in a separate back building. The best rooms in the house might be wainscotted or painted or covered with hangings; they are sometimes identified as "the red parlour" or "the green chamber." The hall was the focal point, as in oldfashioned English houses. In large plantation houses the hall held dozens of chairs for balls and receptions. The hall also served another purpose; it was the custom in Jamaica, at least, for the plantation slaves to assemble once a week in this room and patiently squat on the floor to receive their doles of rum. In 1683 Col. William Ivey, a member of the Jamaica Council, was tipped off by a faithful slave that the other blacks on his plantation were plotting a revolt. Ivey quietly gathered as many armed white men as he could and secreted them in the lower rooms of his house; then he summoned his 180 Negroes for their rum ration. The blacks came into Ivey's hall and sat down unsuspectingly, whereupon the whites rushed in, nabbed

48. Labat, *Nouveau voyage aux isles de l'Amérique*, IV, 392, 409.
49. Waterman, "Some Early Buildings of Barbados," *Jour. Bar. Mus. Hist. Soc.*, XIII (1945–1946), 141–144.

the ringleaders, and took them off to be whipped, maimed, or killed. This grim story tells us, among other things, that Colonel Ivey had a very large hall in his house.[50]

The planters' furniture and silver that Father Labat admired has disappeared almost completely. In Barbados, though the curators of the Barbados Museum have assembled a particularly choice collection of island silver, glass, china, and furniture, practically none of it predates 1700. Yet the inventories of rich Jamaicans include such things as cabinets inlaid with ivory and tortoise shell, flowered satin chairs, a "pair of harpsichords," oil paintings, and framed maps. The most costly piece of furniture was generally the master's four-posted bed, its mattress stuffed with feathers, flock, or plantain leaves, a canopy overhead, and the sides hung with curtains to keep out the bad night air. Up in the Jamaica mountains the nights were chilly, but it is hard to see why Capt. Thomas Barrett in Port Royal needed two sets of curtains, three quilts, and five blankets for his two beds. Sir Henry Morgan, the buccaneer king, must have nearly suffocated inside his mohair hangings with persian lining and his "musketo nett." His servants, who slept in plebian hammocks, and even his slaves, who slept on the ground, were very likely more comfortable.[51]

Two early buildings in the islands deserve special mention. One is the parsonage built in 1679 for the minister of St. John parish, Barbados, at a cost of £437 10s. The vestry set down precise specifications for this house and listed every piece of lumber to be used in its construction. It was a stone building with walls two feet thick, two stories in height, plus a garret floor under the tiled roof. This house, superbly sited next to the church on a tall bluff overlooking the Atlantic, was intelligently designed for the climate. On the ground floor the parson had a hall twenty by seventeen feet, a parlor seventeen by sixteen, a porch ten by ten, a staircase twelve by twelve, and two "shades" twelve by ten feet. These shades were verandas, equipped with jalousies or louvers, and were placed at the ends or

50. Taylor MS, 549–550. Among the inventories in Jam. Inv., Vols. 1–3, 5, those of William Barber, Edmund Duck (another victim of slave rebellion), Judith Freeman, Robert Freeman, William Hall, Samuel Long, Sir Thomas Lynch, Thomas Martyn, Robert Norris, and Gifford Pennant are particularly helpful in reconstructing the layout of a 17th-century plantation house.

51. Jam. Hist. Rev., II, no. 2 (1952), 58; Sloane, Voyage, I, xxx–xxxi. The following Jamaican inventories are especially good on furniture and bedding: Thomas Barrett, Robert Freeman, William Jud, Samuel Long, Sir Thomas Lynch, Thomas Matthews, Sir Henry Morgan, and Abraham Oakshott.

sides of the house so as to catch the breeze and ward off the full sun.[52] The six ground-floor rooms had eight doors and nine glazed windows, brick floors, plastered walls, and rather low ceilings about eight feet high. Cooking was done in one of the shades, where there was an oven and chimney. The second story, floored with mastic boards, contained five sleeping chambers of exactly the same dimensions as the rooms below. The stairs continued up to the garret, which was probably used only for storage. Very likely the present parsonage, a spacious and airy structure of about the same dimensions as the 1679 house, is built on its foundations. The present building differs in many respects from the 1679 design, but it is pleasant to find in the cellar (there was no cellar in 1679) large numbers of ancient paving bricks that fit the specifications in the vestry records for the bricks that covered the parsonage ground floor three centuries ago.[53]

If the plan for St. John parsonage shows us how an islander of middling rank and wealth lived during the late seventeenth century, the imposing ruins of Colbeck Castle in Jamaica possibly show us how a big planter lived. Colbeck Castle stands in an unkempt pasture a few miles from Old Harbour on the south coast of the island. The date of this curious structure is much in doubt. Popular tradition has it that Col. John Colbeck (d. 1683), one of the principal early planters in Jamaica, built the place.[54] But more probably it was built in the mid-eighteenth century. Colbeck Castle is a grand, gloomy pile of gray limestone trimmed with brick, so singular in its design as to defy architectural periodization. It is a much larger building than any of the other surviving early island houses. In scale and plan it resembles a seventeenth-century English aristo-

52. Porches are frequently mentioned in the island inventories, but shades, only toward the close of the century. In St. Christopher in 1706, Philip Verchild had a house valued at £250 with dimensions 30 x 18 feet—considerably smaller than the St. John, Barbados, parsonage—and a shade at either end of the house. C.O. 243/2.

53. In 1683 the St. John vestry ordered a much smaller house, 30 x 20 x 8 feet, built for the parish clerk. The specifications for this building, as for the parsonage, are enumerated in the St. John vestry book, 1649–1699, Bar. Mus. Hist. Soc. I am much indebted to Neville Connell, the director of the Museum, for helping me to interpret these plans, as also to the Rev. E. L. Payne for letting me inspect his house at St. John on Aug. 12, 1969.

54. Colbeck came to Jamaica with the army in 1655, patented 7,732 acres (including the land where the castle stands), became speaker of the Assembly, and died shortly after being elevated to the Council, leaving no male descendants. His land grants are in Jam. Land Pat., some Colbeck papers are in the Institute of Jamaica in Kingston, and his tombstone is in the Spanish Town Cathedral.

crat's great house. The three-storied central block is almost square, ninety-four by eighty-four feet, with walls three feet thick and thirty-six feet high. There are four massive corner towers, with distinctive round porthole windows at ground level. These towers are joined by aqueduct-style double arcades, which provide shaded terraces and balconies on all sides of the building. Inside there is abundant display space; the grand staircase and terraces occupy twice the area of the six rooms on each floor. The kitchen, bakery, and other service rooms are far removed, placed in four symmetrically arranged outbuildings situated at the outer perimeter of the castle's two-acre compound. On a street plan of Kingston, circa 1740, there is a picture of a town house strikingly similar to Colbeck Castle, with much the same corner towers, arcades, and round porthole windows.[55] Corner towers are a feature of early eighteenth-century Jamaican houses; Stokes Hall and Halse Hall both have them. Colbeck Castle, with its many large apertures, was poorly designed for a fort, but very well designed for tropical living. If, as present evidence suggests, it was built in 1748, the building illustrates a new and better approach toward tropical architecture, providing far more cool shade and ventilation than the stuffy houses Ligon and Sloane complained about.[56]

There is no mystery about the year in which the town of Kingston in Jamaica was founded; the date was 1692. And the street plan for this new town, devised in the 1690s, gives us further evidence that the English colonists were changing their ideas about how to live in the tropics. The earthquake of June 7, 1692, wrecked the town of Port Royal so thoroughly that the colony leaders elected to move their port to a new site across the harbor. On June 28 the Jamaica Council arranged to place the new town on a two-hundred-acre waterfront tract belonging to William Beeston, and in August the Council approved "the Draught laid out by Mr. John Goffe of the Town of Kingston." [57] This draft may have been modified in the next few years, but the plan worked out in the 1690s has scarcely

55. Plan of Kingston under Gov. Trelawny (1738–1752), reproduced by Frank Cundall, *The Governors of Jamaica in the First Half of the Eighteenth Century* (London, 1937), facing p. 206.

56. T. A. L. Concannon, the leading architectural historian in Jamaica, found a date—either 1748 or 1848—cut into the undercoat of plaster on a wall of Colbeck Castle. Writing in a Jamaica periodical, *The Masterbuilder* (June 1965), he leans toward 1748 as the more probable date of construction.

57. Jamaica Council minutes, 1692, C.O. 140/5/195–196, 201. See also J. G. Young, "Who Planned Kingston?," *Jam. Hist. Rev.*, I (1945–1948), 144–153.

been altered since. The central district of modern Kingston still retains the network of streets, block dimensions, and street names—though not the buildings—which are detailed in a chart of the town, dated 1702, in the Public Record Office.[58]

The men who built Kingston had to work fast, without leisure for studied rumination about city planning. Still, they had been complaining for years about the hot and uncomfortable layout of Port Royal, a higgledy-piggledy crowded place like Bridgetown in Barbados, and the plan they devised for Kingston was a conscious effort at improvement. It is a symmetrical gridiron scheme utilizing a rectangular tract of land nearly half a mile wide along the harbor front and a mile deep. There are thirteen uniformly spaced streets and lanes running north from the waterfront and eleven cross streets, more widely spaced, running east and west. In the center of town is a large open square (now Victoria Park), bordered by the church and other public buildings. Since the harbor entrance to the town was securely fortified, the inhabitants of Kingston could afford to arrange their building lots more openly and generously than in other West Indian towns.[59] Despite English scorn for the Spanish way of building in the Indies, the layout of Kingston clearly imitates the standard features of Spanish town planning in America, with its grid of streets and central plaza. But the design possibly also reflects the notions of William Penn, who publicized his plan for Philadelphia in the previous decade. Trade relations between Jamaica and Pennsylvania were close in the 1690s, and it may not be pure coincidence that Penn's plan for Philadelphia, published in London in 1683, so closely resembles the 1702 plan for Kingston.

The new Jamaica town was only one quarter the area of Philadelphia, but it shared the Quaker city's symmetrical street pattern, inward-facing central square, overall rectangular boundaries, and relatively narrow space for commercial wharfage along the waterfront. In both towns the early settlers—being practical businessmen—refused to spread inland as the design called for. Instead they took up all the building lots close to the docks and then spilled out

58. "A Plan of Kingston," 1702, endorsed by Gov. Handasyd, the Council, and the Assembly, P.R.O., reproduced by Cundall, *Governors of Jamaica, Eighteenth Century*, facing p. 48.

59. The French towns, in particular, were scarcely more than forts. The plans of towns in Martinique and Guadeloupe which illustrate Labat's *Nouveau voyage aux isles de l'Amérique* (I, 68, II, 2, III, 360) show the streets and houses huddled behind massive fortified walls.

beyond the original town limits to stake out additional waterfront lots. The old streets in both cities seem narrow and congested in modern traffic conditions, but by seventeenth-century standards they are unusually broad as well as straight. In London, even when the streets were widened after the fire of 1666, few of the main arteries were as wide as forty feet, and many side lanes were barely fourteen feet. Kingston boasts no hundred-foot thoroughfares like Broad Street or Market Street in Philadelphia, but all of the principal streets in the town were made fifty or sixty feet wide, and no side lane was made less than twenty.

One amusing difference between the two new towns is that the Jamaica politicians named most of the streets in Kingston after themselves—Barry Street, Beckford Street, Beeston Street, Heywood Street, Laws Street, Sutton Street, Tower Street, and so forth— whereas the Quaker proprietor named his streets for local trees or merely numbered them in keeping with his taste for simplicity and order. A more telling difference is in the provision for trees, gardens, and open space. William Penn announced that he wanted "a green country town, which will never be burnt, and always be wholesome." Accordingly, he provided four residential parks and individual building lots so generous in size that every householder would have room to plant a garden and orchard. In fact, Penn made his building lots too large, for the purposeful people who swarmed into his town soon chopped them up into a great number of very small lots.[60] The planners of Kingston, less idealistic than Penn, nevertheless provided far more breathing space than in Bridgetown or Port Royal. They offered no residential parks, and the building lots close to the harbor had frontages of only 30 feet, but the bulk of the Kingston lots were 50 feet wide and 150 feet deep, and they seem to have remained this size after the town began to grow.

Kingston today does not have the patina of an old city. The earthquake of 1907 obliterated most early remains, and the modern business district is nondescript, shabby, and depressing. But Kingston must have been an attractive place to live in during the eighteenth century. Old views of the town show rows of graceful

60. For further discussion of Penn's plan for Philadelphia, see Anthony N. B. Garvan, "Proprietary Philadelphia as Artifact," in Oscar Handlin and John Burchard, eds., *The Historian and the City* (Cambridge, Mass. 1963), 189–191; John W. Reps, *The Making of Urban America* (Princeton, N.J., 1965), 15–19, 161–164; and Albert Cook Myers, ed., *Narratives of Early Pennsylvania, West New Jersey and Delaware* (New York, 1912), 239–244.

buildings, the streets lined with arcaded passageways, so that pedestrians could avoid the sun, and plenty of louvered balconies to let the breeze into the houses and keep out the heat. The four Kingston houses that decorate a map of the town, drawn around 1740, differ utterly in appearance from the Port Royal houses described by John Taylor in 1688 or the Bridgetown houses pictured by Samuel Copen in 1695. They are built much lower and wider, with ample verandas and arcades and tall windows the height of the rooms within.[61] These Kingston houses express the development of a Georgian architectural style in Jamaica, surviving examples of which today include the handsome group of government buildings surrounding the square in Spanish Town, several streets of elegant (though rapidly decaying) town houses in Falmouth, and planters' mansions such as Rose Hall. These Jamaican Georgian buildings are not blind copies of English models. The classical components of the English Georgian style are carefully modulated to achieve coolness and comfort in a hot climate.

Everywhere in the English islands by the early eighteenth century the colonists were working toward a practical, indigenous building style. In St. Christopher the compensation claims of 1706 show us dozens of examples of long, narrow, one-story wooden houses, built low to resist hurricanes, built narrow so that the breeze could pass through every room, built long so as to incorporate porches and shades at either end. In Barbados the splendid range of mid-eighteenth-century buildings at Codrington College is a particularly good example of Georgian architecture freely adapted to fit the West Indian climate. And in Antigua the elegant Admiral's House in English Harbor, where Nelson lived in the 1780s, abandons any sort of "English style" altogether. The Admiral's House would look completely out of place in England, enveloped as it is with wide double balconies, the walls of the principal rooms completely fitted with tall jalousied windows, the lofty, white-painted interior admirably designed to retain cool air and evade the heat. It took over a hundred years, but the English did eventually learn how to live in the tropics.

61. Plan of Kingston under Gov. Trelawny, reproduced by Cundall, *Governors of Jamaica, Eighteenth Century,* facing p. 206.

9 ❧ *Death in the Tropics*

Historical demography is in high fashion these days, nowhere more so than among students of early modern European and colonial American history. Utilizing such long-neglected reservoirs of vital statistics as parish registers, demographers in France, England, and America have been able to pinpoint population trends in the seventeenth century with a new exactitude and to correct and amplify old assumptions about marriage habits, childbearing, family structure, and generational conflict. One of the prime points to emerge so far is that when Englishmen moved to America in the seventeenth century their demographic profiles tended to change. Those who migrated to New England, and probably to the other mainland colonies as well, had a better chance of living to a ripe old age and producing a large brood of children than their countrymen who stayed at home. What of Englishmen who came to the sugar islands?

Unfortunately the sources for historical demography in the Caribbean colonies leave much to be desired. If the Puritans and Quakers compiled the best vital records in English America, the sugar planters compiled the worst. West Indian parish registers for the seventeenth century are too patchy and unreliable to permit the techniques of aggregative analysis or family reconstitution employed by demographers in England and New England. Vital statistics for the slaves are almost nonexistent. Population experts who have worked with West Indian vital records have wisely concentrated on the modern era, where the statistical evidence is far more solid. This chapter constitutes an unwise attempt to explore the earliest demographic information about the island population, white and black. Though buttressed by impressive-looking figures and tables, my calculations are always shaky and my conclusions frankly conjectural.

One thing is certain: mortality in the sugar islands was frightfully high for whites and blacks alike in the seventeenth century. The mortality rate was bad enough in England; life expectancy at birth was about thirty-five years in the seventeenth century. But Englishmen who moved to the Caribbean shortened their life expectancy significantly. Though they married in the islands and raised families, they did not increase and multiply; rather they depended on constant in-migration to sustain the white population. For the blacks the situation was if anything worse. Negroes imported to the sugar islands died much faster than they were born. West Indian slave masters soon gave up trying to keep their Negroes alive long enough to breed up a new generation and instead routinely bought replacement slaves year in and year out.

Thus the demographic contrast between the early West Indian and New England settlements is very striking. Recent microcosmic studies of Andover, Dedham, and Plymouth by Philip Greven, Kenneth Lockridge, and John Demos demonstrate how remarkably healthy, settled, and stable these communities were in the seventeenth century.[1] Families were close-knit: grown children clung to and deferred to their parents. Hence, despite the much advertised perils and disorders of frontier life, the New England towns rapidly increased in size and maintained rather more cohesive discipline than contemporary villages back in England.[2] This being so, the New Englanders did not need to recreate the elaborate institutional fabric they left behind in the mother country. The pioneers in this corner of the New World found in their families and in their communities effective vehicles for socialization. It was quite otherwise in the Caribbean colonies. The sugar planters lived in pomp and

1. Philip J. Greven, Jr., "Family Structure in Seventeenth-Century Andover, Massachusetts," *Wm. and Mary Qtly.*, 3d Ser., XXIII (1966), 234–256; Greven, *Four Generations;* Kenneth A. Lockridge, "The Population of Dedham, Massachusetts, 1636–1736," *Econ. Hist. Rev.*, 2d Ser., XIX (1966), 318–344; Lockridge, *A New England Town: The First Hundred Years* (New York, 1970); John Demos, "Notes on Life in Plymouth Colony," *Wm. and Mary Qtly.*, 3d Ser., XXII (1965), 264–286; Demos, *A Little Commonwealth: Family Life in Plymouth Colony* (New York, 1970).

2. As described in such studies as Peter Laslett and John Harrison, "Clayworth and Cogenhoe," in H. E. Bell and R. L. Ollard, eds., *Historical Essays, 1600–1750, Presented to David Ogg* (London, 1963), 157–184; and E. A. Wrigley, "Mortality in Pre-Industrial England: The Example of Colyton, Devon, Over Three Centuries," *Daedalus* (Spring 1968), 546–580.

kept their slaves and servants in awe, but their social system was neither stable nor settled. Omnipresent disease and death kept dissolving the island families and driving the most successful and valued members of the planter class into absenteeism. Those who stuck it out in the islands often died emptily rich, with no direct, legitimate heirs to receive their wealth. In the seventeenth century the Caribbean was truly the white man's grave—and the black man's, too.

§⮞

What did the English planters and their slaves die of? By moving to the tropics the colonists escaped some of the worst English killers: bubonic plague, smallpox, and influenza, in particular. Tuberculosis and venereal disease were apparently less rampant in the Indies during the seventeenth century than at home. But the colonists encountered a powerful battery of new ailments. Though they described their symptoms vaguely and did not use the modern medical terms, it is clear from their accounts that they experienced nearly the full range of deadly diseases still endemic in hot and humid parts of the world: malaria, yellow fever, dysentery, dropsy, leprosy, yaws, hookworm and elephantiasis, to name the chief seventeenth-century killers and cripplers. The early colonists were helpless to guard against these maladies, not realizing that they were caused by parasites, bacteria, and viruses, that malaria and yellow fever were transmitted by mosquitoes, or that hygenic and nutritional disorders produced dysentery and dropsy.[3] Considering the state of medical knowledge in the seventeenth century, short life expectancy was inevitable in the West Indian settlements. But the early planters aggravated their health problems by practicing foolish habits of diet, drink, dress, and housing, and they killed their slaves unnecessarily fast by providing inadequate food and filthy living conditions.

In the loose terminology of the seventeenth century, the English suffered chiefly from fevers of various descriptions: intermittent

3. For fuller discussion of the diseases endemic in the West Indies during the 17th century, see H. Harrold Scott, *A History of Tropical Medicine*, 2d ed. (Baltimore, 1942), and such medical textbooks as L. Everard Napier, *The Principles and Practice of Tropical Medicine* (New York, 1946), and George Cheever Shattuck, *Diseases of the Tropics* (New York, 1951).

and remittent fever; quotidian, tertian, or quartan agues; Barbados fever and bleeding fever. Most of these fevers appear to have been variants of malaria and yellow fever. Malaria, with its sudden and repeated fits of freezing chills, burning heat, and drenching sweat, left the patient jaundiced and aching—if he recovered. Malaria ran rampant in Jamaica. John Helyar had three bouts within his first year at Bybrook. The colonists traced their fevers to bad air, or miasma, that was thought to rise at night from moist and swampy soil, so they endeavored to shut out the night air by enveloping their beds with curtains, sometimes adding netting to fend off the mosquitoes. Bites from mosquitoes were a minor irritant to them, for they did not understand that Anopheles mosquitoes, bred in the swamps, transmitted the malaria parasite to man through their bites. The early colonists inadvertently created new mosquito breeding places by cutting the forests. Military commanders had a genius for putting barracks adjacent to swamps, sometimes on the lee side, fully exposed to windblown Anopheles, which helps explain the specially high mortality rate among English soldiers garrisoned in the islands.

Barbados was free from malaria in the seventeenth century, but subject to another virulent disease—yellow fever, probably introduced from Africa in the slave ships. Richard Ligon arrived in the midst of the first major yellow-fever epidemic in 1647 and thought it as bad as the plague in England. The victim, having been bitten several days previously by an infected mosquito, experienced a sudden splitting headache followed by burning fever, jaundice, falling pulse, nausea, and—in fatal cases—hemorrhages, black vomit, and delirium. At Bridgetown the corpses of yellow-fever victims were tossed into the swamp next to the town, which infected the drinking water! Thousands of Barbadians died of yellow fever in the 1640s and again in the 1690s. The disease was appropriately known as the Barbados distemper or the bleeding fever.[4]

The slaves caught yellow fever and malaria also, of course. In addition they picked up tuberculosis and venereal disease from their English masters and brought a number of African diseases with them: hookworm, yaws, guinea worm, leprosy, elephantiasis, and "a

4. Sloane, *Voyage,* I, *xc, cxxxiv–cxxxv;* Ligon, *True History of Barbados,* 21, 25. Isaac Norris, who had lived in the West Indies, told Jonathan Dickinson that a new pestilential fever had broken out in Philadelphia: "I think it is exactly the Barbados distemper. We vomit and void Blood." Aug. 15, 1699, Maria Dickinson Logan Collection, Hist. Soc. of Pa.

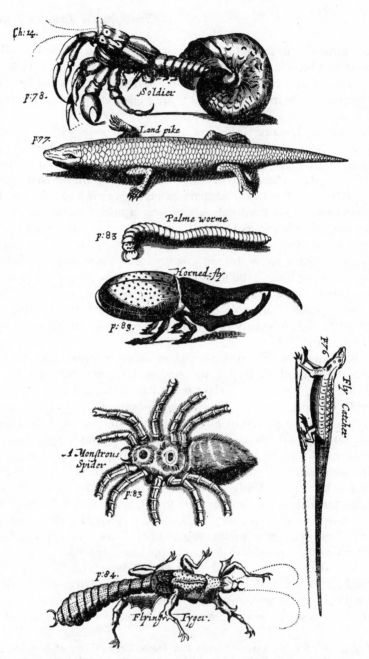

FIG. *10. West Indian insects and reptiles. The* Fly Catcher *came onto planters' tables during meal times to catch insects. The* Soldier *was a hermit crab. The* Monstrous Spider *was far less harmful than the Anopheles mosquito, not pictured here. (From figure facing p. 78 in John Davies of Kidwelly, trans.,* The History of the Caribby-Islands . . . [London, *1666*]; *courtesy of the Library Company of Philadelphia.)*

sleepy disease." Sleeping sickness could not spread in the Indies because it is transmitted solely by the African tsetse fly, but incoming slaves who turned hopelessly lethargic and brooding were likely infected with it before they arrived. In guinea-worm disease the parasite could grow four feet long in the subcutaneous tissue under a man's skin; Dr. Sloane observed the time-honored African method of extracting the guinea worm by winding its head around a twig and twisting the twig daily until the whole worm is pulled out. Yaws, clinically similar to syphilis, was a common affliction among the slaves in the English islands. The repulsive skin ulcers characteristic of yaws could develop into bone lesions and destroy or deform the nose, lips, hands, and feet. Hookworm was even more insidious, because more hidden. In this disease the hookworm larvae burrow into a man's foot and pass eventually into his intestine, where the adult worm avariciously sucks blood. The victim turns sluggish, bloated, and ravenously hungry and acquires a depraved taste for eating dirt. Most of the big slave gangs had several dirt eaters, acute hookworm sufferers. The slave masters regarded these people as inveterate malingerers or supposed they were trying to commit suicide.[5] In any case, the physic they administered did little or no good.

The English and their slaves were always falling prey to dysentery and dropsy in the seventeenth century, which means that they suffered from gastrointestinal disorders. Bad hygiene promoted the "bloody flux," or dysentery. The colonists came to the islands on crowded, filthy ships. They seldom bathed and wore dirty, vermin-infested garments. They drank contaminated water and ate half-rotten meat and fish, weevily biscuit, rancid butter and cheese, unwashed raw fruits and root vegetables. Excrement and garbage lay everywhere, especially around the slave quarters, to be picked over by the rats and vultures.[6] As for the dropsy, or "country disease," this term covered a multitude of sins. The islanders were subject to

5. For example, a Barbados plantation manager told the owner in 1693 that he had "upwards of twenty notorious runaway negroes and such that do eat dirt etc., and whose service is worse than not any, or ill example to others, a continual trouble in nursing and physicking the one sort and daily hunting and seeking after the other." This manager's recipe for hookworm was to sell the dirt-eaters and buy new slaves. Richard Pares, ed., "Barbados History from the Records of the Prize Courts," *Jour. Bar. Mus. Hist. Soc.*, VI (1939–1940), 20. For a discussion of guinea worms and yaws, see Sloane, *Voyage*, I, cxv, cxxvi.

6. A visitor to Barbados in 1718 was horrified to see a mastiff gnawing the bowels and thighs of a dead Negro left lying in the highway. *Jour. Bar. Mus. Hist. Soc.*, X (1942–1943), 123.

all sorts of bodily swellings that reflected a variety of ailments. Slaves with swollen legs were likely victims of protein deficiency. Planters with distended abdomens possibly had cirrhosis of the liver. Many of Dr. Sloane's Jamaican patients seem to have suffered from liver trouble: they had jaundiced complexions and pot bellies, drank very heavily, and took little rest.

The most mysterious Caribbean malady of the seventeenth century was the dry bellyache, or dry gripes, perhaps induced by drinking rum processed in lead pipes. The victim caught cold and suffered excruciating cramps in the pit of his stomach and bowels. He lost the use of his limbs temporarily or permanently and often died. The dry bellyache even affected Barbados politics in 1684. Governor Dutton returned that year from a visit to England to discover his deputy, Sir John Witham, seemingly at death's door with the bellyache. So he judged it safe to prosecute Witham for maladministration in order to avoid paying him any salary. Dutton threw the unfortunate man in jail and appointed a special court, which fined him £5,000. But Witham unexpectedly recovered his health and complained to the home authorities, and in 1685 Dutton was dismissed from his post.[7]

A special health problem for the English colonists, largely self-induced, was lack of exercise. The wealthy planters not merely delegated all physical labor to the Negroes; they avoided walking and riding by making their slaves drive them from place to place in coaches or carry them in litters. The most popular outdoor sports in seventeenth-century England were less enjoyable in the tropics. A good index to the sporting tastes of the landed gentry at home is Richard Blome's *The Gentlemans Recreation*, a profusely illustrated folio volume, a copy of which was lost by a St. Christopher planter during the French raid of 1706.[8] Blome devotes chapters to horsemanship, hawking, hunting, fowling, angling, gardening, and cockfighting. The islanders practiced some of these recreations. In Jamaica the horsemen from Old Harbour raced twice a year against the horsemen from Withywood for a silver cup. The islanders

7. The Dutton-Witham quarrel can be traced in Barbados Council Journal, 1660–1686, C.O. 31/1/549–553, 564, 593; Barbados Entry Book, 1680–1686, C.O. 29/3/247, 252–258, 266–282; and Edwin Stede's letters of Nov. 11, 1684, Feb. 6, 1684/5, May 30, 1685, and July 9, 1685, to William Blathwayt, Blathwayt Papers, XXXIII.
8. [Richard Blome], *The Gentlemans Recreation* (London, 1686). This volume is valued at £3 in the St. Christopher compensation claims, C.O. 243/2/381. There was a second edition in 1710.

hunted for small game, held cockfights, played at bowls, and shot at butts. Billiards, shuffleboard, gaming, and dancing were popular indoor sports.

Sea bathing might seem an obvious and attractive form of exercise for the gentry, but not so. Swimming was not among Richard Blome's gentlemanly recreations; it was considered unhealthy in the seventeenth century. The swimmer spread infections and caught chills from overexertion, so the argument ran, and swimming in the sparkling Caribbean exposed him to more direct sunlight than he cared for.[9] Bathing in mineral springs was a different story; mineral baths were fashionable in England, and the island planters used the hot springs at Nevis and those near Morant in Jamaica. The citizens of Port Royal may have tried some sea bathing inside roofed and sheltered bath houses of the sort that became popular in the next century; several "bathing houses" are listed as lost in the earthquake of 1692. Dr. Trapham of Jamaica recommended frequent tub baths in 1679 to open the pores and forestall the ague, dropsy, and dry bellyache. But eighty years later Dr. Hilary of Barbados was still warning against the dangers of sea bathing when overheated.[10]

The premier sport in the islands (sex aside) was heavy drinking. One evening a patient of Dr. Sloane's managed to down eight quarts of madeira before he collapsed into a stupor. Sir James Modyford, asked if he had met another such spark, replied: "Mr. Chase happened to die before I could see him; the usual consequence of young Blades coming into this hott clymate and playing too much the good fellowes on their first arrivall." [11]

Island planters who could not shake off their fevers and stomach troubles or spare the time or money for the long journey home to England might travel to the mainland colonies or to neighboring islands in an effort to recover their health. The Cayman Islands were a convenient health spa for Jamaicans: "What with the change of the climent and the Turtle which is all the foode there," William

9. A newcomer at Bybrook was warned not to exercise violently by shooting water fowl or swimming in the Rio Cobre, but he bathed in the river notwithstanding and contracted a violent fever. Robert Hall to William Helyar, Apr. 29, 1702, Helyar MSS.

10. *Port Royal Real Estate Index*, card 76; Trapham, *A Discourse of the State of Health in Jamaica*, 136, 140; William Hilary, *Observations on the Changes of the Air and the Concomitant Epidemical Diseases, in the Island of Barbados* (London, 1759), *v*.

11. Sir James Modyford to Andrew King, July 3, 1671, *Jam. Hist. Rev.*, II, no. 2 (1952), 57.

Whaley reported, "it generally kills or cures." The turtle, it seems, had great therapeutic properties. Richard Ligon recovered from a serious illness by imbibing "the Pisle of a green Turtle," which had been dried, powdered, and mixed with beer or white wine—probably as effective a remedy as the infusion of goose dung that Sir Henry Morgan's buccaneers took to rid themselves of jaundice at Porto Bello.[12]

Physicians, surgeons, and apothecaries were plentiful, perhaps too plentiful, in the English islands. The slave ships employed doctors who were paid so many shillings for every living Negro at the close of the voyage, as a way of inspiring them to keep the cargo alive. The planters employed doctors to dose the slaves and dress their sores. At Bybrook the Negro doctor was paid £35 per annum. The island doctors who treated white patients charged much fancier fees: £5 for a house call in town, according to John Helyar, and £10 for a visit to a plantation. In Montserrat, where the small planters were unable to pay this kind of money, the doctors were ordered by the Assembly to treat anyone who offered £2.[13] The Bridgetown vestry built a pesthouse and an almshouse for the sick poor and hired a doctor to visit the almshouse twice a week. When an almshouse inmate named Augustine Kelly wanted his diseased leg amputated, Dr. James Sharpe was asked "with the assistance of some other Churchgoers [to] dismember the said Kelly." Whether all these medical men did more good than harm is problematical. John Taylor thought that the quacks, empirics, and illiterate pretenders who practiced in Jamaica had "distroyd many a stout Man." [14]

The doctors whose medicines, instruments, and books are itemized in the Jamaica inventories do not inspire confidence. A surgeon named Robert Hudson left a set of large rusty instruments and a collection of chemical pots and glasses filled with decayed physic. Few of the island doctors appear to have owned any medical books —not necessarily a handicap, since medical learning in the seventeenth century often impeded the natural healing process. Probably they were generally content to mix the herbal nostrums used in folk medicine since antiquity. Though the English were contemptuous

12. William Whaley to William Helyar, Apr. 30, 1676, Helyar MSS; Ligon, *True History of Barbados*, 119; Sloane, *Voyage*, I, lxxxii.

13. Pares, ed., "Barbados History from the Records of the Prize Courts," *Jour. Bar. Mus. Hist. Soc.*, V (1937–1938), 188; John Helyar to William Helyar, Sept. 16, 1686, Helyar MSS; *Acts of Assembly, Montserrat*, 32.

14. St. Michael vestry records, *Jour. Bar. Mus. Hist. Soc.*, XV (1947–1948), 207–209, XVI (1948–1949), 136–138; Taylor MS, 506–507.

of the medical practices brought from Africa by their slaves, there seems to have been little essential difference between the two methods of doctoring. Dr. Sloane saw the slaves administer herbal potions, draw blood, cup, and scarify—all standard techniques in his own practice.

The basic problem with seventeenth-century doctors, in the tropics as elsewhere, was that they still believed, with Hippocrates and Galen, in the humoral theory of medicine. They thought that man's physical environment was compounded of four competing elements—earth, water, air, and fire—which in human physiology had their counterparts in four invisible fluids known as humors—melancholy, phlegm, blood, and choler—passing through the veins from the liver to the heart. Life required all four humors, and health depended on keeping them in proper balance. Dr. Thomas Trapham, who published a treatise in 1679 on how to stay healthy in Jamaica, was an avid believer in the four humors. He supposed that women had more moisture in their systems than men, which gave them a different humoral balance, better attuned to the humid tropical climate. This explained why women outlived men in Jamaica. For men in particular, the tropical nights, with too much earth and water in the air and not enough fire, were very dangerous. Dysentery was "a colliquation of humours" that made the blood too thick or too thin. Dropsy was an excess of water in the system from sweat entering the pores. Fever was an excess of choler. Hookworms were generated by moisture in the stomach, and one could catch the dry bellyache by sleeping in the moisture-laden moonshine. Confusing yaws with gonorrhea, Trapham concluded that African slaves were particularly susceptible to venereal disease. The explanation for this was that they were "animal People," badly out of humoral balance because of their "unhappy jumble of the rational with the brutal Nature." For most tropical maladies Dr. Trapham recommended bloodletting or purges to restore the humoral balance.[15] With doctors like this in attendance, no wonder the colonists were in trouble!

On the other hand, Dr. Hans Sloane (1660–1753) represents medical practice in the islands at its best. Sloane was by far the most distinguished physician to practice in the English islands during the seventeenth century. He was a young man when he went to Ja-

15. Trapham, *A Discourse of the State of Health in Jamaica*, 5–7, 13, 72–75, 79–80, 93–97, 101–103, 113–117, 129–132.

maica as the duke of Albemarle's physician, but he had a French medical degree, was a member of the Royal Society, and had lived in the house of Thomas Sydenham, the premier English practitioner of the day. Sydenham's common-sense clinical method, his efforts to comprehend the natural history of infectious diseases, and his particular work with malaria were very useful guides for young Sloane in the West Indies. Sloane spent a bare fifteen months in Jamaica, devoting much of this time to collecting botanical specimens for his natural history of the island. However, he maintained an extensive medical practice in Spanish Town. His lengthy report, "Of the Diseases I observed in Jamaica, and the Method by which I used to Cure them," records his treatment of several hundred widely variegated patients, English and Negro, men and women, children and adults, rich and poor—altogether a fair cross section of ailing islanders.[16]

"I never saw a Disease in Jamaica," Sloane insisted, "which I had not met with in Europe." In this he was mistaken, for yaws, elephantiasis, and sleeping sickness are strictly tropical disorders, and Europe has been spared the yellow fever. Sloane was too dogmatic, also, in asserting that his European remedies always worked in Jamaica and that his patients died only when they refused to follow his directions. Sloane lost many patients, including the two leading personages on the island, the duke of Albemarle and Sir Henry Morgan. These gentlemen were certainly difficult to handle. The duke, already jaundiced from liver disease before he came to the Indies, speedily drank himself into the grave. Morgan rejected Sloane's medications and tried a black doctor who gave him injections of urine and plastered him all over with moist clay, after which the buccaneer soon died.[17] But other patients probably died because they *did* accept Sloane's medications.

Sloane treated some diseases with notably greater success than others. Following his mentor, Sydenham, he gave malarial patients a newly discovered drug, Peruvian bark or Jesuit's powder (quinine), with excellent results. Quinine is still the preferred drug for treating malaria. Again applying Sydenham's method, Sloane cured dysentery cases by the use of laudanum and a bland, nutritious diet. He learned how to distinguish yaws from syphilis and said he was

16. Sloane, *Voyage*, I, xc–cliv.
17. For Morgan's case history, see *ibid.*, xcviii–xcic; for Albemarle's case history, see Sloane MSS, 3984/282–286. Morgan was 45 when he died, and Albemarle was 33.

able to cure yaws by purging the patient in a hothouse. Beyond this Dr. Sloane was rather conservative, preferring traditional herbal decoctions to new mineral drugs like mercury. And he was completely conservative in his penchant for bloodletting. Like most seventeenth-century doctors, Sloane was a great bleeder. Almost any complaint—fevers, hemorrhages, apoplexy, drunkenness, menstrual pains, pleurisy, convulsions, hemorrhoids, blindness, gout, and heart palpitations—he treated by bloodletting. This course of action was disastrously wrongheaded. Extreme anemia is characteristic of many tropical disorders, and bloodletting only aggravates this condition. In treating such diseases as malaria and hookworm, modern practice calls for an opposite approach; doses of iron, vitamins, nutritious diet, and—in severe cases—blood transfusions to rebuild the patient's vitality.

Like Dr. Trapham, Dr. Sloane still believed in the humoral theory of medicine. Like Trapham, he characterized his Jamaican patients as overly melancholic, phlegmatic, sanguine, or choleric and bled, blistered, or dosed them to redress their humoral balance. With such an outlook, the best doctors of the seventeenth century were ill equipped to diagnose or cure tropical disease. Improvements in hygiene and diet in the late eighteenth century arrested some West Indian diseases and strengthened the inhabitants' resistance. But until doctors discovered the germ theory of disease in the nineteenth century and developed effective drugs for combating tropical parasites, bacteria, and viruses in the twentieth century, the sugar islanders could never enjoy thoroughly sound health.

How large was the island population, white and black, in the seventeenth century? This most basic demographic question can be answered in a general way only for the period after 1660. During the first generation of settlement the island governments did not attempt to compile census returns. The early figures on taxables and militiamen are too scattered to be worth much, and the population estimates by visitors to the islands are wildly exaggerated. Thus any conjecture about population trends up to the Restoration is little more than guesswork.

From 1660 onwards the situation improves. The Plantation Office began to agitate for statistical information of all sorts, and the island governors developed the habit of tabulating population figures and reporting the results home. There are census returns for Barbados in 1673, 1676, 1680, 1684, 1696, 1712, and 1715; for Jamaica in 1661, 1662, 1670, 1673, 1680, 1698, and 1703; and for the Leeward Islands in 1672, 1674, 1678, 1708, and 1720. Some of these census returns are systematic and elaborate head counts—notably the Barbados returns of 1680 and 1715, the Jamaica returns of 1680, and the Leeward returns of 1678 and 1708. Others are impressionistic and worthless guesses. Past commentators have tended to dismiss all of these tabulations, but as we have seen, the only early census that can be checked and double-checked—the Barbados census of 1680—turns out to be honest and accurate as well as richly informa-

Table 26. Estimated Population of the English Sugar Islands, 1660–1713

	Barbados		Jamaica		Leeward Islands	
Year	White	Black	White	Black	White	Black
1660	22,000	20,000	3,000	500	8,000	2,000
1670	20,000	30,000	7,000	7,000	8,000	3,000
1680	20,000	40,000	12,000	15,000	11,000	9,000
1690	18,000	50,000	10,000	30,000	10,000	15,000
1700	15,000	40,000	7,000	40,000	7,000	20,000
1713	16,000	45,000	7,000	55,000	9,000	30,000

tive. The Barbados census of 1715, to be discussed shortly, is for demographic purposes an even more precisely detailed document. All in all, the West Indian census returns compiled between 1660 and 1720 appear to be at least as accurate as contemporary counts taken for religious or tax purposes in England,[18] and they are certainly more exact and comprehensive than the population estimates made in the English mainland colonies during these years.[19]

Table 26 draws upon these census figures to conjecture in round numbers the population pattern in the English islands between the Restoration and Utrecht. The most striking feature of this table is

18. Such as the ecclesiastical enumerations of 1676 and 1688, the hearth tax returns of 1662–1674 and 1690, and the data provided by the marriage duty act of 1695. See T. H. Hollingsworth, *Historical Demography* (Ithaca, N.Y., 1969), 80–88, 124–128.

19. For a survey of the mainland census returns, tax rolls, and militia lists for this period, see Evarts B. Greene and Virginia D. Harrington, *American Population Before the Federal Census of 1790* (New York, 1932).

the contrast between black and white population trends. On every island the number of white inhabitants climbed gradually for several decades and then dropped. Barbados probably reached its maximum white population as early as the 1650s; the total at the Restoration was higher than it has ever been since. In Jamaica and the Leewards the white population peaked a generation later, around 1680. In Jamaica, settled after the sugar and slave system had taken root in the eastern islands, the white population was never as large as in Barbados even though the island contained far more room for settlement. Overall the white population pattern was static at best. There were no more Englishmen in the sugar islands in 1713 than in 1660, whereas the English population of the mainland colonies increased fivefold during this span. Initially, back in the tobacco days, Barbados had been as populous as Virginia or Massachusetts, but by Utrecht the North American settlements contained ten times as many white inhabitants as the sugar islands.

The black population in the islands was certainly not static. As table 26 shows, the number of slaves rose rapidly and continually from 1660 to 1713—except in Barbados after 1690. On this island the slave population leveled off at about forty-five thousand for half a century, from the 1680s to the 1730s, before it began to climb again. But in Jamaica and the Leewards the number of blacks swelled steadily decade by decade, until by the mid-eighteenth century the masters were outnumbered by their slaves ten to one in Jamaica, seven to one in the Leewards, and four to one in Barbados.

It would be a mistake to conclude from these figures that the slaves adjusted better than their masters to life in the tropics. The black population rose only because of the huge volume of the slave trade, and the white population stopped growing in part because so many whites moved away from the islands. Overall there is little doubt that the blacks died faster than the whites in the English islands. It is far from easy to assay slave demography in the seventeenth century, since the planters kept no record of Negro births, marriages, and deaths, except for the handful of free Christian Negroes. But something can be attempted, and all the evidence points toward demographic catastrophy for the slaves.

The simplest way to demonstrate the scale of black mortality in the English islands is to compare the number of slaves imported during the course of the seventeenth century with the number of slaves living in the islands at the close of the century. Between 1640 and 1700, according to Philip Curtin's careful calculation, the English sugar planters brought some 264,000 slaves from Africa into Barbados, Jamaica, and the Leeward Islands. In 1700, according to the census returns, the black population of these islands was barely 100,000—about 40,000 apiece in Barbados and Jamaica and 20,000 in the Leeward Islands. These figures are all approximate, of course, but they prove without question that the island slaves suffered an appalling natural decrease during the seventeenth century. Negro mortality rose even higher in the English islands in the next century. Between 1708 and 1735 the Barbadians imported 85,000 new slaves in order to lift the black population on this island from 42,000 to 46,000. By 1790 Barbados, Jamaica, and the Leewards had taken a total of some 1,230,000 slaves from Africa in order to achieve a collective black population of about 387,000.

This pattern of human spoliation in the English sugar islands was by no means unique. The Negro slaves in Portuguese Brazil, in Dutch Surinam, in French St. Domingue, and in Spanish Cuba died off equally fast in the seventeenth and eighteenth centuries. But in the mainland English colonies Negro slaves from the outset had a much better chance of surviving and multiplying. Between 1607 and 1790 the North American settlers imported 275,000 slaves—a total very little higher than the number imported to the sugar islands in the seventeenth century alone. Yet the first United States census of 1790 shows a Negro population of 757,000, seven times the size of the Negro population in Barbados, Jamaica, and the Leeward Islands in 1700 and twice the size of the island black population in 1790.[20] Clearly climate is not the factor here. Blacks transported from equatorial Africa survived much better in the frozen North than in the tropical Caribbean. They did so because they escaped diseases endemic in the Caribbean and because mainland slave masters treated them less brutally.

Surviving West Indian slave records for the seventeenth century tell some interesting things about the sex ratio between men and women and about the age distribution between adults and children. To begin with, K. G. Davies has analyzed sixty thousand slaves delivered to the West Indies by the Royal African Company be-

20. My slave importation figures are drawn from Curtin, *Atlantic Slave Trade*, 52–64, 72–73, 119, 216. North American Negro population figures are drawn from U.S. Bureau of the Census, *Historical Statistics*, 9, 756.

tween 1673 and 1711; he reports that "51 per cent were men and 35 percent were women; of the remainder 9 per cent were boys and 4 percent girls." [21] The dividing line between adults and children in slave tabulations is always vague. Generally the sugar planters categorized black children up to about age ten as "pickaninnies," youths from about ten to fifteen as "working boys" or "working girls," and anyone over sixteen as "men" or "women." In any case, Davies's figures show that very few children were brought over from Africa. And though 86 percent of the arriving slaves appear to have been old enough for procreation, the 60:40 sex ratio in favor of men would hamper effective breeding. The low proportion of females imported into the islands might seem to explain the stunted character of Negro family life in the Caribbean, but this explanation turns out to be too easy. For the sex and age characteristics of the slave population began to change as soon as the blacks were led off the slave ships and put to work in the sugar plantations.

For documentation of this change we must turn to the early island census returns. The Barbados returns of 1673 and 1676, the Leeward Islands census of 1678, and the Nevis and St. Christopher returns of 1708 all give totals for the number of Negro males and females or for the number of Negro men, women, and children. Since these census totals can be challenged as pure guesswork, I have tested them against two other kinds of evidence that are more certainly trustworthy. The Jamaica inventories of 1674 to 1701 identify the slaves attached to each probated estate as men, women, boys, girls, or pickaninnies and appraise each category differently, men being worth the most and pickaninnies the least. The records for Bybrook plantation in Jamaica include nine lists of slaves, classified as men, women, and children, taken between 1676 and 1709. As table 27 demonstrates, the Jamaica inventories and Bybrook records confirm the census returns. All of these variegated sources yield very much the same ratio between male and female slaves and between adult and child slaves. The most obvious point to emerge from this table is that the male preponderance among incoming slaves quickly melted away. Female slaves survived better in the sugar islands and righted the sexual imbalance. Even though the Royal African Company delivered 60 percent male cargoes, the women slightly outnumbered the men in the island slave gangs. As

21. K. G. Davies, *Royal African Company*, 299. These figures only add up to 99%.

Table 27. Sex and Age Distribution of West Indian Slaves, 1673–1708

Colony	No. of Slaves	Percentage			Percentage	
		Men	Women	Children	Males	Females
Barbados, 1673	33,184	30.8	35.9	33.3	48.4	51.6
Barbados, 1676	32,473	32.4			50.4	49.6
Leeward Is., 1678	8,560	37.7	35.3	27.0		
Jamaica inventories, 1674–1701	1,467	36.4	36.3	27.0	50.7	49.3
Bybrook, Jamaica, 1676–1709	1,030	37.5	34.1	28.4		
St. Christopher, 1708	3,252	31.9	38.0	30.1	48.3	51.7
Nevis, 1708	3,676				48.0	52.0

NOTE: The Barbados census of 1673 is reported in *Cal.S.P.Col.*, *1669–1674*, #1101; the Barbados census of 1676 is summarized in C.O. 318/2/115; the Leeward Islands census of 1678 is summarized in C.O. 1/42/239; the Jamaica figures are tabulated from a cross section of inventories in Jam. Inv., Vols. 1-3, 5; the Bybrook figures come from Helyar MSS; and the St. Christopher and Nevis census returns for 1708 are summarized in Oliver, ed., *Caribbeana*, III, 138–139, 179, 256. If we add to the St. Christopher total for 1708 the 350 males and 224 females lost to the French in 1706 (see table 28), the percentage of men on this island climbs to 35, and the sex balance becomes 50:50.

we have seen, the large planters (at least in Jamaica) kept their gangs as evenly matched as possible, so as to provide each adult male with a wife. Clearly the slave couples produced a sizable number of babies. For though only about 13 percent of the incoming blacks were children, this percentage more than doubled once the slaves were settled in the islands.[22]

22. The 17th-century 50:50 sex ratio in the island slave gangs seems to have changed in the next century, as the planters stopped trying to provide a wife for every male and bought only male slaves as much as possible. On four Price plantations the male preponderance rose to 70:30. See Patterson, *Sociology of Slavery*, 107; Craton and Walvin, *A Jamaican Plantation*, 127, 151.

Why did the male slaves die faster than the women? Doubtless they were forced to work harder. Some tropical diseases strike men more frequently than women. The men may have suffered more from malnutrition and from fatal accidents in the sugar works. The men were far more likely than the women to run away or steal or rebel; they were far more frequently flogged, maimed, and executed. Rebellion took many forms: a new Negro might pretend that he did not know how to use a hoe and refuse to be taught; an old slave, feeling hopelessly cornered, might malinger or kill himself. In protesting so often against their captivity, the male slaves expressed their deep psychological maladjustment. For the women the plantation regimen was probably somewhat less degrading and repressive, for they were accustomed in West Africa to perform most of the routine agricultural labor and domestic drudgery. Whatever the reasons, the pressures of the slave system bore most heavily against the men, and this helped to promote the well-known matriarchal character of black family life in the Caribbean.[23]

Plantation slaves, when they grew old or ornery, might be sold as refuse. When young and healthy they might be grabbed by enemy raiders during wartime. The French raiders who sacked St. Christopher in 1706 made off with over six hundred of the best slaves—61 percent of them males. The English planters, when they filed compensation claims, identified 574 of the missing Negroes by name, sex, age, occupation, and value. The affidavits concerning this batch of stolen slaves are unique in telling just how old the missing Negroes were. Census returns and inventories classify slaves by rough age groups at best, but these affidavits identify 360 males and 224 females by exact age. The planters were surprisingly precise in fixing the ages of their young Negroes, though they lost track after age twenty-five and generally gave approximations for the older ones: thirty, thirty-five, forty, and so on. No slave in this group was listed as over fifty-five years old.

It must be emphasized that table 28 does not constitute a true sample. The French probably stole selectively, taking Negroes of prime working age and males in preference to females. Furthermore St. Christopher had only fairly recently been resettled by the English after the devastation of the 1690s, and it may be that an

23. Patterson, *Sociology of Slavery*, chap. 4, thinks the black women survived better because the whites who exploited them sexually treated them better. To explain the low Negro birth rate, he puts special stress on the slave women's infertility and their hostility to child-rearing.

exceptionally high proportion of the slave population had recently arrived from Africa. In any case, the very small number of youngsters aged five to nine in this group and the almost total absence of young teenagers is striking. Sixty percent of these Negroes were between the ages of eighteen and thirty. We cannot deduce from this table that the English slaves all died by age fifty-five. Dr. Sloane claimed that blacks in Jamaica very commonly attained

Table 28. Age of 574 St. Christopher Slaves, 1706

Age	Number			Percentage		
	Males	Females	Total	Males	Females	Total
0–4	25	20	45	7.1	8.9	7.9
5–9	13	9	22	3.7	4.0	3.9
10–14	6	2	8	1.7	0.9	1.4
15–19	31	10	41	8.9	4.5	7.1
20–24	63	31	94	18.0	13.8	16.4
25–29	82	53	135	23.4	23.7	23.5
30–34	66	43	109	18.9	19.2	19.0
35–39	27	27	54	7.7	12.1	9.4
40–44	22	17	39	6.3	7.6	6.8
45–49	5	5	10	1.4	2.2	1.7
50–54	7	7	14	2.0	3.1	2.4
55–59	3	0	3	0.9	0.0	0.5
Total	350	224	574	100.0	100.0	100.0

NOTE: Compiled from Account of Losses sustained by the Proprietors and Inhabitants of the Island of St. Christophers . . . when the French Invaded the said Island and the Island of Nevis in the months of February and March 1705 [i.e., 1706], C.O. 243/2.

the age of one hundred—though how they knew themselves to be so old in the absence of vital records he does not say.

The St. Christopher planters valued their slaves on a rather complicated scale, determined by sex, age, and occupation. Males commanded a somewhat higher price than females, and slaves in their twenties and thirties commanded a much higher price than children and old people. A Negro boy was appraised at only £5 when one year old, but his value rose to £16 at age nine, £30 at age seventeen, and £40 at age twenty. Past the age of forty he began de-

preciating in value: a healthy male of fifty was worth only £25.[24]
In appraising a slave the planter seems to have correlated working
ability with life expectancy. He valued a boy of twelve well below a
boy of seventeen not merely because the younger boy could do less
work but because he had less chance of reaching manhood. And he
valued a field worker in his forties well below a field worker in his
twenties who labored no better but could be expected to live longer.

Some of the slaves in the St. Christopher affidavits held specialized jobs on large plantations, while others were the sole employees of very small planters. Altogether, 450 of them can be

Table 29. *Occupations of 450 St. Christopher Slaves, 1706*

Men		Women	
Overseers	5	Domestics	42
Domestics	20	Distillers	2
Craftsmen	19	Field hands	131
Boilers, distillers	42	Total	175
Carters	22		
Shepherds	5		
Fishermen	5		
Field hands	157		
Total	275		

identified by occupation (see table 29). The youngest worker in
this group was a nine-year-old footboy. Teenagers of both sexes
were often assigned household jobs, though one fifteen-year-old
was a boiler. Slaves trained to operate the sugar works or to perform plantation crafts were generally valued at about £60, well
above the field hands. Among the crafts open to male slaves were
cooper, potter, mason, carpenter, smith, tailor, shoemaker, basket-
maker, and pewterer. Some of the female house slaves also had
specialties as cooks, laundresses, and seamstresses. The handful of
black overseers, valued at about £80 each, were surprisingly young,
in their twenties. The only slave identified in these claims as a
mulatto was a twenty-three-year-old shoemaker appraised at £100.

24. The Jamaica inventories show the same scale and in addition set low
values on sick and maimed Negroes. One old Jamaican slave belonging to John
Waller, described as about 80 years old, was valued at only £1. Jam. Inv., Vol. 1.

But even in this picked group of slaves, 81 percent of the women and 57 percent of the men were simple field laborers.

Above all, the St. Christopher affidavits document the human wastage inherent in slavery. The master who owned a slave and his posterity only really wanted the best years out of a slave's life. In the seventeenth century this was a very brief span. The French, when they raided St. Christopher, grabbed Negroes in their twenties and thirties. The English, in appraising their losses, downgraded blacks who were younger than eighteen or older than forty. The sugar planters were always businessmen first and foremost, and from a business viewpoint it was more efficient to import new slaves of prime working age from Africa than to breed up a creole generation of Negroes in the Caribbean. A planter encumbered by numerous pickaninnies, suckling mothers, and decrepit old slaves found himself running an almshouse as well as a business enterprise. Some of the slave masters found it hard to resist the temptation to get rid of the young and old by systematic neglect and underfeeding.

If this judgment sounds too harsh, consider the record of slave usage at Bybrook plantation in Jamaica. The health of the Negroes on this plantation fluctuated amazingly over a forty-year span, and there seems to be a close correlation between periods of extreme sickness and periods of brutal or careless management. Bybrook was a large plantation by seventeenth-century standards. Cary Helyar and William Whaley quickly built up the slave force from zero in 1669 to 104 in 1676, and their successors kept the force at this size or larger. Seven times between 1691 and 1709 the Bybrook managers took head counts of the black men, women, and children on the estate.[25] Overall the proportion of men to women to children at Bybrook was standard for the time, but the interesting thing to see is how radically the composition of the slave population changed, year by year, as Negroes died and the managers bought replacements. Graph 1 shows that the number of children fluctuated the most, suggesting how susceptible young Negroes were to disease and neglect. Over the twenty-year span the number of men declined appreciably, while the number of women held steady. The

25. There are also two earlier head counts, in 1676 and 1678. These lists are all in the Helyar MSS. As usual, the definition of a "child" is hopelessly vague. Some lists speak of men, women, and pickaninnies; others of men, women, boys, and girls; others of men, women, male children, and female children; still others of men, women, boys, girls, and suckling children!

Bybrook slaves were healthiest under the management of Cary Helyar (1669–1672), John Helyar (1687–1691), and John Halstead (1705–1713). These men, being part owners of the plantation, had a personal stake in the well-being of their laborers. In

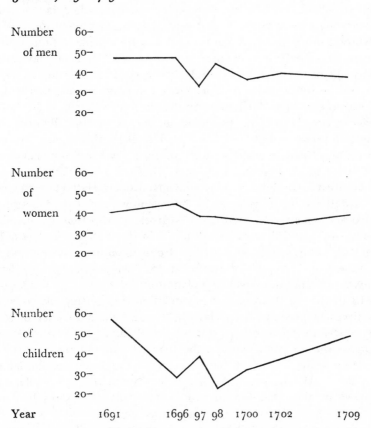

Graph 1. *Fluctuations in the Slave Population at Bybrook Plantation, Jamaica, 1691–1709*

Cary Helyar's time Bybrook was brand new and not yet fully operating, the Negroes were fresh and given enough to eat, and in consequence no slaves died. Conditions were never this good again. After 1672 deaths greatly outnumbered births at Bybrook, and the managers bought five or ten new Negroes every year or so in order to keep the working force at effective strength. Incomplete records show that 169 blacks were added to the Bybrook slave gang between

1672 and 1713: the full total was undoubtedly much higher. But at least under the supervision of John Helyar and John Halstead the slaves were well enough treated so that they bred effectively, as is shown by the large number of children in 1691 and 1709.

The worst times for the Bybrook slaves came in the late 1670s and mid-1690s, when the plantation was managed by irresponsible overseers. It is no coincidence that 13 Negroes from Bybrook were implicated in a rebellion in 1678, for the slaves died fast at this point and stole or ran away for want of food. The execution of the Bybrook rebels crippled the productivity of the plantation; never again did the Helyars own as many as 50 adult male slaves. In the wake of this disaster Squire Helyar begged his manager in 1678 to care for the Negroes "by yor beinge constantly among them, and usinge them with that humanity that every good man will afford even to his very beast." John Austin, who supervised Bybrook in the mid-1690s, would have done well to heed this advice. He reduced the Negroes to such a starved and filthy condition that they fell prey to dropsy and dysentery. Between 1691 and 1696, 80 slaves died at Bybrook. A new manager, Robert Hall, claimed that he fed the Negroes generously, but 22 more slaves died between 1700 and 1702. Hall hired extra Negroes at crop time because he found the Bybrook workers too feeble to do the job. In 1703 only 42 field hands could be mustered from among 110 slaves, and a number of these were good for little, "being some of the first negroes that began to settle the plantation." [26]

In truth, the Bybrook slave population was getting old as well as tired. Inspection of the slave lists show that a number of seasoned veterans from the 1670s were still alive thirty years later. Among the forty-four men on the Bybrook force in 1678, fourteen turn up again in 1696 and eight in 1709, all identified as old, lame, or past hard labor. Of the thirty-nine women in 1678, twelve reappear in 1696 and five in 1709.[27] These aged Negroes had arrived at Bybrook when the place was new and well managed. Slaves added to the Bybrook force in the 1680s and 1690s stood a much poorer chance of long life, being buffeted from the outset

26. William Helyar to Thomas Hillyard, Aug. 26, 1678, John Austin to William Helyar, Aug. 16, 1696, Robert Hall to William Helyar, Jr., Apr. 16, 1700, and 1702, James Seviour to William Helyar, Jr., Nov. 22, 1703, Helyar MSS.

27. Comparison of the names on these slave lists is of course a dubious procedure. "Jack the overseer" in 1678 and 1696 may not be the same person as "Old Jack" in 1709.

by infectious diseases, poor food, and low morale. When any new Negro was brought from Africa, the first year or two of captivity, the so-called "seasoning" stage, was critical. The shock of forced transfer to America, the exposure to new diseases, and the rigors of chattel slavery always winnowed out the weak from the strong. At Bybrook by the 1690s the unhealthy environment was winnowing out most new arrivals. Thus through stupid management the Helyars' labor force became a collection of over-aged and under-aged blacks—the exact opposite of what a sugar planter wanted.

My impression is that the story of slave usage at Bybrook reflects a more general process, namely that the treatment of Negroes in the sugar islands gradually deteriorated during the closing decades of the seventeenth century. Slaves seem to have fared better and lived longer when the sugar industry was brand new than later when the plantation system became thoroughly institutionalized. Initially in Barbados, Negroes were scarce enough to be handled with some consideration, and the mix of black and white laborers protected the blacks from extreme overwork and underfeeding. Plantations were generally small, the owners were personally in charge, and epidemics of yellow fever and malaria were just beginning. In 1671 Cary Helyar naively supposed that the Negroes he brought to Bybrook would propagate like rabbits and enable him soon to staff a second plantation, "for as negroes will begett negroes so one plantation will begett another." [28] His successors soon learned otherwise.

By 1689 a leading Barbados planter named Edward Littleton (who owned 120 slaves) was arguing in an influential pamphlet that the master of a hundred slaves had to buy six new ones a year in order to maintain his stock. If this were true, a slave on Littleton's plantation had a life expectancy of only seventeen years. "One of the great Burdens of our Lives is the going to buy Negroes," Littleton groaned. "But we must have them; we cannot be without them, and the best Men in those Countries must in their own Persons submit to the Indignity." [29] Actually Littleton—being an absentee—did not have to submit to this indignity in his own person. Like many another sugar planter at the close of the century he let his factor or overseer buy the new Negroes and tend to the old ones. Though he complained about the Royal African Com-

28. Cary Helyar to William Helyar, Jan. 12, 1670/1, Helyar MSS.
29. Littleton, *Groans of the Plantations*, 6, 18.

pany monopoly, new slaves were far more readily available than ever before. In all of the English islands plantation units were growing in size and becoming more impersonal. Sugar profits were shrinking, and planters hated to spend money on slave food, which in Barbados and the Leewards had to be largely imported. Slave revolts and conspiracies, though so far completely ineffectual, had touched a raw nerve, and the masters kept tightening up their policing laws. None of these late-seventeenth-century developments benefited the black man.

From the 1690s onward new slaves cost much more, surely an inducement for keeping them alive longer. But what governed the slave system in the English islands from about 1660 to 1760 was the superabundant supply of new Negroes, not their high cost. Slave mortality on the ocean passage from Africa did indeed decline, but slave mortality in the English islands seems to have reached an all time high during the first half of the eighteenth century. On the Codrington estate in Barbados, the largest and finest on the island, 450 new Negroes were added to the slave force between 1712 and 1761 at an average price of £33 each. Yet the black population of this plantation fell by a third during this span of years. Six Negroes died at Codrington for every Negro born. Codrington plantation, operated by the Society for the Propagation of the Gospel, exemplifies the full-blown West Indian slave system, in which several hundred blacks, kept docile and dumb through systematic semistarvation and a stupefying round of brute chores, functioned as dehumanized cogs in a very inefficient machine. Symbolically, one overseer at Codrington branded the Negroes with the letters SOCIETY on their breasts. Productivity was well below seventeenth-century standards, but so was the risk of rebellion.[30]

At length, around 1760, the English sugar planters made a great discovery. By funneling a small part of the money they had been spending on new slaves into ameliorating the living conditions of those they already had, they could significantly reduce the rate of natural decrease within the West Indian slave population. At Codrington and elsewhere the planters launched a new policy of "amelioration," which gradually raised the Negro birth rate, lowered the Negro death rate, freed the slaveholders from dependence on the African slave trade, and cut costs.[31] Thus when Englishmen

---

30. For a full discussion of Codrington, see Bennett, *Bondsmen and Bishops.*
31. For the demographic change in the Codrington slave population, see *ibid.*, 91, 96, 102–103, 139. Pares discusses a parallel change in the slave population of

at home came to see the slave trade as immoral, the sugar interest came to see it as uneconomic. With the collapse of the sugar industry in the nineteenth century, the island planters suddenly discovered that their pool of Negro laborers was too large. By the emancipation era the black population was finally stabilized and births began to exceed deaths. And in the twentieth century, with further improvements in health conditions and medical knowledge, the black population in Jamaica and Barbados has grown so fast that both nations are now severely overcrowded and hundreds of thousands of West Indians have emigrated abroad—the exact opposite of the population pattern in the days of slavery.[32]

The demographic data for whites living in the sugar islands in the seventeenth century are more ample than for the blacks, but also more contradictory and confusing. A great deal of miscellaneous information about births, deaths, and family structure can be garnered from early census returns, parish registers, and churchyard tombstones. But most of these sources are radically defective, and they tell us little for sure beyond a few obvious points: the sugar planters died young, married irregularly, and had too few children to maintain the population. There is some evidence to suggest that the health of the whites improved over time while the health of the blacks was deteriorating and considerable evidence to suggest that the English always fared rather better than their slaves.

Peter Laslett has proposed that nascent colonial communities such as the sugar islands in the seventeenth century "must have been in sexual unbalance, more men than women, more bridegrooms than brides, whilst in Europe and England the sexes were much more nearly in balance."[33] But this proposition applies only for the first few decades in the English islands. The aggressively exploitive frontier milieu of the Caribbean was assuredly a man's

---

the Pinney plantations in Nevis, *A West-India Fortune*, 123–125; Craton and Walvin discuss amelioration at Worthy Park in *A Jamaican Plantation*, 129–131, 195–197.

32. For modern population patterns in the islands, see George W. Roberts, *The Population of Jamaica* (Cambridge, Eng., 1957); Lowenthal, "Population of Barbados," *Soc. and Econ. Studies*, VI (1957), 445–501.

33. Peter Laslett, "The Numerical Study of English Society," in E. A. Wrigley, ed., *An Introduction to English Historical Demography* (New York, 1966), 8.

world, and far more men than women came out from England. Nearly all of the colonists who first planted Barbados and St. Christopher were males: 94 percent of the 1,408 migrants from London in 1635, for example. Most of the English settlers of Jamaica were also males: 85 percent of the white inhabitants in 1661, for example. Even in the second half of the century, the Bristol register of indentured servants shows that 76 percent of the 2,678 servants who came to Barbados between 1654 and 1686 were still young males.[34] As a result census returns for the 1660s and 1670s show a very unbalanced sex ratio in Jamaica, and even in Barbados and the Leewards white women were scarce enough so that many men had to choose between monasticism and slave girls. But—as with the incoming Negroes—the male preponderance disappeared once the English had lived for some time in the islands. Table 30, drawing upon census returns, shows the trend very clearly. By the early eighteenth century the sexes were balanced, with the women forging ahead of the men.

Comparing this computation for whites with the parallel computation for blacks in table 27, we find the same tendency in both population groups for the women to outlast the men. As the number of white women increased there were naturally more marriages and children. Family life among the whites appears to have been more robust than among the slaves. The proportion of slave children remained stationary at about 30 percent, while the proportion of white children kept rising until, by 1720, 45 percent of the Leeward whites were classified as children. But the most striking thing about table 30 is the dwindling percentage of white men. By 1720 the effective white working force in the islands was much smaller than it had been fifty years before. The parish registers in Barbados for 1678–1679 show that 53 percent of the whites buried were men, 26 percent women, 11 percent boys, and 10 percent girls.[35] All of the victims of drowning listed in these registers were men, and it can be assumed that men were more likely to kill one another in brawls or undermine their constitutions through hard drinking. Men were of course also drawn into dangerous duty as

34. The London figures for 1635 are compiled from Hotten, ed., *Original Lists*, 33–145; the Jamaica figures for 1661 are in *Cal.S.P.Col., 1661–1668,* #204; the Bristol registry figures are compiled from *Jour. Bar. Mus. Hist. Soc.,* XIV (1946–1947) through XIX (1951–1952), *passim.*

35. These percentages are compiled from the registers of St. Michael, St. George, St. Andrew, Christchurch and St. James, Mar. 1678–Sept. 1679, printed by Hotten, ed., *Original Lists,* 425–438, 466–472, 493–499.

buccaneers, privateers, or soldiers in the French wars. Male colonists were probably more transient than the females, more likely to pick up and move on to better job opportunities elsewhere—unchivalrously leaving their women and children behind.[36] But out-migration is certainly not the only explanation for the white male shrinkage. It is evident that men died faster than women in the tropics.

Table 30. Sex and Age Distribution of the White Population in the English Islands, 1662–1720

Colony	Whites	Men	Percentage Women	Children	Percentage Males	Females
Jamaica, 1662	3,653	71.2	17.6	11.2		
Jamaica, 1673	7,768	52.1	25.9	22.0		
Barbados, 1673	21,309	43.5			60.4	39.6
Barbados, 1676	21,725	46.1			60.0	40.0
Leeward Is., 1678	11,132	42.8	24.3	32.9		
Barbados, 1684	19,568	36.9			55.8	44.2
Leeward Is., 1708 *	5,853	33.7	27.8	38.5	53.4	46.6
Barbados, 1715	16,888	27.7	29.4	42.9	49.9	50.1
Leeward Is., 1720	8,361	26.3	29.1	44.6	48.7	51.3

* exclusive of Nevis

NOTE: As with the preceding slave tabulations, the dividing line between adults and children is vague. The best approximation is age 16, when boys became eligible for militia duty. The Jamaica figures are taken from *Jours. of Jam. Assembly*, I, Appendix, 20, 40. The Barbados figures for 1673 come from *Cal.S.P.Col., 1669–1674*, #1101; for 1676 from C.O. 318/2/115; for 1684 from Sloane MSS, 2441/17–22; for 1715 from C.O. 28/16. The Leeward Islands figures for 1678 come from C.O. 1/42/239; for 1708 from C.O. 318/2/7; for 1720 from Pitman, *Development of the British West Indies*, 378.

Perhaps Dr. Trapham's theory about moist women in humid climates has something to it after all!

Parish registers give some additional information, but not very much, about white baptisms, marriages, and burials in the seventeenth century. Only three parishes in the islands—St. Michael in Barbados, St. Andrew, and St. Catherine in Jamaica—have lengthy series of vital records for this early period. The registers were kept by Church of England vicars who charged a fee for registering each

36. In Barbados during 1679, 88% of the whites who obtained tickets to leave the island were males.

marriage, baptism or burial, which surely discouraged compliance by nonchurchgoers. Jews, Quakers, Baptists, and practically all Negroes were excluded altogether. I suspect that deaths were always better recorded than births in these registers, for corpses had to be buried, and the churchyard was the most convenient place. Nonetheless, it may be significant that all three surviving registers record many more burials than baptisms during the seventeenth century.[37]

St. Michael parish, which embraces Bridgetown, has the gloomiest set of figures. In the years between 1648 and 1694 four whites were buried in this church for every one baptized. In the yellow-fever year of 1694, the worst of the century, 354 persons were buried and only 40 baptized. But it must be remembered that Bridgetown was atypical, being by far the unhealthiest place on the island, and filled with unseasoned transients who were particularly susceptible to island fevers.[38] In most years rather more burials were recorded in the hottest summer months. At first the dead were mainly servants, but after 1660, as expected, they were more usually identified as husbands, wives, and children. Some entries are pathetic: "a maid that died in the street," "a child out of the woods," or "Poor Patrick the foole." [39] It is interesting to find that Barbadian vital statistics from the eighteenth century, which appear to be much more complete, show the birth-death ratio on the island in much closer equilibrium. An average of 542 births and 562 deaths are reported for forty-one years between 1710 and 1803. These figures suggest that the Barbadians were learning how to survive better in the tropics.[40]

In Jamaica the parishes of St. Andrew (near Kingston) and St. Catherine (Spanish Town and environs) kept registers from the 1660s onward. At first births outnumber deaths in both registers, but after 1680 the burials always outnumber the baptisms, generally by two to one. Not surprisingly, the worst year of the century was

37. Baptisms were not synonymous with births; sometimes older children and adults were baptized.

38. In 1678–1679, 581 baptisms and 1,087 burials are reported for the island as a whole. C.O. 1/44/159–241. In 1683, 407 baptisms and 1,026 burials are reported. Sloane MSS, 2441/17–22. In both cases, St. Michael had much the worst record.

39. St. Michael Parish Register: Baptisms, Marriages, and Burials, Vol. 1A, RL 1/1. I have surveyed 15 years in this register: 1648–1650, 1657–1658, 1661–1662, 1670, 1674, 1678–1679, 1682, 1686, 1690, and 1694.

40. F. W. Pitman tabulates the 18-century vital statistics in *Development of the British West Indies*, 385.

the earthquake year of 1692: 185 persons were buried and 47 baptized in St. Andrew. Unlike Barbados the Jamaican vital records show no improvement after 1700. According to these two registers, at least, the Jamaicans in the eighteenth century continued to die much faster than they were born.[41] The parish registers do not permit systematic reconstitution of island families, though it is occasionally possible to trace all the children in one generation of a family. William and Mary Archbold of Jamaica baptized twelve children at annual intervals between 1676 and 1688, until the arrival of the last of these offspring killed his mother. Eight of the Archbold children survived infancy, and four lived long enough to get married. Another Jamaican planter couple with a big family, Charles and Sarah Price, had about the same batting average: of their thirteen children, three died in infancy, five in childhood, and five reached maturity.[42]

The funerals that were so plentiful in the islands were ritualistic occasions for the English planters, as for their slaves. When a man left any assets at his death, the executors spent some of his estate on a burial feast. Nathaniel Hickes of Jamaica had a funeral costing £155, most of which went into gold rings, gloves, madeira, and brandy for the mourners. The Kingston merchant William Parke did a brisk business in black hats and gloves for funerals. "As soon as the Corps are interr'd," said a Barbadian in 1710, "they sit around the Liquor in the Church porch [and] drinke to the obsequies of the defunct . . . until they are as drunk as Tinckers." If the dead man was of gentle birth, or if his family wished to invent a suitable heraldic device, a coat of arms was proudly incised on his tombstone.[43]

Many hundred weathered tombstones to the early planters are still to be found in the island graveyards. The inscriptions on these ancient monuments have a certain demographic interest, for they often record the subject's age at death. But tomb counting, even

41. The St. Andrew and St. Catherine Copy Registers of Baptisms, Marriages, and Burials are in the Island Registry Office, Spanish Town. I have surveyed the St. Andrew register from 1664 to 1750, the St. Catherine register from 1669 to 1750.

42. The Archbolds can be traced in the St. Catherine register, the Prices partially in the St. Andrew register. For the Prices, see Craton and Walvin, *A Jamaican Plantation*, 65–67.

43. Inventory of Nathaniel Hickes, Jam. Inv., Vol. 2; William Parke to John and Thomas Eyre, Sept. 27, 1706, Jamaica Commercial Papers, 1662–1788, New York Public Library; T. Walduck to James Petiver, 1710, *Jour. Bar. Mus. Hist. Soc.*, XV (1947–1948), 44–45.

more than the tabulation of parish registers, has built-in statistical defects. A grave marker in the West Indies was a status symbol at this time, and the people memorialized were mostly from the planter or merchant classes. The young and the old were inadequately represented, the young because their parents seldom bothered to set up stones for them, the old because they frequently retired to England. But since the people commemorated by grave monuments were by and large the island leaders, it is worth checking their life expectancy. Drawing upon Philip Wright's collection of monumental inscriptions from Jamaica graveyards and E. M. Shilstone's collection of monumental inscriptions from an old Jewish burying ground in Bridgetown, I have tabulated the ages of 354 persons who died between 1660 and 1750.[44] Because of the shortage of children's tombstones, I have excluded youngsters under sixteen from this computation. Thus everyone in the sample lived long enough to procreate or enter a career. But very few lived to a ripe old age. Seven percent of these people died in their late teens, 20 percent in their twenties, 24 percent in their thirties, and 13 percent in their forties. More of the Bridgetown Jews reached old age than the Jamaica Christians, but only 14 percent of the total sample lived to age sixty-five. There is, however, a great problem with these figures, for they show that the males died at a median age of forty-five while the females died at a median age of thirty-three. This gaping twelve-year sex differential conflicts head on with evidence from the census returns and the parish registers that females outlived males in the islands, and it leads one to question the validity of graveyard research for demographic purposes.[45]

The best demographic data by far for the white population in the islands come at the close of our period, from a Barbados census taken in 1715. Parish by parish the churchwardens enumerated the 16,888 white inhabitants, listing the age and sex of all persons and categorizing them as men, women, boys, and girls.[46] As might be

44. The Jamaica figures for 191 men and 114 women are tabulated from Philip Wright, *Monumental Inscriptions of Jamaica* (London, 1966). The Barbados figures for 26 men and 23 women are tabulated from Shilstone, *Monumental Inscriptions*.

45. See Hollingsworth's caustic comments on tombstone counting in *Historical Demography*, 272–274.

46. The Barbados census of 1715 occupies a manuscript volume, C.O. 28/16, in the P.R.O. There is another copy in the Bridgetown Registration Office. Molen has analyzed this census in "Population and Social Patterns in Barbados,"

expected, many colonists did not know exactly how old they were and thus gave their ages as twenty, twenty-five, thirty, and so forth. The white population of the island had shrunk by several thousand since the census of 1680; it was still distributed in much the same way, parish by parish, except that more of the inhabitants now lived in Bridgetown and the southeastern parish of St. Philip and fewer in the barren northern parish of St. Lucy, where so many of the small planters had lived in 1680. One quarter of the whites

Table 31. Sex and Age of the White Population in Barbados, 1715

Age	Number of Males	Percentage of Males	Number of Females	Percentage of Females
0–9	2,382	28.5	2,392	28.8
10–19	1,824	21.9	1,858	22.4
20–29	1,648	19.7	1,494	18.0
30–39	1,296	15.5	1,076	12.9
40–49	731	8.8	781	9.4
50–59	288	3.5	424	5.1
60–69	128	1.5	174	2.1
70+	49	0.6	112	1.3

NOTE: Drawn from tables II and III in Molen, "Population and Social Patterns in Barbados," *Wm. and Mary Qtly.*, 3d Ser., XXVIII (1971), 293–294.

lived in St. Michael (Bridgetown) in 1715, and the census indicates that this port town was now just about as healthy—or unhealthy—as the rest of the island. Slightly fewer young children and old people are found in Bridgetown than in the country parishes and a slightly larger proportion of young adults. Bridgetown had a significant surplus of women, however, while most of the country parishes had a surplus of men. Overall the sexes were very evenly balanced. As table 31 shows, Barbados girls survived childhood diseases a little better than boys; women in their twen-

Wm. and Mary Qtly., 3d Ser., XXVIII (1971), 287–300. The following paragraphs draw upon her analysis and upon my inspection of the return for Christ church parish in 1715, printed in *Jour. Bar. Mus. Hist. Soc.*, V (1937–1938) through VII (1939–1940), *passim*.

ties and thirties—the prime childbearing years—died faster than men; but women who survived to age forty were more likely to attain old age.

Overall the Barbados population in 1715 was exceedingly youthful, yet it was not growing in the way most young populations do. The median age for both sexes was nineteen. Only 16 percent of the inhabitants had passed their fortieth birthdays, and only 3 percent had passed their sixtieth birthdays—which corroborates the evidence garnered from island tombstones that the sugar planters' life expectancy was very low. As in 1680 family life was stunted. Despite the large number of young people, only half of the adults were married in 1715. Those Barbadians who married seem to have done so at much the same age as in contemporary England and New England: the women in their early twenties, the men in their late twenties. Back in 1671 George Fox had upbraided the Barbados Quakers for marrying their children "too young, as at thirteen or fourteen years of age." [47] But there is no sign of child brides and grooms in 1715. In Christchurch parish only sixteen wives and three husbands out of 250 married couples are under twenty-one. Given the high mortality rate, marriages tended to be short. The census lists in 1715 (as in 1680) are studded with widows, widowers, and orphans. In Christchurch there were eighty-seven widows and nine widowers—a discrepancy suggesting that men found it easier than women to remarry in this community. Sixty-four children under the age of ten in this parish were placed in strangers' households as wards or servants; many of these children must have been orphans.

In one respect conditions in Barbados do seem to have improved since 1680. The 250 married couples in Christchurch had 802 living children; the 200 married couples in St. Peter had 619 living children. Both of these parishes had many more large families than in Bridgetown thirty-five years before. The colonists seem to have shepherded their children through the perils of infant mortality more successfully than in the past. But since so many colonists did not marry and so many marriages were dissolved by early death, the population was probably continuing to decline. In Barbados broken family life was still the rule.

John Taylor thought the creole colonists, born in the islands, were geared to a shorter, faster life cycle than Englishmen born at

47. Penney, ed., *Journal of George Fox*, 276.

home. "They grow generally tall, and slendor, of a spare thin body, and pale Complection; haveing all light flaxen haire, being at the full growth and prime strength, att fiften years old: and seldom live to be above five and thirty years, for as sone as they are twenty, they begin to decline." [48] Certainly the islanders, whether native born or immigrants, were collectively more youthful than the English population at home. Because the planters were generally so young, men were often elected to the island assemblies in their twenties and elevated to the island councils in their thirties, in contrast to the New England governments, dominated by long-lived patriarchs. In Plymouth Colony men were first elected to such posts as selectman, deputy, assistant, and governor when they were already in their forties, and once elected they tended to stay in office until they died. Thus Plymouth was managed by relatively old men; the average age of the governor and assistants throughout the seventeenth century was fifty-five [49]—by which age almost all Barbadians would be in their graves. "We have assistant Judges sitts upon the bench that are minors," a Barbados colonist complained in 1710. "They shall jump from a boy and a hobby horse to a Collonel of a troope of horse at once. There is no age of Adolescens here; they are either Children or men." [50]

Everyone seemed caught up in a race between quick wealth and quick death. Charles Atkinson came to Jamaica in his early twenties, took out patents for twenty-five thousand acres of land, and was felled by "an invidious and malignant fever" (according to his tombstone) at age thirty-one. William Bent built up in only seven years a Jamaica plantation valued at £2,500 stocked with sixty-five slaves, before he too was "struck down by a mortal blow" at age thirty. The surest recipe for eminence in the sugar islands was survival past middle life. Samuel Long died relatively young, at forty-five, but since he came to Jamaica as a boy, he had a twenty-eight-year career, long enough to accumulate an estate worth £12,-000 and most of the top political posts in the island. Christopher Codrington the elder was a Barbados councillor at twenty-six and deputy governor at twenty-nine; years later, when he was governor of the Leeward Islands and had reached the venerable age of fifty-seven, the Antigua Assembly reminded him that he had already

48. Taylor MS, 504.
49. Demos, *A Little Commonwealth*, 172–175.
50. T. Walduck to James Petiver, 1710, *Jour. Bar. Mus. Hist. Soc.*, XV (1947–1948), 48.

far exceeded the normal West Indian life expectancy, so they urged him to choose a deputy governor in case he died unexpectedly, "which God forbid." [51] William Beeston and Peter Beckford, who lived into their sixties, were able to devote more than forty years each to Jamaican business and politics and climaxed their careers as governors of the island. Sir Thomas Modyford survived to the grand old age of sixty-nine, which enabled him to amass a solid fortune in Barbados and Jamaica, to govern both islands in turn, and then to spend nearly a decade in retirement.

Modyford, Beeston, and Beckford were rarities. In general the masters and the slaves in the English islands shared the same demographic characteristics: short life expectancy, a high proportion of young adults, stunted families, a shrinking proportion of males and many fewer births than deaths. But if whites and blacks alike adjusted poorly to life in the Indies and fell prey to the same diseases, their reasons for maladjustment were certainly different. In essence the slaves were overdisciplined and underfed, while their masters were underdisciplined and overfed. The blacks, the male blacks in particular, were shocked into early death by captivity, forced labor, and neglect. The whites, the male whites in particular, catapulted themselves into early death by their strident, showy mode of behavior. The specter of death helps to explain the frenetic tempo and the mirage-like quality of West Indian life— gorgeously opulent today, gone tomorrow. No wonder the blacks looked forward longingly to their afterlife in the pleasant mountains of West Africa. No wonder the whites looked forward longingly to an early retirement in England. It was impossible to think of the sugar islands as home when they were such a demographic disaster area.

51. Antigua Assembly to Codrington, Dec. 16, 1697, C.O. 155/2/224. The point was well taken, for Codrington died seven months later.

10 ❧ The Legacy

The sugar and slave system of plantation life matured quickly in the English islands under the tropical sun. In Barbados as early as 1650, in Jamaica and the Leewards by 1680, the colonists worked out the distinctive social and economic formula by which they and their successors lived and died. This social mode, a small cadre of white masters driving an army of black slaves, was totally without precedent in English experience. Once established, it shaped three centuries of Caribbean life. The plantation system lasted without significant alteration throughout the eighteenth century, continued in modified form even after the slaves were freed in the nineteenth century, and still survives in large measure in Jamaica, Barbados, and the Leeward Islands today. The scrabbling pioneer planters we have traced in this book created for better or worse a strongly articulated and very durable social pattern.

It is hardly surprising that posterity has ignored the creators of the West Indian plantation system. Ever since the eighteenth century the sugar planters have deservedly received a bad press. Englishmen at home never quite accepted the glittering, decadent absentee magnates as proper gentry, and the mainland colonists looked askance at visitors from the islands with their "carbuncled faces, slender legs and thighs, and large prominent bellies." [1] When the sugar planters sided with Britain in 1775 the mainlanders dismissed them as un-American and paid them little further heed. Once the English abolitionists began exposing the crassly materialistic, exploitive, spendthrift character of the Caribbean slave system, the planter class fell into permanent disrepute at home. Naturally the

1. W. Sandiford to James Pemberton, May 30, 1774, quoted by Pares, *Yankees and Creoles*, 3.

336 / Sugar and Slaves

black citizens of Jamaica, Barbados, and the Leewards can take no pride in the attainments of their first slave masters. Yet these anti-heroes deserve our attention. Study of the Caribbean social system is essential to a full understanding of the English colonizing experience in the New World, to a full understanding of American chattel slavery, to a full understanding of developments in the thirteen mainland colonies.

The Englishmen who came to the West Indies in the seventeenth century shared much in common with their North American cousins. As early as the 1640s the two sections established the famous triangular trading pattern that made the island and mainland settlements economically interdependent and kept them in close touch. Thousands of planters, servants, and slaves migrated from the islands, Barbados in particular, to North America during the course of the century. They led the early settlement of South Carolina, as we have seen. The Carpenters, Norrises, and Dickinsons came to the new town of Philadelphia from Bridgetown and Port Royal. One of the earliest settlements in East Jersey was called New Barbados, and we find Capt. John Berry of Barbados staking out a plantation in 1669 manned by thirty-two slaves on the banks of the Hackensack River.[2] The tie with New England was particularly close. "It pleased the Lord," Governor Winthrop of Massachusetts reported in 1647, "to open to us a trade with Barbados and other Islands in the West Indies." By the 1680s nearly half the ships that served the islands came from New England, and over half of the ships entering and clearing Boston were in the West Indian trade.[3] Two of John Winthrop's sons planted in the Indies —Henry Winthrop briefly in Barbados and Samuel Winthrop permanently in Antigua. A pair of cousins both named John Turner from Massachusets and Barbados shared ownership in a ketch; in the 1660s the Massachusetts cousin built the House of the Seven Gables in Salem while the Barbados cousin was selling half of a 421-acre sugar plantation for £5,728.[4] Answering the islanders'

2. Capt. Berry's land claims, East Jersey Records, III, 220, New Jersey State Library, Trenton; John E. Pomfret, *The Province of East New Jersey, 1609–1702* (Princeton, N.J., 1962), 54.

3. Winthrop, *Journal*, ed. Hosmer, II, 328; Harlow, *Barbados*, 288–289. Shipping returns for Jamaica, C.O. 1/43/59; Nevis, C.O. 1/42/270, C.O. 1/47/67–72; St. Christopher, C.O. 1/46/85–89, C.O. 1/54/230–235; and Montserrat, C.O. 1/49/66, C.O. 1/55/26–27.

4. G. Andrews Moriarty, "The Turners of New England and Barbados," *Jour. Bar. Mus. Hist. Soc.*, X (1942–1943), 7–14.

pleas for a supply of learned clergy, a number of New England parsons spent short tours of duty preaching in the Indies, including such notable figures as John Oxenbridge of Boston and Solomon Stoddard of Northhampton.[5] Another clergyman, Samuel Parris, brought two Indian slaves—John and Tituba—with him from Barbados to Salem Village, and it was John's witch cake and Tituba's incantations that launched the Salem witchcraft frenzy in 1692.

Despite these close contacts the islanders rapidly diverged from the mainlanders, most particularly from the Puritan colonists in New England. The contrast in life-style between the sugar planters and the Puritans in the seventeenth century goes way beyond religion, slavery, and climate. To begin with demography, the early New Englanders were exceptionally healthy and fertile people; in the village of Andover the average couple died at age seventy, having raised seven children to maturity, while in Barbados hardly anyone lived to age seventy and the average white couple raised one or two children to maturity.[6] The family was the prime instrument for socialization in New England, with parents training their children in habits of restraint and introspection, but the West Indian colonists lacked effective family guidance and were much more undisciplined, exhibitionist, and freewheeling. The New England villages were stable, cohesive little communities, where children habitually settled near their parents and few planters moved away, while the West Indian parishes were in constant flux, as we have seen with St. Mary in Antigua and St. John in Jamaica; few families stayed or survived for more than a generation, and the most successful planters retired to England. Most of the New Englanders lived in frugal but modest comfort, whereas the Jamaica inventories and St. Christopher compensation claims show far more stratification, with ostentatious wealth at the top and desperate poverty at the bottom. The New Englanders, through their numerous elective offices and frequent town meetings, encouraged (indeed almost required) every inhabitant to participate in public life, but in the Indies the big sugar planters completely dominated politics, and at least in Barbados the bottom half of the property

---

5. Babette M. Levy, "Early Puritanism in the Southern and Island Colonies," American Antiquarian Society, *Proceedings*, LXX (Worcester, Mass., 1960), 293–298.

6. Compare Greven, *Four Generations*, 26–30, with tables 9, 31 above.

holders were disfranchised.[7] In New England the young were deferential to their elders, repressed their adolescent rebelliousness, and often waited into their thirties to marry and set up on their own, while in the islands there were no elders, the young were in control, and many a planter made his fortune and died by age thirty. In short, the Caribbean and New England planters were polar opposites; they represented the outer limits of English social expression in the seventeenth century.

The islanders brought with them a whole panoply of English institutions: the common law, the representative assembly, the militia, the church, the parish, the school. None of these institutions worked as they did at home or in North America. Superficially constitutional developments in the island colonies paralleled developments on the mainland. In Barbados, Jamaica, and the Leewards, as Frederick G. Spurdle has shown, the assemblies steadily gained power at the expense of the royal governors. The island legislators in the seventeenth and eighteenth centuries secured control over the appropriation, audit, and issue of public finance, supervised fortifications and other public works, regulated fees, and appointed colony officers. One can thus speak of "the rise of the assembly" in the Indies as in the thirteen mainland colonies, or what Spurdle calls the planters' "radical" quest for "popular liberties." [8] But this is to miss the point. It was not the assembly but the planter class that rose in the English sugar islands; the assembly was the planters' political platform—or rather, one of their several platforms. In Barbados twenty of the twenty-two assemblymen in 1680 were big planters, owning sixty slaves apiece. At least 85 percent of the seats in the ten Barbadian assemblies elected between 1674 and 1685 went to big planters, and the remaining 15 percent were taken by only slightly less substantial slaveholders or rich Bridgetown merchants. The big Barbados planters also controlled the Council, the courts of common pleas, the panel of justices of the peace, and the parish vestries.[9] And while one can find almost as much concentrated oligarchic control in certain eighteenth-century mainland colonies such as Virginia, the big tobacco squires in the House of Burgesses were chosen by a broad electorate and had to respond to popular opinion

7. See table 6 above.
8. Spurdle, *Early West Indian Government*, 10–11, 215. See also Whitson, *Constitutional Development of Jamaica*, 158–167.
9. See table 8 above.

and pressure. The big sugar planters spoke for no one but themselves. The representative assembly in the sugar islands represented only the master class.

As with the assembly, so with other English institutions. The planters designed their legal system so as to exclude three-quarters of the inhabitants—the slaves—from due process, for they considered the blacks "an heathenish, brutish and an uncertaine, dangerous kinde of people" who could not be governed by English principles of justice.[10] The big planters effectively sabotaged the island militia system by expropriating the lands of the small peasant planters and hiring a minimum number of white servants. The island assemblies curtailed militia drills, because they interfered with sugar production, and economized on fortifications as much as possible.[11] And during the French wars, the big planters who commanded the militia in the Leeward Islands surrendered to the enemy rather than risk fighting.

Organized religion was not so much sabotaged as muzzled by the planters, who controlled the parish vestries and made sure that the Anglican clergy tried no mission work among their slaves. Quaker efforts to convert the blacks were fiercely resisted, as we have seen. Nor were the planters enthusiastic patrons of education and culture for the white inhabitants. Perhaps the most elaborate gesture they made in this direction came in 1684 when the young gentlemen of Barbados put on a theatrical performance for Governor Dutton. "This weeke," reported Dutton, "I was entertained with a play which was prepared for my reception here which was acted by the best of the Island, and I will assure you performed to admiration with musick both vocall and instrumentall[,] scenes and machines which cost them above twelve hundred pounds."[12] Twelve hundred pounds for stage props, but no money for schools. Poor Ebenezer Hicks, the Jamaican schoolmaster, left nothing when he died except two years' back salary. The islanders had no printing press in the seventeenth century, and they owned few books. Many of the whites could not read. Nearly half of the St. Christopher planters who filed compensation claims in 1706 were unable to sign their names, and 70 percent of the small planters in this

10. Barbados Act for the better ordering and governing of Negroes, Sept. 27, 1661, Barbados MSS Laws, 1645–1682, C.O. 30/2/16.
11. Spurdle, *Early West Indian Government*, 57–62, 96–100, 129–134, 168–173; Pares, *War and Trade in the West Indies*, 227–252.
12. Dutton to Col. Oglethorp, Nov. 4, 1684, Blathwayt Papers, XXX.

group, with claims under £100, were illiterate. The creoles, or native-born islanders, were considered to be decidedly more ignorant and corrupt than the English-born colonists. Governor Beeston of Jamaica protested in 1694 against having to appoint creoles to public office, for he held these people to be "very vitious in their Moralls, and loose in their lives for want of Education, not Naturall parts, for they are Pregnant enough." [13]

In 1710 a Barbadian named Thomas Walduck wrote a series of letters to a London friend in which he described the history, topography, economy, and society of his colony. Looking back from the perspective of nearly a century's settlement, Walduck extolled the industry and integrity of the first planters who had brought Barbados to such a flourishing state in the 1660s and roundly condemned the debauched people who now managed the place, accusing them of driving the colony into economic decay and moral bankruptcy. He summed up his feelings about the character of life in Barbados with an acrostic on the name of the island:

> Barbadoes Isle inhabited by Slaves
> And for one honest man ten thousand knaves
> Religion to thee's a Romantick storey
> Barbarity and ill got wealth thy glory
> All Sodom's Sins are Centred in thy heart
> Death is thy look and Death in every part
> Oh! Glorious Isle in Vilany Excell
> Sin to the Height—thy fate is Hell. [14]

We may agree with Thomas Walduck that Barbados and the other English sugar colonies had turned into disastrous social failures, but there is small point in excoriating the colonists as knaves and villains. The English planters were not consciously bad men. They had sailed beyond the line to the Indies in search of adventure and wealth at a time when both were in short supply at home. They had tried to plant the islands in the only way they knew, drawing upon the huge reservoir of unskilled servile labor in England. Finding that English servants did not work well in the tropics, they turned to African slaves. The concept of slavery was new to them, but not horrifying, for Englishmen in the seventeenth

13. Beeston to William Blathwayt, Aug. 26, 1694, *ibid.*, XXI.
14. T. Walduck to James Petiver, Nov. 12, 1710, *Jour. Bar. Mus. Hist. Soc.*, XV (1947–1948), 50.

century were accustomed to extreme social polarity and stratification. At home the distance between the privileged property holders
and the unprivileged laboring class was great—and steadily widen-
ing. As I have argued elsewhere,[15] seventeenth-century conditions of
chronically low productivity and burgeoning capitalistic expectations had the psychological effect of accentuating class conscious-
ness. Since there was clearly not enough wealth and comfort for
everyone to share, the privileged few who possessed riches luxuri-
ated in conspicuous consumption and waste, while the unprivileged
masses received nothing—and were taught to expect nothing—beyond bare subsistence.

Englishmen who came to America in the seventeenth century rang
varied changes on these themes of wealth and status. In the North
American settlements the early colonists worked out a relatively un-
differentiated social pattern in which traditional class lines were
considerably blunted. No one was really rich or privileged in early
Massachusetts or Virginia. Few were really poor and oppressed.
But in the Caribbean settlements the contrary happened. For all
their boisterous pioneer crudity, these island colonies evolved a
more extreme pattern of social stratification than in England: rich
versus poor, big planter versus small planter, master versus slave,
white versus black. The stark dichotomy between the all-powerful
sugar magnate and his abject army of black bondsmen was the ultimate expression in seventeenth-century English society of man's
strenuous search for wealth in an era of primitive productive
techniques.

15. Richard S. Dunn, *The Age of Religious Wars, 1559–1689* (New York,
1970) , chap. 3.

Index